A
SOCIAL HISTORY
OF THE
AMERICAN NEGRO

BENJAMIN BRAWLEY

DOVER PUBLICATIONS, INC.
Mineola, New York

Published in Canada by General Publishing Company, Ltd., 895 Don Mills Road, 400-2 Park Centre, Toronto, Ontario M3C 1W3.
Published in the United Kingdom by David & Charles, Brunel House, Forde Close, Newton Abbot, Devon TQ12 4PU.

Bibliographical Note

This Dover edition, first published in 2001, is an unabridged republication of the work originally published in 1921 by The Macmillan Company, New York.

Library of Congress Cataloging-in-Publication Data

Brawley, Benjamin Griffith, 1882–1939.
    A social history of the American Negro / Benjamin Brawley.
        p. cm.
    Originally published: New York : Macmillan, 1921.
    Includes bibliographical references and index.
    ISBN 0-486-41821-9 (pbk.)
    1. African Americans–History. 2. African Americans–Social conditions. 3. Slavery–United States–History. 4. United States–Race relations. 5. Liberia–History. I. Title.

E185 .B825 2001
973'.0496073–dc21

                                       2001028650

Manufactured in the United States of America
Dover Publications, Inc., 31 East 2nd Street, Mineola, N.Y. 11501

TO THE MEMORY OF

NORWOOD PENROSE HALLOWELL

PATRIOT

1839-1914

———

These all died in faith, not having received the promises, but having seen them afar off.

Norwood Penrose Hallowell was born in Philadelphia April 13, 1839. He inherited the tradition of the Quakers and grew to manhood in a strong anti-slavery atmosphere. The home of his father, Morris L. Hallowell—the "House called Beautiful," in the phrase of Oliver Wendell Holmes—was a haven of rest and refreshment for wounded soldiers of the Union Army, and hither also, after the assault upon him in the Senate, Charles Sumner had come for succor and peace. Three brothers in one way or another served the cause of the Union, one of them, Edward N. Hallowell, succeeding Robert Gould Shaw in the Command of the Fifty-Fourth Regiment of Massachusetts Volunteers. Norwood Penrose Hallowell himself, a natural leader of men, was Harvard class orator in 1861; twenty-five years later he was the marshal of his class; and in 1896 he delivered the Memorial Day address in Sanders Theater. Entering the Union Army with promptness in April, 1861, he served first in the New England Guards, then as First Lieutenant in the Twentieth Massachusetts, won a Captain's commission in November, and within the next year took part in numerous engagements, being wounded at Glendale and even more severely at Antietam. On April 17, 1863, he became Lieutenant-Colonel of the Fifty-Fourth Massachusetts, and on May 30 Colonel of the newly organized Fifty-Fifth. Serving in the investment of Fort Wagner, he was one of the first to enter the fort after its evacuation. His wounds ultimately forced him to resign his commission, and in November, 1863, he retired from the service. He engaged in business in New York, but after a few years removed to Boston, where he became eminent for his public spirit. He was one of God's noblemen, and to the last he preserved his faith in the Negro whom he had been among the first to lead toward the full heritage of American citizenship. He died April 11, 1914.

CONTENTS

CHAPTER I

CHAPTER II

CHAPTER III

CHAPTER IV

CHAPTER V

PREFACE

In the following pages an effort is made to give fresh treatment to the history of the Negro people in the United States, and to present this from a distinct point of view, the social. It is now forty years since George W. Williams completed his *History of the Negro Race in America,* and while there have been many brilliant studies of periods or episodes since that important work appeared, no one book has again attempted to treat the subject comprehensively, and meanwhile the race has passed through some of its most critical years in America. The more outstanding political phases of the subject, especially in the period before the Civil War, have been frequently considered; and in any account of the Negro people themselves the emphasis has almost always been upon political and military features. Williams emphasizes this point of view, and his study of legal aspects is not likely soon to be superseded. A noteworthy point about the history of the Negro, however, is that laws on the statute-books have not necessarily been regarded, public opinion and sentiment almost always insisting on being considered. It is necessary accordingly to study the actual life of the Negro people in itself and in connection with that of the nation, and something like this the present work endeavors to do. It thus becomes not only a Social History of the race, but also the first formal effort toward a History of the Negro Problem in America.

With this aim in mind, in view of the enormous amount of material, we have found it necessary to confine ourselves within very definite limits. A thorough study of all the questions relating to the Negro in the United States would fill volumes, for sooner or later it would touch upon all the great problems of American life. No attempt is made to perform such a task; rather is it intended to fix attention upon the race itself as definitely as possible. Even with this limitation there are

xiii

some topics that might be treated at length, but that have already been studied so thoroughly that no very great modification is now likely to be made of the results obtained. Such are many of the questions revolving around the general subject of slavery. Wars are studied not so much to take note of the achievement of Negro soldiers, vital as that is, as to record the effect of these events on the life of the great body of people. Both wars and slavery thus become not more than incidents in the history of the ultimate problem.

In view of what has been said, it is natural that the method of treatment should vary with the different chapters. Sometimes it is general, as when we touch upon the highways of American history. Sometimes it is intensive, as in the consideration of insurrections and early effort for social progress; and Liberia, as a distinct and much criticized experiment in government by American Negroes, receives very special attention. For the first time also an effort is now made to treat consecutively the life of the Negro people in America for the last fifty years.

This work is the result of studies on which I have been engaged for a number of years and which have already seen some light in *A Short History of the American Negro* and *The Negro in Literature and Art;* and acquaintance with the elementary facts contained in such books as these is in the present work very largely taken for granted. I feel under a special debt of gratitude to the New York State Colonization Society, which, coöperating with the American Colonization Society and the Board of Trustees of Donations for Education in Liberia, in 1920 gave me opportunity for some study at first hand of educational and social conditions on the West Coast of Africa; and most of all do I remember the courtesy and helpfulness of Dr. E. C. Sage and Dr. J. H. Dillard in this connection. In general I have worked independently of Williams, but any student of the subject must be grateful to that pioneer, as well as to Dr. W. E. B. DuBois, who has made contributions in so many ways. My obligations to such scholarly dissertations as those by Turner and Russell are manifest, while to Mary Stoughton Locke's *Anti-Slavery in America*—a model monograph—I feel indebted more than to any other thesis. Within the last few years, of course, the *Crisis,* the *Journal of Negro History,* and the *Negro Year-Book* have in their special fields become indispensable, and to Dr. Carter G. Woodson and Professor M. N. Work much credit is due for the faith which has prompted their respective ventures. I take this occasion also to thank Professor W. E. Dodd, of the University of Chicago, who from the time of my entrance upon this field has generously placed at my disposal his unrivaled knowledge of the history of the South; and as always I must be grateful to my father, Rev. E. M. Brawley, for that stimulation and criticism which all my life have been most valuable to me. Finally, the work has been dedicated to the memory of a distinguished soldier, who, in his youth, in the nation's darkest hour, helped to lead a struggling people to freedom and his country to victory. It is now submitted to the consideration of all who are interested in the nation's problems, and indeed in any effort that tries to keep in mind the highest welfare of the country itself.

BENJAMIN BRAWLEY.

Cambridge,
   January 1, 1921.

CHAPTER I

THE COMING OF NEGROES TO AMERICA

1. *African Origins*

An outstanding characteristic of recent years has been an increasing recognition of the cultural importance of Africa to the world. From all that has been written three facts are prominent: (1) That at some time early in the Middle Ages, perhaps about the seventh century, there was a considerable infiltration of Arabian culture into the tribes living below the Sahara, something of which may to-day most easily be seen among such people as the Haussas in the Soudan and the Mandingoes along the West Coast; (2) That, whatever influences came in from the outside, there developed in Africa an independent culture which must not be underestimated; and (3) That, perhaps vastly more than has been supposed, this African culture had to do with early exploration and colonization in America. The first of these three facts is very important, but is now generally accepted and need not here detain us. For the present purpose the second and third demand more attention.

The development of native African art is a theme of never-ending fascination for the ethnologist. Especially have striking resemblances between Negro and Oceanian culture been pointed out. In political organization as well as certain forms of artistic endeavor the Negro people have achieved creditable results, and especially have they been honored as the originators of the iron technique.* It has further been shown that fetish-

* Note article "Africa" in *New International Encyclopædia,* referring especially to the studies of Von Luschan.

1

ism, which is especially well developed along the West Coast and its hinterland, is at heart not very different from the manitou beliefs of the American Indians; and it is this connection that furnishes the key to some of the most striking results of the researches of the latest and most profound student of this and related problems.*

From the Soudan radiated a culture that was destined to affect Europe and in course of time to extend its influence even beyond the Atlantic Ocean. It is important to remember that throughout the early history of Europe and up to the close of the fifteenth century the approach to the home of the Negro was by land. The Soudan was thought to be the edge of the then known world; Homer speaks of the Ethiopians as "the farthest removed of men, and separated into two divisions." Later Greek writers carry the description still further and speak of the two divisions as Eastern and Western—the Eastern occupying the countries eastward of the Nile, and the Western stretching from the western shores of that river to the Atlantic Coast. "One of these divisions," says Lady Lugard, "we have to acknowledge, was perhaps itself the original source of the civilization which has through Egypt permeated the Western world. . . . When the history of Negroland comes to be written in detail, it may be found that the kingdoms lying toward the eastern end of the Soudan were the home of races who inspired, rather than of races who received, the traditions of civilization associated for us with the name of ancient Egypt." †

If now we come to America, we find the Negro influence upon the Indian to be so strong as to call in question all current conceptions of American archæology and so early as to suggest the coming of men from the Guinea Coast perhaps even before the coming of Columbus.‡ The first natives of Africa to come were Mandingoes; many of the words used by the Indians in their daily life appear to be not more than corruptions or adaptations of words used by the tribes of Africa;

---

* Leo Wiener: *Africa and the Discovery of America,* Vol. I, Innes & Sons, Philadelphia, 1920.
† *A Tropical Dependency,* James Nisbet & Co., Ltd., London, 1906, p. 17.
‡ See Wiener, I, 178.

and the more we study the remains of those who lived in America before 1492, and the far-reaching influence of African products and habits, the more must we acknowledge the strength of the position of the latest thesis. This whole subject will doubtless receive much more attention from scholars, but in any case it is evident that the demands of Negro culture can no longer be lightly regarded or brushed aside, and that as a scholarly contribution to the subject Wiener's work is of the very highest importance.

2. The Negro in Spanish Exploration

When we come to Columbus himself, the accuracy of whose accounts has so recently been questioned, we find a Negro, Pedro Alonso Niño, as the pilot of one of the famous three vessels. In 1496 Niño sailed to Santo Domingo and he was also with Columbus on his third voyage. With two men, Cristóbal de la Guerra, who served as pilot, and Luís de la Guerra, a Spanish merchant, in 1499 he planned what proved to be the first successful commercial voyage to the New World.

The revival of slavery at the close of the Middle Ages and the beginning of the system of Negro slavery were due to the commercial expansion of Portugal in the fifteenth century. The very word *Negro* is the modern Spanish and Portuguese form of the Latin *niger*. In 1441 Prince Henry sent out one Gonzales, who captured three Moors on the African coast. These men offered as ransom ten Negroes whom they had taken. The Negroes were taken to Lisbon in 1442, and in 1444 Prince Henry regularly began the European trade from the Guinea Coast. For fifty years his country enjoyed a monopoly of the traffic. By 1474 Negroes were numerous in Spain, and special interest attaches to Juan de Valladolid, probably the first of many Negroes who in time came to have influence and power over their people under the authority of a greater state. He was addressed as "judge of all the Negroes and mulattoes, free or slaves, which are in the very loyal and noble city of Seville, and throughout the whole archbishopric thereof." After 1500 there are frequent references to Negroes, especially in the Spanish West Indies. Instructions to Ovando, governor of Hispaniola, in 1501, prohibited the passage to the Indies of Jews, Moors, or recent converts, but authorized him to take over Negro slaves who had been born in the power of Christians. These orders were actually put in force the next year. Even the restricted importation Ovando found inadvisable, and he very soon requested that Negroes be not sent, as they ran away to the Indians, with whom they soon made friends. Isabella accordingly withdrew her permission, but after her death Ferdinand reverted to the old plan and in 1505 sent to Ovando seventeen Negro slaves for work in the copper-mines, where the severity of the labor was rapidly destroying the Indians. In 1510 Ferdinand directed that fifty Negroes be sent immediately, and that more be sent later; and in April of this year over a hundred were bought in the Lisbon market. This, says Bourne,* was the real beginning of the African slave-trade to America. Already, however, as early as 1504, a considerable number of Negroes had been introduced from Guinea because, as we are informed, "the work of one Negro was worth more than that of four Indians." In 1513 thirty Negroes assisted Balboa in building the first ships made on the Pacific Coast of America. In 1517 Spain formally entered upon the traffic, Charles V on his accession to the throne granting "license for the introduction of Negroes to the number of four hundred," and thereafter importation to the West Indies became a thriving industry. Those who came in these early years were sometimes men of considerable intelligence, having been trained as Mohammedans or Catholics. By 1518 Negroes were at work in the sugar-mills in Hispaniola, where they seem to have suffered from indulgence in drinks made from sugarcane. In 1521 it was ordered that Negro slaves should not be employed on errands as in general these tended to cultivate too close acquaintance with the Indians. In 1522 there was a rebellion on the sugar plantations in Hispaniola, primarily because the services of certain Indians were discontinued. Twenty Negroes from the Admiral's mill, uniting with twenty others who spoke the same language, killed a

* *Spain in America,* Vol. 3 in American Nation Series, p. 270.

number of Christians. They fled and nine leagues away they killed another Spaniard and sacked a house. One Negro, assisted by twelve Indian slaves, also killed nine other Christians. After much trouble the Negroes were apprehended and several of them hanged. It was about 1526 that Negroes were first introduced within the present limits of the United States, being brought to a colony near what later became Jamestown, Va. Here the Negroes were harshly treated and in course of time they rose against their oppressors and fired their houses. The settlement was broken up, and the Negroes and their Spanish companions returned to Hispaniola, whence they had come. In 1540, in Quivira, in Mexico, there was a Negro who had taken holy orders; and in 1542 there were established at Guamanga three brotherhoods of the True Cross of Spaniards, one being for Indians and one for Negroes.

The outstanding instance of a Negro's leading in exploration is that of Estévanico (or Estévanillo, or Estévan, that is, Stephen), one of the four survivors of the ill-fated expedition of De Narvaez, who sailed from Spain, June 17, 1527. Having returned to Spain after many years of service in the New World, Pánfilo de Narvaez petitioned for a grant, and accordingly the right to conquer and colonize the country between the Rio de las Palmas, in eastern Mexico, and Florida was accorded him.* His force originally consisted of six hundred soldiers and colonists. The whole conduct of the expedition—incompetent in the extreme—furnished one of the most appalling tragedies of early exploration in America. The original number of men was reduced by half by storms and hurricanes and desertions in Santo Domingo and Cuba, and those who were left landed in April, 1528, near the entrance to Tampa Bay, on the west coast of Florida. One disaster followed another in the vicinity of Pensacola Bay and the mouth of the Mississippi until at length only four men survived. These were Alvar Nuñez Cabeza de Vaca; Andrés Dorantes de Carranza, a captain of infantry; Alonzo del Cas-

* Frederick W. Hodge, 3, in *Spanish Explorers in the Southern United States*, 1528-1543, in "Original Narratives of Early American History," Scribner's, New York, 1907. Both the Narrative of Alvar Nuñez Cabeza de Vaca and the Narrative of the Expedition of Coronado, by Pedro de Casteñada, are edited by Hodge, with illuminating introductions.

tillo Maldonado; and Estévanico, who had originally come
from the west coast of Morocco and who was a slave of Dorantes. These men had most remarkable adventures in the
years between 1528 and 1536, and as a narrative of suffering and privation Cabeza de Vaca's *Journal* has hardly an
equal in the annals of the continent. Both Dorantes and
Estévanico were captured, and indeed for a season or two all
four men were forced to sojourn among the Indians. They
treated the sick, and with such success did they work that
their fame spread far and wide among the tribes. Crowds
followed them from place to place, showering presents upon
them. With Alonzo de Castillo, Estévanico sojourned for
a while with the Yguazes, a very savage tribe that killed its
own male children and bought those of strangers. He at
length escaped from these people and spent several months
with the Avavares. He afterwards went with De Vaca to
the Maliacones, only a short distance from the Avavares, and
still later he accompanied Alonzo de Castillo in exploring the
country toward the Rio Grande. He was unexcelled as a
guide who could make his way through new territory. In
1539 he went with Fray Marcos of Nice, the Father Provincial of the Franciscan order in New Spain, as a guide to
the Seven Cities of Cibola, the villages of the ancestors of
the present Zuñi Indians in western New Mexico. Preceding
Fray Marcos by a few days and accompanied by natives who
joined him on the way, he reached Háwikuh, the southern-
most of the seven towns. Here he and all but three of his
Indian followers were killed.

3. *Development of the Slave-Trade*

Portugal and Spain having demonstrated that the slave-
trade was profitable, England also determined to engage
in the traffic; and as early as 1530 William Hawkins, a merchant of Plymouth, visited the Guinea Coast and took away a
few slaves. England really entered the field, however, with
the voyage in 1562 of Captain John Hawkins, son of William,
who in October of this year also went to the coast of Guinea.
He had a fleet of three ships and one hundred men, and part-

ly by the sword and partly by other means he took three hundred or more Negroes, whom he took to Santo Domingo and sold profitably.*   He was richly laden going homeward and some of his stores were seized by Spanish vessels.   Hawkins made two other voyages, one in 1564, and another, with Drake, in 1567.   On his second voyage he had four armed ships, the largest being the *Jesus,* a vessel of seven hundred tons, and a force of one hundred and seventy men.   December and January (1564-5) he spent in picking up freight, and by sickness and fights with the Negroes he lost many of his men. Then at the end of January he set out for the West Indies. He was becalmed for twenty-one days, but he arrived at the Island of Dominica March 9.   He traded along the Spanish coasts and on his return to England he touched at various points in the West Indies and sailed along the coast of Florida. On his third voyage he had five ships.   He himself was again in command of the *Jesus,* while Drake was in charge of the *Judith,* a little vessel of fifty tons.   He got together between four and five hundred Negroes and again went to Dominica. He had various adventures and at last was thrown by a storm on the coast of Mexico.   Here after three days he was attacked by a Spanish fleet of twelve vessels, and all of his ships were destroyed except the *Judith* and another small vessel, the *Minion,* which was so crowded that one hundred men risked the dangers on land rather than go to sea with her.   On this last voyage Hawkins and Drake had among their companions the Earls of Pembroke and Leicester, who were then, like other young Elizabethans, seeking fame and fortune.   It is noteworthy that in all that he did Hawkins seems to have had no sense of cruelty or wrong.   He held religious services morning and evening, and in the spirit of the later Cromwell he enjoined upon his men to "serve God daily, love one another, preserve their victuals, beware of fire, and keep good company."   Queen Elizabeth evidently regarded the opening of the slave-trade as a worthy achievement, for after his second voyage she made Hawkins a knight, giving him for

* Edward E. Hale in Justin Winsor's *Narrative and Critical History of America,* III, 60.

a crest the device of a Negro's head and bust with the arms securely bound.

France joined in the traffic in 1624, and then Holland and Denmark, and the rivalry soon became intense. England, with her usual aggressiveness, assumed a commanding position, and, much more than has commonly been supposed, the Navigation Ordinance of 1651 and the two wars with the Dutch in the seventeenth century had as their basis the struggle for supremacy in the slave-trade. The English trade proper began with the granting of rights to special companies, to one in 1618, to another in 1631, and in 1662 to the "Company of Royal Adventurers," rechartered in 1672 as the "Royal African Company," to which in 1687 was given the exclusive right to trade between the Gold Coast and the British colonies in America. James, Duke of York, was interested in this last company, and it agreed to supply the West Indies with three thousand slaves annually. In 1698, on account of the incessant clamor of English merchants, the trade was opened generally, and any vessel carrying the British flag was by act of Parliament permitted to engage in it on payment of a duty of 10 per cent on English goods exported to Africa. New England immediately engaged in the traffic, and vessels from Boston and Newport went forth to the Gold Coast laden with hogsheads of rum. In course of time there developed a three-cornered trade by which molasses was brought from the West Indies to New England, made into rum to be taken to Africa and exchanged for slaves, the slaves in turn being brought to the West Indies or the Southern colonies.* A slave purchased for one hundred gallons of rum worth £10 brought from £20 to £50 when offered for sale in America.† Newport soon had twenty-two still houses, and even these could not satisfy the demand. England regarded the slave-trade as of such importance that when in 1713 she accepted the Peace of Utrecht she insisted on having awarded to her for thirty years the exclusive right to transport slaves to the Spanish colonies in America. When in the course of the eighteenth century the trade became fully

* Bogart: *Economic History*, 72.
† Coman: *Industrial History*, 78.

developed, scores of vessels went forth each year to engage
in it; but just how many slaves were brought to the present
United States and how many were taken to the West Indies
or South America, it is impossible to say. In 1726 the three
cities of London, Bristol, and Liverpool alone had 171 ships
engaged in the traffic, and the profits were said to warrant a
thousand more, though such a number was probably never
reached so far as England alone was concerned.*

4. *Planting of Slavery in the Colonies*

It is only for Virginia that we can state with definiteness
the year in which Negro slaves were first brought to an English colony on the mainland. When legislation on the subject
of slavery first appears elsewhere, slaves are already present.
"About the last of August (1619)," says John Rolfe in John
Smith's *Generall Historie,* "came in a Dutch man of warre,
that sold us twenty Negars." These Negroes were sold into
servitude, and Virginia did not give statutory recognition to
slavery as a system until 1661, the importations being too
small to make the matter one of importance. In this year,
however, an act of assembly stated that Negroes were "incapable of making satisfaction for the time lost in running away
by addition of time"; † and thus slavery gained a firm place in
the oldest of the colonies.

Negroes were first imported into Massachusetts from Barbadoes a year or two before 1638, but in John Winthrop's
Journal, under date February 26 of this year, we have positive
evidence on the subject as follows: "Mr. Pierce in the Salem
ship, the *Desire,* returned from the West Indies after seven
months. He had been at Providence, and brought some cotton, and tobacco, and Negroes, etc., from thence, and salt
from Tertugos. Dry fish and strong liquors are the only
commodities for those parts. He met there two men-of-war,
sent forth by the lords, etc., of Providence with letters of
mart, who had taken divers prizes from the Spaniard and
many Negroes." It was in 1641 that there was passed in

* Ballagh: *Slavery in Virginia,* 12.
† Hening: *Statutes,* II, 26.

Massachusetts the first act on the subject of slavery, and this was the first positive statement in any of the colonies with reference to the matter.   Said this act: "There shall never be any bond slavery, villeinage, nor captivity among us, unless it be lawful captives, taken in just wars, and such strangers as willingly sell themselves or are sold to us, and these shall have all the liberties and Christian usages which the law of God established in Israel requires."   This article clearly sanctioned slavery.   Of the three classes of persons referred to, the first was made up of Indians, the second of white people under the system of indenture, and the third of Negroes.   In this whole matter, as in many others, Massachusetts moved in advance of the other colonies.   The first definitely to legalize slavery, in course of time she became also the foremost representative of sentiment against the system.   In 1646 one John Smith brought home two Negroes from the Guinea Coast, where we are told he "had been the means of killing near a hundred more."   The General Court, "conceiving themselves bound by the first opportunity to bear witness against the heinous and crying sin of man-stealing," ordered that the Negroes be sent at public expense to their native country.*   In later cases, however, Massachusetts did not find herself able to follow this precedent.   In general in these early years New England was more concerned about Indians than about Negroes, as the presence of the former in large numbers was a constant menace, while Negro slavery had not yet assumed its most serious aspects.

In New York slavery began under the Dutch rule and continued under the English.   Before or about 1650 the Dutch West India Company brought some Negroes to New Netherland.   Most of these continued to belong to the company, though after a period of labor (under the common system of indenture) some of the more trusty were permitted to have small farms, from the produce of which they made return to the company.   Their children, however, continued to be slaves.   In 1664 New Netherland became New York.   The next year, in the code of English laws that was drawn up, it

---

* Coffin: *Slave Insurrections*, 8.

was enacted that "no Christian shall be kept in bond slavery, villeinage, or captivity, except who shall be judged thereunto by authority, or such as willingly have sold or shall sell themselves." As at first there was some hesitancy about making Negroes Christians, this act, like the one in Massachusetts, by implication permitted slavery.

It was in 1632 that the grant including what is now the states of Maryland and Delaware was made to George Calvert, first Lord Baltimore. Though slaves are mentioned earlier, it was in 1663-4 that the Maryland Legislature passed its first enactment on the subject of slavery. It was declared that "all Negroes and other slaves within this province, and all Negroes and other slaves to be hereinafter imported into this province, shall serve during life; and all children born of any Negro or other slave, shall be slaves as their fathers were, for the term of their lives."

In Delaware and New Jersey the real beginnings of slavery are unusually hazy. The Dutch introduced the system in both of these colonies. In the laws of New Jersey the word *slaves* occurs as early as 1664, and acts for the regulation of the conduct of those in bondage began with the practical union of the colony with New York in 1702. The lot of the slave was somewhat better here than in most of the colonies. Although the system was in existence in Delaware almost from the beginning of the colony, it did not receive legal recognition until 1721, when there was passed an act providing for the trial of slaves in a special court with two justices and six freeholders.

As early as 1639 there are incidental reference to Negroes in Pennsylvania, and there are frequent references after this date.* In this colony there were strong objections to the importing of Negroes in spite of the demand for them. Penn in his charter to the Free Society of Traders in 1682 enjoined upon the members of this company that if they held black slaves these should be free at the end of fourteen years, the Negroes then to become the company's tenants.† In 1688 there originated in Germantown a protest against Negro

* Turner: *The Negro in Pennsylvania*, 1.
† *Ibid.*, 21.

slavery that was "the first formal action ever taken against the barter in human flesh within the boundaries of the United States." *   Here a small company of Germans was assembled April 18, 1688, and there was drawn up a document signed by Garret Hendericks, Franz Daniel Pastorius, Dirck Op den Graeff, and Abraham Op den Graeff.   The protest was addressed to the monthly meeting of the Quakers about to take place in Lower Dublin.   The monthly meeting on April 30 felt that it could not pretend to take action on such an important matter and referred it to the quarterly meeting in June. This in turn passed it on to the yearly meeting, the highest tribunal of the Quakers.   Here it was laid on the table, and for the next few years nothing resulted from it.   About 1696, however, opposition to slavery on the part of the Quakers began to be active.   In the colony at large before 1700 the lot of the Negro was regularly one of servitude.   Laws were made for servants, white or black, and regulations and restrictions were largely identical.   In 1700, however, legislation began more definitely to fix the status of the slave.   In this year an act of the legislature forbade the selling of Negroes out of the province without their consent, but in other ways it denied the personality of the slave.   This act met further formal approval in 1705, when special courts were ordained for the trial and punishment of slaves, and when importation from Carolina was forbidden on the ground that it made trouble with the Indians nearer home.   In 1700 a maximum duty of 20s. was placed on each Negro imported, and in 1705 this was doubled, there being already some competition with white labor. In 1712 the Assembly sought to prevent importation altogether by a duty of £20 a head.   This act was repealed in England, and a duty of £5 in 1715 was also repealed.   In 1729, however, the duty was fixed at £2, at which figure it remained for a generation.

It was almost by accident that slavery was officially recognized in Connecticut in 1650.   The code of laws compiled for the colony in this year was especially harsh on the Indians. It was enacted that certain of them who incurred the displeas-

* Faust: *The German Element in the United States*, Boston, 1909, I, 45.

ure of the colony might be made to serve the person injured or "be shipped out and exchanged for Negroes." In 1680 the governor of the colony informed the Board of Trade that "as for blacks there came sometimes three or four in a year from Barbadoes, and they are usually sold at the rate of £22 apiece." These people were regarded rather as servants than as slaves, and early legislation was mainly in the line of police regulations designed to prevent their running away.

In 1652 it was enacted in Rhode Island that all slaves brought into the colony should be set free after ten years of service. This law was not designed, as might be supposed, to restrict slavery. It was really a step in the evolution of the system, and the limit of ten years was by no means observed. "The only legal recognition of the law was in the series of acts beginning January 4, 1703, to control the wandering of African slaves and servants, and another beginning in April, 1708, in which the slave-trade was indirectly legalized by being taxed." * "In course of time Rhode Island became the greatest slave-trader in the country, becoming a sort of clearing-house for the other colonies."†

New Hampshire, profiting by the experience of the neighboring colony of Massachusetts, deemed it best from the beginning to discourage slavery. There were so few Negroes in the colony as to form a quantity practically negligible. The system was recognized, however, an act being passed in 1714 to regulate the conduct of slaves, and another four years later to regulate that of masters.

In North Carolina, even more than in most of the colonies, the system of Negro slavery was long controlled by custom rather than by legal enactment. It was recognized by law in 1715, however, and police regulations to govern the slaves were enacted. In South Carolina the history of slavery is particularly noteworthy. The natural resources of this colony offered a ready home for the system, and the laws here formulated were as explicit as any ever enacted. Slaves were first imported from Barbadoes, and their status received official

---

* William T. Alexander: *History of the Colored Race in America,* New Orleans, 1887, p. 136.

† DuBois: *Suppression of the Slave-Trade,* 34.

confirmation in 1682. By 1720 the number had increased to 12,000, the white people numbering only 9,000. By 1698 such was the fear from the preponderance of the Negro population that a special act was passed to encourage white immigration. Legislation "for the better ordering of slaves" was passed in 1690, and in 1712 the first regular slave law was enacted. Once before 1713, the year of the Assiento Contract of the Peace of Utrecht, and several times after this date, prohibitive duties were placed on Negroes to guard against their too rapid increase. By 1734, however, importation had again reached large proportions; and in 1740, in consequence of recent insurrectionary efforts, a prohibitive duty several times larger than the previous one was placed upon Negroes brought into the province.

The colony of Georgia was chartered in 1732 and actually founded the next year. Oglethorpe's idea was that the colony should be a refuge for persecuted Christians and the debtor classes of England. Slavery was forbidden on the ground that Georgia was to defend the other English colonies from the Spaniards on the South, and that it would not be able to do this if like South Carolina it dissipated its energies in guarding Negro slaves. For years the development of Georgia was slow, and the prosperous condition of South Carolina constantly suggested to the planters that "the one thing needful" for their highest welfare was slavery. Again and again were petitions addressed to the trustees, George Whitefield being among those who most urgently advocated the innovation. Moreover, Negroes from South Carolina were sometimes hired for life, and purchases were openly made in Savannah. It was not until 1749, however, that the trustees yielded to the request. In 1755 the legislature passed an act that regulated the conduct of the slaves, and in 1765 a more regular code was adopted. Thus did slavery finally gain a foothold in what was destined to become one of the most important of the Southern states.

For the first fifty or sixty years of the life of the colonies the introduction of Negroes was slow; the system of white servitude furnished most of the labor needed, and England had not yet won supremacy in the slave-trade. It was in the last quarter of the seventeenth century that importations began to be large, and in the course of the eighteenth century the numbers grew by leaps and bounds. In 1625, six years after the first Negroes were brought to the colony, there were in Virginia only 23 Negroes, 12 male, 11 female.* In 1659 there were 300; but in 1683 there were 3,000 and in 1708, 12,000. In 1680 Governor Simon Bradstreet reported to England with reference to Massachusetts that "no company of blacks or slaves" had been brought into the province since its beginning, for the space of fifty years, with the exception of a small vessel that two years previously, after a twenty months' voyage to Madagascar, had brought hither between forty and fifty Negroes, mainly women and children, who were sold for £10, £15, and £20 apiece; occasionally two or three Negroes were brought from Barbadoes or other islands, and altogether there were in Massachusetts at the time not more than 100 or 120.

The colonists were at first largely opposed to the introduction of slavery, and numerous acts were passed prohibiting it in Virginia, Massachusetts, and elsewhere; and in Georgia, as we have seen, it had at first been expressly forbidden. English business men, however, had no scruples about the matter. About 1663 a British Committee on Foreign Plantations declared that "black slaves are the most useful appurtenances of a plantation," † and twenty years later the Lords Commissioners of Trade stated that "the colonists could not possibly subsist" without an adequate supply of slaves. Laws passed in the colonies were regularly disallowed by the crown, and royal governors were warned that the colonists would not be permitted to "discourage a traffic so beneficial to the nation." Before 1772 Virginia passed not less than thirty-three acts looking toward the prohibition of the importation of slaves, but in every instance the act was annulled by England. In the far South, especially in South Carolina, we have seen that there were increasingly heavy duties. In spite of all such efforts for restriction, however, the system of Negro slavery, once well started, developed apace.

* *Virginia Magazine of History*, VII, 364.
† Bogart: *Economic History*, 73.

In two colonies not among the original thirteen but important in the later history of the United States, Negroes were present at a very early date, in the Spanish colony of Florida from the very first, and in the French colony of Louisiana as soon as New Orleans really began to grow. Negroes accompanied the Spaniards in their voyages along the South Atlantic coast early in the sixteenth century, and specially trained Spanish slaves assisted in the founding of St. Augustine in 1565. The ambitious schemes in France of the great adventurer, John Law, and especially the design of the Mississippi Company (chartered 1717) included an agreement for the importation into Louisiana of six thousand white persons and three thousand Negroes, the Company having secured among other privileges the exclusive right to trade with the colony for twenty-five years and the absolute ownership of all mines in it. The sufferings of some of the white emigrants from France—the kidnapping, the revenge, and the chicanery that played so large a part—all make a story complete in itself. As for the Negroes, it was definitely stipulated that these should not come from another French colony without the consent of the governor of that colony. The contract had only begun to be carried out when Law's bubble burst. However, in June, 1721, there were 600 Negroes in Louisiana; in 1745 the number had increased to 2020. The stories connected with these people are as tragic and wildly romantic as are most of the stories in the history of Louisiana. In fact, this colony from the very first owed not a little of its abandon and its fascination to the mysticism that the Negroes themselves brought from Africa. In the midst of much that is apocryphal one or two events or episodes stand out with distinctness. In 1729, Perier, governor at the time, testified with reference to a small company of Negroes who had been sent against the Indians as follows: "Fifteen Negroes in whose hands we had put weapons, performed prodigies of valor. If the blacks did not cost so much, and if their labors were not so necessary to the colony, it would be better to turn them into soldiers, and to dismiss those we have, who are so bad and so cowardly that they seem to have been manufactured purposely for this colony." *   Not always, however, did the Negroes fight against the Indians.   In 1730 some representatives of the powerful Banbaras had an understanding with the Chickasaws by which the latter were to help them in exterminating all the white people and in setting up an independent republic.†   They were led by a strong and desperate Negro named Samba.   As a result of this effort for freedom Samba and seven of his companions were broken on the wheel and a woman was hanged.   Already, however, there had been given the suggestion of the possible alliance in the future of the Indian and the Negro.   From the very first also, because of the freedom from restraint of all the elements of population that entered into the life of the colony, there was the beginning of that mixture of the races which was later to tell so vitally on the social life of Louisiana and whose effects are so readily apparent even to-day.

5.   *The Wake of the Slave-Ship*

Thus it was that Negroes came to America.   Thus it was also, we might say, that the Negro Problem came, though it was not for decades, not until the budding years of American nationality, that the ultimate reaches of the problem were realized.   Those who came were by no means all of exactly the same race stock and language.   Plantations frequently exhibited a variety of customs, and sometimes traditional enemies became brothers in servitude.   The center of the colonial slave-trade was the African coast for about two hundred miles east of the great Niger River.   From this comparatively small region came as many slaves as from all the rest of Africa together.   A number of those who came were of entirely different race stock from the Negroes; some were Moors, and a very few were Malays from Madagascar.

The actual procuring of the slaves was by no means as easy a process as is sometimes supposed.   In general the slave mart brought out the most vicious passions of all who were in any way connected with the traffic.   The captain of a vessel

* Gayarré: *History of Louisiana*, I, 435.
† *Ibid.*, I, 440.

had to resort to various expedients to get his cargo. His commonest method was to bring with him a variety of gay cloth, cheap ornaments, and whiskey, which he would give in exchange for slaves brought to him. His task was most simple when a chieftain of one tribe brought to him several hundred prisoners of war. Ordinarily, however, the work was more toilsome, and kidnapping a favorite method, though individuals were sometimes enticed on vessels. The work was always dangerous, for the natives along the slave-coast soon became suspicious. After they had seen some of their tribesmen taken away, they learned not to go unarmed while a slave-vessel was on the coast, and very often there were hand-to-hand encounters. It was not long before it began to be impressed upon those interested in the trade that it was not good business to place upon the captain of a vessel the responsibility of getting together three or four hundred slaves, and that it would be better if he could find his cargo waiting for him when he came. Thus arose the so-called factories, which were nothing more than warehouses. Along the coast were placed small settlements of Europeans, whose business it was to stimulate slave-hunting expeditions, negotiate for slaves brought in, and see that they were kept until the arrival of the ships. Practically every nation engaged in the traffic planted factories of this kind along the West Coast from Cape Verde to the equator; and thus it was that this part of Africa began to be the most flagrantly exploited region in the world; thus whiskey and all the other vices of civilization began to come to a simple and home-loving people.

Once on board the slaves were put in chains two by two. When the ship was ready to start, the hold of the vessel was crowded with moody and unhappy wretches who most often were made to crouch so that their knees touched their chins, but who also were frequently made to lie on their sides "spoon-fashion." Sometimes the space between floor and ceiling was still further diminished by the water-barrels; on the top of these barrels boards were placed, on the boards the slaves had to lie, and in the little space that remained they had to subsist as well as they could. There was generally only one entrance to the hold, and provision for only the smallest amount of air through the gratings on the sides. The clothing of a captive, if there was any at all, consisted of only a rag about the loins. The food was half-rotten rice, yams, beans, or soup, and sometimes bread and meat; the cooking was not good, nor was any care taken to see that all were fed. Water was always limited, a pint a day being a generous allowance; frequently no more than a gill could be had. The rule was to bring the slaves from the hold twice a day for an airing, about eight o'clock in the morning and four in the afternoon; but this plan was not always followed. On deck they were made to dance by the lash, and they were also forced to sing. Thus were born the sorrow-songs, the last cry of those who saw their homeland vanish behind them—forever.

Sometimes there were stern fights on board. Sometimes food was refused in order that death might be hastened. When opportunity served, some leaped overboard in the hope of being taken back to Africa. Throughout the night the hold resounded with the moans of those who awoke from dreams of home to find themselves in bonds. Women became hysterical, and both men and women became insane. Fearful and contagious diseases broke out. Smallpox was one of these. More common was ophthalmia, a frightful inflammation of the eyes. A blind, and hence a worthless, slave was thrown to the sharks. The putrid atmosphere, the melancholy, and the sudden transition from heat to cold greatly increased the mortality, and frequently when morning came a dead and a living slave were found shackled together. A captain always counted on losing one-fourth of his cargo. Sometimes he lost a great deal more.

Back on the shore a gray figure with strained gaze watched the ship fade away—an old woman sadly typical of the great African mother. With her vision she better than any one else perceived the meaning of it all. The men with hard faces who came to buy and sell might deceive others, but not her. In a great vague way she felt that something wrong had attacked the very heart of her people. She saw men wild with the whiskey of the Christian nations commit crimes undreamed of before. She did not like the coast towns; the girl who went thither came not home again, and a young man was lost to all that Africa held dear.   In course of time she saw every native craft despised, and instead of the fabric that her own fingers wove her children yearned for the tinsel and the gew-gaws of the trader.   She cursed this man, and she called upon all her spirits to banish the evil.   But when at last all was of no avail—when the strongest youth or the dearest maiden had gone—she went back to her hut and ate her heart out in the darkness.   She wept for her children and would not be comforted because they were not.   Then slowly to the un-tutored mind somehow came the promise: "These are they which came out of great tribulation, and have washed their robes and made them white in the blood of the Lamb. . . They shall hunger no more, neither thirst any more; neither shall the sun light on them, nor any heat.   For the Lamb which is in the midst of the throne shall feed them, and shall lead them unto living fountains of waters; and God shall wipe away all tears from their eyes."

CHAPTER II

THE NEGRO IN THE COLONIES

The Negroes who were brought from Africa to America were brought hither to work, and to work under compulsion; hence any study of their social life in the colonial era must be primarily a study of their life under the system of slavery, and of the efforts of individuals to break away from the same.

1. *Servitude and Slavery*

For the antecedents of Negro slavery in America one must go back to the system of indentured labor known as servitude. This has been defined as "a legalized status of Indian, white, and Negro servants preceding slavery in most, if not all, of the English mainland colonies." * A study of servitude will explain many of the acts with reference to Negroes, especially those about intermarriage with white people. For the origins of the system one must go back to social conditions in England in the seventeenth century. While villeinage had been formally abolished in England at the middle of the fourteenth century, it still lingered in remote places, and even if men were not technically villeins they might be subjected to long periods of service. By the middle of the fifteenth century the demand for wool had led to the enclosure of many farms for sheep-raising, and accordingly to distress on the part of many agricultural laborers. Conditions were not improved early in the sixteenth century, and they were in fact made more acute, the abolition of the monasteries doing away with many of the sources of relief. Men out of work were thrown upon the highways and thus became a menace to society. In 1564 the price of wheat was 19s. a quarter and wages were 7d. a

* *New International Encyclopædia*, Article "Slavery."

day. The situation steadily grew worse, and in 1610, while wages were still the same, wheat was 35s. a quarter. Rents were constantly rising, moreover, and many persons died from starvation. In the course of the seventeenth century paupers and dissolute persons more and more filled the jails and workhouses.

Meanwhile in the young colonies across the sea labor was scarce, and it seemed to many an act of benevolence to bring from England persons who could not possibly make a living at home and give them some chance in the New World. From the very first, children, and especially young people between the ages of twelve and twenty, were the most desired. The London Company undertook to meet half of the cost of the transportation and maintenance of children sent out by parish authorities, the understanding being that it would have the service of the same until they were of age.* The Company was to teach each boy a trade and when his freedom year arrived was to give to each one fifty acres, a cow, some seed corn, tools, and firearms. He then became the Company's tenant, for seven years more giving to it one-half of his produce, at the end of which time he came into full possession of twenty-five acres. After the Company collapsed individuals took up the idea. Children under twelve years of age might be bound for seven years, and persons over twenty-one for no more than four; but the common term was five years.

Under this system fell servants voluntary and involuntary. Hundreds of people, too poor to pay for their transportation, sold themselves for a number of years to pay for the transfer. Some who were known as "freewillers" had some days in which to dispose of themselves to the best advantage in America; if they could not make satisfactory terms, they too were sold to pay for the passage. More important from the standpoint of the system itself, however, was the number of involuntary servants brought hither. Political offenders, vagrants, and other criminals were thus sent to the colonies, and many persons, especially boys and girls, were kidnapped in the streets of London and "spirited" away. Thus came

* Coman: *Industrial History*, 42.

Irishmen or Scotchmen who had incurred the ire of the crown,
Cavaliers or Roundheads according as one party or the other
was out of power, and farmers who had engaged in Mon-
mouth's rebellion; and in the year 1680 alone it was estimated that not less than ten thousand persons were "spirited"
away from England. It is easy to see how such a system became a highly profitable one for shipmasters and those in
connivance with them. Virginia objected to the criminals,
and in 1671 the House of Burgesses passed a law against
the importing of such persons, and the same was approved
by the governor. Seven years later, however, it was set
aside for the transportation of political offenders.

As having the status of an apprentice the servant could sue
in court and he was regularly allowed "freedom dues" at the
expiration of his term. He could not vote, however, could
not bear weapons, and of course could not hold office. In
some cases, especially where the system was voluntary,
servants sustained kindly relations with their masters, a few
even becoming secretaries or tutors. More commonly, however, the lot of the indentured laborer was a hard one, his
food often being only coarse Indian meal, and water mixed
with molasses. The moral effect of the system was bad in
the fate to which it subjected woman and in the evils resulting
from the sale of the labor of children. In this whole connection, however, it is to be remembered that the standards
of the day were very different from those of our own. The
modern humanitarian impulse had not yet moved the heart
of England, and flogging was still common for soldiers and
sailors, criminals and children alike.

The first Negroes brought to the colonies were technically
servants, and generally as Negro slavery advanced white servitude declined. James II, in fact, did whatever he could to
hasten the end of servitude in order that slavery might become
more profitable. Economic forces were with him, for while
a slave varied in price from £10 to £50, the mere cost of
transporting a servant was from £6 to £10. "Servitude became
slavery when to such incidents as alienation, disfranchisement, whipping, and limited marriage were added those of
perpetual service and a denial of civil, juridical, marital and

property rights as well as the denial of the possession of children." *   Even after slavery was well established, however, white men and women were frequently retained as domestic servants, and the system of servitude did not finally pass in all of its phases before the beginning of the Revolutionary War.

Negro slavery was thus distinctively an evolution. As the first Negroes were taken by pirates, the rights of ownership could not legally be given to those who purchased them; hence slavery by custom preceded slavery by statute. Little by little the colonies drifted into the sterner system. The transition was marked by such an act as that in Rhode Island, which in 1652 permitted a Negro to be bound for ten years. We have already referred to the Act of Assembly in Virginia in 1661 to the effect that Negroes were incapable of making satisfaction for time lost in running away by addition of time. Even before it had become generally enacted or understood in the colonies, however, that a child born of slave parents should serve for life, a new question had arisen, that of the issue of a free person and a slave. This led Virginia in 1662 to lead the way with an act declaring that the status of a child should be determined by that of the mother,† which act both gave to slavery the sanction of law and made it hereditary. From this time forth Virginia took a commanding lead in legislation; and it is to be remembered that when we refer to this province we by no means have reference to the comparatively small state of to-day, but to the richest and most populous of the colonies. This position Virginia maintained until after the Revolutionary War, and not only the present West Virginia but the great Northwest Territory were included in her domain.

The slave had none of the ordinary rights of citizenship; in a criminal case he could be arrested, tried, and condemned with but one witness against him, and he could be sentenced without a jury. In Virginia in 1630 one Hugh Davis was ordered to be "soundly whipped before an assembly of Negroes and others, for abusing himself to the dishonor of God and the shame of Christians, by defiling his body in lying with

---

* New International Encyclopædia, Article "Slavery."
† Hening: Statutes, II, 170.

a Negro." * Just ten years afterwards, in 1640, one Robert Sweet was ordered "to do penance in church, according to the laws of England, for getting a Negro woman with child, and the woman to be whipped." † Thus from the very beginning the intermixture of the races was frowned upon and went on all the same. By the time, moreover, that the important acts of 1661 and 1662 had formally sanctioned slavery, doubt had arisen in the minds of some Virginians as to whether one Christian could legitimately hold another in bondage; and in 1667 it was definitely stated that the conferring of baptism did not alter the condition of a person as to his bondage or freedom, so that masters, freed from this doubt, could now "more carefully endeavor the propagation of Christianity." In 1669 an "act about the casual killing of slaves" provided that if any slave resisted his master and under the extremity of punishment chanced to die, his death was not to be considered a felony and the master was to be acquitted. In 1670 it was made clear that none but freeholders and housekeepers should vote in the election of burgesses, and in the same year provision was taken against the possible ownership of a white servant by a free Negro, who nevertheless "was not debarred from buying any of his own nation." In 1692 there was legislation "for the more speedy prosecution of slaves committing capital crimes"; and this was reënacted in 1705, when some provision was made for the compensation of owners and when it was further declared that Negro, mulatto, and Indian slaves within the dominion were "real estate" and "incapable in law to be witnesses in any cases whatsoever"; and in 1723 there was an elaborate and detailed act "directing the trial of slaves committing capital crimes, and for the more effectual punishing conspiracies and insurrections of them, and for the better government of Negroes, mulattoes, and Indians, bond or free." This last act specifically stated that no slave should be set free upon any pretense whatsoever "except for some meritorious services, to be adjudged and allowed by the governor and council." All this legislation was soon found to be too drastic and too difficult

* Hening: *Statutes,* I, 146.
† *Ibid.,* I, 552.

to enforce, and modification was inevitable. This came in
1732, when it was made possible for a slave to be a witness
when another slave was on trial for a capital offense, and
in 1744 this provision was extended to civil cases as well.
In 1748 there was a general revision of all existing legislation, with special provision against attempted insurrections.

Thus did Virginia pave the way, and more and more slave
codes took on some degree of definiteness and uniformity.
Very important was the act of 1705, which provided that
a slave might be inventoried as real estate. As property
henceforth there was nothing to prevent his being separated
from his family. Before the law he was no longer a person
but a thing.

2.   The Indian, the Mulatto, and the Free Negro

All along, it is to be observed, the problem of the Negro
was complicated by that of the Indian. At first there was
a feeling that Indians were to be treated not as Negroes but
as on the same basis as Englishmen. An act in Virginia of
1661-2 summed up this feeling in the provision that they
were not to be sold as servants for any longer time than
English people of the same age, and injuries done to them
were to be duly remedied by the laws of England. About
the same time a Powhatan Indian sold for life was ordered
to be set free. An interesting enactment of 1670 attempted
to give the Indian an intermediate status between that of
the Englishman and the Negro slave, as "servants not being
Christians, imported into the colony by shipping" (i.e.,
Negroes) were to be slaves for their lives, but those that
came by land were to serve "if boys or girls until thirty years
of age; if men or women, twelve years and no longer." All
such legislation, however, was radically changed as a result
of Nathaniel Bacon's rebellion of 1676, in which the aid of
the natives was invoked against the English governor. Henceforth Indians taken in war became the slaves for life of their
captors. An elaborate act of 1682 summed up the new status,
and Indians sold by other Indians were to be "adjudged,
deemed, and taken to be slaves, to all intents and purposes,

any law, usage, or custom to the contrary notwithstanding."
Indian women were to be "tithables," * and they were required
to pay levies just as Negro women. From this time forth
enactments generally included Indians along with Negroes,
but of course the laws placed on the statute books did not
always bear close relation to what was actually enforced, and
in general the Indian was destined to be a vanishing rather
than a growing problem. Very early in the eighteenth century,
in connection with the wars between the English and the
Spanish in Florida, hundreds of Indians were shipped to
the West Indies and some to New England. Massachusetts
in 1712 prohibited such importation, as the Indians were
"malicious, surly, and very ungovernable," and she was followed to similar effect by Pennsylvania in 1712, by New
Hampshire in 1714, and by Connecticut and Rhode Island
in 1715.

If the Indian was destined to be a vanishing factor, the
mulatto and the free Negro most certainly were not. In spite
of all the laws to prevent it, the intermixture of the races
increased, and manumission somehow also increased. Sometimes a master in his will provided that several of his slaves
should be given their freedom. Occasionally a slave became
free by reason of what was regarded as an act of service
to the commonwealth, as in the case of one Will, slave belonging to Robert Ruffin, of the county of Surry in Virginia,
who in 1710 divulged a conspiracy.† There is, moreover,
on record a case of an indentured Negro servant, John Gea-
ween, who by his unusual thrift in the matter of some hogs
which he raised on the share system with his master, was
able as early as 1641 to purchase his own son from another
master, to the perfect satisfaction of all concerned.‡ Of special

---

* Hurd, commenting on an act of 1649 declaring all imported male
servants to be tithables, speaks as follows (230): *"Tithables* were persons assessed for a poll-tax, otherwise called the 'county levies.' At
first, only free white persons were tithable. The law of 1645 provided
for a tax on property and tithable persons. By 1648 property was
released and taxes levied only on the tithables, at a specified poll-tax.
Therefore by classing servants or slaves as tithables, the law attributes
to them legal personality, or a membership in the social state inconsistent with the condition of a chattel or property."

† Hening: *Statutes,* III, 537.

‡ *Virginia Magazine of History,* X, 281.

importance for some years were those persons who were descendants of Negro fathers and indentured white mothers, and who at first were of course legally free. By 1691 the problem had become acute in Virginia. In this year "for prevention of that abominable mixture and spurious issue, which hereafter may increase in this dominion, as well by Negroes, mulattoes and Indians intermarrying with English or other white women, as by their unlawful accompanying with one another," it was enacted that "for the time to come whatsoever English or other white man or woman being free shall intermarry with a Negro, mulatto, or Indian man or woman, bond or free, shall within three months after such marriage be banished and removed from this dominion forever, and that the justices of each respective county within this dominion make it their particular care that this act be put in effectual execution." *   A white woman who became the mother of a child by a Negro or mulatto was to be fined £15 sterling, in default of payment was to be sold for five years, while the child was to be bound in servitude to the church wardens until thirty years of age.   It was further provided that if any Negro or mulatto was set free, he was to be transported from the country within six months of his manumission (which enactment is typical of those that it was difficult to enforce and that after a while were only irregularly observed).   In 1705 it was enacted that no "Negro, mulatto, or Indian shall from and after the publication of this act bear any office ecclesiastical, civil or military, or be in any place of public trust or power, within this her majesty's colony and dominion of Virginia"; and to clear any doubt that might arise as to who should be accounted a mulatto, it was provided that "the child of an Indian, and the child, grandchild, or great-grandchild of a Negro shall be deemed, accounted, held, and taken to be a mulatto."   It will be observed that while the act of 1670 said that "none but freeholders and housekeepers" could vote, this act of 1705 did not specifically legislate against voting by a mulatto or a free Negro, and that some such privi-

---

* The penalty was so ineffective that in 1705 it was changed simply to imprisonment for six months "without bail or mainprise."

lege was exercised for a while appears from the definite
provision in 1723 that "no free Negro, mulatto, or Indian,
whatsoever, shall hereafter have any vote at the election of
burgesses, or any other election whatsoever." In the same
year it was provided that free Negroes and mulattoes might
be employed as drummers or trumpeters in servile labor, but
that they were not to bear arms; and all free Negroes above
sixteen years of age were declared tithable. In 1769, however, all free Negro and mulatto women were exempted from
levies as tithables, such levies having proved to be burden-
some and "derogatory to the rights of freeborn subjects."

More than other colonies Maryland seems to have been
troubled about the intermixture of the races; certainly no other
phase of slavery here received so much attention. This was
due to the unusual emphasis on white servitude in the colony.
In 1663 it was enacted that any freeborn woman intermarrying with a slave should serve the master of the slave during
the life of her husband and that any children resulting from
the union were also to be slaves. This act was evidently
intended to frighten the identured woman from such a marriage. It had a very different effect. Many masters, in order
to prolong the indenture of their white female servants, encouraged them to marry Negro slaves. Accordingly a new law
in 1681 threw the responsibility not on the indentured woman
but on the master or mistress; in case a marriage took place
between a white woman-servant and a slave, the woman was
to be free at once, any possible issue was to be free, and
the minister performing the ceremony and the master or mistress were to be fined ten thousand pounds of tobacco. This
did not finally dispose of the problem, however, and in 1715,
in response to a slightly different situation, it was enacted
that a white woman who became the mother of a child by
a free Negro father should become a servant for seven years,
the father also a servant for seven years, and the child a
servant until thirty-one years of age. Any white man who
begot a Negro woman with child, whether a free woman
or a slave, was to undergo the same penalty as a white
woman—a provision that in course of time was notoriously

disregarded. In 1717 the problem was still unsettled, and in this year it was enacted that Negroes or mulattoes of either sex intermarrying with white people were to be slaves for life, except mulattoes born of white women, who were to serve for seven years, and the white person so intermarrying also for seven years. It is needless to say that with all these changing and contradictory provisions many servants and Negroes did not even know what the law was. In 1728, however, free mulatto women having illegitimate children by Negroes and other slaves, and free Negro women having illegitimate children by white men, and their issue, were subjected to the same penalties as in the former act were provided against white women. Thus vainly did the colony of Maryland struggle with the problem of race intermixture. Generally throughout the South the rule in the matter of the child of the Negro father and the indentured white mother was that the child should be bound in servitude for thirty or thirty-one years.

In the North as well as in the South the intermingling of the blood of the races was discountenanced. In Pennsylvania as early as 1677 a white servant was indicted for cohabiting with a Negro. In 1698 the Chester County court laid it down as a principle that the mingling of the races was not to be allowed. In 1722 a woman was punished for promoting a secret marriage between a white woman and a Negro; a little later the Assembly received from the inhabitants of the province a petition inveighing against cohabiting; and in 1725-6 a law was passed positively forbidding the mixture of the races.* In Massachusetts as early as 1705 and 1708 restraining acts to prevent a "spurious and mixt issue" ordered the sale of offending Negroes and mulattoes out of the colony's jurisdiction, and punished Christians who intermarried with them by a fine of £50. After the Revolutionary War such marriages were declared void and the penalty of £50 was still exacted, and not until 1843 was this act repealed. Thus was the color-line, with its social and legal distinctions, extended beyond the conditions of servitude and slavery, and thus early

* Turner: *The Negro in Pennsylvania*, 29-30.

was an important phase of the ultimate Negro Problem foreshadowed.

Generally then, in the South, in the colonial period, the free Negro could not vote, could not hold civil office, could not give testimony in cases involving white men, and could be employed only for fatigue duty in the militia. He could not purchase white servants, could not intermarry with white people, and had to be very circumspect in his relations with slaves. No deprivation of privilege, however, relieved him of the obligation to pay taxes. Such advantages as he possessed were mainly economic. The money gained from his labor was his own; he might become skilled at a trade; he might buy land; he might buy slaves; * he might even buy his wife and child if, as most frequently happened, they were slaves; and he might have one gun with which to protect his home.† Once in a long while he might even find some opportunity for education, as when the church became the legal warden of Negro apprentices. Frequently he found a place in such a trade as that of the barber or in other personal service, and such work accounted very largely for the fact that he was generally permitted to remain in communities where technically he had no right to be. In the North his situation was little better than in the South, and along economic lines even harder. Everywhere his position was a difficult one. He was most frequently regarded as idle and shiftless, and as a breeder of mischief; but if he showed unusual thrift he might even be forced to leave his home and go elsewhere. Liberty, the boon of every citizen, the free Negro did not possess. For all the finer things of life—the things that make life worth living—the lot that was his was only less hard than that of the slave.

---

* Russell: *The Free Negro in Virginia,* 32-33, cites from the court records of Northampton County, 1651-1654 and 1655-1658, the noteworthy case of a free negro, Anthony Johnson, who had come to Virginia not later than 1622 and who by 1650 owned a large tract of land on the Eastern Shore. To him belonged a Negro, John Casor. After several years of labor Casor demanded his freedom on the ground that from the first he had been an indentured servant and not a slave. When the case came up in court, however, not only did Johnson win the verdict that Casor was his slave, but he also won his suit against Robert Parker, a white man, who he asserted had illegally detained Casor.

† Hening: *Statutes,* IV, 131.

3. *First Effort for Social Betterment*

If now we turn aside from laws and statutes and consider the ordinary life and social intercourse of the Negro, we shall find more than one contradiction, for in the colonial era codes affecting slaves and free Negroes had to grope their way to uniformity. Especially is it necessary to distinguish between the earlier and the later years of the period, for as early as 1760 the liberalism of the Revolutionary era began to be felt. If we consider what was strictly the colonial epoch, we may find it necessary to make a division about the year 1705. Before this date the status of the Negro was complicated by the incidents of the system of servitude; after it, however, in Virginia, Pennsylvania, and Massachusetts alike, special discrimination against him on account of race was given formal recognition.

By 1715 there were in Virginia 23,000 Negroes, and in all the colonies 58,850, or 14 per cent of the total population.* By 1756, however, the Negroes in Virginia numbered 120,156 and the white people but 173,316.† Thirty-eight of the forty-nine counties had more Negro than white tithables, and eleven of the counties had a Negro population varying from one-fourth to one-half more than the white. A great many of the Negroes had only recently been imported from Africa, and they were especially baffling to their masters of course when they conversed in their native tongues. At first only men were brought, but soon women came also, and the treatment accorded these people varied all the way from occasional indulgence to the utmost cruelty. The hours of work regularly extended from sunrise to sunset, though corn-husking and rice-beating were sometimes continued after dark, and overseers were almost invariably ruthless, often having a share in the crops. Those who were house-servants would go about only partially clad, and the slave might be marked or branded like one of the lower animals; he was not thought to have a soul, and the law sought to deprive him of all human attributes. Holiday amusement consisted largely of the dances

---

* Blake: *History of Slavery and the Slave-Trade,* 378.
† Ballagh: *Slavery in Virginia,* 12.

that the Negroes had brought with them, these being accompanied by the beating of drums and the blowing of horns; and funeral ceremonies featured African mummeries. For those who were criminal offenders simple execution was not always considered severe enough; the right hand might first be amputated, the criminal then hanged and his head cut off, and his body quartered and the parts suspended in public places. Sometimes the hanging was in chains, and several instances of burning are on record. A master was regularly reimbursed by the government for a slave legally executed, and in 1714 there was a complaint in South Carolina that the treasury had become almost exhausted by such reimbursements. In Massachusetts hanging was the worst legal penalty, but the obsolete common-law punishment was revived in 1755 to burn alive a slave-woman who had killed her master in Cambridge.*

The relations between the free Negro and the slave might well have given cause for concern. Above what was after all only an artificial barrier spoke the call of race and frequently of kindred. Sometimes at a later date jealousy arose when a master employed a free Negro to work with his slaves, the one receiving pay and the others laboring without compensation. In general, however, the two groups worked like brothers, each giving the other the benefit of any temporary advantage that it possessed. Sometimes the free Negro could serve by reason of the greater freedom of movement that he had, and if no one would employ him, or if, as frequently happened, he was browbeaten and cheated out of the reward of his labor, the slave might somehow see that he got something to eat. In a state of society in which the relation of master and slave was the rule, there was of course little place for either the free Negro or the poor white man. When the pressure became too great the white man moved away; the Negro, finding himself everywhere buffeted, in the colonial era at least had little choice but to work out his salvation at home as well as he could. More and more character told, and if a man had made himself known for his industry

* Edward Eggleston: "Social Conditions in the Colonies," in *Century Magazine,* October, 1884, p. 863.

and usefulness, a legislative act might even be passed permitting him to remain in the face of a hostile law. Even before 1700 there were in Virginia families in which both parents were free colored persons and in which every effort was made to bring up the children in honesty and morality. When some prosperous Negroes found themselves able to do so, they occasionally purchased Negroes, who might be their own children or brothers, in order to give them that protection without which on account of recent manumission they might be required to leave the colony in which they were born.   Thus, whatever the motive, the tie that bound the free Negro and the slave was a strong one; and in spite of the fact that Negroes who owned slaves were generally known as hard masters, as soon as any men of the race began to be really prominent their best endeavor was devoted to the advancement of their people.   It was not until immediately after the Revolutionary War, however, that leaders of vision and statesmanship began to be developed.

It was only the materialism of the eighteenth century that accounted for the amazing development of the system of Negro slavery, and only this that defeated the benevolence of Oglethorpe's scheme for the founding of Georgia.   As yet there was no united protest—no general movement for freedom; and as Von Holst said long afterwards, "If the agitation had been wholly left to the churches, it would have been long before men could have rightly spoken of 'a slavery question.'" The Puritans, however, were not wholly unmindful of the evil, and the Quakers were untiring in their opposition, though it was Roger Williams who in 1637 made the first protest that appears in the colonies.*   Both John Eliot and Cotton Mather were somewhat generally concerned about the harsh treatment of the Negro and the neglect of his spiritual welfare. Somewhat more to the point was Richard Baxter, the eminent English nonconformist, who was a contemporary of both of these men.   "Remember," said he, in speaking of Negroes and other slaves, "that they are of as good a kind as you; that is, they are reasonable creatures as well as you, and born to

* For this and the references immediately following note Locke: *Anti-Slavery in America*, 11-45.

as much natural liberty. If their sin have enslaved them to you, yet Nature made them your equals." On the subject of man-stealing he is even stronger: "To go as pirates and catch up poor Negroes or people of another land, that never forfeited life or liberty, and to make them slaves, and sell them, is one of the worst kinds of thievery in the world." Such statements, however, were not more than the voice of individual opinion. The principles of the Quakers carried them far beyond the Puritans, and their history shows what might have been accomplished if other denominations had been as sincere and as unselfish as the Society of Friends. The Germantown protest of 1688 has already been remarked. In 1693 George Keith, in speaking of fugitives, quoted with telling effect the text, "Thou shalt not deliver unto his master the servant which is escaped from his master unto thee" (Deut. 23.15). In 1696 the Yearly Meeting in Pennsylvania first took definite action in giving as its advice "that Friends be careful not to encourage the bringing in of any more Negroes; and that such that have Negroes, be careful of them, bring them to meetings, have meetings with them in their families, and restrain them from loose and lewd living as much as in them lies, and from rambling abroad on First-days or other times." * As early as 1713 the Quakers had in mind a scheme for freeing the Negroes and returning them to Africa, and by 1715 their efforts against importation had seriously impaired the market for slaves in Philadelphia. Within a century after the Germantown protest the abolition of slavery among the Quakers was practically accomplished.

In the very early period there seems to have been little objection to giving a free Negro not only religious but also secular instruction; indeed he might be entitled to this, as in Virginia, where in 1691 the church became the agency through which the laws of Negro apprenticeship were carried out; thus in 1727 it was ordered that David James, a free Negro boy, be bound to Mr. James Isdel, who was to "teach him to read the Bible distinctly, also the trade of a gunsmith" and "carry him to the clerk's office and take indenture to that

* *Brief Statement of the Rise and Progress of the Testimony of the Religious Society of Friends against Slavery and the Slave-Trade,* 8.

purpose." * In general the English church did a good deal
to provide for the religious instruction of the free Negro;
"the reports made in 1724 to the English bishop by the Virginia parish ministers are evidence that the few free Negroes
in the parishes were permitted to be baptized, and were received
into the church when they had been taught the catechism." †
Among Negroes, moreover, as well as others in the colonies
the Society for the Propagation of the Gospel in Foreign Parts
was active. As early as 1705, in Goose Creek Parish in South
Carolina, among a population largely recently imported from
Africa, a missionary had among his communicants twenty
blacks who well understood the English tongue.‡ The most
effective work of the Society, however, was in New York,
where as early as 1704 a school was opened by Elias Neau,
a Frenchman who after several years of imprisonment because
of his Protestant faith had come to New York to try his fortune as a trader. In 1703 he had called the attention of the
Society to the Negroes who were "without God in the world,
and of whose souls there was no manner of care taken," and
had suggested the appointment of a catechist. He himself
was prevailed upon to take up the work and he accordingly
resigned his position as an elder in the French church and
conformed to the Church of England. He worked with
success for a number of years, but in 1712 was embarrassed
by the charge that his school fomented the insurrection that
was planned in that year. He finally showed, however, that
only one of his students was in any way connected with
the uprising.

From slave advertisements of the eighteenth century § we
may gain many sidelights not only on the education of Negroes
in the colonial era, but on their environment and suffering
as well. One slave "can write a pretty good hand; plays on
the fife extremely well." Another "can both read and write
and is a good fiddler." Still others speak "Dutch and good
English," "good English and High Dutch," or "Swede and

* Russell: *The Free Negro in Virginia*, 138-9.
† *Ibid.*, 138.
‡ C. E. Pierre, in *Journal of Negro History*, October, 1916, p. 350.
§ See documents, "Eighteenth Century Slave Advertisements," *Journal
of Negro History*, April, 1916, 163-216.

English well." Charles Thomas of Delaware bore the following remarkable characterization: "Very black, has white teeth
. . . has had his left leg broke . . . speaks both French and
English, and is a very great rogue." One man who came
from the West Indies "was born in Dominica and speaks
French, but very little English; he is a very ill-natured fellow
and has been much cut in his back by often whipping." A
Negro named Simon who in 1740 ran away in Pennsylvania
"could bleed and draw teeth pretending to be a great doctor."
Worst of all the incidents of slavery, however, was the lack
of regard for home ties, and this situation of course obtained
in the North as well as the South. In the early part of the
eighteenth century marriages in New York were by mutual
consent only, without the blessing of the church, and burial
was in a common field without any Christian office. In Massachusetts in 1710 Rev. Samuel Phillips drew up a marriage
formulary especially designed for slaves and concluding as
follows: "For you must both of you bear in mind that you
remain still, as really and truly as ever, your master's property,
and therefore it will be justly expected, both by God and
man, that you behave and conduct yourselves as obedient and
faithful servants." * In Massachusetts, however, as in New
York, marriage was most often by common consent simply,
without the office of ministers.

As yet there was no racial consciousness, no church, no business organization, and the chief coöperative effort was in
insurrection. Until the great chain of slavery was thrown
off, little independent effort could be put forth. Even in the
state of servitude or slavery, however, the social spirit of
the race yearned to assert itself, and such an event as a funeral
was attractive primarily because of the social features that
it developed. As early as 1693 there is record of the formation of a distinct society by Negroes. In one of his manuscript diaries, preserved in the library of the Massachusetts
Historical Society,† Cotton Mather in October of this year
wrote as follows: "Besides the other praying and pious meet-

* Quoted from Williams: Centennial Oration, "The American Negro
from 1776 to 1876," 10.
† See *Rules for the Society of Negroes*, 1693, by Cotton Mather,
reprinted, New York, 1888, by George H. Moore.

ings which I have been continually serving in our neighborhood, a little after this period a company of poor Negroes, of
their own accord, addressed me, for my countenance to a
design which they had, of erecting such a meeting 'for the
welfare of their miserable nation, that were servants among
us. I allowed their design and went one evening and prayed
and preached (on Ps. 68.31) with them; and gave them the
following orders, which I insert duly for the curiosity of
the occasion." The Rules to which Mather here refers are
noteworthy as containing not one suggestion of anti-slavery
sentiment, and as portraying the altogether abject situation
of the Negro at the time he wrote; nevertheless the text used
was an inspiring one, and in any case the document must have
historical importance as the earliest thing that has come down
to us in the nature of the constitution or by-laws for a distinctively Negro organization. It is herewith given entire:

RULES FOR THE SOCIETY OF NEGROES.

1693.

We the Miserable Children of *Adam,* and of *Noah,* thankfully
Admiring and Accepting the Free-Grace of GOD, that Offers to
Save us from our Miseries, by the Lord Jesus Christ, freely Resolve,
with His Help, to become the Servants of that Glorious LORD.

And that we may be Assisted in the Service of our *Heavenly
Master,* we now join together in a SOCIETY, wherein the following RULES are to be observed.

I.   It shall be our Endeavor, to Meet in the *Evening* after the
      Sabbath; and Pray together by Turns, one to Begin, and
      another to Conclude the Meeting; And between the two
      Prayers, a *Psalm* shall be sung, and a *Sermon* Repeated.

II.   Our coming to the Meeting, shall never be without the *Leave*
      of such as have Power over us: And we will be Careful,
      that our Meeting may Begin and Conclude between the
      Hours of *Seven* and *Nine;* and that we may not be *un-
      seasonably Absent* from the Families whereto we pertain.

III. As we will, with the help of God, at all Times avoid all
      Wicked Company, so we will Receive none into our Meet-
      ing, but such as have sensibly *Reformed* their lives from
      all manner of Wickedness. And, therefore, None shall be
      Admitted, without the Knowledge and Consent of the *Min-
      ister* of God in this place; unto whom we will also carry

every Person, that seeks for *Admission* among us; to be by Him Examined, Instructed and Exhorted.

IV. We will, as often as may be, Obtain some Wise and Good Man, of the English in the Neighborhood, and especially the Officers of the Church, to look in upon us, and by their Presence and Counsel, do what they think fitting for us.

V. If any of our Number fall into the Sin of *Drunkenness,* or *Swearing,* or *Cursing,* or *Lying,* or *Stealing,* or notorious *Disobedience* or *Unfaithfulness* unto their Masters, we will *Admonish* him of his Miscarriage, and Forbid his coming to the Meeting, for at least *one Fortnight;* And except he then come with great Signs and Hopes of his *Repentance,* we will utterly Exclude him, with Blotting his *Name* out of our list.

VI. If any of our Society Defile himself with *Fornication,* we will give him our *Admonition;* and so, debar him from the Meeting, at least half a Year: Nor shall he Return to it, ever any more, without Exemplary Testimonies of his becoming a *New Creature.*

VII. We will, as we have Opportunity, set ourselves to do all the Good we can, to the other *Negro-Servants* in the Town; And if any of them should, at unfit Hours, be *Abroad,* much more, if any of them should *Run away* from their Masters, we will afford them *no Shelter:* But we will do what in us lies, that they may be discovered, and punished. And if any *of us* are found Faulty in this matter, they shall be no longer *of us.*

VIII. None of our Society shall be *Absent* from our Meeting, without giving a Reason of the Absence; and if it be found, that any have pretended unto their *Owners,* that they came unto the Meeting, when they were otherwise and elsewhere Employed, we will faithfully *Inform* their Owners, and also do what we can to Reclaim such Person from all such Evil Courses for the Future.

IX. It shall be expected from every one in the Society, that he learn the Catechism; And therefore, it shall be one of our usual Exercises, for one of us, to ask the *Questions,* and for all the rest in their Order, to say the *Answers* in the Catechism; Either, The *New English* Catechism, or the *Assemblies* Catechism, or the Catechism in the *Negro Christianized.*

4. *Early Insurrections*

The Negroes who came to America directly from Africa in the eighteenth century were strikingly different from those whom generations of servitude later made comparatively docile.   They were wild and turbulent in disposition and were likely at any moment to take revenge for the great wrong that had been inflicted upon them.   The planters in the South knew this and lived in constant fear of uprisings.   When the situation became too threatening, they placed prohibitive duties on importations, and they also sought to keep their slaves in subjection by barbarous and cruel modes of punishment, both crucifixion and burning being legalized in some early codes. On sea as well as on land Negroes frequently rose upon those who held them in bondage, and sometimes they actually won their freedom.   More and more, however, in any study of Negro insurrections it becomes difficult to distinguish between a clearly organized revolt and what might be regarded as simply a personal crime, so that those uprisings considered in the following discussion can only be construed as the more representative of the many attempts for freedom made by Negro slaves in the colonial era.

In 1687 there was in Virginia a conspiracy among the Negroes in the Northern Neck that was detected just in time to prevent slaughter, and in Surry County in 1710 there was a similar plot, betrayed by one of the conspirators.   In 1711, in South Carolina, several Negroes ran away from their masters and "kept out, armed, robbing and plundering houses and plantations, and putting the inhabitants of the province in great fear and terror"; * and Governor Gibbes more than once wrote to the legislature about amending the Negro Act, as the one already in force did "not reach up to some of the crimes" that were daily being committed.   For one Sebastian, "a Spanish Negro," alive or dead, a reward of £50 was offered, and he was at length brought in by the Indians and taken in triumph to Charleston.   In 1712 in New York occurred an outbreak that occasioned greater excitement than any uprising that had preceded it in the colonies.   Early in the morning of April 7 some slaves of the Carmantee and Pappa tribes who had suffered ill-usage, set on fire the house of Peter van Tilburgh, and, armed with guns and knives, killed and wounded several persons who came to extinguish

* Holland: *A Refutation of Calumnies,* 63.

the flames. They fled, however, when the Governor ordered the cannon to be fired to alarm the town, and they got away to the woods as well as they could, but not before they had killed several more of the citizens. Some shot themselves in the woods and others were captured. Altogether eight or ten white persons were killed, and, aside from those Negroes who had committed suicide, eighteen or more were executed, several others being transported. Of those executed one was hanged alive in chains, some were burned at the stake, and one was left to die a lingering death before the gaze of the town.

In May, 1720, some Negroes in South Carolina were fairly well organized and killed a man named Benjamin Cattle, one white woman, and a little Negro boy. They were pursued and twenty-three taken and six convicted. Three of the latter were executed, the other three escaping. In October, 1722, the Negroes near the mouth of the Rappahannock in Virginia undertook to kill the white people while the latter were assembled in church, but were discovered and put to flight. On this occasion, as on most others, Sunday was the day chosen for the outbreak, the Negroes then being best able to get together. In April, 1723, it was thought that some fires in Boston had been started by Negroes, and the select-men recommended that if more than two Negroes were found "lurking together" on the streets they should be put in the house of correction. In 1728 there was a well organized attempt in Savannah, then a place of three thousand white people and two thousand seven hundred Negroes. The plan to kill all the white people failed because of disagreement as to the exact method; but the body of Negroes had to be fired on more than once before it dispersed. In 1730 there was in Williamsburg, Va., an insurrection that grew out of a report that Colonel Spotswood had orders from the king to free all baptized persons on his arrival; men from all the surrounding counties had to be called in before it could be put down.

The first open rebellion in South Carolina in which Negroes were "actually armed and embodied" * took place in 1730.

* Holland: *A Refutation of Calumnies,* 68.

The plan was for each Negro to kill his master in the dead of night, then for all to assemble supposedly for a dancing-bout, rush upon the heart of the city, take possession of the arms, and kill any white man they saw. The plot was discovered and the leaders executed. In this same colony three formidable insurrections broke out within the one year 1739 —one in St. Paul's Parish, one in St. John's, and one in Charleston. To some extent these seem to have been fomented by the Spaniards in the South, and in one of them six houses were burned and as many as twenty-five white people killed. The Negroes were pursued and fourteen killed. Within two days "twenty more were killed, and forty were taken, some of whom were shot, some hanged, and some gibbeted alive." * This "examplary punishment," as Governor Gibbes called it, was by no means effective, for in the very next year, 1740, there broke out what might be considered the most formidable insurrection in the South in the whole colonial period. A number of Negroes, having assembled at Stono, first surprised and killed two young men in a warehouse, from which they then took guns and ammunition.† They then elected as captain one of their own number named Cato, whom they agreed to follow, and they marched towards the southwest, with drums beating and colors flying, like a disciplined company. They entered the home of a man named Godfrey, and having murdered him and his wife and children, they took all the arms he had, set fire to the house, and proceeded towards Jonesboro. On their way they plundered and burned every house to which they came, killing every white person they found and compelling the Negroes to join them. Governor Bull, who happened to be returning to Charleston from the southward, met them, and observing them armed, spread the alarm, which soon reached the Presbyterian Church at Wilton, where a number of planters was assembled. The women were left in the church trembling with fear, while the militia formed and marched in quest of the Negroes, who by this time had become formidable from the number that had joined them. They had marched twelve miles and spread desolation

* Coffin.
† The following account follows mainly Holland, quoting Hewitt.

through all the plantations on their way. They had then halted in an open field and too soon had begun to sing and drink and dance by way of triumph. During these rejoicings the militia discovered them and stationed themselves in different places around them to prevent their escape. One party then advanced into the open field and attacked the Negroes. Some were killed and the others were forced to the woods. Many ran back to the plantations, hoping thus to avoid suspicion, but most of them were taken and tried. Such as had been forced to join the uprising against their will were pardoned, but all of the chosen leaders and the first insurgents were put to death. All Carolina, we are told, was struck with terror and consternation by this insurrection, in which more than twenty white persons were killed. It was followed immediately by the famous and severe Negro Act of 1740, which among other provisions imposed a duty of £100 on Africans and £150 on colonial Negroes. This remained technically in force until 1822, and yet as soon as security and confidence were restored, there was a relaxation in the execution of the provisions of the act and the Negroes little by little regained confidence in themselves and again began to plan and act in concert.

About the time of Cato's insurrection there were also several uprisings at sea. In 1731, on a ship returning to Rhode Island from Guinea with a cargo of slaves, the Negroes rose and killed three of the crew, all the members of which died soon afterwards with the exception of the captain and his boy. The next year Captain John Major of Portsmouth, N. H., was murdered with all his crew, his schooner and cargo being seized by the slaves. In 1735 the captives on the *Dolphin* of London, while still on the coast of Africa, overpowered the crew, broke into the powder room, and finally in the course of their effort for freedom blew up both themselves and the crew.

A most remarkable design—as an insurrection perhaps not as formidable as that of Cato, but in some ways the most important single event in the history of the Negro in the colonial period—was the plot in the city of New York in 1741. New York was at the time a thriving town of twelve thousand inhabitants, and the calamity that now befell it was unfortunate in every way. It was not only a Negro insurrection, though the Negro finally suffered most bitterly. It was also a strange compound of the effects of whiskey and gambling, of the designs of abandoned white people, and of prejudice against the Catholics.

Prominent in the remarkable drama were John Hughson, a shoemaker and alehouse keeper; Sarah Hughson, his wife; John Romme, also a shoemaker and alehouse keeper; Margaret Kerry, alias Salinburgh, commonly known as Peggy; John Ury, a priest; and a number of Negroes, chief among whom were Cæsar, Prince, Cuffee, and Quack.* Prominent among those who helped to work out the plot were Mary Burton, a white servant of Hughson's, sixteen years of age; Arthur Price, a young white man who at the time of the proceedings happened to be in prison on a charge of stealing; a young seaman named Wilson; and two white women, Mrs. Earle and Mrs. Hogg, the latter of whom assisted in the store kept by her husband, Robert Hogg. Hughson's house on the outskirts of the town was a resort for Negroes, and Hughson himself aided and abetted the Negro men in any crime that they might commit. Romme was of similar quality. Peggy was a prostitute, and it was Cæsar who paid for her board with the Hughsons. In the previous summer she had found lodging with these people, a little later she had removed to Romme's, and just before Christmas she had come back to Hughson's, and a few weeks thereafter she became a mother. At both the public houses the Negroes would engage in drinking and gambling; and importance also attaches to an organization of theirs known as the Geneva Society, which had angered some of the white citizens by its imitation of the rites and forms of freemasonry.

Events really began on the night of Saturday, February 28, 1741, with a robbery in the house of Hogg, the merchant, from which were taken various pieces of linen and other goods,

* The sole authority on the plot is "A Journal of the Proceedings in the Detection of the Conspiracy formed by Some White People, in Conjunction with Negro and other Slaves, for Burning the City of New York in America, and Murdering the Inhabitants (by Judge Daniel Horsemanden). New York, 1744."

several silver coins, chiefly Spanish, and medals, to the value of about £60. On the day before, in the course of a simple purchase by Wilson, Mrs. Hogg had revealed to the young seaman her treasure. He soon spoke of the same to Cæsar, Prince, and Cuffee, with whom he was acquainted; he gave them the plan of the house, and they in turn spoke of the matter to Hughson. Wilson, however, when later told of the robbery by Mrs. Hogg, at once turned suspicion upon the Negroes, especially Cæsar; and Mary Burton testified that she saw some of the speckled linen in question in Peggy's room after Cæsar had gone thither

On Wednesday, March 18, a fire broke out on the roof of His Majesty's House at Fort George. One week later, on March 25, there was a fire at the home of Captain Warren in the southwest end of the city, and the circumstances pointed to incendiary origin. One week later, on April 1, there was a fire in the storehouse of a man named Van Zant; on the following Saturday evening there was another fire, and while the people were returning from this there was still another; and on the next day, Sunday, there was another alarm, and by this time the whole town had been worked up to the highest pitch of excitement. As yet there was nothing to point to any connection between the stealing and the fires. On the day of the last one, however, Mrs. Earle happened to overhear remarks by three Negroes that caused suspicion to light upon them; Mary Burton was insisting that stolen goods had been brought by Prince and Cæsar to the house of her master; and although a search of the home of Hughson failed to produce a great deal, arrests were made right and left. The case was finally taken to the Supreme Court, and because of the white persons implicated, the summary methods ordinarily used in dealing with Negroes were waived for the time being.

Peggy at first withstood all questioning, denying any knowledge of the events that had taken place. One day in prison, however, she remarked to Arthur Price that she was afraid the Negroes would tell but that she would not forswear herself unless they brought her into the matter. "How forswear?" asked Price. "There are fourteen sworn," she said. "What, is it about Mr. Hogg's goods?" he asked. "No," she replied, "about the fire." "What, Peggy," asked Price, "were you going to set the town on fire?" "No," she replied, "but since I knew of it they made me swear." She also remarked that she had faith in Prince, Cuff, and Cæsar. All the while she used the vilest possible language, and at last, thinking suddenly that she had revealed too much, she turned upon Price and with an oath warned him that he had better keep his counsel. That afternoon she said further to him that she could not eat because Mary had brought her into the case.

A little later Peggy, much afraid, voluntarily confessed that early in May she was at the home of John Romme, where in the course of December the Negroes had had several meetings; among other things they had conspired to burn the fort first of all, then the city, then to get all the goods they could and kill anybody who had money. One evening just about Christmas, she said, Romme and his wife and ten or eleven Negroes had been together in a room. Romme had talked about how rich some people were, gradually working on the feelings of the Negroes and promising them that if they did not succeed in their designs he would take them to a strange country and set them free, meanwhile giving them the impression that he bore a charmed life. A little later, it appeared, Cæsar gave to Hughson £12; Hughson was then absent for three days, and when he came again he brought with him seven or eight guns, some pistols, and some swords.

As a result of these and other disclosures it was seen that not only Hughson and Romme but also Ury, who was not so much a priest as an adventurer, had instigated the plots of the Negroes; and Quack testified that Hughson was the first contriver of the plot to burn the houses of the town and kill the people, though he himself, he confessed, did fire the fort with a lighted stick. The punishment was terrible. Quack and Cuffee, the first to be executed, were burned at the stake on May 30. All through the summer the trials and the executions continued, harassing New York and indeed the whole country. Altogether twenty white persons were arrested; four—Hughson, his wife, Peggy, and Ury—were executed, and some of their acquaintances were forced to leave the province. One hundred and fifty-four Negroes were arrested. Thirteen were burned, eighteen were hanged, and seventy-one transported.

It is evident from these events and from the legislation of the era that, except for the earnest work of such a sect as the Quakers, there was little genuine effort for the improvement of the social condition of the Negro people in the colonies. They were not even regarded as potential citizens, and both in and out of the system of slavery were subjected to the harshest regulations. Towards amicable relations with the other racial elements that were coming to build up a new country only the slightest measure of progress was made. Instead, insurrection after insurrection revealed the sharpest antagonism, and any outbreak promptly called forth the severest and frequently the most cruel punishment.

CHAPTER III

1. *Sentiment in England and America*

The materialism of the eighteenth century, with all of its evils, at length produced a liberalism of thought that was to shake to their very foundations old systems of life in both Europe and America. The progress of the cause of the Negro in this period is to be explained by the general diffusion of ideas that made for the rights of man everywhere. Cowper wrote his humanitarian poems; in close association with the romanticism of the day the missionary movement in religion began to gather force; and the same impulse which in England began the agitation for a free press and for parliamentary reform, and which in France accounted for the French Revolution, in America led to the revolt from Great Britain. No patriot could come under the influence of any one of these movements without having his heart and his sense of justice stirred to some degree in behalf of the slave. At the same time it must be remembered that the contest of the Americans was primarily for the definite legal rights of Englishmen rather than for the more abstract rights of mankind which formed the platform of the French Revolution; hence arose the great inconsistency in the position of men who were engaged in a stern struggle for liberty at the same time that they themselves were holding human beings in bondage.

In England the new era was formally signalized by an epoch-making decision. In November, 1769, Charles Stewart, once a merchant in Norfolk and later receiver general of the customs of North America, took to England his Negro slave, James Somerset, who, being sick, was turned adrift by his master. Later Somerset recovered and Stewart seized him, intending to have him borne out of the country and sold in Jamaica. Somerset objected to this and in so doing raised the important legal question, Did a slave by being brought to England become free? The case received an extraordinary amount of attention, for everybody realized that the decision would be far-reaching in its consequences. After it was argued at three different sittings, Lord Mansfield, Chief Justice of England, in 1772 handed down from the Court of King's Bench the judgment that as soon as ever any slave set his foot upon the soil of England he became free.

This decision may be taken as fairly representative of the general advance that the cause of the Negro was making in England at the time. Early in the century sentiment against the slave-trade had begun to develop, many pamphlets on the evils of slavery were circulated, and as early as 1776 a motion for the abolition of the trade was made in the House of Commons. John Wesley preached against the system, Adam Smith showed its ultimate expensiveness, and Burke declared that the slavery endured by the Negroes in the English settlements was worse than that ever suffered by any other people. Foremost in the work of protest were Thomas Clarkson and William Wilberforce, the one being the leader in investigation and in the organization of the movement against slavery while the other was the parliamentary champion of the cause. For years, assisted by such debaters as Burke, Fox, and the younger Pitt, Wilberforce worked until on March 25, 1807, the bill for the abolition of the slave-trade received the royal assent, and still later until slavery itself was abolished in the English dominions (1833).

This high thought in England necessarily found some reflection in America, where the logic of the position of the patriots frequently forced them to take up the cause of the slave. As early as 1751 Benjamin Franklin, in his *Observations concerning the Increase of Mankind,* pointed out the evil effects of slavery upon population and the production of wealth; and in 1761 James Otis, in his argument against the Writs of Assistance, spoke so vigorously of the rights of black men as to leave no doubt as to his own position. To Patrick Henry slavery was a practice "totally repugnant to the first impressions of right and wrong," and in 1777 he was interested in a plan for gradual emancipation received from his friend, Robert Pleasants. Washington desired nothing more than "to see some plan adopted by which slavery might be abolished by law"; while Joel Barlow in his *Columbiad* gave significant warning to Columbia of the ills that she was heaping up for herself.

Two of the expressions of sentiment of the day, by reason of their deep yearning and philosophic calm, somehow stand apart from others. Thomas Jefferson in his *Notes on Virginia* wrote: "The whole commerce between master and slave is a perpetual exercise of the most boisterous passions; the most unremitting despotism on the one part, and degrading submission on the other. . . . The man must be a prodigy who can retain his manners and morals undepraved by such circumstances. . . . I tremble for my country when I reflect that God is just; that his justice can not sleep forever; that considering numbers, nature, and natural means only, a revolution of the wheel of fortune, an exchange of situation, is among possible events; that it may become probable by supernatural interference! The Almighty has no attribute which can take side with us in such a contest." * Henry Laurens, that fine patriot whose business sense was excelled only by his idealism, was harassed by the problem and wrote to his son, Colonel John Laurens, as follows: "You know, my dear son, I abhor slavery. I was born in a country where slavery had been established by British kings and parliaments, as well as by the laws of that country ages before my existence. I found the Christian religion and slavery growing under the same authority and cultivation. I nevertheless disliked it. In former days there was no combating the prejudices of men supported by interest; the day I hope is approaching when, from principles of gratitude as well as justice, every man will strive to be foremost in showing his readiness to comply with the golden rule. Not less than twenty thousand pounds sterling would all my Negroes produce if sold at public auction to-morrow. I am

* "The Writings of Thomas Jefferson, issued under the auspices of the Thomas Jefferson Memorial Association," 20 vols., Washington, 1903, II, 226-227.

not the man who enslaved them; they are indebted to Englishmen for that favor; nevertheless I am devising means for manumitting many of them, and for cutting off the entail of slavery. Great powers oppose me—the laws and customs of my country, my own and the avarice of my countrymen. What will my children say if I deprive them of so much estate? These are difficulties, but not insuperable. I will do as much as I can in my time, and leave the rest to a better hand." * Stronger than all else, however, were the immortal words of the Declaration of Independence: "We hold these truths to be self-evident: That all men are created equal; that they are endowed by their Creator with certain inalienable rights; that among these are life, liberty, and the pursuit of happiness." Within the years to come these words were to be denied and assailed as perhaps no others in the language; but in spite of all they were to stand firm and justify the faith of 1776 before Jefferson himself and others had become submerged in a gilded opportunism.

It is not to be supposed that such sentiments were by any means general; nevertheless these instances alone show that some men at least in the colonies were willing to carry their principles to their logical conclusion. Naturally opinion crystallized in formal resolutions or enactments. Unfortunately most of these were in one way or another rendered ineffectual after the war; nevertheless the main impulse that they represented continued to live. In 1769 Virginia declared that the discriminatory tax levied on free Negroes and mulattoes since 1668 was "derogatory to the rights of freeborn subjects" and accordingly should be repealed. In October, 1774, the First Continental Congress declared in its Articles of Association that the united colonies would "neither import nor purchase any slave imported after the first day of December next" and that they would "wholly discontinue the trade." On April 16, 1776, the Congress further resolved that "no slaves be imported into any of the thirteen colonies"; and the first draft of the Declaration of Independence contained a strong passage

* "A South Carolina Protest against Slavery (being a letter written from Henry Laurens, second president of the Continental Congress, to his son, Colonel John Laurens; dated Charleston, S. C., August 14th, 1776)." Reprinted by G. P. Putnam, New York, 1861.

censuring the King of England for bringing slaves into the country and then inciting them to rise against their masters. On April 14, 1775, the first abolition society in the country was organized in Pennsylvania; in 1778 Virginia once more passed an act prohibiting the slave-trade; and the Methodist Conference in Baltimore in 1780 strongly expressed its disapproval of slavery.

2. The Negro in the War

As in all the greater wars in which the country has engaged, the position of the Negro was generally improved by the American Revolution. It was not by reason of any definite plan that this was so, for in general the disposition of the government was to keep him out of the conflict. Nevertheless between the hesitating policy of America and the overtures of England the Negro made considerable advance.

The American cause in truth presented a strange and embarrassing dilemma, as we have remarked. In the war itself, moreover, began the stern cleavage between the North and the South. At the moment the rift was not clearly discerned, but afterwards it was to widen into a chasm. Massachusetts bore more than her share of the struggle, and in the South the combination of Tory sentiment and the aristocratic social system made enlistment especially difficult. In this latter section, moreover, there was always the lurking fear of an uprising of the slaves, and before the end of the war came South Carolina and Georgia were very nearly demoralized. In the course of the conflict South Carolina lost not less than 25,000 slaves,* about one-fifth of all she had. Georgia did not lose so many, but proportionally suffered even more. Some of the Negroes went into the British army, some went away with the loyalists, and some took advantage of the confusion and escaped to the Indians. In Virginia, until they were stopped at least, some slaves entered the Continental Army as free Negroes.

Three or four facts are outstanding. The formal policy

* Historical Notes on the Employment of Negroes in the American Army of the Revolution, by G. H. Moore, New York, 1862, p. 15.

of Congress and of Washington and his officers was against the enlistment of Negroes and especially of slaves; nevertheless, while things were still uncertain, some Negroes entered the regular units. The inducements offered by the English, moreover, forced a modification of the American policy in actual operation; and before the war was over the colonists were so hard pressed that in more ways than one they were willing to receive the assistance of Negroes. Throughout the North Negroes served in the regular units; but while in the South especially there was much thought given to the training of slaves, in only one of all the colonies was there a distinctively Negro military organization, and that one was Rhode Island. In general it was understood that if a slave served in the war he was to be given his freedom, and it is worthy of note that many slaves served in the field instead of their masters.

In Massachusetts on May 29, 1775, the Committee of Safety passed an act against the enlistment of slaves as "inconsistent with the principles that are to be supported." Another resolution of June 6 dealing with the same matter was laid on the table. Washington took command of the forces in and about Boston July 3, 1775, and on July 10 issued instructions to the recruiting officers in Massachusetts against the enlisting of Negroes. Toward the end of September there was a spirited debate in Congress over a letter to go to Washington, the Southern delegates, led by Rutledge of South Carolina, endeavoring to force instructions to the commander-in-chief to discharge all slaves and free Negroes in the army. A motion to this effect failed to win a majority; nevertheless, a council of Washington and his generals on October 8 "agreed unanimously to reject all slaves, and, by a great majority, to reject Negroes altogether," and in his general orders of November 12 Washington acted on this understanding. Meanwhile, however, Lord Dunmore issued his proclamation declaring free those indentured servants and Negroes who would join the English army, and in great numbers the slaves in Virginia flocked to the British standard. Then on December 14—somewhat to the amusement of both the Negroes and the English—the Virginia Convention issued a proclamation offering pardon to those slaves who returned to their duty within ten days. On December 30 Washington gave instructions for the enlistment of free Negroes, promising later to lay the matter before Congress; and a congressional committee on January 16, 1776, reported that those free Negroes who had already served faithfully in the army at Cambridge might reënlist but no others, the debate in this connection having drawn very sharply the line between the North and the South. Henceforth for all practical purposes the matter was left in the hands of the individual colonies. Massachusetts on January 6, 1777, passed a resolution drafting every seventh man to complete her quota "without any exception, save the people called Quakers," and this was as near as she came at any time in the war to the formal recognition of the Negro. The Rhode Island Assembly in 1778 resolved to raise a regiment of slaves, who were to be freed at enlistment, their owners in no case being paid more than £120. In the Battle of Rhode Island August 29, 1778, the Negro regiment under Colonel Greene distinguished itself by deeds of desperate valor, repelling three times the assaults of an overwhelming force of Hessian troops. A little later, when Greene was about to be murdered, some of these same soldiers had to be cut to pieces before he could be secured. Maryland employed Negroes as soldiers and sent them into regiments along with white men, and it is to be remembered that at the time the Negro population of Maryland was exceeded only by that of Virginia and South Carolina. For the far South there was the famous Laurens plan for the raising of Negro regiments.

In a letter to Washington of March 16, 1779, Henry Laurens suggested the raising and training of three thousand Negroes in South Carolina. Washington was rather conservative about the plan, having in mind the ever-present fear of the arming of Negroes and wondering about the effect on those slaves who were not given a chance for freedom. On June 30, 1779, however, Sir Henry Clinton issued a proclamation only less far-reaching than Dunmore's, threatening Negroes if they joined the "rebel" army and offering them security if they came within the British lines. This was effective; assistance of any kind that the Continental Army could now get was acceptable; and the plan for the raising of several battalions of Negroes in the South was entrusted to Colonel John Laurens, a member of Washington's staff. In his own way Colonel Laurens was a man of parts quite as well as his father; he was thoroughly devoted to the American cause and Washington said of him that his only fault was a courage that bordered on rashness. He eagerly pursued his favorite project; able-bodied slaves were to be paid for by Congress at the rate of $1,000 each, and one who served to the end of the war was to receive his freedom and $50 in addition. In South Carolina, however, Laurens received little encouragement, and in 1780 he was called upon to go to France on a patriotic mission. He had not forgotten the matter when he returned in 1782; but by that time Cornwallis had surrendered and the country had entered upon the critical period of adjustment to the new conditions. Washington now wrote to Laurens: "I must confess that I am not at all astonished at the failure of your plan. That spirit of freedom which, at the commencement of this contest, would have gladly sacrificed everything to the attainment of its object, has long since subsided, and every selfish passion has taken its place. It is not the public but private interest which influences the generality of mankind; nor can the Americans any longer boast an exception. Under these circumstances, it would rather have been surprising if you had succeeded; nor will you, I fear, have better success in Georgia." *

From this brief survey we may at least see something of the anomalous position occupied by the Negro in the American Revolution. Altogether not less than three thousand, and probably more, members of the race served in the Continental army. At the close of the conflict New York, Rhode Island, and Virginia freed their slave soldiers. In general, however, the system of slavery was not affected, and the English were bound by the treaty of peace not to carry away any Negroes. As late as 1786, it is nevertheless interesting to note, a band of Negroes calling themselves "The King of England's soldiers" harassed and alarmed the people on both sides of the Savannah River.

* Sparks's *Washington*, VIII, 322-323.

Slavery remained; but people could not forget the valor of the Negro regiment in Rhode Island, or the courage of individual soldiers.   They could not forget that it was a Negro, Crispus Attucks, who had been the patriot leader in the Boston Massacre, or the scene when he and one of his companions, Jonas Caldwell, lay in Faneuil Hall.   Those who were at Bunker Hill could not fail to remember Peter Salem, who, when Major Pitcairn of the British army was exulting in his expected triumph, rushed forward, shot him in the breast, and killed him; or Samuel Poor, whose officers testified that he performed so many brave deeds that "to set forth particulars of his conduct would be tedious."   These and many more, some with very humble names, in a dark day worked for a better country.   They died in faith, not having received the promises, but having seen them afar off.

3.   The Northwest Territory and the Constitution

The materialism and selfishness which rose in the course of the war to oppose the liberal tendencies of the period, and which Washington felt did so much to embarrass the government, became pronounced in the debates on the Northwest Territory and the Constitution.   At the outbreak of the Revolutionary War the region west of Pennsylvania, east of the Mississippi River, north of the Ohio River, and south of Canada, was claimed by Virginia, New York, Connecticut, and Massachusetts.   This territory afforded to these states a source of revenue not possessed by the others for the payment of debts incurred in the war, and Maryland and other seaboard states insisted that in order to equalize matters these claimants should cede their rights to the general government.   The formal cessions were made and accepted in the years 1782-6.   In April, 1784, after Virginia had made her cession, the most important, Congress adopted a temporary form of government drawn up by Thomas Jefferson for the territory south as well as north of the Ohio River.   Jefferson's most significant provision, however, was rejected.   This declared that "after the year 1800 there shall be neither slavery nor involuntary servitude in any of the said states other than in the punishment

of crimes whereof the party shall have been duly convicted
to have been personally guilty." This early ordinance, although
it did not go into effect, is interesting as an attempt to exclude
slavery from the great West that was beginning to be opened
up. On March 3, 1786, moreover, the Ohio Company was
formed in Boston by a group of New England business men
for the purpose of purchasing land in the West and promoting
settlement; and early in June, 1787, Dr. Manasseh Cutler, one
of the chief promoters of the company, appeared in New York,
where the last Continental Congress was sitting, for the concrete purpose of buying land. He doubtless did much to hasten
action by Congress, and on July 13 was passed "An Ordinance
for the Government of the Territory of the United States,
Northwest of the Ohio," the Southern states not having ceded
the area south of the river. It was declared that "There
shall be neither slavery nor involuntary servitude in the said
territory, otherwise than in punishment of crimes, whereof
the parties shall be duly convicted." To this was added the
stipulation (soon afterwards embodied in the Federal Constitution) for the return of any person escaping into the territory from whom labor or service was "lawfully claimed in
any one of the original states." In this shape the ordinance
was adopted, even South Carolina and Georgia concurring;
and thus was paved the way for the first fugitive slave law.

Slavery, already looming up as a dominating issue, was
the cause of two of the three great compromises that entered
into the making of the Constitution of the United States (the
third, which was the first made, being the concession to the
smaller states of equal representation in the Senate). These
were the first but not the last of the compromises that were
to mark the history of the subject; and, as some clear-headed
men of the time perceived, it would have been better and
cheaper to settle the question at once on the high plane of
right rather than to leave it indefinitely to the future. South
Carolina, however, with able representation, largely controlled
the thought of the convention, and she and Georgia made the
most extreme demands, threatening not to accept the Constitution if there was not compliance with them. An important
question was that of representation, the Southern states advo-

cating representation according to numbers, slave and free, while the Northern states were in favor of the representation of free persons only.   Williamson of North Carolina advocated the counting of three-fifths of the slaves, but this motion was at first defeated, and there was little real progress until Gouverneur Morris suggested that representation be according to the principle of wealth.   Mason of Virginia pointed out practical difficulties which caused the resolution to be made to apply to direct taxation only, and in this form it began to be generally acceptable.   By this time, however, the deeper feelings of the delegates on the subject of slavery had been stirred, and they began to speak plainly.   Davie of North Carolina declared that his state would never enter the Union on any terms that did not provide for counting at least three-fifths of the slaves and that "if the Eastern states meant to exclude them altogether the business was at an end."   It was finally agreed to reckon three-fifths of the slaves in estimating taxes and to make taxation the basis of representation.   The whole discussion was renewed, however, in connection with the question of importation.   There were more threats from the far South, and some of the men from New England, prompted by commercial interest, even if they did not favor the sentiments expressed, were at least disposed to give them passive acquiescence.   From Maryland and Virginia, however, came earnest protest.   Luther Martin declared unqualifiedly that to have a clause in the Constitution permitting the importation of slaves was inconsistent with the principles of the Revolution and dishonorable to the American character, and George Mason could foresee only a future in which a just Providence would punish such a national sin as slavery by national calamities. Such utterances were not to dominate the convention, however; it was a day of expediency, not of morality.   A bargain was made between the commercial interests of the North and the slave-holding interests of the South, the granting to Congress of unrestricted power to enact navigation laws being conceded in exchange for twenty years' continuance of the slave-trade.   The main agreements on the subject of slavery were thus finally expressed in the Constitution: "Representatives and direct taxes shall be apportioned among the several states which may be included within this Union, according to their respective numbers, which shall be determined by adding to the whole number of free persons, including those bound to servitude for a term of years, and excluding Indians not taxed, three-fifths of all other persons" (Art. I, Sec. 2); "The migration or importation of such persons as any of the states now existing shall think proper to admit, shall not be prohibited by the congress prior to the year 1808; but a tax or duty may be imposed, not exceeding ten dollars on each person" (Art. I, Sec. 9); "No person held to service or labor in one state, under the laws thereof, escaping into another, shall, in consequence of any law or regulation therein, be discharged from such service or labor, but shall be delivered up on claim of the party to whom such service or labor may be due" (Art. IV, Sec. 2). With such provisions, though without the use of the question-begging word *slaves,* the institution of human bondage received formal recognition in the organic law of the new republic of the United States.

"Just what is the light in which we are to regard the slaves?" wondered James Wilson in the course of the debate. "Are they admitted as citizens?" he asked; "then why are they not admitted on an equality with white citizens? Are they admitted as property? then why is not other property admitted into the computation?" Such questions and others to which they gave rise were to trouble more heads than his in the course of the coming years, and all because a great nation did not have the courage to do the right thing at the right time.

4. *Early Steps toward Abolition*

In spite, however, of the power crystallized in the Constitution, the moral movement that had set in against slavery still held its ground, and it was destined never wholly to languish until slavery ceased altogether to exist in the United States. Throughout the century the Quakers continued their good work; in the generation before the war John Woolman of New Jersey traveled in the Southern colonies preaching that "the practice of continuing slavery is not right"; and Anthony Benezet opened in Philadelphia a school for Negroes which he himself taught without remuneration, and otherwise influenced Pennsylvania to begin the work of emancipation. In general the Quakers conducted their campaign along the lines on which they were most likely to succeed, attacking the slave-trade first of all but more and more making an appeal to the central government; and the first Abolition Society, organized in Pennsylvania in 1775 and consisting mainly of Quakers, had for its original object merely the relief of free Negroes unlawfully held in bondage.* The organization was forced to suspend its work in the course of the war, but in 1784 it renewed its meetings, and men of other denominations than the Quakers now joined in greater numbers. In 1787 the society was formally reorganized as "The Pennsylvania Society for Promoting the Abolition of Slavery, the Relief of Free Negroes unlawfully held in Bondage, and for Improving the Condition of the African Race." Benjamin Franklin was elected president and there was adopted a constitution which was more and more to serve as a model for similar societies in the neighboring states.

Four years later, by 1791, there were in the country as many as twelve abolition societies, and these represented all the states from Massachusetts to Virginia, with the exception of New Jersey, where a society was formed the following year. That of New York, formed in 1785 with John Jay as president, took the name of the Manumission Society, limiting its aims at first to promoting manumission and protecting those Negroes who had already been set free. All of the societies had very clear ideas as to their mission. The prevalence of kidnaping made them emphasize "the relief of free Negroes unlawfully held in bondage," and in general each one in addition to its executive committee had committees for inspection, advice, and protection; for the guardianship of children; for the superintending of education, and for employment. While the societies were originally formed to attend to local matters, their efforts naturally extended in course of time to national affairs, and on December 8, 1791, nine of them prepared petitions to Congress for the limitation of the

* Locke: *Anti-Slavery in America*, 97.

slave-trade. These petitions were referred to a special committee and nothing more was heard of them at the time. After two years accordingly the organizations decided that a more vigorous plan of action was necessary, and on January 1, 1794, delegates from nine societies organized in Philadelphia the American Convention of Abolition Societies. The object of the Convention was twofold, "to increase the zeal and efficiency of the individual societies by its advice and encouragement . . . and to take upon itself the chief responsibility in regard to national affairs." It prepared an address to the country and presented to Congress a memorial against the fitting out of vessels in the United States to engage in the slave-trade, and it had the satisfaction of seeing Congress in the same year pass a bill to this effect.

Some of the organizations were very active and one as far South as that in Maryland was at first very powerful. Always were they interested in suits in courts of law. In 1797 the New York Society reported 90 complaints, 36 persons freed, 21 cases still in suit, and 19 under consideration. The Pennsylvania Society reported simply that it had been instrumental in the liberation of "many hundreds" of persons. The different branches, however, did not rest with mere liberation; they endeavored generally to improve the condition of the Negroes in their respective communities, each one being expected to report to the Convention on the number of freedmen in its state and on their property, employment, and conduct. From time to time also the Convention prepared addresses to these people, and something of the spirit of its work and also of the social condition of the Negro at the time may be seen from the following address of 1796:

TO THE FREE AFRICANS AND OTHER FREE PEOPLE OF COLOR IN THE UNITED STATES.

The Convention of Deputies from the Abolition Societies in the United States, assembled at Philadelphia, have undertaken to address you upon subjects highly interesting to your prosperity.

They wish to see you act worthily of the rank you have acquired as freemen, and thereby to do credit to yourselves, and to justify the friends and advocates of your color in the eyes of the world.

As the result of our united reflections, we have concluded to call your attention to the following articles of advice. We trust they are dictated by the purest regard for your welfare, for we view you as Friends and Brethren.

In the first place, We earnestly recommend to you, a regular attention to the important duty of public worship; by which means you will evince gratitude to your Creator, and, at the same time, promote knowledge, union, friendship, and proper conduct among yourselves.

Secondly, We advise such of you, as have not been taught reading, writing, and the first principles of arithmetic, to acquire them as early as possible. Carefully attend to the instruction of your children in the same simple and useful branches of education. Cause them, likewise, early and frequently to read the holy Scriptures; these contain, amongst other great discoveries, the precious record of the original equality of mankind, and of the obligations of universal justice and benevolence, which are derived from the relation of the human race to each other in a common Father.

Thirdly, Teach your children useful trades, or to labor with their hands in cultivating the earth. These employments are favorable to health and virtue. In the choice of masters, who are to instruct them in the above branches of business, prefer those who will work with them; by this means they will acquire habits of industry, and be better preserved from vice than if they worked alone, or under the eye of persons less interested in their welfare. In forming contracts, for yourselves or children, with masters, it may be useful to consult such persons as are capable of giving you the best advice, and who are known to be your friends, in order to prevent advantages being taken of your ignorance of the laws and customs of our country.

Fourthly, Be diligent in your respective callings, and faithful in all the relations you bear in society, whether as husbands, wives, fathers, children or hired servants. Be just in all your dealings. Be simple in your dress and furniture, and frugal in your family expenses. Thus you will act like Christians as well as freemen, and, by these means, you will provide for the distresses and wants of sickness and old age.

Fifthly, Refrain from the use of spirituous liquors; the experience of many thousands of the citizens of the United States has proved that these liquors are not necessary to lessen the fatigue of labor, nor to obviate the effects of heat or cold; nor can they, in any degree, add to the innocent pleasures of society.

Sixthly, Avoid frolicking, and amusements which lead to expense and idleness; they beget habits of dissipation and vice, and thus expose you to deserved reproach amongst your white neighbors.

Seventhly, We wish to impress upon your minds the moral and religious necessity of having your marriages legally performed; also to have exact registers preserved of all the births and deaths which occur in your respective families.

Eighthly, Endeavor to lay up as much as possible of your earnings for the benefit of your children, in case you should die before they are able to maintain themselves—your money will be safest and most beneficial when laid out in lots, houses, or small farms.

Ninthly, We recommend to you, at all times and upon all occasions, to behave yourselves to all persons in a civil and respectful manner, by which you may prevent contention and remove every just occasion of complaint. We beseech you to reflect, that it is by your good conduct alone that you can refute the objections which have been made against you as rational and moral creatures, and remove many of the difficulties which have occurred in the general emancipation of such of your brethren as are yet in bondage.

With hearts anxious for your welfare, we commend you to the guidance and protection of that *Being* who is able to keep you from all evil, and who is the common Father and Friend of the whole family of mankind.

By order, and in behalf, of the Convention,

THEODORE FOSTER, President.

Philadelphia, January 6th, 1796.

THOMAS P. COPE, Secretary.

The general impulse for liberty which prompted the Revolution and the early Abolition societies naturally found some reflection in formal legislation. The declarations of the central government under the Confederation were not very effective, and for more definite enactments we have to turn to the individual states. The honor of being the first actually to prohibit and abolish slavery really belongs to Vermont, whose constitution, adopted in 1777, even before she had come into the Union, declared very positively against the system. In 1782 the old Virginia statute forbidding emancipation except for meritorious services was repealed. The repeal was in force ten years, and in this time manumissions were numerous. Maryland soon afterwards passed acts similar to those in Virginia prohibiting the further introduction of slaves and removing restraints on emancipation, and New York and New Jersey also prohibited the further introduction of slaves from Africa or from other states. In 1780, in spite of considerable opposition because of the course of the war, the Penn-

sylvania Assembly passed an act forbidding the further introduction of slaves and giving freedom to all persons thereafter
born in the state. Similar provisions were enacted in Connecticut and Rhode Island in 1784. Meanwhile Massachusetts
was much agitated, and beginning in 1766 there were before
the courts several cases in which Negroes sued for their freedom.* Their general argument was that the royal charter
declared that all persons residing in the province were to be as
free as the king's subjects in Great Britain, that by Magna
Carta no subject could be deprived of liberty except by the
judgment of his peers, and that any laws that may have been
passed in the province to mitigate or regulate the evil of
slavery did not authorize it. Sometimes the decisions were
favorable, but at the beginning of the Revolution Massachusetts still recognized the system by the decision that no slave
could be enlisted in the army. In 1777, however, some slaves
brought from Jamaica were ordered to be set at liberty, and
it was finally decided in 1783 that the declaration in the
Massachusetts Bill of Rights to the effect that "all men are
born free and equal" prohibited slavery. In this same year
New Hampshire incorporated in her constitution a prohibitive
article. By the time the convention for the framing of the
Constitution of the United States met in Philadelphia in 1787,
two of the original thirteen states (Massachusetts and New
Hampshire) had positively prohibited slavery, and in three
others (Pennsylvania, Connecticut, and Rhode Island) gradual
abolition was in progress.

The next decade was largely one of the settlement of new
territory, and by its close the pendulum seemed to have swung
decidedly backward. In 1799, however, after much effort and
debating, New York at last declared for gradual abolition, and
New Jersey did likewise in 1804. In general, gradual emancipation was the result of the work of people who were humane
but also conservative and who questioned the wisdom of thrust-
ing upon the social organism a large number of Negroes suddenly emancipated. Sometimes, however, a gradual emanci-

* See Williams: *History of the Negro Race in America,* I, 228-
236.

pation act was later followed by one for immediate manumission, as in New York in 1817. At first those who favored gradual emancipation were numerous in the South as well as in the North, but in general after Gabriel's insurrection in 1800, though some individuals were still outstanding, the South was quiescent. The character of the acts that were really put in force can hardly be better stated than has already been done by the specialist in the subject.* We read:

Gradual emancipation is defined as the extinction of slavery by depriving it of its hereditary quality. In distinction from the clauses in the constitutions of Vermont, Massachusetts, and New Hampshire, which directly or indirectly affected the condition of slavery as already existing, the gradual emancipation acts left this condition unchanged and affected only the children born after the passage of the act or after a fixed date. Most of these acts followed that of Pennsylvania in providing that the children of a slave mother should remain with her owner as servants until they reached a certain age, of from twenty-one to twenty-eight years, as stated in the various enactments. In Pennsylvania, however, they were to be regarded as free. In Connecticut, on the other hand, they were to be "held in servitude" until twenty-five years of age and after that to be free. The most liberal policy was that of Rhode Island, where the children were pronounced free but were to be supported by the town and educated in reading, writing, and arithmetic, morality and religion. The latter clauses, however, were repealed the following year, leaving the children to be supported by the owner of the mother until twenty-one years of age, and only if he abandoned his claims to the mother to become a charge to the town. In New York and New Jersey they were to remain as servants until a certain age, but were regarded as free, and liberal opportunities were given the master for the abandonment of his claims, the children in such cases to be supported at the common charge. . . . The manumission and emancipation acts were naturally followed, as in the case of the constitutional provision in Vermont, by the attempts of some of the slave-owners to dispose of their property outside the State. Amendments to the laws were found necessary, and the Abolition Societies found plenty of occasion for their exertions in protecting free blacks from seizure and illegal sale and in looking after the execution and amendment of the laws. The process of gradual emancipation was also unsatisfactory on account of the length of time it would require, and in Pennsylvania and Connecticut attempts were made to obtain acts for immediate emancipation.

* Locke, 124-126.

5. *Beginning of Racial Consciousness*

Of supreme importance in this momentous period, more important perhaps in its ultimate effect than even the work of the Abolition Societies, was what the Negro was doing for himself. In the era of the Revolution began that racial consciousness on which almost all later effort for social betterment has been based.

By 1700 the only coöperative effort on the part of the Negro was such as that in the isolated society to which Cotton Mather gave rules, or in a spasmodic insurrection, or a rather crude development of native African worship. As yet there was no genuine basis of racial self-respect. In one way or another, however, in the eighteenth century the idea of association developed, and especially in Boston about the time of the Revolution Negroes began definitely to work together; thus they assisted individuals in test cases in the courts, and when James Swan in his *Dissuasion from the Slave Trade* made such a statement as that "no country can be called free where there is one slave," it was "at the earnest desire of the Negroes in Boston" that the revised edition of the pamphlet was published.

From the very beginning the Christian Church was the race's foremost form of social organization. It was but natural that the first distinctively Negro churches should belong to the democratic Baptist denomination. There has been much discussion as to which was the very first Negro Baptist church, and good claims have been put forth by the Harrison Street Baptist Church of Petersburg, Va., and for a church in Williamsburg, Va., organization in each case going back to 1776. A student of the subject, however, has shown that there was a Negro Baptist church at Silver Bluff, "on the South Carolina side of the Savannah River, in Aiken County, just twelve miles from Augusta, Ga.," founded not earlier than 1773, not later than 1775.* In any case special interest attaches to the First Bryan Baptist Church, of Savannah, founded in January, 1788. The origin of this body goes back

* Walter H. Brooks: *The Silver Bluff Church.*

to George Liele, a Negro born in Virginia, who might justly lay claim to being America's first foreign missionary. Converted by a Georgia Baptist minister, he was licensed as a probationer and was known to preach soon afterwards at a white quarterly meeting.* In 1783 he preached in the vicinity of Savannah, and one of those who came to hear him was Andrew Bryan, a slave of Jonathan Bryan. Liele then went to Jamaica and in 1784 began to preach in Kingston, where with four brethren from America he formed a church. At first he was subjected to persecution; nevertheless by 1791 he had baptized over four hundred persons. Eight or nine months after he left for Jamaica, Andrew Bryan began to preach, and at first he was permitted to use a building at Yamacraw, in the suburbs of Savannah. Of this, however, he was in course of time dispossessed, the place being a rendezvous for those Negroes who had been taken away from their homes by the British. Many of these men were taken before the magistrates from time to time, and some were whipped and others imprisoned. Bryan himself, having incurred the ire of the authorities, was twice imprisoned and once publicly whipped, being so cut that he "bled abundantly"; but he told his persecutors that he "would freely suffer death for the cause of Jesus Christ," and after a while he was permitted to go on with his work. For some time he used a barn, being assisted by his brother Sampson; then for £50 he purchased his freedom, and afterwards he began to use for worship a house that Sampson had been permitted to erect. By 1791 his church had two hundred members, but over a hundred more had been received as converted members though they had not won their masters' permission to be baptized. An interesting sidelight on these people is furnished by the statement that probably fifty of them could read though only three could write. Years afterwards, in 1832, when the church had grown to great numbers, a large part of the congregation left the Bryan Church and formed what is now the First African Baptist Church of Savannah. Both congregations, however, remembered their early leader as one "clear in the

* See letters in *Journal of Negro History*, January, 1916, 69-97.

grand doctrines of the Gospel, truly pious, and the instrument of doing more good among the poor slaves than all the learned doctors in America."

While Bryan was working in Savannah, in Richmond, Va., rose Lott Cary, a man of massive and erect frame and of great personality. Born a slave in 1780, Cary worked for a number of years in a tobacco factory, leading a wicked life. Converted in 1807, he made rapid advance in education and he was licensed as a Baptist preacher. He purchased his own freedom and that of his children (his first wife having died), organized a missionary society, and then in 1821 himself went as a missionary to the new colony of Liberia, in whose interest he worked heroically until his death in 1828.

More clearly defined than the origin of Negro Baptist churches are the beginnings of African Methodism. Almost from the time of its introduction in the country Methodism made converts among the Negroes and in 1786 there were nearly two thousand Negroes in the regular churches of the denomination, which, like the Baptist denomination, it must be remembered, was before the Revolution largely overshadowed in official circles by the Protestant Episcopal Church. The general embarrassment of the Episcopal Church in America in connection with the war, and the departure of many loyalist ministers, gave opportunity to other denominations as well as to certain bodies of Negroes. The white members of St. George's Methodist Episcopal Church in Philadelphia, however, determined to set apart its Negro membership and to segregate it in the gallery. Then in 1787 came a day when the Negroes, choosing not to be insulted, and led by Richard Allen and Absalom Jones, left the edifice, and with these two men as overseers on April 17 organized the Free African Society. This was intended to be "without regard to religious tenets," the members being banded together "to support one another in sickness and for the benefit of their widows and fatherless children." The society was in the strictest sense fraternal, there being only eight charter members: Absalom Jones, Richard Allen, Samuel Boston, Joseph Johnson, Cato Freeman, Cæsar Cranchell, James Potter, and William White. By 1790 the society had on deposit in the Bank of North

America £42 9s. 1d., and that it generally stood for racial enterprise may be seen from the fact that in 1788 an organization in Newport known as the Negro Union, in which Paul Cuffe was prominent, wrote proposing a general exodus of the Negroes to Africa. Nothing came of the suggestion at the time, but at least it shows that representative Negroes of the day were beginning to think together about matters of general policy.

In course of time the Free African Society of Philadelphia resolved into an "African Church," and this became affiliated with the Protestant Episcopal Church, whose bishop had exercised an interest in it. Out of this organization developed St. Thomas's Episcopal Church, organized in 1791 and formally opened for service July 17, 1794. Allen was at first selected for ordination, but he decided to remain a Methodist and Jones was chosen in his stead and thus became the first Negro rector in the United States. Meanwhile, however, in 1791, Allen himself had purchased a lot at the corner of Sixth and Lombard Streets; he at once set about arranging for the building that became Bethel Church; and in 1794 he formally sold the lot to the church and the new house of worship was dedicated by Bishop Asbury of the Methodist Episcopal Church. With this general body Allen and his people for a number of years remained affiliated, but difficulties arose and separate churches having come into being in other places, a convention of Negro Methodists was at length called to meet in Philadelphia April 9, 1816. To this came sixteen delegates —Richard Allen, Jacob Tapsico, Clayton Durham, James Champion, Thomas Webster, of Philadelphia; Daniel Coker, Richard Williams, Henry Harden, Stephen Hill, Edward Williamson, Nicholas Gailliard, of Baltimore; Jacob Marsh, Edward Jackson, William Andrew, of Attleborough, Penn.; Peter Spencer, of Wilmington, Del., and Peter Cuffe, of Salem, N. J.—and these were the men who founded the African Methodist Episcopal Church. Coker, of whom we shall hear more in connection with Liberia, was elected bishop, but resigned in favor of Allen, who served until his death in 1831.

In 1796 a congregation in New York consisting of James Varick and others also withdrew from the main body of the

Methodist Episcopal Church, and in 1800 dedicated a house of worship. For a number of years it had the oversight of the older organization, but after preliminary steps in 1820, on June 21, 1821, the African Methodist Episcopal Zion Church was formally organized. To the first conference came 19 preachers representing 6 churches and 1,426 members. Varick was elected district chairman, but soon afterwards was made bishop. The polity of this church from the first differed somewhat from that of the A. M. E. denomination in that representation of the laity was a prominent feature and there was no bar to the ordination of women.

Of denominations other than the Baptist and the Methodist, the most prominent in the earlier years was the Presbyterian, whose first Negro ministers were John Gloucester and John Chavis. Gloucester owed his training to the liberal tendencies that about 1800 were still strong in eastern Tennessee and Kentucky, and in 1810 took charge of the African Presbyterian Church which in 1807 had been established in Philadelphia. He was distinguished by a rich musical voice and the general dignity of his life, and he himself became the father of four Presbyterian ministers. Chavis had a very unusual career. After passing "through a regular course of academic studies" at Washington Academy, now Washington and Lee University, in 1801 he was commissioned by the General Assembly of the Presbyterians as a missionary to the Negroes. He worked with increasing reputation until Nat Turner's insurrection caused the North Carolina legislature in 1832 to pass an act silencing all Negro preachers. Then in Wake County and elsewhere he conducted schools for white boys until his death in 1838. In these early years distinction also attaches to Lemuel Haynes, a Revolutionary patriot and the first Negro preacher of the Congregational denomination. In 1785 he became the pastor of a white congregation in Torrington, Conn., and in 1818 began to serve another in Manchester, N. H.

After the church the strongest organization among Negroes has undoubtedly been that of secret societies commonly known as "lodges." The benefit societies were not necessarily secret and call for separate consideration. On March 6, 1775, an army lodge attached to one of the regiments stationed under

General Gage in or near Boston initiated Prince Hall and fourteen other colored men into the mysteries of Freemasonry.* These fifteen men on March 2, 1784, applied to the Grand Lodge of England for a warrant. This was issued to "African Lodge, No. 459," with Prince Hall as master, September 29, 1784. Various delays and misadventures befell the warrant, however, so that it was not actually received before April 29, 1787. The lodge was then duly organized May 6. From this beginning developed the idea of Masonry among the Negroes of America. As early as 1792 Hall was formally styled Grand Master, and in 1797 he issued a license to thirteen Negroes to "assemble and work" as a lodge in Philadelphia; and there was also at this time a lodge in Providence. Thus developed in 1808 the "African Grand Lodge" of Boston, afterwards known as "Prince Hall Lodge of Massachusetts"; the second Grand Lodge, called the "First Independent African Grand Lodge of North America in and for the Commonwealth of Pennsylvania," organized in 1815; and the "Hiram Grand Lodge of Pennsylvania."

Something of the interest of the Masons in their people, and the calm judgment that characterized their procedure, may be seen from the words of their leader, Prince Hall.† Speaking in 1797, and having in mind the revolution in Hayti and recent indignities inflicted upon the race in Boston, he said:

When we hear of the bloody wars which are now in the world, and thousands of our fellowmen slain; fathers and mothers bewailing the loss of their sons; wives for the loss of their husbands; towns and cities burnt and destroyed; what must be the heartfelt sorrow and distress of these poor and unhappy people! Though we can not help them, the distance being so great, yet we may sympathize with them in their troubles, and mingle a tear of sorrow with them, and do as we are exhorted to—weep with those that weep. . . .

Now, my brethren, as we see and experience that all things here are frail and changeable and nothing here to be depended upon: Let us seek those things which are above, which are sure and steadfast, and unchangeable, and at the same time let us pray to Almighty God, while we remain in the tabernacle, that he would give us the grace

---

* William H. Upton: *Negro Masonry*, Cambridge, 1899, 10.
† "A Charge Delivered to the African Lodge, June 24, 1797, at Menotomy. By the Right Worshipful Prince Hall." (Boston?) 1797.

and patience and strength to bear up under all our troubles, which at this day God knows we have our share. Patience I say, for were we not possessed of a great measure of it you could not bear up under the daily insults you meet with in the streets of Boston; much more on public days of recreation, how are you shamefully abused, and that at such a degree, that you may truly be said to carry your lives in your hands; and the arrows of death are flying about your heads; helpless old women have their clothes torn off their backs, even to the exposing of their nakedness; and by whom are these disgraceful and abusive actions committed? Not by the men born and bred in Boston, for they are better bred; but by a mob or horde of shameless, low-lived, envious, spiteful persons, some of them not long since, servants in gentlemen's kitchens, scouring knives, tending horses, and driving chaise. 'Twas said by a gentleman who saw that filthy behavior in the Common, that in all the places he had been in he never saw so cruel behavior in all his life, and that a slave in the West Indies, on Sundays or holidays, enjoys himself and friends without molestation. Not only this man, but many in town who have seen their behavior to you, and that without any provocations twenty or thirty cowards fall upon one man, have wondered at the patience of the blacks: 'tis not for want of courage in you, for they know that they dare not face you man for man, but in a mob, which we despise, and had rather suffer wrong than do wrong, to the disturbance of the community and the disgrace of our reputation; for every good citizen does honor to the laws of the State where he resides. . . .

My brethren, let us not be cast down under these and many other abuses we at present labor under: for the darkest is before the break of day. My brethren, let us remember what a dark day it was with our African brethren six years ago, in the French West Indies. Nothing but the snap of the whip was heard from morning to evening; hanging, breaking on the wheel, burning, and all manner of tortures inflicted on those unhappy people, for nothing else but to gratify their masters' pride, wantonness, and cruelty: but blessed be God, the scene is changed; they now confess that God hath no respect of persons, and therefore receive them as their friends, and treat them as brothers. Thus doth Ethiopia begin to stretch forth her hand, from a sink of slavery to freedom and equality.

An African Society was organized in New York in 1808 and chartered in 1810, and out of it grew in course of time three or four other organizations. Generally close to the social aim of the church and sometimes directly fathered by the secret societies were the benefit organizations, which even in the days of slavery existed for aid in sickness or at death; in fact, it was the hopelessness of the general situation coupled with the yearning for care when helpless that largely called these societies into being. Their origin has been explained somewhat as follows:

Although it was unlawful for Negroes to assemble without the presence of a white man, and so unlawful to allow a congregation of slaves on a plantation without the consent of the master, these organizations existed and held these meetings on the "lots" of some of the law-makers themselves. The general plan seems to have been to select some one who could read and write and make him the secretary. The meeting-place having been selected, the members would come by ones and twos, make their payments to the secretary, and quietly withdraw. The book of the secretary was often kept covered up on the bed. In many of the societies each member was known by number and in paying simply announced his number. The president of such a society was usually a privileged slave who had the confidence of his or her master and could go and come at will. Thus a form of communication could be kept up between all members. In event of death of a member, provision was made for decent burial, and all the members as far as possible obtained permits to attend the funeral. Here and again their plan of getting together was brought into play. In Richmond they would go to the church by ones and twos and there sit as near together as convenient. At the close of the service a line of march would be formed when sufficiently far from the church to make it safe to do so. It is reported that the members were faithful to each other and that every obligation was faithfully carried out. This was the first form of insurance known to the Negro from which his family received a benefit.*

All along of course a determining factor in the Negro's social progress was the service that he was able to render to any community in which he found himself as well as to his own people. Sometimes he was called upon to do very hard work, sometimes very unpleasant or dangerous work; but if he answered the call of duty and met an actual human need, his service had to receive recognition. An example of such work was found in his conduct in the course of the yellow fever epidemic in Philadelphia in 1793. Knowing that fever in general was not quite as severe in its ravages upon Negroes as upon white people, the daily papers of Philadelphia called upon the colored people in the town to come forward and assist with the sick. The Negroes consented, and Absalom Jones

* Hampton Conference Report, No. 8

and William Gray were appointed to superintend the operations, though as usual it was upon Richard Allen that much of the real responsibility fell. In September the fever increased and upon the Negroes devolved also the duty of removing corpses. In the course of their work they encountered much opposition; thus Jones said that a white man threatened to shoot him if he passed his house with a corpse. This man himself the Negroes had to bury three days afterwards. When the epidemic was over, under date January 23, 1794, Matthew Clarkson, the mayor, wrote the following testimonial: "Having, during the prevalence of the late malignant disorder, had almost daily opportunities of seeing the conduct of Absalom Jones and Richard Allen, and the people employed by them to bury the dead, I with cheerfulness give this testimony of my approbation of their proceedings, as far as the same came under my notice. Their diligence, attention, and decency of deportment, afforded me, at the time, much satisfaction." After the lapse of years it is with something of the pathos of martyrdom that we are impressed by the service of these struggling people, who by their self-abnegation and patriotism endeavored to win and deserve the privileges of American citizenship.

All the while, in one way or another, the Negro was making advance in education. As early as 1704 we have seen that Neau opened a school in New York; there was Benezet's school in Philadelphia before the Revolutionary War, and in 1798 one for Negroes was established in Boston. In the first part of the century, we remember also, some Negroes were apprenticed in Virginia under the oversight of the church. In 1764 the editor of a paper in Williamsburg, Va., established a school for Negroes, and we have seen that as many as one-sixth of the members of Andrew Bryan's congregation in the far Southern city of Savannah could read by 1790. Exceptional men, like Gloucester and Chavis, of course availed themselves of such opportunities as came their way. All told, by 1800 the Negro had received much more education than is commonly supposed.

Two persons—one in science and one in literature—because of their unusual attainments attracted much attention. The first was Benjamin Banneker of Maryland, and the second Phillis Wheatley of Boston. Banneker in 1770 constructed the first clock striking the hours that was made in America, and from 1792 to 1806 published an almanac adapted to Maryland and the neighboring states. He was thoroughly scholarly in mathematics and astronomy, and by his achievements won a reputation for himself in Europe as well as in America. Phillis Wheatley, after a romantic girlhood of transition from Africa to a favorable environment in Boston, in 1773 published her *Poems on Various Subjects,* which volume she followed with several interesting occasional poems.* For the summer of this year she was the guest in England of the Countess of Huntingdon, whose patronage she had won by an elegiac poem on George Whitefield; in conversation even more than in verse-making she exhibited her refined taste and accomplishment, and presents were showered upon her, one of them being a copy of the magnificent 1770 Glasgow folio edition of *Paradise Lost,* which was given by Brook Watson, Lord Mayor of London, and which is now preserved in the library of Harvard University. In the earlier years of the next century her poems found their way into the common school readers. One of those in her representative volume was addressed to Scipio Moorhead, a young Negro of Boston who had shown some talent for painting. Thus even in a dark day there were those who were trying to struggle upward to the light.

* For a full study see Chapter II of *The Negro in Literature and Art.*

CHAPTER IV

The twenty years of the administrations of the first three presidents of the United States—or, we might say, the three decades between 1790 and 1820—constitute what might be considered the "Dark Ages" of Negro history; and yet, as with most "Dark Ages," at even a glance below the surface these years will be found to be throbbing with life, and we have already seen that in them the Negro was doing what he could on his own account to move forward. After the high moral stand of the Revolution, however, the period seems quiescent, and it was indeed a time of definite reaction. This was attributable to three great events: the opening of the Southwest with the consequent demand for slaves, the Haytian revolution beginning in 1791, and Gabriel's insurrection in 1800.

In no way was the reaction to be seen more clearly than in the decline of the work of the American Convention of Delegates from the Abolition Societies. After 1798 neither Connecticut nor Rhode Island sent delegates; the Southern states all fell away by 1803; and while from New England came the excuse that local conditions hardly made aggressive effort any longer necessary, the lack of zeal in this section was also due to some extent to a growing question as to the wisdom of interfering with slavery in the South. In Virginia, that just a few years before had been so active, a statute was now passed imposing a penalty of one hundred dollars on any person who assisted a slave in asserting his freedom, provided he failed to establish the claim; and another provision enjoined that no member of an abolition society should serve as a juror in a freedom suit. Even the Pennsylvania society showed signs of faintheartedness, and in 1806 the Convention decided upon triennial rather than annual meetings. It did not again become really vigorous until after the War of 1812.

1. The Cotton-Gin, the New Southwest, and the First Fugitive Slave Law

Of incalculable significance in the history of the Negro in America was the series of inventions in England by Arkwright, Hargreaves, and Crompton in the years 1768-79. In the same period came the discovery of the power of steam by James Watt of Glasgow and its application to cotton manufacture, and improvements followed quickly in printing and bleaching. There yet remained one final invention of importance for the cultivation of cotton on a large scale. Eli Whitney, a graduate of Yale, went to Georgia and was employed as a teacher by the widow of General Greene on her plantation. Seeing the need of some machine for the more rapid separating of cotton-seed from the fiber, he labored until in 1793 he succeeded in making his cotton-gin of practical value. The tradition is persistent, however, that the real credit of the invention belongs to a Negro on the plantation. The cotton-gin created great excitement throughout the South and began to be utilized everywhere. The cultivation and exporting of the staple grew by leaps and bounds. In 1791 only thirty-eight bales of standard size were exported from the United States; in 1816, however, the cotton sent out of the country was worth $24,106,000 and was by far the most valuable article of export. The current price was 28 cents a pound. Thus at the very time that the Northern states were abolishing slavery, an industry that had slumbered became supreme, and the fate of hundreds of thousands of Negroes was sealed.

Meanwhile the opening of the West went forward, and from Maine and Massachusetts, Carolina and Georgia journeyed the pioneers to lay the foundations of Ohio, Indiana, and Illinois, and Alabama and Mississippi. It was an eager, restless caravan that moved, and sometimes more than a hundred persons in a score of wagons were to be seen going from a single town in the East—"Baptists and Methodists and

Democrats." The careers of Boone and Sevier and those who went with them, and the story of their fights with the Indians, are now a part of the romance of American history. In 1790 a cluster of log huts on the Ohio River was named in honor of the Society of the Cincinnati. In 1792 Kentucky was admitted to the Union, the article on slavery in her constitution encouraging the system and discouraging emancipation, and Tennessee also entered as a slave state in 1796.

Of tremendous import to the Negro were the questions relating to the Mississippi Territory. After the Revolution Georgia laid claim to great tracts of land now comprising the states of Alabama and Mississippi, with the exception of the strip along the coast claimed by Spain in connection with Florida. This territory became a rich field for speculation, and its history in its entirety makes a complicated story. A series of sales to what were known as the Yazoo Companies, especially in that part of the present states whose northern boundary would be a line drawn from the mouth of the Yazoo to the Chattahoochee, resulted in conflicting claims, the last grant sale being made in 1795 by a corrupt legislature at the price of a cent and a half an acre. James Jackson now raised the cry of bribery and corruption, resigned from the United States Senate, secured a seat in the state legislature, and on February 13, 1796, carried through a bill rescinding the action of the previous year,* and the legislature burned the documents concerned with the Yazoo sale in token of its complete repudiation of them. The purchasers to whom the companies had sold lands now began to bombard Congress with petitions and President Adams helped to arrive at a settlement by which Georgia transferred the lands in question to the Federal Government, which undertook to form of them the Mississippi Territory and to pay any damages involved. In 1802 Georgia threw the whole burden upon the central government by transferring to it *all* of her land beyond her present boundaries, though for this she exacted an article favorable to slavery. All was now made into the Mississippi Territory, to which Congress held out the promise that it would be ad-

* Phillips in *The South in the Building of the Nation,* II, 154.

mitted as a state as soon as its population numbered 60,000; but Alabama was separated from Mississippi in 1816. The old matter of claims was not finally disposed of until an act of 1814 appropriated $5,000,000 for the purpose. In the same year Andrew Jackson's decisive victories over the Creeks at Talladega and Horseshoe Bend—of which more must be said —resulted in the cession of a vast tract of the land of that unhappy nation and thus finally opened for settlement three-fourths of the present state of Alabama.

It was in line with the advance that slavery was making in new territory that there was passed the first Fugitive Slave Act (1793). This grew out of the discussion incident to the seizure in 1791 at Washington, Penn., of a Negro named John, who was taken to Virginia, and the correspondence between the Governor of Pennsylvania and the Governor of Virginia with reference to the case. The important third section of the act read as follows:

And be it also enacted, That when a person held to labor in any of the United States, or in either of the territories on the northwest or south of the river Ohio, under the laws thereof, shall escape into any other of the said states or territory, the person to whom such labor or service may be due, his agent or attorney, is hereby empowered to seize or arrest such fugitive from labor, and to take him or her before any judge of the circuit or district courts of the United States, residing or being within the state, or before any magistrate of a county, city or town corporate, wherein such seizure or arrest shall be made, and upon proof to the satisfaction of such judge or magistrate, either by oral testimony or affidavit taken before and certified by a magistrate of any such state or territory, that the person so seized or arrested, doth, under the laws of the state or territory from which he or she fled, owe service or labor to the person claiming him or her, it shall be the duty of such judge or magistrate to give a certificate thereof to such claimant, his agent or attorney, which shall be sufficient warrant for removing the said fugitive from labor, to the state or territory from which he or she fled.

It will be observed that by the terms of this enactment a master had the right to recover a fugitive slave by proving his ownership before a magistrate without a jury or any other of the ordinary forms of law. A human being was thus placed at the disposal of the lowest of courts and subjected to such procedure as was not allowed even in petty property suits. A great field for the bribery of magistrates was opened up, and opportunity was given for committing to slavery Negro men about whose freedom there should have been no question.

By the close of the decade 1790-1800 the fear occasioned by the Haytian revolution had led to a general movement against the importation of Negroes, especially of those from the West Indies. Even Georgia in 1798 prohibited the importation of all slaves, and this provision, although very loosely enforced, was never repealed. In South Carolina, however, to the utter chagrin and dismay of the other states, importation, prohibited in 1787, was again legalized in 1803; and in the four years immediately following 39,075 Negroes were brought to Charleston, most of these going to the territories.* When in 1803 Ohio was carved out of the Northwest Territory as a free state, an attempt was made to claim the rest of the territory for slavery, but this failed. In the congressional session of 1804-5 the matter of slavery in the newly acquired territory of Louisiana was brought up, and slaves were allowed to be imported if they had come to the United States before 1798, the purpose of this provision being to guard against the consequences of South Carolina's recent act, although such a clause never received rigid enforcement. The mention of Louisiana, however, brings us concretely to Toussaint L'Ouverture, the greatest Negro in the New World in the period and one of the greatest of all time.

2.   *Toussaint L'Ouverture, Louisiana, and the Formal Closing of the Slave-Trade*

When the French Revolution broke out in 1789, it was not long before its general effects were felt in the West Indies. Of special importance was Santo Domingo because of the commercial interests centered there. The eastern end of the island was Spanish, but the western portion was French, and in this latter part was a population of 600,000, of which number 50,000 were French creoles, 50,000 mulattoes, and 500,000 pure Negroes. All political and social privileges were monopo-

*DuBois: *Suppression of the Slave-Trade,* 90.

lized by the creoles, while the Negroes were agricultural laborers and slaves; and between the two groups floated the restless element of the free people of color.

When the General Assembly in France decreed equality of rights to all citizens, the mulattoes of Santo Domingo made a petition for the enjoyment of the same political privileges as the white people—to the unbounded consternation of the latter. They were rewarded with a decree which was so ambiguously worded that it was open to different interpretations and which simply heightened the animosity that for years had been smoldering. A new petition to the Assembly in 1791 primarily for an interpretation brought forth on May 15 the explicit decree that the people of color were to have all the rights and privileges of citizen „ provided they had been born of free parents on both sides. The white people were enraged by the decision, turned royalist, and trampled the national cockade underfoot; and throughout the summer armed strife and conflagration were the rule. To add to the confusion the black slaves struck for freedom and on the night of August 23, 1791, drenched the island in blood. In the face of these events the Conventional Assembly rescinded its order, then announced that the original decree must be obeyed, and it sent three commissioners with troops to Santo Domingo, real authority being invested in Santhonax and Polverel.

On June 20, 1793, at Cape François trouble was renewed by a quarrel between a mulatto and a white officer in the marines. The seamen came ashore and loaned their assistance to the white people, and the Negroes now joined forces with the mulattoes. In the battle of two days that followed the arsenal was taken and plundered, thousands were killed in the streets, and more than half of the town was burned. The French commissioners were the unhappy witnesses of the scene, but they were practically helpless, having only about a thousand troops. Santhonax, however, issued a proclamation offering freedom to all slaves who were willing to range themselves under the banner of the Republic. This was the first proclamation for the freeing of slaves in Santo Domingo, and as a result of it many of the Negroes came in and were enfranchised.

Soon after this proclamation Polverel left his colleague at the Cape and went to Port au Prince, the capital of the West. Here things were quiet and the cultivation of the crops was going forward as usual. The slaves were soon unsettled, however, by the news of what was being done elsewhere, and Polverel was convinced that emancipation could not be delayed and that for the safety of the planters themselves it was necessary to extend it to the whole island. In September (1793) he set in circulation from Aux Cayes a proclamation to this effect, and at the same time he exhorted all the planters in the vicinity who concurred in his work to register their names. This almost all of them did, as they were convinced of the need of measures for their personal safety; and on February 4, 1794, the Conventional Assembly in Paris formally approved all that had been done by decreeing the abolition of slavery in all the colonies of France.

All the while the Spanish and the English had been looking on with interest and had even come to the French part of the island as if to aid in the restoration of order. Among the former, at first in charge of a little royalist band, was the Negro, Toussaint, later called L'Ouverture. He was then a man in the prime of life, forty-eight years old, and already his experience had given him the wisdom that was needed to bring peace in Santo Domingo. In April, 1794, impressed by the decree of the Assembly, he returned to the jurisdiction of France and took service under the Republic. In 1796 he became a general of brigade; in 1797 general-in-chief, with the military command of the whole colony.

He at once compelled the surrender of the English who had invaded his country. With the aid of a commercial agreement with the United States, he next starved out the garrison of his rival, the mulatto Rigaud, whom he forced to consent to leave the country. He then imprisoned Roume, the agent of the Directory, and assumed civil as well as military authority. He also seized the Spanish part of the island, which had been ceded to France some years before but had not been actually surrendered. He then, in May, 1801, gave to Santo

Domingo a constitution by which he not only assumed power for life but gave to himself the right of naming his successor; and all the while he was awakening the admiration of the world by his bravery, his moderation, and his genuine instinct for government.

Across the ocean, however, a jealous man was watching with interest the career of the "gilded African." None knew better than Napoleon that it was because he did not trust France that Toussaint had sought the friendship of the United States, and none read better than he the logic of events. As Adams says, "Bonaparte's acts as well as his professions showed that he was bent on crushing democratic ideas, and that he regarded St. Domingo as an outpost of American republicanism, although Toussaint had made a rule as arbitrary as that of Bonaparte himself. . . . By a strange confusion of events, Toussaint L'Ouverture, because he was a Negro, became the champion of republican principles, with which he had nothing but the instinct of personal freedom in common. Toussaint's government was less republican than that of Bonaparte; he was doing by necessity in St. Domingo what Bonapart was doing by choice in France." *

This was the man to whom the United States ultimately owes the purchase of Louisiana. On October 1, 1801, Bonaparte gave orders to General Le Clerc for a great expedition against Santo Domingo. In January, 1802, Le Clerc appeared and war followed. In the course of this, Toussaint—who was ordinarily so wise and who certainly knew that from Napoleon he had most to fear—made the great mistake of his life and permitted himself to be led into a conference on a French vessel. He was betrayed and taken to France, where within the year he died of pneumonia in the dungeon of Joux. Immediately there was a proclamation annulling the decree of 1794 giving freedom to the slaves. Bonaparte, however, had not estimated the force of Toussaint's work, and to assist the Negroes in their struggle now came a stalwart ally, yellow fever. By the end of the summer only one-seventh of Le Clerc's army remained, and he himself died in November. At

* *History of the United States*, I, 391-392.

once Bonaparte planned a new expedition.   While he was arranging for the leadership of this, however, the European war broke out again.   Meanwhile the treaty for the retrocession of the territory of Louisiana had not yet received the signature of the Spanish king, because Godoy, the Spanish representative, would not permit the signature to be affixed until all the conditions were fulfilled; and toward the end of 1802 the civil officer at New Orleans closed the Mississippi to the United States.   Jefferson, at length moved by the plea of the South, sent a special envoy, no less a man than James Monroe, to France to negotiate the purchase; Bonaparte, disgusted by the failure of his Egyptian expedition and his project for reaching India, and especially by his failure in Santo Domingo, in need also of ready money, listened to the offer; and the people of the United States—who within the last few years have witnessed the spoliation of Hayti—have not yet realized how much they owe to the courage of 500,000 Haytian Negroes who refused to be slaves.

The slavery question in the new territory was a critical one.   It was on account of it that the Federalists had opposed the acquisition; the American Convention endeavored to secure a provision like that of the Northwest Ordinance; and the Yearly Meeting of the Society of Friends in Philadelphia in 1805 prayed "that effectual measures may be adopted by Congress to prevent the introduction of slavery into any of the territories of the United States."   Nevertheless the whole territory without regard to latitude was thrown open to the system March 2, 1805.

In spite of this victory for slavery, however, the general force of the events in Hayti was such as to make more certain the formal closing of the slave-trade at the end of the twenty-year period for which the Constitution had permitted it to run.   The conscience of the North had been profoundly stirred, and in the far South was the ever-present fear of a reproduction of the events in Hayti.   The agitation in England moreover was at last about to bear fruit in the act of 1807 forbidding the slave-trade.   In America it seems from the first to have been an understood thing, especially by the Southern representatives, that even if such an act passed it would be only irregularly enforced, and the debates were concerned rather with the disposal of illegally imported Africans and with the punishment of those concerned in the importation than with the proper limitation of the traffic by water.* On March 2, 1807, the act was passed forbidding the slave-trade after the close of the year. In course of time it came very near to being a dead letter, as may be seen from presidential messages, reports of cabinet officers, letters of collectors of revenue, letters of district attorneys, reports of committees of Congress, reports of naval commanders, statements on the floor of Congress, the testimony of eye-witnesses, and the complaints of home and foreign anti-slavery societies. Fernandina and Galveston were only two of the most notorious ports for smuggling. A regular chain of posts was established from the head of St. Mary's River to the upper country, and through the Indian nation, by means of which the Negroes were transferred to every part of the country.† If dealers wished to form a caravan they would give an Indian alarm, so that the woods might be less frequented, and if pursued in Georgia they would escape into Florida. One small schooner contained one hundred and thirty souls. "They were almost packed into a small space, between a floor laid over the water-casks and the deck—not near three feet—insufficient for them to sit upright—and so close that chafing against each other their bones pierced the skin and became galled and ulcerated by the motion of the vessel." Many American vessels were engaged in the trade under Spanish colors, and the traffic to Africa was pursued with uncommon vigor at Havana, the crews of vessels being made up of men of all nations, who were tempted by the high wages to be earned. Evidently officials were negligent in the discharge of their duty, but even if offenders were apprehended it did not necessarily follow that they would receive effective punishment. President Madison in his message of December 5, 1810, said, "It appears that American citizens are instrumental in carrying on a traffic in enslaved Africans, equally in violation of the laws of humanity, and in defiance of those of their own country"; and on Janu-

* See DuBois, 95, ff.
† Niles's *Register*, XIV, 176 (May 2, 1818).

ary 7, 1819, the Register of the Treasury made to the House
the amazing report that "it doth not appear, from an examination of the records of this office, and particularly of the accounts (to the date of their last settlement) of the collectors
of the customs, and of the several marshals of the United
States, that any forfeitures had been incurred under the said
act." A supplementary and compromising and ineffective act
of 1818 sought to concentrate efforts against smuggling by
encouraging informers; and one of the following year that
authorized the President to "make such regulations and arrangements as he may deem expedient for the safe keeping,
support, and removal beyond the limits of the United States"
of recaptured Africans, and that bore somewhat more fruit,
was in large measure due to the colonization movement and
of importance in connection with the founding of Liberia.

Thus, while the formal closing of the slave-trade might seem
to be a great step forward, the laxness with which the decree
was enforced places it definitely in the period of reaction.

3.   Gabriel's Insurrection and the Rise of the Negro Problem

Gabriel's insurrection of 1800 was by no means the most
formidable revolt that the Southern states witnessed. In design it certainly did not surpass the scope of the plot of Denmark Vesey twenty-two years later, and in actual achievement it was insignificant when compared not only with Nat
Turner's insurrection but even with the uprisings sixty years
before. At the last moment in fact a great storm that came
up made the attempt to execute the plan a miserable failure.
Nevertheless coming as it did so soon after the revolution in
Hayti, and giving evidence of young and unselfish leadership,
the plot was regarded as of extraordinary significance.

Gabriel himself * was an intelligent slave only twenty-four
years old, and his chief assistant was Jack Bowler, aged
twenty-eight. Throughout the summer of 1800 he matured
his plan, holding meetings at which a brother named Martin
interpreted various texts from Scripture as bearing on the
situation of the Negroes. His insurrection was finally set

* His full name was Gabriel Prosser.

for the first day of September. It was well planned. The rendezvous was to be a brook six miles from Richmond. Under cover of night the force of 1,100 was to march in three columns on the city, then a town of 8,000 inhabitants, the right wing to seize the penitentiary building which had just been converted into an arsenal, while the left took possession of the powder-house. These two columns were to be armed with clubs, and while they were doing their work the central force, armed with muskets, knives, and pikes, was to begin the carnage, none being spared except the French, whom it is significant that the Negroes favored. In Richmond at the time there were not more than four or five hundred men with about thirty muskets; but in the arsenal were several thousand guns, and the powder-house was well stocked. Seizure of the mills was to guarantee the insurrectionists a food supply; and meanwhile in the country districts were the new harvests of corn, and flocks and herds were fat in the fields.

On the day appointed for the uprising Virginia witnessed such a storm as she had not seen in years. Bridges were carried away, and roads and plantations completely submerged. Brook Swamp, the strategic point for the Negroes, was inundated; and the country Negroes could not get into the city, nor could those in the city get out to the place of rendezvous. The force of more than a thousand dwindled to three hundred, and these, almost paralyzed by fear and superstition, were dismissed. Meanwhile a slave who did not wish to see his master killed divulged the plot, and all Richmond was soon in arms.

A troop of United States cavalry was ordered to the city and arrests followed quickly. Three hundred dollars was offered by Governor Monroe for the arrest of Gabriel, and as much more for Jack Bowler. Bowler surrendered, but it took weeks to find Gabriel. Six men were convicted and condemned to be executed on September 12, and five more on September 18. Gabriel was finally captured on September 24 at Norfolk on a vessel that had come from Richmond; he was convicted on October 3 and executed on October 7. He showed no disposition to dissemble as to his own plan; at the same time he said not one word that incriminated anybody else.

After him twenty-four more men were executed; then it began to appear that some "mistakes" had been made and the killing ceased. About the time of this uprising some Negroes were also assembled for an outbreak in Suffolk County; there were alarms in Petersburg and in the country near Edenton, N. C.; and as far away as Charleston the excitement was intense.

There were at least three other Negro insurrections of importance in the period 1790-1820. When news came of the uprising of the slaves in Santo Domingo in 1791, the Negroes in Louisiana planned a similar effort.* They might have succeeded better if they had not disagreed as to the hour of the outbreak, when one of them informed the commandant. As a punishment twenty-three of the slaves were hanged along the banks of the river and their corpses left dangling for days; but three white men who assisted them and who were really the most guilty of all, were simply sent out of the colony. In Camden, S. C., on July 4, 1816, some other Negroes risked all for independence.† On various pretexts men from the country districts were invited to the town on the appointed night, and different commands were assigned, all except that of commander-in-chief, which position was to be given to him who first forced the gates of the arsenal. Again the plot was divulged by "a favorite and confidential slave," of whom we are told that the state legislature purchased the freedom, settling upon him a pension for life. About six of the leaders were executed. On or about May 1, 1819, there was a plot to destroy the city of Augusta, Ga.‡ The insurrectionists were to assemble at Beach Island, proceed to Augusta, set fire to the place, and then destroy the inhabitants. Guards were posted, and a white man who did not answer when hailed was shot and fatally wounded. A Negro named Coot was tried as being at the head of the conspiracy and sentenced to be executed a few days later. Other trials followed his. Not a muscle moved when the verdict was pronounced upon him.

* Gayarré: *History of Louisiana,* III, 355.
† Holland: *Refutation of Calumnies.*
‡ Niles's *Register,* XVI, 213 (May 22, 1819).

The deeper meaning of such events as these could not escape the discerning. More than one patriot had to wonder just whither the country was drifting. Already it was evident that the ultimate problem transcended the mere question of slavery, and many knew that human beings could not always be confined to an artificial status. Throughout the period the slave-trade seemed to flourish without any real check, and it was even accentuated by the return to power of the old royalist houses of Europe after the fall of Napoleon. Meanwhile it was observed that slave labor was driving out of the South the white man of small means, and antagonism between the men of the "up-country" and the seaboard capitalists was brewing. The ordinary social life of the Negro in the South left much to be desired, and conditions were not improved by the rapid increase. As for slavery itself, no one could tell when or where or how the system would end; all only knew that it was developing apace: and meanwhile there was the sinister possibility of the alliance of the Negro and the Indian. Sincere plans of gradual abolition were advanced in the South as well as the North, but in the lower section they seldom got more than a respectful hearing. In his "Dissertation on Slavery, with a Proposal for the Gradual Abolition of it in the State of Virginia," St. George Tucker, a professor of law in the University of William and Mary, and one of the judges of the General Court of Virginia, in 1796 advanced a plan by which he figured that after sixty years there would be only one-third as many slaves as at first. At this distance his proposal seems extremely conservative; at the time, however, it was laid on the table by the Virginia House of Delegates, and from the Senate the author received merely "a civil acknowledgment."

Two men of the period—widely different in temper and tone, but both earnest seekers after truth—looked forward to the future with foreboding, one with the eye of the scientist, the other with the vision of the seer. Hezekiah Niles had full sympathy with the groping and striving of the South; but he insisted that slavery must ultimately be abolished throughout the country, that the minds of the slaves should be exalted, and that reasonable encouragement should be given free Negroes.* Said he: *"We are ashamed of the thing we practice; . . .* there is no attribute of heaven that takes part with us, and *we know it.* And in the contest that must come and *will come,* there will be a heap of sorrows such as the world has rarely seen." †

On the other hand rose Lorenzo Dow, the foremost itinerant preacher of the time, the first Protestant who expounded the gospel in Alabama and Mississippi, and a reformer who at the very moment that cotton was beginning to be supreme, presumed to tell the South that slavery was wrong.‡ Everywhere he arrested attention—with his long hair, his harsh voice, and his wild gesticulation startling all conservative hearers. But he was made in the mold of heroes. In his lifetime he traveled not less than two hundred thousand miles, preaching to more people than any other man of his time. Several times he went to Canada, once to the West Indies, and three times to England, everywhere drawing great crowds about him. In *A Cry from the Wilderness* he more than once clothed his thought in enigmatic garb, but the meaning was always ultimately clear. At this distance, when slavery and the Civil War are alike viewed in the perspective, the words of the oracle are almost uncanny: "In the rest of the Southern states the influence of these Foreigners will be known and felt in its time, and the seeds from the HORY ALLIANCE and the DECAPI-GANDI, who have a hand in those grades of Generals, from the Inquisitor to the Vicar General and down . . . ! ! ! ☞ The STRUGGLE will be DREADFUL! the CUP will be BITTER! and when the agony is over, those who survive may see better days! FAREWELL!"

Register, XVI, 177 (May 8, 1819).
† *Ibid.,* XVI, 213 (May 22, 1819).
‡ For full study see article "Lorenzo Dow," in *Methodist Review* and *Journal of Negro History,* July, 1916, the same being included in *Africa and the War,* New York, 1918.

CHAPTER V

It is not the purpose of the present chapter to give a history of the Seminole Wars, or even to trace fully the connection of the Negro with these contests. We do hope to show at least, however, that the Negro was more important than anything else as an immediate cause of controversy, though the general pressure of the white man upon the Indian would in time of course have made trouble in any case. Strange parallels constantly present themselves, and incidentally it may be seen that the policy of the Government in force in other and even later years with reference to the Negro was at this time also very largely applied in the case of the Indian.

1. *Creek, Seminole, and Negro to 1817: The War of 1812*

On August 7, 1786, the Continental Congress by a definite and far-reaching ordinance sought to regulate for the future the whole conduct of Indian affairs. Two great districts were formed, one including the territory north of the Ohio and west of the Hudson, and the other including that south of the Ohio and east of the Mississippi; and for anything pertaining to the Indian in each of these two great tracts a superintendent was appointed. As affecting the Negro the southern district was naturally of vastly more importance than the northern. In the eastern portion of this, mainly in what are now Georgia, eastern Tennessee, and eastern Alabama, were the Cherokees and the great confederacy of the Creeks, while toward the west, in the present Mississippi and western Alabama, were the Chickasaws and the Choctaws. Of Muskhogean stock, and originally a part of the Creeks, were the Seminoles ("runaways"), who about 1750, under the leader-

ship of a great chieftain, Secoffee, separated from the main
confederacy, which had its center in southwest Georgia just
a little south of Columbus, and overran the peninsula of
Florida.   In 1808 came another band under Micco Hadjo to
the present site of Tallahassee.   The Mickasukie tribe was
already on the ground in the vicinity of this town, and at first
its members objected to the newcomers, who threatened to
take their lands from them; but at length all abode peace-
ably together under the general name of Seminoles.   About
1810 these people had twenty towns, the chief ones being
Mikasuki and Tallahassee.   From the very first they had received occasional additions from the Yemassee, who had been
driven out of South Carolina, and of fugitive Negroes.

By the close of the eighteenth century all along the frontier
the Indian had begun to feel keenly the pressure of the white
man, and in his struggle with the invader he recognized in
the oppressed Negro a natural ally.   Those Negroes who by
any chance became free were welcomed by the Indians, fugitives from bondage found refuge with them, and while Indian chiefs commonly owned slaves, the variety of servitude
was very different from that under the white man.   The
Negroes were comparatively free, and intermarriage was frequent; thus a mulatto woman who fled from bondage married
a chief and became the mother of a daughter who in course
of time became the wife of the famous Osceola.   This very
close connection of the Negro with the family life of the
Indian was the determining factor in the resistance of the
Seminoles to the demands of the agents of the United States,
and a reason, stronger even than his love for his old hunting-
ground, for his objection to removal to new lands beyond the
Mississippi.   Very frequently the Indian could not give up
his Negroes without seeing his own wife and children led
away into bondage; and thus to native courage and pride was
added the instinct of a father for the preservation of his own.

In the two wars between the Americans and the English it
was but natural that the Indian should side with the English,
and it was in some measure but a part of the game that he
should receive little consideration at the hands of the victor.
In the politics played by the English and the French, the

English and the Spaniards, and finally between the Americans and all Europeans, the Indian was ever the loser. In the very early years of the Carolina colonies, some effort was made to enslave the Indians; but such servants soon made their way to the Indian country, and it was not long before they taught the Negroes to do likewise. This constant escape of slaves, with its attendant difficulties, largely accounted for the establishing of the free colony of Georgia between South Carolina and the Spanish possession, Florida. It was soon evident, however, that the problem had been aggravated rather than settled. When Congress met in 1776 it received from Georgia a communication setting forth the need of "preventing slaves from deserting their masters"; and as soon as the Federal Government was organized in 1789 it received also from Georgia an urgent request for protection from the Creeks, who were charged with various ravages, and among other documents presented was a list of one hundred and ten Negroes who were said to have left their masters during the Revolution and to have found refuge among the Creeks. Meanwhile by various treaties, written and unwritten, the Creeks were being forced toward the western line of the state, and in any agreement the outstanding stipulation was always for the return of fugitive slaves. For a number of years the Creeks retreated without definitely organized resistance. In the course of the War of 1812, however, moved by the English and by a visit from Tecumseh, they suddenly rose, and on August 30, 1813, under the leadership of Weathersford, they attacked Fort Mims, a stockade thirty-five miles north of Mobile. The five hundred and fifty-three men, women, and children in this place were almost completely massacred. Only fifteen white persons escaped by hiding in the woods, a number of Negroes being taken prisoner. This occurrence spurred the whole Southwest to action. Volunteers were called for, and the Tennessee legislature resolved to exterminate the whole tribe. Andrew Jackson with Colonel Coffee administered decisive defeats at Talladega and Tohopeka or Horseshoe Bend on the Tallapoosa River, and the Creeks were forced to sue for peace. By the treaty of Fort Jackson (August 9, 1814) the future president, now a major general in the regular army and in command at Mobile, demanded that the unhappy nation give up more than half of its land as indemnity for the cost of the war, that it hold no communication with a Spanish garrison or town, that it permit the necessary roads to be made or forts to be built in any part of the territory, and that it surrender the prophets who had instigated the war. This last demand was ridiculous, or only for moral effect, for the so-called prophets had already been left dead on the field of battle. The Creeks were quite broken, however, and Jackson passed on to fame and destiny at the Battle of New Orleans, January 8, 1815. In April of this year he was made commander-in-chief of the Southern Division.* It soon developed that his chief task in this capacity was to reckon with the Seminoles.

On the Appalachicola River the British had rebuilt an old fort, calling it the British Post on the Appalachicola. Early in the summer of 1815 the commander, Nicholls, had occasion to go to London, and he took with him his troops, the chief Francis, and several Creeks, leaving in the fort seven hundred and sixty-three barrels of cannon powder, twenty-five hundred muskets, and numerous pistols and other weapons of war. The Negroes from Georgia who had come to the vicinity, who numbered not less than a thousand, and who had some well kept farms up and down the banks of the river, now took charge of the fort and made it their headquarters. They were joined by some Creeks, and the so-called Negro Fort soon caused itself to be greatly feared by any white people who happened to live near. Demands on the Spanish governor for its suppression were followed by threats of the use of the soldiery of the United States; and General Gaines, under orders in the section, wrote to Jackson asking authority to build near the boundary another post that might be used as

---

* In his official capacity Jackson issued two addresses which have an important place in the history of the Negro soldier. From his headquarters at Mobile, September 21, 1814, he issued an appeal "To the Free Colored Inhabitants of Louisiana," offering them an honorable part in the war, and this was later followed by a "Proclamation to the Free People of Color" congratulating them on their achievement. Both addresses are accessible in many books.

the base for any movement that had as its aim to overawe the
Negroes. Jackson readily complied with the request, saying,
"I have no doubt that this fort has been established by some
villains for the purpose of murder, rapine, and plunder, and
that it ought to be blown up regardless of the ground it
stands on. If you have come to the same conclusion, destroy
it, and restore the stolen Negroes and property to their right-
ful owners." Gaines accordingly built Fort Scott not far from
where the Flint and the Chattahoochee join to form the Appalachicola. It was necessary for Gaines to pass the Negro
Fort in bringing supplies to his own men; and on July 17,
1816, the boats of the Americans were within range of the
fort and opened fire. There was some preliminary shooting,
and then, since the walls were too stubborn to be battered down
by a light fire, "a ball made red-hot in the cook's galley was put
in the gun and sent screaming over the wall and into the magazine. The roar, the shock, the scene that followed, may be
imagined, but not described. Seven hundred barrels of gunpowder tore the earth, the fort, and all the wretched creatures
in it to fragments. Two hundred and seventy men, women,
and children died on the spot. Of sixty-four taken out alive,
the greater number died soon after." *

The Seminoles—in the West more and more identified with
the Creeks—were angered by their failure to recover the lands
lost by the treaty of Fort Jackson and also by the building
of Fort Scott. One settlement, Fowltown, fifteen miles east
of Fort Scott, was especially excited and in the fall of 1817
sent a warning to the Americans "not to cross or cut a stick
of timber on the east side of the Flint." The warning was
regarded as a challenge; Fowltown was taken on a morning in
November, and the Seminole Wars had begun.

2. *First Seminole War and the Treaties of Indian Spring and
Fort Moultrie*

In the course of the First Seminole War (1817-18) Jackson
ruthlessly laid waste the towns of the Indians; he also took
Pensacola, and he awakened international difficulties by his

* McMaster, IV, 431.

rather summary execution of two British subjects, Arbuthnot and Ambrister, who were traders to the Indians and sustained generally pleasant relations with them. For his conduct, especially in this last instance, he was severely criticized in Congress, but it is significant of his rising popularity that no formal vote of censure could pass against him. On the cession of Florida to the United States he was appointed territorial governor; but he served for a brief term only. As early as 1822 he was nominated for the presidency by the legislature of Tennessee, and in 1823 he was sent to the United States Senate.

Of special importance in the history of the Creeks about this time was the treaty of Indian Spring, of January 8, 1821, an iniquitous agreement in the signing of which bribery and firewater were more than usually present. By this the Creeks ceded to the United States, for the benefit of Georgia, five million acres of their most valuable land. In cash they were to receive $200,000, in payments extending over fourteen years. The United States Government moreover was to hold $250,000 as a fund from which the citizens of Georgia were to be reimbursed for any "claims" (for runaway slaves of course) that the citizens of the state had against the Creeks prior to the year 1802.* In the actual execution of this agreement a slave was frequently estimated at two or three times his real value, and the Creeks were expected to pay whether the fugitive was with them or not. All possible claims, however, amounted to $101,000. This left $149,000 of the money in the hands of the Government. This sum was not turned over to the Indians, as one might have expected, but retained until 1834, when the Georgia citizens interested petitioned for a division. The request was referred to the Commission on Indian Affairs, and the chairman, Gilmer of Georgia, was in favor of dividing the money among the petitioners as compensation for "the offspring which the slaves would have borne had they remained in bondage." This suggestion was rejected at the time, but afterwards the division was made

---

* See J. R. Giddings: *The Exiles of Florida*, 63-66; also speech in House of Representatives February 9, 1841.

nevertheless; and history records few more flagrant violations of all principles of honor and justice.

The First Seminole War, while in some ways disastrous to the Indians, was in fact not much more than the preliminary skirmish of a conflict that was not to cease until 1842. In general the Indians, mindful of the ravages of the War of 1812, did not fully commit themselves and bided their time. They were in fact so much under cover that they led the Americans to underestimate their real numbers. When the cession of Florida was formally completed, however (July 17, 1821), they were found to be on the very best spots of land in the territory. On May 20, 1822, Colonel Gad Humphreys was appointed agent to them, William P. Duval as governor of the territory being ex-officio superintendent of Indian affairs. Altogether the Indians at this time, according to the official count, numbered 1,594 men, 1,357 women, and 993 children, a total of 3,944, with 150 Negro men and 650 Negro women and children.* In the interest of these people Humphreys labored faithfully for eight years, and not a little of the comparative quiet in his period of service is to be credited to his own sympathy, good sense, and patience.

In the spring of 1823 the Indians were surprised by the suggestion of a treaty that would definitely limit their boundaries and outline their future relations with the white man. The representative chiefs had no desire for a conference, were exceedingly reluctant to meet the commissioners, and finally came to the meeting prompted only by the hope that such terms might be arrived at as would permanently guarantee them in the peaceable possession of their homes. Over the very strong protest of some of them a treaty was signed at Fort Moultrie, on the coast five miles below St. Augustine, September 18, 1823, William P. Duval, James Gadsden, and Bernard Segui being the representatives of the United States. By this treaty we learn that the Indians, in view of the fact that they have "thrown themselves on, and have promised to continue under, the protection of the United States, and of no other nation, power, or sovereignty; and in consideration of the promises

* Sprague, 19.

and stipulations hereinafter made, do cede and relinquish all claim or title which they have to the whole territory of Florida, with the exception of such district of country as shall herein be allotted to them." They are to have restricted boundaries, the extreme point of which is nowhere to be nearer than fifteen miles to the Gulf of Mexico. The United States promises to distribute, as soon as the Indians are settled on their new land, under the direction of their agent, "implements of husbandry, and stock of cattle and hogs to the amount of six thousand dollars, and an annual sum of five thousand dollars a year for twenty successive years"; and "to restrain and prevent all white persons from hunting, settling, or otherwise intruding" upon the land set apart for the Indians, though any American citizen, lawfully authorized, is to pass and re-pass within the said district and navigate the waters thereof "without any hindrance, toll or exactions from said tribes." For facilitating removal and as compensation for any losses or inconvenience sustained, the United States is to furnish rations of corn, meat, and salt for twelve months, with a special appropriation of $4,500 for those who have made improvements, and $2,000 more for the facilitating of transportation. The agent, sub-agent, and interpreter are to reside within the Indian boundary "to watch over the interests of said tribes"; and the United States further undertake "as an evidence of their humane policy towards said tribes" to allow $1,000 a year for twenty years for the establishment of a school and $1,000 a year for the same period for the support of a gun- and blacksmith. Of supreme importance is Article 7: "The chiefs and warriors aforesaid, for themselves and tribes, stipulate to be active and vigilant in the preventing the retreating to, or passing through, the district of country assigned them, of any absconding slaves, or fugitives from justice; and further agree to use all necessary exertions to apprehend and deliver the same to the agent, who shall receive orders to compensate them agreeably to the trouble and expense incurred."

We have dwelt at length upon the provisions of this treaty because it contained all the seeds of future trouble between the white man and the Indian. Six prominent chiefs—Nea Mathla, John Blunt, Tuski Hajo, Mulatto King, Emathlochee,

and Econchattimico—refused absolutely to sign, and their
marks were not won until each was given a special reserva-
tion of from two to four square miles outside the Seminole
boundaries. Old Nea Mathla in fact never did accept the treaty
in good faith, and when the time came for the execution of
the agreement he summoned his warriors to resistance. Governor Duval broke in upon his war council, deposed the war
leaders, and elevated those who favored peaceful removal.
The Seminoles now retired to their new lands, but Nea Mathla
was driven into practical exile. He retired to the Creeks, by
whom he was raised to the dignity of a chief. It was soon
realized by the Seminoles that they had been restricted to some
pine woods by no means as fertile as their old lands, nor were
matters made better by one or two seasons of drought. To
allay their discontent twenty square miles more, to the north,
was given them, but to offset this new cession their rations
were immediately reduced.

3. From the Treaty of Fort Moultrie to the Treaty of Payne's Landing

Now succeeded ten years of trespassing, of insult, and of
increasing enmity. Kidnapers constantly lurked near the
Indian possessions, and instances of injury unredressed increased the bitterness and rancor. Under date May 20, 1825,
Humphreys * wrote to the Indian Bureau that the white settlers were already thronging to the vicinity of the Indian reser-
vation and were likely to become troublesome. As to some
recent disturbances, writing from St. Augustine February 9,
1825, he said: "From all I can learn here there is little doubt
that the disturbances near Tallahassee, which have of late occasioned so much clamor, were brought about by a course of
unjustifiable conduct on the part of the whites, similar to that
which it appears to be the object of the territorial legislature
to legalize. In fact, it is stated that one Indian had been so
severely whipped by the head of the family which was destroyed in these disturbances, as to cause his death; if such

* The correspondence is readily accessible in Sprague, 30-37.

be the fact, the subsequent act of the Indians, however lamentable, must be considered as one of retaliation, and I can not but think it is to be deplored that they were afterwards 'hunted' with so unrelenting a revenge." The word *hunted* was used advisedly by Humphreys, for, as we shall see later, when war was renewed one of the common means of fighting employed by the American officers was the use of bloodhounds. Sometimes guns were taken from the Indians so that they had nothing with which to pursue the chase. On one occasion, when some Indians were being marched to headquarters, a woman far advanced in pregnancy was forced onward with such precipitancy as to produce a premature delivery, which almost terminated her life. More far-reaching than anything else, however, was the constant denial of the rights of the Indian in court in cases involving white men. As Humphreys said, the great disadvantage under which the Seminoles labored as witnesses "destroyed everything like equality of rights." Some of the Negroes that they had, had been born among them, and some others had been purchased from white men and duly paid for. No receipts were given, however, and efforts were frequently made to recapture the Negroes by force. The Indian, conscious of his rights, protested earnestly against such attempts and naturally determined to resist all efforts to wrest from him his rightfully acquired property.

By 1827, however, the territorial legislature had begun to memorialize Congress and to ask for the complete removal of the Indians. Meanwhile the Negro question was becoming more prominent, and orders from the Department of War, increasingly peremptory, were made on Humphreys for the return of definite Negroes. For Duval and Humphreys, however, who had actually to execute the commissions, the task was not always so easy. Under date March 20, 1827, the former wrote to the latter: "Many of the slaves belonging to the whites are now in the possession of the white people; these slaves can not be obtained for their Indian owners without a lawsuit, and I see no reason why the Indians shall be compelled to surrender all slaves claimed by our citizens when this surrender is not mutual." Meanwhile the annuity began to be withheld from the Indians in order to force them to return

Negroes, and a friendly chief, Hicks, constantly waited upon Humphreys only to find the agent little more powerful than himself. Thus matters continued through 1829 and 1830. In violation of all legal procedure, the Indians were constantly *required to relinquish beforehand property in their possession to settle a question of claim.* On March 21, 1830, Humphreys was informed that he was no longer agent for the Indians. He had been honestly devoted to the interest of these people, but his efforts were not in harmony with the policy of the new administration.

Just what that policy was may be seen from Jackson's special message on Indian affairs of February 22, 1831. The Senate had asked for information as to the conduct of the Government in connection with the act of March 30, 1802, "to regulate trade and intercourse with the Indian tribes and to preserve peace on the frontiers." The Nullification controversy was in everybody's mind, and already friction had arisen between the new President and the abolitionists. In spite of Jackson's attitude toward South Carolina, his message in the present instance was a careful defense of the whole theory of state rights. Nothing in the conduct of the Federal Government toward the Indian tribes, he insisted, had ever been intended to attack or even to call in question the rights of a sovereign state. In one way the Southern states had seemed to be an exception. "As early as 1784 the settlements within the limits of North Carolina were advanced farther to the west than the authority of the state to enforce an obedience of its laws." After the Revolution the tribes desolated the frontiers. "Under these circumstances the first treaties, in 1785 and 1790, with the Cherokees, were concluded by the Government of the United States." Nothing of all this, said Jackson, had in any way affected the relation of any Indians to the state in which they happened to reside, and he concluded as follows: "Toward this race of people I entertain the kindest feelings, and am not sensible that the views which I have taken of their true interests are less favorable to them than those which oppose their emigration to the West. Years since I stated to them my belief that if the States chose to extend their laws over them it would not be in the power of the Federal Government to prevent it. My opinion remains the same, and I can see no alternative for them but that of their removal to the West or a quiet submission to the state laws. If they prefer to remove, the United States agree to defray their expenses, to supply them the means of transportation and a year's support after they reach their new homes—a provision too liberal and kind to bear the stamp of injustice. Either course promises them peace and happiness, whilst an obstinate perseverance in the effort to maintain their possessions independent of the state authority can not fail to render their condition still more helpless and miserable. Such an effort ought, therefore, to be discountenanced by all who sincerely sympathize in the fortunes of this peculiar people, and especially by the political bodies of the Union, as calculated to disturb the harmony of the two Governments and to endanger the safety of the many blessings which they enable us to enjoy."

The policy thus formally enunciated was already in practical operation. In the closing days of the administration of John Quincy Adams a delegation came to Washington to present to the administration the grievances of the Cherokee nation. The formal reception of the delegation fell to the lot of Eaton, the new Secretary of War. The Cherokees asserted that not only did they have no rights in the Georgia courts in cases involving white men, but that they had been notified by Georgia that all laws, usages, and agreements in force in the Indian country would be null and void after June 1, 1830; and naturally they wanted the interposition of the Federal Government. Eaton replied at great length, reminding the Cherokees that they had taken sides with England in the War of 1812, that they were now on American soil only by sufferance, and that the central government could not violate the rights of the state of Georgia; and he strongly advised immediate removal to the West. The Cherokees, quite broken, acted in accord with this advice; and so in 1832 did the Creeks, to whom Jackson had sent a special talk urging removal as the only basis of Federal protection.

To the Seminoles as early as 1827 overtures for removal had been made; but before the treaty of Fort Moultrie had really become effective they had been intruded upon and they in turn had become more slow about returning runaway slaves. From some of the clauses in the treaty of Fort Moultrie, as some of the chiefs were quick to point out, the understanding was that the same was to be in force for twenty years; and they felt that any slowness on their part about the return of Negroes was fully nullified by the efforts of the professional Negro stealers with whom they had to deal.

Early in 1832, however, Colonel James Gadsden of Florida was directed by Lewis Cass, the Secretary of War, to enter into negotiation for the removal of the Indians of Florida. There was great opposition to a conference, but the Indians were finally brought together at Payne's Landing on the Ocklawaha River just seventeen miles from Fort King. Here on May 9, 1832, was wrested from them a treaty which is of supreme importance in the history of the Seminoles. The full text was as follows:

Treaty of Payne's Landing,
May 9, 1832

Whereas, a treaty between the United States and the Seminole nation of Indians was made and concluded at Payne's Landing, on the Ocklawaha River, on the 9th of May, one thousand eight hundred and thirty-two, by James Gadsden, commissioner on the part of the United States, and the chiefs and headmen of said Seminole nation of Indians, on the part of said nation; which treaty is in the words following, to wit:

The Seminole Indians, regarding with just respect the solicitude manifested by the President of the United States for the improvement of their condition, by recommending a removal to the country more suitable to their habits and wants than the one they at present occupy in the territory of Florida, are willing that their confidential chiefs, Jumper, Fuch-a-lus-to-had-jo, Charley Emathla, Coi-had-jo, Holati-Emathla, Ya-ha-had-jo, Sam Jones, accompanied by their agent, Major John Phagan, and their faithful interpreter, Abraham, should be sent, at the expense of the United States, as early as convenient, to examine the country assigned to the Creeks, west of the Mississippi River, and should they be satisfied with the character of the country, and of the favorable disposition of the Creeks to re-unite with the Seminoles as one people; the articles of the compact and agreement herein stipulated, at Payne's Landing, on the Ocklawaha River, this ninth day of May, one thousand eight hundred and thirty-two, between James Gadsden, for and in behalf of the government of the United States, and the undersigned chiefs and headmen, for and in behalf of the Seminole Indians, shall be binding on the respective parties.

Article I. The Seminole Indians relinquish to the United States all claim to the land they at present occupy in the territory of Florida, and agree to emigrate to the country assigned to the Creeks, west of the Mississippi River, it being understood that an additional extent of country, proportioned to their numbers, will be added to the Creek territory, and that the Seminoles will be received as a constituent part of the Creek nation, and be re-admitted to all the privileges as a member of the same.

Article II. For and in consideration of the relinquishment of claim in the first article of this agreement, and in full compensation for all the improvements which may have been made on the lands thereby ceded, the United States stipulate to pay to the Seminole Indians fifteen thousand four hundred ($15,400) dollars, to be divided among the chiefs and warriors of the several towns, in a ratio proportioned to their population, the respective proportions of each to be paid on their arrival in the country they consent to remove to; it being understood that their faithful interpreters, Abraham and Cudjo, shall receive two hundred dollars each, of the above sum, in full remuneration of the improvements to be abandoned on the lands now cultivated by them.

Article III. The United States agree to distribute, as they arrive at their new homes in the Creek territory, west of the Mississippi River, a blanket and a homespun frock to each of the warriors, women and children, of the Seminole tribe of Indians.

Article IV. The United States agree to extend the annuity for the support of a blacksmith, provided for in the sixth article of the treaty at Camp Moultrie, for ten (10) years beyond the period therein stipulated, and in addition to the other annuities secured under that treaty, the United States agree to pay the sum of three thousand ($3,000) dollars a year for fifteen (15) years, commencing after the removal of the whole tribe; these sums to be added to the Creek annuities, and the whole amount to be so divided that the chiefs and warriors of the Seminole Indians may receive their equitable proportion of the same, as members of the Creek confederation.

Article V. The United States will take the cattle belonging to the Seminoles, at the valuation of some discreet person, to be appointed by the President, and the same shall be paid for in money to the respective owners, after their arrival at their new homes; or other cattle, such as may be desired, will be furnished them; notice being given through their agent, of their wishes upon this subject, before their removal, that time may be afforded to supply the demand.

Article VI. The Seminoles being anxious to be relieved from the repeated vexatious demands for slaves, and other property, alleged to have been stolen and destroyed by them, so that they may remove unembarrassed to their new homes, the United States stipulate to have the same property (properly) investigated, and to liquidate such as may be satisfactorily established, provided the amount does not exceed seven thousand ($7,000) dollars.

Article VII. The Seminole Indians will remove within three (3) years after the ratification of this agreement, and the expenses of their removal shall be defrayed by the United States, and such subsistence shall also be furnished them, for a term not exceeding twelve (12) months after their arrival at their new residence, as in the opinion of the President their numbers and circumstances may require; the emigration to commence as early as practicable in the year eighteen hundred and thirty-three (1833), and with those Indians at present occupying the Big Swamp, and other parts of the country beyond the limits, as defined in the second article of the treaty concluded at Camp Moultrie Creek, so that the whole of that proportion of the Seminoles may be removed within the year aforesaid, and the remainder of the tribe, in about equal proportions, during the subsequent years of eighteen hundred and thirty-four and five (1834 and 1835).

In testimony whereof, the commissioner, James Gadsden, and the undersigned chiefs and head-men of the Seminole Indians, have hereunto subscribed their names and affixed their seals.

Done at camp, at Payne's Landing, on the Ocklawaha River, in the territory of Florida, on this ninth day of May, one thousand eight hundred and thirty-two, and of the independence of the United States of America, the fifty-sixth.

(Signed)	James Gadsden	L. S.
	Holati Emathlar,	his X mark.
	Jumper,	his X mark.
	Fuch-ta-lus-ta-Hadjo,	his X mark.
	Charley Emathla,	his X mark.
Witnesses.	Coi Hadjo,	his X mark.
Douglass Vass, Sec. to Comm.	Ar-pi-uck-i, or Sam	
John Phagan, Agent.	Jones,	his X mark.
Stephen Richards, Interpreter.	Ya-ha-Hadjo,	his X mark.
Abraham, Interpreter, his X	Mico-Noha,	his X mark.
mark.	Tokose Emathla, or	
Cudjo, Interpreter, his X mark.	John Hicks,	his X mark.
Erastus Rodgers.	Cat-sha-Tustenuggee,	his X mark.
B. Joscan.	Holat-a-Micco,	his X mark.
	Hitch-it-i-Micco,	his X mark.
	E-na-hah,	his X mark.
	Ya-ha-Emathla-	
	Chopco,	his X mark.
	Moki-his-she-lar-ni,	his X mark.

Now, therefore, be it known that I, Andrew Jackson, President of the United States of America, having seen and considered said treaty, do, by and with the advice and consent of the Senate, as expressed by their resolution of the eighth day of April, one thousand eight hundred and thirty-four, accept, ratify, and confirm the same, and every clause and article thereof.

In witness whereof, I have caused the seal of the United States to be hereunto affixed, having signed the same with my hand.

Done at the city of Washington, this twelfth day of April, in the year of our Lord one thousand eight hundred and thirty-four, and of the independence of the United States of America, the fifty-eighth.

(Signed) ANDREW JACKSON.

By the President,
LOUIS McLANE, Secretary of State.

It will be seen that by the terms of this document seven chiefs were to go and examine the country assigned to the Creeks, and that they were to be accompanied by Major John Phagan, the successor of Humphreys, and the Negro interpreter Abraham. The character of Phagan may be seen from the facts that he was soon in debt to different ones of the Indians and to Abraham, and that he was found to be short in his accounts. While the Indian chiefs were in the West, three United States commissioners conferred with them as to the suitability of the country for a future home, and at Fort Gibson, Arkansas, March 28, 1833, they were beguiled into signing an additional treaty in which occurred the following sentence: "And the undersigned Seminole chiefs, delegated as aforesaid, on behalf of their nation, hereby declare themselves well satisfied with the location provided for them by the commissioners, and agree that their nation shall commence the removal to their new home as soon as the government will make arrangements for their emigration, satisfactory to the Seminole nation." They of course had no authority to act on their own initiative, and when all returned in April, 1833, and Phagan explained what had happened, the Seminoles expressed themselves in no uncertain terms. The chiefs who had gone West denied strenuously that they had signed away any rights to land, but they were nevertheless upbraided as the agents of deception. Some of the old chiefs, of whom Micanopy was the highest authority, resolved to resist the efforts to dispossess them; and John Hicks, who seems to have been substituted for Sam Jones on the commission, was killed because he argued too strongly for migration. Meanwhile the treaty of Payne's Landing was ratified by the Senate of the United States and proclaimed as in force by President Jackson April 12, 1834, and in connection with it the supplementary treaty of Fort Gibson was also ratified. The Seminoles, however, were not showing any haste about removing, and ninety of the white citizens of Alachua County sent a protest to the President alleging that the Indians were not returning their fugitive slaves. Jackson was made angry, and without even waiting for the formal ratification of the treaties, he sent the document to the Secretary of War, with an endorsement on the back directing him "to inquire into the alleged facts, and if found to be true, to direct the Seminoles to prepare to remove West and join the Creeks." General Wiley Thompson was appointed to succeed Phagan as agent, and General Duncan L. Clinch was placed in command of the troops whose services it was thought might be needed. It was at this juncture that Osceola stepped forward as the leading spirit of his people.

4. *Osceola and the Second Seminole War*

Osceola (Asseola, or As-se-he-ho-lar, sometimes called Powell because after his father's death his mother married a white man of that name *) was not more than thirty years of age. He was slender, of only average height, and slightly round-shouldered; but he was also well proportioned, muscular, and capable of enduring great fatigue. He had light, deep, restless eyes, and a shrill voice, and he was a great admirer of order and technique. He excelled in athletic contests and in his earlier years had taken delight in engaging in military practice with the white men. As he was neither by descent nor formal election a chief, he was not expected to have a voice in important deliberations; but he was a natural leader and

* Hodge's *Handbook of American Indians,* II, 159.

he did more than any other man to organize the Seminoles to resistance. It is hardly too much to say that to his single influence was due a contest that ultimately cost $10,000,000 and the loss of thousands of lives. Never did a patriot fight more valiantly for his own, and it stands to the eternal disgrace of the American arms that he was captured under a flag of truce.

It is well to pause for a moment and reflect upon some of the deeper motives that entered into the impending contest. A distinguished congressman,* speaking in the House of Representatives a few years later, touched eloquently upon some of the events of these troublous years. Let us remember that this was the time of the formation of anti-slavery societies, of pronounced activity on the part of the abolitionists, and recall also that Nat Turner's insurrection was still fresh in the public mind. Giddings stated clearly the issue as it appeared to the people of the North when he said, "I hold that if the slaves of Georgia or any other state leave their masters, the Federal Government has no constitutional authority to employ our army or navy for their recapture, or to apply the national treasure to repurchase them." There could be no question of the fact that the war was very largely one over fugitive slaves. Under date October 28, 1834, General Thompson wrote to the Commissioner of Indian Affairs: "There are many very likely Negroes in this nation [the Seminole]. Some of the whites in the adjacent settlements manifest a restless desire to obtain them, and I have no doubt that Indian raised Negroes are now in the possession of the whites." In a letter dated January 20, 1834, Governor Duval had already said to the same official: "The slaves belonging to the Indians have a controlling influence over the minds of their masters, and are entirely opposed to any change of residence." Six days later he wrote: "The slaves belonging to the Indians must be made to fear for themselves before they will cease to influence the minds of their masters. . . . The first step towards the emigration of these Indians must be the breaking up of the runaway slaves and the outlaw In-

* Joshua R. Giddings, of Ohio. His exhaustive speech on the Florida War was made February 9, 1841.

dians." And the New Orleans *Courier* of July 27, 1839, revealed all the fears of the period when it said, "Every day's delay in subduing the Seminoles increases the danger of a rising among the serviles."

All the while injustice and injury to the Indians continued. Econchattimico, well known as one of those chiefs to whom special reservations had been given by the treaty of Fort Moultrie, was the owner of twenty slaves valued at $15,-000. Observing Negro stealers hovering around his estate, he armed himself and his men. The kidnapers then furthered their designs by circulating the report that the Indians were arming themselves for union with the main body of Seminoles for the general purpose of massacring the white people. Face to face with this charge Econchattimico gave up his arms and threw himself on the protection of the government; and his Negroes were at once taken and sold into bondage.

A similar case was that of John Walker, an Appalachicola chief, who wrote to Thompson under date July 28, 1835: "I am induced to write you in consequence of the depredations making and attempted to be made upon my property, by a company of Negro stealers, some of whom are from Columbus, Ga., and have connected themselves with Brown and Douglass. . . . I should like your advice how I am to act. I dislike to make or to have any difficulty with the white people. But if they trespass upon my premises and my rights, I must defend myself the best way I can. If they do make this attempt, and I have no doubt they will, they must bear the consequences. *But is there no civil law to protect me?* Are the free Negroes and the Negroes belonging to this town to be stolen away publicly, and in the face of law and justice, carried off and sold to fill the pockets of these worse than land pirates? Douglass and his company hired a man who has two large trained dogs for the purpose to come down and take Billy. He is from Mobile and follows for a livelihood catching runaway Negroes."

Such were the motives, fears and incidents in the years immediately after the treaty of Payne's Landing. Beginning at the close of 1834 and continuing through April, 1835,

Thompson had a series of conferences with the Seminole chiefs. At these meetings Micanopy, influenced by Osceola and other young Seminoles, took a more definite stand than he might otherwise have assumed. Especially did he insist with reference to the treaty that he understood that the chiefs who went West were to *examine* the country, and for his part he knew that when they returned they would report unfavorably. Thompson then, becoming angry, delivered an ultimatum to the effect that if the treaty was not observed the annuity from the great father in Washington would cease. To this, Osceola, stepping forward, replied that he and his warriors did not care if they never received another dollar from the great father, and drawing his knife, he plunged it in the table and said, "The only treaty I will execute is with this." Henceforward there was deadly enmity between the young Seminole and Thompson. More and more Osceola made his personality felt, constantly asserting to the men of his nation that whoever recommended emigration was an enemy of the Seminoles, and he finally arrived at an understanding with many of them that the treaty would be resisted with their very lives. Thompson, however, on April 23, 1835, had a sort of secret conference with sixteen of the chiefs who seemed favorably disposed toward migration, and he persuaded them to sign a document "freely and fully" assenting to the treaties of Payne's Landing and Fort Gibson. The next day there was a formal meeting at which the agent, backed up by Clinch and his soldiers, upbraided the Indians in a very harsh manner. His words were met by groans, angry gesticulations, and only half-muffled imprecations. Clinch endeavored to appeal to the Indians and to advise them that resistance was both unwise and useless. Thompson, however, with his usual lack of tact, rushed onward in his course, and learning that five chiefs were unalterably opposed to the treaty, he arbitrarily struck their names off the roll of chiefs, an action the highhandedness of which was not lost on the Seminoles. Immediately after the conference moreover he forbade the sale of any more arms and powder to the Indians. To the friendly chiefs the understanding had been given that the nation might have until January 1, 1836, to make preparation for removal, by which time all were to assemble at Fort Brooke, Tampa Bay, for emigration.

About the first of June Osceola was one day on a quiet errand of trading at Fort King. With him was his wife, the daughter of a mulatto slave woman who had run away years before and married an Indian chief. By Southern law this woman followed the condition of her mother, and when the mother's former owner appeared on the scene and claimed the daughter, Thompson, who desired to teach Occeola a lesson, readily agreed that she should be remanded into captivity.* Osceola was highly enraged, and this time it was his turn to upbraid the agent. Thompson now had him overpowered and put in irons, in which situation he remained for the better part of two days. In this period of captivity his soul plotted revenge and at length he too planned a *"ruse de guerre."* Feigning assent to the treaty he told Thompson that if he was released not only would he sign himself but he would also bring his people to sign. The agent was completely deceived by Osceola's tactics. "True to his professions," wrote Thompson on June 3, "he this day appeared with seventy-nine of his people, men, women, and children, including some who had joined him since his conversion, and redeemed his promise. He told me many of his friends were out hunting, whom he could and would bring over on their return. I have now no doubt of his sincerity, and as little, that the greatest difficulty is surmounted."

Osceola now rapidly urged forward preparations for war, which, however, he did not wish actually started until after the crops were gathered. By the fall he was ready, and one day in October when he and some other warriors met Charley Emathla, who had upon him the gold and silver that he had

* This highly important incident, which was really the spark that started the war, is absolutely ignored even by such well informed writers as Drake and Sprague. Drake simply gives the impression that the quarrel between Osceola and Thompson was over the old matter of emigration, saying (413), "Remonstrance soon grew into altercation, which ended in a *ruse de guerre,* by which Osceola was made prisoner by the agent, and put in irons, in which situation he was kept one night and part of two days." The story is told by McMaster, however. Also note M. M. Cohen as quoted in *Quarterly Anti-Slavery Magazine,* Vol. II, p. 419 (July, 1837).

received from the sale of his cattle preparatory to migration, they killed this chief, and Osceola threw the money in every direction, saying that no one was to touch it, as it was the price of the red man's blood. The true drift of events became even more apparent to Thompson and Clinch in November, when five chiefs friendly to migration with five hundred of their people suddenly appeared at Fort Brooke to ask for protection. When in December Thompson sent final word to the Seminoles that they must bring in their horses and cattle, the Indians did not come on the appointed day; on the contrary they sent their women and children to the interior and girded themselves for battle. To Osceola late in the month a runner brought word that some troops under the command of Major Dade were to leave Fort Brooke on the 25th and on the night of the 27th were to be attacked by some Seminoles in the Wahoo Swamp. Osceola himself, with some of his men, was meanwhile lying in the woods near Fort King, waiting for an opportunity to kill Thompson. On the afternoon of the 28th the agent dined not far from the fort at the home of the sutler, a man named Rogers, and after dinner he walked with Lieutenant Smith to the crest of a neighboring hill. Here he was surprised by the Indians, and both he and Smith fell pierced by numerous bullets. The Indians then pressed on to the home of the sutler and killed Rogers, his two clerks, and a little boy. On the same day the command of Major Dade, including seven officers and one hundred and ten men, was almost completely annihilated, only three men escaping. Dade and his horse were killed at the first onset. These two attacks began the actual fighting of the Second Seminole War. That the Negroes were working shoulder to shoulder with the Indians in these encounters may be seen from the report of Captain Belton,* who said, "Lieut. Keays, third artillery, had both arms broken from the first shot; was unable to act, and was tomahawked the latter part of the second attack, by a Negro"; and further: "A Negro named Harry controls the Pea Band of about a hundred warriors, forty miles southeast of us, who have done most of the mischief, and keep this post

* Accessible in Drake, 416-418.

constantly observed." Osceola now joined forces with those
Indians who had attacked Dade, and in the early morning of
the last day of the year occurred the Battle of Ouithlecoochee,
a desperate encounter in which both Osceola and Clinch gave
good accounts of themselves. Clinch had two hundred regulars and five or six hundred volunteers. The latter fled early
in the contest and looked on from a distance; and Clinch had
to work desperately to keep from duplicating the experience
of Dade. Osceola himself was conspicuous in a red belt and
three long feathers, but although twice wounded he seemed to
bear a charmed life. He posted himself behind a tree, from
which station he constantly sallied forth to kill or wound an
enemy with almost infallible aim.

After these early encounters the fighting became more and
more bitter and the contest more prolonged. Early in the
war the disbursing agent reported that there were only three
thousand Indians, including Negroes, to be considered; but this
was clearly an understatement. Within the next year and a
half the Indians were hard pressed, and before the end of
this period the notorious Thomas S. Jessup had appeared on
the scene as commanding major general. This man seems
to have determined never to use honorable means of warfare
if some ignoble instrument could serve his purpose. In a letter
sent to Colonel Harvey from Tampa Bay under date May 25,
1837, he said: "If you see Powell (Osceola), tell him I shall
send out and take all the Negroes who belong to the white
people. And he must not allow the Indian Negroes to mix
with them. Tell him I am sending to Cuba for bloodhounds
to trail them; and I intend to hang every one of them who
does not come in." And it might be remarked that for his
bloodhounds Jessup spent—or said he spent—as much as
$5,000, a fact which thoroughly aroused Giddings and other
persons from the North, who by no means cared to see such an
investment of public funds. By order No. 160, dated August 3,
1837, Jessup invited his soldiers to plunder and rapine, saying,
"All Indian property captured from this date will belong to
the corps or detachment making it." From St. Augustine,
under date October 20, 1837, in a "confidential" communication he said to one of his lieutenants: "Should Powell and his

warriors come within the fort, seize him and the whole party. It is important that he, Wild Cat, John Cowagee, and Tustenuggee, be secured. Hold them until you have my orders in relation to them." * Two days later he was able to write to the Secretary of War that Osceola was actually taken. Said he: "That chief came into the vicinity of Fort Peyton on the 20th, and sent a messenger to General Hernandez, desiring to see and converse with him. The sickly season being over, and there being no further necessity to temporize, I sent a party of mounted men, and seized the entire body, and now have them securely lodged in the fort." Osceola, Wild Cat, and others thus captured were marched to St. Augustine; but Wild Cat escaped. Osceola was ultimately taken to Fort Moultrie, in the harbor of Charleston, where in January (1838) he died.

Important in this general connection was the fate of the deputation that the influential John Ross, chief of the Cherokees, was persuaded to send from his nation to induce the Seminoles to think more favorably of migration. Micanopy, twelve other chieftains, and a number of warriors accompanied the Cherokee deputation to the headquarters of the United States Army at Fort Mellon, where they were to discuss the matter. These warriors also Jessup seized, and Ross wrote to the Secretary of War a dignified but bitter letter protesting against this "unprecedented violation of that sacred rule which has ever been recognized by every nation, civilized and uncivilized, of treating with all due respect those who had ever presented themselves under a flag of truce before the enemy, for the purpose of proposing the termination of warfare." He had indeed been most basely used as the agent of deception.

This chapter, we trust, has shown something of the real nature of the points at issue in the Seminole Wars. In the course of these contests the rights of Indian and Negro alike were ruthlessly disregarded. There was redress for neither before the courts, and at the end in dealing with them every honorable principle of men and nations was violated. It is

---

* This correspondence, and much more bearing on the point, may be found in House Document 327 of the Second Session of the Twenty-fifth Congress.

interesting that the three representatives of colored peoples who in the course of the nineteenth century it was most difficult to capture—Toussaint L'Ouverture, the Negro, Osceola, the Indian, and Aguinaldo, the Filipino—were all taken through treachery; and on two of the three occasions this treachery was practiced by responsible officers of the United States Army.

CHAPTER VI

EARLY APPROACH TO THE NEGRO PROBLEM

1. *The Ultimate Problem and the Missouri Compromise*

In a previous chapter* we have already indicated the rise
of the Negro Problem in the last decade of the eighteenth
and the first two decades of the nineteenth century. And what
was the Negro Problem? It was certainly not merely a question of slavery; in the last analysis this institution was hardly
more than an incident. Slavery has ceased to exist, but even
to-day the Problem is with us. The question was rather what
was to be the final place in the American body politic of the
Negro population that was so rapidly increasing in the country.
In the answering of this question supreme importance attached
to the Negro himself; but the problem soon transcended the
race. Ultimately it was the destiny of the United States
rather than of the Negro that was to be considered, and all
the ideals on which the country was based came to the testing.
If one studied those ideals he soon realized that they were
based on Teutonic or at least English foundations. By 1820,
however, the young American republic was already beginning
to be the hope of all of the oppressed people of Europe, and
Greeks and Italians as well as Germans and Swedes were turning their faces toward the Promised Land. The whole background of Latin culture was different from the Teutonic, and
yet the people of Southern as well as of Northern Europe
somehow became a part of the life of the United States. In
this life was it also possible for the children of Africa to have
a permanent and an honorable place? With their special tradition and gifts, with their shortcomings, above all with their
distinctive color, could they, too, become genuine American

* IV, Section 3.

citizens? Some said No, but in taking this position they denied not only the ideals on which the country was founded but also the possibilities of human nature itself. In any case the answer to the first question at once suggested another, What shall we do with the Negro? About this there was very great difference of opinion, it not always being supposed that the Negro himself had anything whatever to say about the matter. Some said send the Negro away, get rid of him by any means whatsoever; others said if he must stay, keep him in slavery; still others said not to keep him permanently in slavery, but emancipate him only gradually; and already there were beginning to be persons who felt that the Negro should be emancipated everywhere immediately, and that after this great event had taken place he and the nation together should work out his salvation on the broadest possible plane.

Into the agitation was suddenly thrust the application of Missouri for entrance into the Union as a slave state. The struggle that followed for two years was primarily a political one, but in the course of the discussion the evils of slavery were fully considered. Meanwhile, in 1819, Alabama and Maine also applied for admission. Alabama was allowed to enter without much discussion, as she made equal the number of slave and free states. Maine, however, brought forth more talk. The Southern congressmen would have been perfectly willing to admit this as a free state if Missouri had been admitted as a slave state; but the North felt that this would have been to concede altogether too much, as Missouri from the first gave promise of being unusually important. At length, largely through the influence of Henry Clay, there was adopted a compromise whose main provisions were (1) that Maine was to be admitted as a free state; (2) that in Missouri there was to be no prohibition of slavery; but (3) that slavery was to be prohibited in any other states that might be formed out of the Louisiana Purchase north of the line of 36° 30'.

By this agreement the strife was allayed for some years; but it is now evident that the Missouri Compromise was only a postponement of the ultimate contest and that the social questions involved were hardly touched. Certainly the significance of the first clear drawing of the line between the sections was not lost upon thoughtful men. Jefferson wrote from Monticello in 1820: "This momentous question, like a fire-bell in the night, awakened and filled me with terror. I considered it at once as the knell of the Union. It is hushed, indeed, for the moment. But this is a reprieve only, not a final sentence. . . . I can say, with conscious truth, that there is not a man on earth who would sacrifice more than I would to relieve us from this heavy reproach, in any *practicable* way. The cession of that kind of property, for so it is misnamed, is a bagatelle that would not cost me a second thought, if, in that way, a general emancipation and *expatriation* could be effected; and, gradually, and with due sacrifices, I think it might be." * For the time being, however, the South was concerned mainly about immediate dangers; nor was this section placed more at ease by Denmark Vesey's attempted insurrection in 1822.† A representative South Carolinian,‡ writing after this event, said, "We regard our Negroes as the *Jacobins* of the country, against whom we should always be upon our guard, and who, although we fear no permanent effects from any insurrectionary movements on their part, should be watched with an eye of steady and unremitted observation." Meanwhile from a ratio of 43.72 to 56.28 in 1790 the total Negro population in South Carolina had by 1820 come to outnumber the white 52.77 to 47.23, and the tendency was increasingly in favor of the Negro. The South, the whole country in fact, was more and more being forced to consider not only slavery but the ultimate reaches of the problem.

Whatever one might think of the conclusion—and in this case the speaker was pleading for colonization—no statement of the problem as it impressed men about 1820 or 1830 was clearer than that of Rev. Dr. Nott, President of Union College, at Albany in 1829.§ The question, said he, was by no means local. Slavery was once legalized in New England;

* *Writings*, XV, 249.
† See Chapter VII, Section 1.
‡ Holland: *A Refutation of Calumnies*, 61.
§ See "African Colonization. Proceedings of the Formation of the New York State Colonization Society." Albany, 1829.

and New England built slave-ships and manned these with New England seamen. In 1820 the slave population in the country amounted to 1,500,000. The number doubled every twenty years, and it was easy to see how it would progress from 1,500,000 to 3,000,000; to 6,000,000; to 12,000,000; to 24,000,000. "Twenty-four millions of slaves! What a drawback from our strength; what a tax on our resources; what a hindrance to our growth; what a stain on our character; and what an impediment to the fulfillment of our destiny! Could our worst enemies or the worst enemies of republics, wish us a severer judgment?" How could one know that wakeful and sagacious enemies without would not discover the vulnerable point and use it for the country's overthrow? Or was there not danger that among a people goaded from age to age there might at length arise some second Toussaint L'Ouverture, who, reckless of consequences, would array a force and cause a movement throughout the zone of bondage, leaving behind him plantations waste and mansions desolate? Who could believe that such a tremendous physical force would remain forever spell-bound and quiescent? After all, however, slavery was doomed; public opinion had already pronounced upon it, and the moral energy of the nation would sooner or later effect its overthrow. "But," continued Nott, "the solemn question here arises—in what condition will this momentous change place us? The freed men of other countries have long since disappeared, having been amalgamated in the general mass. Here there can be no amalgamation. Our manumitted bondmen have remained already to the third and fourth, as they will to the thousandth generation—a distinct, a degraded, and a wretched race." After this sweeping statement, which has certainly not been justified by time, Nott proceeded to argue the expediency of his organization. Gerrit Smith, who later drifted away from colonization, said frankly on the same occasion that the ultimate solution was either amalgamation or colonization, and that of the two courses he preferred to choose the latter. Others felt as he did. We shall now accordingly proceed to consider at somewhat greater length the two solutions that about 1820 had the clearest advocates—Colonization and Slavery.

2. *Colonization*

Early in 1773, Rev. Samuel Hopkins, of Newport, called on his friend, Rev. Ezra Stiles, afterwards President of Yale College, and suggested the possibility of educating Negro students, perhaps two at first, who would later go as missionaries to Africa. Stiles thought that for the plan to be worth while there should be a colony on the coast of Africa, that at least thirty or forty persons should go, and that the enterprise should not be private but should have the formal backing of a society organized for the purpose. In harmony with the original plan two young Negro men sailed from New York for Africa, November 12, 1774; but the Revolutionary War followed and nothing more was done at the time. In 1784, however, and again in 1787, Hopkins tried to induce different merchants to fit out a vessel to convey a few emigrants, and in the latter year he talked with a young man from the West Indies, Dr. William Thornton, who expressed a willingness to take charge of the company. The enterprise failed for lack of funds, though Thornton kept up his interest and afterwards became a member of the first Board of Managers of the American Colonization Society. Hopkins in 1791 spoke before the Connecticut Emancipation Society, which he wished to see incorporated as a colonization society, and in a sermon before the Providence society in 1793 he reverted to his favorite theme. Meanwhile, as a result of the efforts of Wilberforce, Clarkson, and Granville Sharp in England, in May, 1787, some four hundred Negroes and sixty white persons were landed at Sierra Leone. Some of the Negroes in England had gained their freedom in consequence of Lord Mansfield's decision in 1772, others had been discharged from the British Army after the American Revolution, and all were leading in England a more or less precarious existence. The sixty white persons sent along were abandoned women, and why Sierra Leone should have had this weight placed upon it at the start history has not yet told. It is not surprising to learn that "disease and disorder were rife, and by 1791 a mere handful survived." * As early as in his *Notes on Virginia,* privately printed in 1781, Thomas Jefferson had suggested a colony for Negroes, perhaps in the new territory of Ohio. The suggestion was not acted upon, but it is evident that by 1800 several persons had thought of the possibility of removing the Negroes in the South to some other place either within or without the country.

Gabriel's insurrection in 1800 again forced the idea concretely forward. Virginia was visibly disturbed by this outbreak, and *in secret session,* on December 21, the House of Delegates passed the following resolution: "That the Governor† be requested to correspond with the President of the United States,‡ on the subject of purchasing land without the limits of this state, whither persons obnoxious to the laws, or dangerous to the peace of society may be removed." The real purpose of this resolution was to get rid of those Negroes who had had some part in the insurrection and had not been executed; but not in 1800, or in 1802 or 1804, was the General Assembly thus able to banish those whom it was afraid to hang. Monroe, however, acted in accordance with his instructions, and Jefferson replied to him under date November 24, 1801. He was not now favorable to deportation to some place within the United States, and thought that the West Indies, probably Santo Domingo, might be better. There was little real danger that the exiles would stimulate vindictive or predatory descents on the American coasts, and in any case such a possibility was "overweighed by the humanity of the measures proposed." "Africa would offer a last and undoubted resort," thought Jefferson, "if all others more desirable should fail." § Six months later, on July 13, 1802, the President wrote about the matter to Rufus King, then minister in London. The course of events in the West Indies, he said, had given an impulse to the minds of Negroes in the United States; there was a disposition to insurgency, and it now seemed that if there was to be colonization, Africa was

* McPherson, 15. (See bibliography on Liberia.)
† Monroe.
‡ Jefferson.
§ *Writings,* X, 297.

by all means the best place. An African company might also engage in commercial operations, and if there was coöperation with Sierra Leone, there was the possibility of "one strong, rather than two weak colonies." Would King accordingly enter into conference with the English officials with reference to disposing of any Negroes who might be sent? "It is material to observe," remarked Jefferson, "that they are not felons, or common malefactors, but persons guilty of what the safety of society, under actual circumstances, obliges us to treat as a crime, but which their feelings may represent in a far different shape. They are such as will be a valuable acquisition to the settlement already existing there, and well calculated to coöperate in the plan of civilization." * King accordingly opened correspondence with Thornton and Wedderbourne, the secretaries of the company having charge of Sierra Leone, but was informed that the colony was in a languishing condition and that funds were likely to fail, and that in no event would they be willing to receive more people from the United States, as these were the very ones who had already made most trouble in the settlement.† On January 22, 1805, the General Assembly of Virginia passed a resolution that embodied a request to the United States Government to set aside a portion of territory in the new Louisiana Purchase "to be appropriated to the residence of such people of color as have been, or shall be, emancipated, or may hereafter become dangerous to the public safety." Nothing came of this. By the close then of Jefferson's second administration the Northwest, the Southwest, the West Indies, and Sierra Leone had all been thought of as possible fields for colonization, but from the consideration nothing visible had resulted.

Now followed the period of Southern expansion and of increasing materialism, and before long came the War of 1812. By 1811 a note of doubt had crept into Jefferson's dealing with the subject. Said he: "Nothing is more to be wished than that the United States would themselves undertake to make such an establishment on the coast of Africa . . . But for this the national mind is not yet prepared. It may

* *Writings*, X, 327-328.
† *Ibid.*, XIII, 11.

perhaps be doubted whether many of these people would voluntarily consent to such an exchange of situation, and very certain that few of those advanced to a certain age in habits of slavery, would be capable of self-government. This should not, however, discourage the experiment, nor the early trial of it; and the proposition should be made with all the prudent cautions and attentions requisite to reconcile it to the interests, the safety, and the prejudices of all parties." *

From an entirely different source, however, and prompted not by expediency but the purest altruism, came an impulse that finally told in the founding of Liberia. The heart of a young man reached out across the sea. Samuel J. Mills, an undergraduate of Williams College, in 1808 formed among his fellow-students a missionary society whose work later told in the formation of the American Bible Society and the Board of Foreign Missions. Mills continued his theological studies at Andover and then at Princeton; and while at the latter place he established a school for Negroes at Parsippany, thirty miles away. He also interested in his work and hopes Rev. Robert Finley, of Basking Ridge, N. J., who "succeeded in assembling at Princeton the first meeting ever called to consider the project of sending Negro colonists to Africa," † and who in a letter to John P. Mumford, of New York, under date February 14, 1815, expressed his interest by saying, "We should send to Africa a population partly civilized and christianized for its benefit; and our blacks themselves would be put in a better condition."

In this same year, 1815, the country was startled by the unselfish enterprise of a Negro who had long thought of the unfortunate situation of his people in America and who himself shouldered the obligation to do something definite in their behalf. Paul Cuffe had been born in May, 1759, on one of the Elizabeth Islands near New Bedford, Mass., the son of a father who was once a slave from Africa and of an Indian mother.‡ Interested in navigation, he made voyages to Russia, England, Africa, the West Indies, and the South; and

* *Writings,* XIII, 11.
† McPherson, 18.
‡ First Annual Report of American Colonization Society.

in time he commanded his own vessel, became generally respected, and by his wisdom rose to a fair degree of opulence. For twenty years he had thought especially about Africa, and in 1815 he took to Sierra Leone a total of nine families and thirty-eight persons at an expense to himself of nearly $4000. The people that he brought were well received at Sierra Leone, and Cuffe himself had greater and more far-reaching plans when he died September 7, 1817. He left an estate valued at $20,000.

Dr. Finley's meeting at Princeton was not very well attended and hence not a great success. Nevertheless he felt sufficiently encouraged to go to Washington in December, 1816, to use his effort for the formation of a national colonization society. It happened that in February of this same year, 1816, General Charles Fenton Mercer, member of the House of Delegates, came upon the secret journals of the legislature for the period 1801-5 and saw the correspondence between Monroe and Jefferson. Interested in the colonization project, on December 14 (Monroe then being President-elect) he presented in the House of Delegates resolutions embodying the previous enactments; and these passed 132 to 14. Finley was generally helped by the effort of Mercer, and on December 21, 1816, there was held in Washington a meeting of public men and interested citizens, Henry Clay, then Speaker of the House of Representatives, presiding. A constitution was adopted at an adjourned meeting on December 28; and on January 1, 1817, were formally chosen the officers of "The American Society for Colonizing the Free People of Color of the United States." At this last meeting Henry Clay, again presiding, spoke in glowing terms of the possibilities of the movement; Elias B. Caldwell, a brother-in-law of Finley, made the leading argument; and John Randolph, of Roanoke, Va., and Robert Wright, of Maryland, spoke of the advantages to accrue from the removal of the free Negroes from the country (which remarks were very soon to awaken much discussion and criticism, especially on the part of the Negroes themselves). It is interesting to note that Mercer had no part at all in the meeting of January 1, not even being present; he did not feel that any but Southern men should be enrolled in the organization. However, Bushrod Washington, the president, was a Southern man; twelve of the seventeen vice-presidents were Southern men, among them being Andrew Jackson and William Crawford; and all of the twelve managers were slaveholders.

Membership in the American Colonization Society originally consisted, first, of such as sincerely desired to afford the free Negroes an asylum from oppression and who hoped through them to extend to Africa the blessings of civilization and Christianity; second, of such as sought to enhance the value of their own slaves by removing the free Negroes; and third, of such as desired to be relieved of any responsibility whatever for free Negroes. The movement was widely advertised as "an effort for the benefit of the blacks in which all parts of the country could unite," it being understood that it was "not to have the abolition of slavery for its immediate object," nor was it to "aim directly at the instruction of the great body of the blacks." Such points as the last were to prove in course of time hardly less than a direct challenge to the different abolitionist organizations in the North, and more and more the Society was denounced as a movement on the part of slaveholders for perpetuating their institutions by doing away with the free people of color. It is not to be supposed, however, that the South, with its usual religious fervor, did not put much genuine feeling into the colonization scheme. One man in Georgia named Tubman freed his slaves, thirty in all, and placed them in charge of the Society with a gift of $10,000; Thomas Hunt, a young Virginian, afterwards a chaplain in the Union Army, sent to Liberia the slaves he had inherited, paying the entire cost of the journey; and others acted in a similar spirit of benevolence. It was but natural, however, for the public to be somewhat uncertain as to the tendencies of the organization when the utterances of representative men were sometimes directly contradictory. On January 20, 1827, for instance, Henry Clay, then Secretary of State, speaking in the hall of the House of Representatives at the annual meeting of the Society, said: "Of all classes of our population, the most vicious is that of the free colored. It is the inevitable result of their moral, political, and civil degradation. Contaminated themselves, they extend their vices to all around them, to the slaves and to the whites." Just a moment later he said: "Every emigrant to Africa is a missionary carrying with him credentials in the holy cause of civilization, religion, and free institutions." How persons contaminated and vicious could be missionaries of civilization and religion was something possible only in the logic of Henry Clay. In the course of the next month Robert Y. Hayne gave a Southern criticism in two addresses on a memorial presented in the United States Senate by the Colonization Society.* The first of these speeches was a clever one characterized by much wit and good-humored raillery; the second was a sober arraignment. Hayne emphasized the tremendous cost involved and the physical impossibility of the whole undertaking, estimating that at least sixty thousand persons a year would have to be transported to accomplish anything like the desired result. At the close of his brilliant attack, still making a veiled plea for the continuance of slavery, he nevertheless rose to genuine statesmanship in dealing with the problem of the Negro, saying, "While this process is going on the colored classes are gradually diffusing themselves throughout the country and are making steady advances in intelligence and refinement, and if half the zeal were displayed in bettering their condition that is now wasted in the vain and fruitless effort of sending them abroad, their intellectual and moral improvement would be steady and rapid." William Lloyd Garrison was untiring and merciless in flaying the inconsistencies and selfishness of the colonization organization. In an editorial in the *Liberator*, July 9, 1831, he charged the Society, first, with persecution in compelling free people to emigrate against their will and in discouraging their education at home; second, with falsehood in saying that the Negroes were natives of Africa when they were no more so than white Americans were natives of Great Britain; third, with cowardice in asserting that the continuance of the Negro population in the country involved dangers; and finally, with infidelity in denying that the Gospel has full power to reach the hatred in the hearts of

* See Jervey: *Robert Y. Hayne and His Times*, 207-8.

men. In *Thoughts on African Colonization* (1832) he developed exhaustively ten points as follows: That the American Colonization Society was pledged not to oppose the system of slavery, that it apologized for slavery and slaveholders, that it recognized slaves as property, that by deporting Negroes it increased the value of slaves, that it was the enemy of immediate abolition, that it was nourished by fear and selfishness, that it aimed at the utter expulsion of the blacks, that it was the disparager of free Negroes, that it denied the possibility of elevating the black people of the country, and that it deceived and misled the nation. Other criticisms were numerous. A broadside, "The Shields of American Slavery" ("Broad enough to hide the wrongs of two millions of stolen men") placed side by side conflicting utterances of members of the Society; and in August, 1830, Kendall, fourth auditor, in his report to the Secretary of the Navy, wondered why the resources of the government should be used "to colonize recaptured Africans, to build homes for them, to furnish them with farming utensils, to pay instructors to teach them, to purchase ships for their convenience, to build forts for their protection, to supply them with arms and munitions of war, to enlist troops to guard them, and to employ the army and navy in their defense."* Criticism of the American Colonization Society was prompted by a variety of motives; but the organization made itself vulnerable at many points. The movement attracted extraordinary attention, but has had practically no effect whatever on the position of the Negro in the United States. Its work in connection with the founding of Liberia, however, is of the highest importance, and must later receive detailed attention.

3. *Slavery*

We have seen that from the beginning there were liberal-minded men in the South who opposed the system of slavery, and if we actually take note of all the utterances of different men and of the proposals for doing away with the system, we

* Cited by McPherson, 22.

shall find that about the turn of the century there was in this section considerable anti-slavery sentiment. Between 1800 and 1820, however, the opening of new lands in the Southwest, the increasing emphasis on cotton, and the rapidly growing Negro population, gave force to the argument of expediency; and the Missouri Compromise drew sharply the lines of the contest. The South now came to regard slavery as its peculiar heritage; public men were forced to defend the institution; and in general the best thought of the section began to be obsessed and dominated by the Negro, just as it is to-day in large measure. In taking this position the South deliberately committed intellectual suicide. In such matters as freedom of speech and literary achievement, and in genuine statesmanship if not for the time being in political influence, this part of the country declined, and before long the difference between it and New England was appalling. Calhoun and Hayne were strong; but between 1820 and 1860 the South had no names to compare with Longfellow and Emerson in literature, or with Morse and Hoe in invention. The foremost college professor, Dew, of William and Mary, and even the outstanding divines, Furman, the Baptist, of South Carolina, in the twenties, and Palmer, the Presbyterian of New Orleans, in the fifties, are all now remembered mainly because they defended their section in keeping the Negro in bonds. William and Mary College, and even the University of Virginia, as compared with Harvard and Yale, became provincial institutions; and instead of the Washington or Jefferson of an earlier day now began to be nourished such a leader as "Bob" Toombs, who for all of his fire and eloquence was a demagogue. In making its choice the South could not and did not blame the Negro *per se,* for it was freely recognized that upon slave labor rested such economic stability as the section possessed. The tragedy was simply that thousands of intelligent Americans deliberately turned their faces to the past, and preferred to read the novels of Walter Scott and live in the Middle Ages rather than study the French Revolution and live in the nineteenth century. One hundred years after we find that the chains are still forged, that thought is not yet free. Thus the Negro Problem began to be, and still is, very largely the prob-

lem of the white man of the South. The era of capitalism
had not yet dawned, and still far in the future was the day
when the poor white man and the Negro were slowly to realize that their interests were largely identical.

The argument with which the South came to support its
position and to defend slavery need not here detain us at
length. It was formally stated by Dew and others* and it was
to be heard on every hand. One could hardly go to church,
to say nothing of going to a public meeting, without hearing
echoes of it. In general it was maintained that slavery had
made for the civilization of the world in that it had mitigated
the evils of war, had made labor profitable, had changed the
nature of savages, and elevated woman. The slave-trade was
of course horrible and unjust, but the great advantages of
the system more than outweighed a few attendant evils. Emancipation and deportation were alike impossible. Even if practicable, they would not be expedient measures, for they meant
the loss to Virginia of one-third of her property. As for
morality, it was not to be expected that the Negro should have
the sensibilities of the white man. Moreover the system had
the advantage of cultivating a republican spirit among the
white people. In short, said Dew, the slaves, in both the economic and the moral point of view, were "entirely unfit for a
state of freedom among the whites." Holland, already cited, in
1822 maintained five points, as follows: 1. That the United
States are one for national purposes, but separate for their
internal regulation and government; 2. That the people of
the North and East "always exhibited an unfriendly feeling
on subjects affecting the interests of the South and West";
3. That the institution of slavery was not an institution of the
South's voluntary choosing; 4. That the Southern sections
of the Union, both before and after the Declaration of Independence, "had uniformly exhibited a disposition to restrict
the extension of the evil—and had always manifested as cor-
dial a disposition to ameliorate it as those of the North and
East"; and 5. That the actual state and condition of the slave
population "reflected no disgrace whatever on the character

* *The Pro-Slavery Argument* (as maintained by the most distinguished writers of the Southern states). Charleston, 1852.

of the country—as the slaves were infinitely better provided for than the laboring poor of other countries of the world, and were generally happier than millions of white people in the world." Such arguments the clergy supported and endeavored to reconcile with Christian precept. Rev. Dr. Richard Furman, president of the Baptist Convention of South Carolina,* after much inquiry and reasoning, arrived at the conclusion that "the holding of slaves is justifiable by the doctrine and example contained in Holy Writ; and is, therefore, consistent with Christian uprightness both in sentiment and conduct." Said he further: "The Christian golden rule, of doing to others as we would they should do to us, has been urged as an unanswerable argument against holding slaves. But surely this rule is never to be urged against that order of things which the Divine government has established; nor do our desires become a standard to us, under this rule, unless they have a due regard to justice, propriety, and the general good. . . . A father may very naturally desire that his son should be obedient to his orders: Is he therefore to obey the orders of his son? A man might be pleased to be exonerated from his debts by the generosity of his creditors; or that his rich neighbor should equally divide his property with him; and in certain circumstances might desire these to be done: Would the mere existence of this desire oblige him to exonerate his debtors, and to make such division of his property?" Calhoun in 1837 formally accepted slavery, saying that the South should no longer apologize for it; and the whole argument from the standpoint of expediency received eloquent expression in the Senate of the United States from no less a man than Henry Clay, who more and more appears in the perspective as a pro-Southern advocate. Said he: "I am no friend of slavery. But I prefer the liberty of my own country to that of any other people; and the liberty of my own race to that of any other race. The liberty of the descendants of Africa in the United States is incompatible with the safety

---

* "Rev. Dr. Richard Furman's Exposition of the Views of the Baptists relative to the Coloured Population in the United States, in a Communication to the Governor of South Carolina." Second edition, Charleston, 1833 (letter bears original date, December 24, 1822).

and liberty of the European descendants. Their slavery forms an exception—an exception resulting from a stern and inexorable necessity—to the general liberty in the United States." * After the lapse of years the pro-slavery argument is pitiful in its numerous fallacies. It was in line with much of the discussion of the day that questioned whether the Negro was actually a human being, and but serves to show to what extremes economic interest will sometimes drive men otherwise of high intelligence and honor.

* Address "On Abolition," February 7, 1839.

CHAPTER VII

We have already seen that on several occasions in colonial times the Negroes in bondage made a bid for freedom, many men risking their all and losing their lives in consequence. In general these early attempts failed completely to realize their aim, organization being feeble and the leadership untrained and exerting only an emotional hold over adherents. In Charleston, S. C., in 1822, however, there was planned an insurrection about whose scope there could be no question. The leader, Denmark Vesey, is interesting as an intellectual insurrectionist just as the more famous Nat Turner is typical of the more fervent sort. It is the purpose of the present chapter to study the attempts for freedom made by these two men, and also those of two daring groups of captives who revolted at sea.

1. *Denmark Vesey's Insurrection*

Denmark Vesey is first seen as one of the three hundred and ninety slaves on the ship of Captain Vesey, who commanded a vessel trading between St. Thomas and Cape François (Santo Domingo), and who was engaged in supplying the French of the latter place with slaves. At the time, the boy was fourteen years old, and of unusual personal beauty, alertness, and magnetism. He was shown considerable favoritism, and was called Télémaque (afterwards corrupted to *Telmak,* and then to *Denmark*). On his arrival at Cape François, Denmark was sold with others of the slaves to a planter who owned a considerable estate. On his next trip, however, Captain Vesey learned that the boy was to be returned to him as unsound and subject to epileptic fits. The

laws of the place permitted the return of a slave in such a
case, and while it has been thought that Denmark's fits may
have been feigned in order that he might have some change
of estate, there was quite enough proof in the matter to impress the king's physician. Captain Vesey never had reason
to regret having to take the boy back. They made several
voyages together, and Denmark served until 1800 as his faithful personal attendant. In this year the young man, now
thirty-three years of age and living in Charleston, won $1,500
in an East Bay Street lottery, $600 of which he devoted imme-
diately to the purchase of his freedom. The sum was much
less than he was really worth, but Captain Vesey liked him
and had no reason to drive a hard bargain with him.

In the early years of his full manhood accordingly Denmark Vesey found himself a free man in his own right and
possessed of the means for a little real start in life. He improved his time and proceeded to win greater standing and
recognition by regular and industrious work at his trade, that
of a carpenter. Over the slaves he came to have unbounded
influence. Among them, in accordance with the standards
of the day, he had several wives and children (none of whom
could he call his own), and he understood perfectly the fervor
and faith and superstition of the Negroes with whom he had
to deal. To his remarkable personal magnetism moreover he
added just the strong passion and the domineering temper that
were needed to make his conquest complete.

Thus for twenty years he worked on. He already knew
French as well as English, but he now studied and reflected
upon as wide a range of subjects as possible. It was not expected at the time that there would be religious classes or congregations of Negroes apart from the white people; but the law
was not strictly observed, and for a number of years a Negro
congregation had a church in Hampstead in the suburbs
of Charleston. At the meetings here and elsewhere Vesey
found his opportunity, and he drew interesting parallels between the experiences of the Jews and the Negroes. He would
rebuke a companion on the street for bowing to a white
person; and if such a man replied, "We are slaves," he would
say, "You deserve to be." If the man then asked what he

could do to better his condition, he would say, "Go and buy a spelling-book and read the fable of Hercules and the wagoner." * At the same time if he happened to engage in conversation with white people in the presence of Negroes, he would often take occasion to introduce some striking remark on slavery. He regularly held up to emulation the work of the Negroes of Santo Domingo; and either he or one of his chief lieutenants clandestinely sent a letter to the President of Santo Domingo to ask if the people there would help the Negroes of Charleston if the latter made an effort to free themselves.† About 1820 moreover, when he heard of the African Colonization scheme and the opportunity came to him to go, he put this by, waiting for something better. This was the period of the Missouri Compromise. Reports of the agitation and of the debates in Congress were eagerly scanned by those Negroes in Charleston who could read; rumor exaggerated them; and some of the more credulous of the slaves came to believe that the efforts of Northern friends had actually emancipated them and that they were being illegally held in bondage. Nor was the situation improved when the city marshal, John J. Lafar, on January 15, 1821, reminded those ministers or other persons who kept night and Sunday schools for Negroes that the law forbade the education of such persons and would have to be enforced. Meanwhile Vesey was very patient. After a few months, however, he ceased to work at his trade in order that all the more he might devote himself to the mission of his life. This was, as he conceived it, an insurrection that would do nothing less than totally annihilate the white population of Charleston.

In the prosecution of such a plan the greatest secrecy and faithfulness were of course necessary, and Vesey waited until about Christmas, 1821, to begin active recruiting. He first sounded Ned and Rolla Bennett, slaves of Governor Thomas Bennett, and then Peter Poyas and Jack Purcell. After Christmas he spoke to Gullah Jack and Monday Gell; and Lot Forrester and Frank Ferguson became his chief agents for

* Official Report, 19.
† Official Report, 96-97, and Higginson, 232-3.

the plantations outside of Charleston.* In the whole matter
of the choice of his chief assistants he showed remarkable
judgment of character. His penetration was almost uncanny.
"Rolla was plausible, and possessed uncommon self-posses-
sion; bold and ardent, he was not to be deterred from his purpose by danger. Ned's appearance indicated that he was a
man of firm nerves and desperate courage. Peter was in-
trepid and resolute, true to his engagements, and cautious in
observing secrecy when it was necessary; he was not to be
daunted or impeded by difficulties, and though confident of
success, was careful in providing against any obstacles or
casualties which might arise, and intent upon discovering
every means which might be in their power if thought of beforehand. Gullah Jack was regarded as a sorcerer, and as such
feared by the natives of Africa, who believe in witchcraft.
He was not only considered invulnerable, but that he could
make others so by his charms; and that he could and certainly would provide all his followers with arms. . . . His
influence amongst the Africans was inconceivable. Monday
was firm, resolute, discreet, and intelligent." † He was also
daring and active, a harness-maker in the prime of life, and
he could read and write with facility; but he was also the only
man of prominence in the conspiracy whose courage failed
him in court and who turned traitor. To these names must
be added that of Batteau Bennett, who was only eighteen
years old and who brought to the plan all the ardor and devotion of youth. In general Vesey sought to bring into the
plan those Negroes, such as stevedores and mechanics, who
worked away from home and who had some free time. He
would not use men who were known to become intoxicated,
and one talkative man named George he excluded from his
meetings. Nor did he use women, not because he did not
trust them, but because in case of mishap he wanted the

* Official Report, 20. Note that Higginson, who was so untiring in
his research, strangely confuses Jack Purcell and Gullah Jack (p. 230).
The men were quite distinct, as appears throughout the report and from
the list of those executed. The name of Gullah Jack's owner was
Pritchard.
† Official Report, 24. Note that this remarkable characterization was
given by the judges, Kennedy and Parker, who afterwards condemned
the men to death.

children to be properly cared for. "Take care," said Peter Poyas, in speaking about the plan to one of the recruits, "and don't mention it to those waiting men who receive presents of old coats, etc., from their masters, or they'll betray us; I will speak to them."

With his lieutenants Vesey finally brought into the plan the Negroes for seventy or eighty miles around Charleston. The second Monday in July, 1822, or Sunday, July 14, was the time originally set for the attack. July was chosen because in midsummer many of the white people were away at different resorts; and Sunday received favorable consideration because on that day the slaves from the outlying plantations were frequently permitted to come to the city. Lists of the recruits were kept. Peter Poyas is said to have gathered as many as six hundred names, chiefly from that part of Charleston known as South Bay in which he lived; and it is a mark of his care and discretion that of all of those afterwards arrested and tried, not one belonged to his company. Monday Gell, who joined late and was very prudent, had forty-two names. All such lists, however, were in course of time destroyed. "During the period that these enlistments were carrying on, Vesey held frequent meetings of the conspirators at his house; and as arms were necessary to their success, each night a hat was handed round, and collections made, for the purpose of purchasing them, and also to defray other necessary expenses. A Negro who was a blacksmith and had been accustomed to make edged tools, was employed to make pike-heads and bayonets with sockets, to be fixed at the ends of long poles and used as pikes. Of these pike-heads and bayonets, one hundred were said to have been made at an early day, and by the 16th June as many as two or three hundred, and between three and four hundred daggers." * A bundle containing some of the poles, neatly trimmed and smoothed off, and nine or ten feet long, was afterwards found concealed on a farm on Charleston Neck, where several of the meetings were held, having been carried there to have the pike-heads and bayonets fixed in place.

* Official Report, 31-32.

Governor Bennett stated that the number of poles thus found was thirteen, but so wary were the Negroes that he and other prominent men underestimated the means of attack. It was thought that the Negroes in Charleston might use their masters' arms, while those from the country were to bring hoes, hatchets, and axes. For their main supply of arms, however, Vesey and Peter Poyas depended upon the magazines and storehouses in the city. They planned to seize the Arsenal in Meeting Street opposite St. Michael's Church; it was the key to the city, held the arms of the state, and had for some time been neglected. Poyas at a given signal at midnight was to move upon this point, killing the sentinel. Two large gun and powder stores were by arrangement to be at the disposal of the insurrectionists; and other leaders, coming from six different directions, were to seize strategic points and thus aid the central work of Poyas. Meanwhile a body of horse was to keep the streets clear. "Eat only dry food," said Gullah Jack as the day approached, "parched corn and ground nuts, and when you join us as we pass put this crab claw in your mouth and you can't be wounded."

On May 25* a slave of Colonel Prioleau, while on an errand at the wharf, was accosted by another slave, William Paul, who remarked: "I have often seen a flag with the number 76, but never one with the number 96 upon it before." As this man showed no knowledge of what was going on, Paul spoke to him further and quite frankly about the plot. The slave afterwards spoke to a free man about what he had heard; this man advised him to tell his master about it; and so he did on Prioleau's return on May 30. Prioleau immediately informed the Intendant, or Mayor, and by five o'clock in the afternoon both the slave and Paul were being examined. Paul was placed in confinement, but not before his testimony had implicated Peter Poyas and Mingo Harth, a man who had been appointed to lead one of the companies of horse. Harth and Poyas were cool and collected, however, they ridiculed the whole idea, and the wardens, completely deceived, discharged them. In general at this time the authorities were

* Higginson, 215.

careful and endeavored not to act hastily. About June 8, however, Paul, greatly excited and fearing execution, confessed that the plan was very extensive and said that it was led by an individual who bore a charmed life. Ned Bennett, hearing that his name had been mentioned, voluntarily went before the Intendant and asked to be examined, thus again completely baffling the officials. All the while, in the face of the greatest danger, Vesey continued to hold his meetings. By Friday, June 14, however, another informant had spoken to his master, and all too fully were Peter Poyas's fears about "waiting-men" justified. This man said that the original plan had been changed, for the night of Sunday, June 16, was now the time set for the insurrection, and otherwise he was able to give all essential information.* On Saturday night, June 15, Jesse Blackwood, an aid sent into the country to prepare the slaves to enter the following day, while he penetrated two lines of guards, was at the third line halted and sent back into the city. Vesey now realized in a moment that all his plans were disclosed, and immediately he destroyed any papers that might prove to be incriminating. "On Sunday, June 16, at ten o'clock at night, Captain Cattle's Corps of Hussars, Captain Miller's Light Infantry, Captain Martindale's Neck Rangers, the Charleston Riflemen and the City Guard were ordered to rendezvous for guard, the whole organized as a detachment under command of Colonel R. Y. Hayne." † It was his work on this occasion that gave Hayne that appeal to the public which was later to help him to pass on to the governorship and then to the United States Senate. On the fateful night twenty or thirty men from the outlying districts who had not been able to get word of the progress of events, came to the city in a small boat, but Vesey sent word to them to go back as quickly as possible.

---

* For reasons of policy the names of these informers were withheld from publication, but they were well known, of course, to the Negroes of Charleston. The published documents said of the chief informer, "It would be a libel on the liberality and gratitude of this community to suppose that this man can be overlooked among those who are to be rewarded for their fidelity and principle." The author has been informed that his reward for betraying his people was to be officially and legally declared "a white man."

† Jervey: *Robert Y. Hayne and His Times,* 131-2.

Two courts were formed for the trial of the conspirators. The first, after a long session of five weeks, was dissolved July 20; a second was convened, but after three days closed its investigation and adjourned August 8.*   All the while the public mind was greatly excited.   The first court, which speedily condemned thirty-four men to death, was severely criticized.   The New York *Daily Advertiser* termed the execution "a bloody sacrifice"; but Charleston replied with the reminder of the Negroes who had been burned in New York in 1741.†   Some of the Negroes blamed the leaders for the trouble into which they had been brought, but Vesey himself made no confession.   He was by no means alone.   "Do not open your lips," said Poyas; "die silent as you shall see me do."   Something of the solicitude of owners for their slaves may be seen from the request of Governor Bennett himself in behalf of Batteau Bennett.   He asked for a special review of the case of this young man, who was among those condemned to death, "with a view to the mitigation of his punishment."   The court did review the case, but it did not change its sentence.   Throughout the proceedings the white people of Charleston were impressed by the character of those who had taken part in the insurrection; "many of them possessed the highest confidence of their owners, and not one was of bad character." ‡

As a result of this effort for freedom one hundred and thirty-one Negroes were arrested; thirty-five were executed and forty-three banished.§   Of those executed, Denmark Vesey, Peter Poyas, Ned Bennett, Rolla Bennett, Batteau Bennett, and Jesse Blackwood were hanged July 2; Gullah Jack and one more on July 12; twenty-two were hanged on a huge gallows Friday, July 26; four more were hanged July 30, and one on August 9.   Of those banished, twelve had been sentenced for execution, but were afterwards given banishment instead; twenty-one were to be transported by their masters beyond the limits of the United States; one, a

* Bennett letter.
† See *City Gazette*, August 14, 1822, cited by Jervey.
‡ Official Report, 44.
§ The figure is sometimes given as 37, but the lists total 43.

free man, required to leave the state, satisfied the court by offering to leave the United States, while nine others who were not definitely sentenced were strongly recommended to their owners for banishment. The others of the one hundred and thirty-one were acquitted. The authorities at length felt that they had executed enough to teach the Negroes a lesson, and the hanging ceased; but within the next year or two Governor Bennett and others gave to the world most gloomy reflections upon the whole proceeding and upon the grave problem at their door. Thus closed the insurrection that for the ambitiousness of its plan, the care with which it was matured, and the faithfulness of the leaders to one another, was never equalled by a similar attempt for freedom in the United States.

2. *Nat Turner's Insurrection*

About noon on Sunday, August 21, 1831, on the plantation of Joseph Travis at Cross Keys, in Southampton County, in Southeastern Virginia, were gathered four Negroes, Henry Porter, Hark Travis, Nelson Williams, and Sam Francis, evidently preparing for a barbecue. They were soon joined by a gigantic and athletic Negro named Will Francis, and by another named Jack Reese. Two hours later came a short, strong-looking man who had a face of great resolution and at whom one would not have needed to glance a second time to know that he was to be the master-spirit of the company. Seeing Will and his companion he raised a question as to their being present, to which Will replied that life was worth no more to him than the others and that liberty was as dear to him. This answer satisfied the latest comer, and Nat Turner now went into conference with his most trusted friends. One can only imagine the purpose, the eagerness, and the firmness on those dark faces throughout that long summer afternoon and evening. When at last in the night the low whispering ceased, the doom of nearly three-score white persons—and it might be added, of twice as many Negroes—was sealed.

Cross Keys was seventy miles from Norfolk, just about as far from Richmond, twenty-five miles from the Dismal

Swamp, fifteen miles from Murfreesboro in North Carolina, and also fifteen miles from Jerusalem, the county seat of Southampton County. The community was settled primarily by white people of modest means. Joseph Travis, the owner of Nat Turner, had recently married the widow of one Putnam Moore.

Nat Turner, who originally belonged to one Benjamin Turner, was born October 2, 1800. He was mentally precocious and had marks on his head and breast which were interpreted by the Negroes who knew him as marking him for some high calling. In his mature years he also had on his right arm a knot which was the result of a blow which he had received. He experimented in paper, gunpowder, and pottery, and it is recorded of him that he was never known to swear an oath, to drink a drop of spirits, or to commit a theft. Instead he cultivated fasting and prayer and the reading of the Bible.

More and more Nat gave himself up to a life of the spirit and to communion with the voices that he said he heard. He once ran away for a month, but felt commanded by the spirit to return. About 1825 a consciousness of his great mission came to him, and daily he labored to make himself more worthy. As he worked in the field he saw drops of blood on the corn, and he also saw white spirits and black spirits contending in the skies. While he thus so largely lived in a religious or mystical world and was immersed, he was not a professional Baptist preacher. On May 12, 1828, he was left no longer in doubt. A great voice said unto him that the Serpent was loosed, that Christ had laid down the yoke, that he, Nat, was to take it up again, and that the time was fast approaching when the first should be last and the last should be first. An eclipse of the sun in February, 1831, was interpreted as the sign for him to go forward. Yet he waited a little longer, until he had made sure of his most important associates. It is worthy of note that when he began his work, while he wanted the killing to be as effective and widespread as possible, he commanded that no outrage be committed, and he was obeyed.

When on the Sunday in August Nat and his companions finished their conference, they went to find Austin, a brother-spirit; and then all went to the cider-press and drank except Nat. It was understood that he as the leader was to spill the first blood, and that he was to begin with his own master, Joseph Travis. Going to the house, Hark placed a ladder against the chimney. On this Nat ascended; then he went downstairs, unbarred the doors, and removed the guns from their places. He and Will together entered Travis's chamber, and the first blow was given to the master of the house. The hatchet glanced off and Travis called to his wife; but this was with his last breath, for Will at once despatched him with his ax. The wife and the three children of the house were also killed immediately. Then followed a drill of the company, after which all went to the home of Salathiel Francis six hundred yards away. Sam and Will knocked, and Francis asked who was there. Sam replied that he had a letter for him. The man came to the door, where he was seized and killed by repeated blows over the head. He was the only white person in the house. In silence all passed on to the home of Mrs. Reese, who was killed while asleep in bed. Her son awoke, but was also immediately killed. A mile away the insurrectionists came to the home of Mrs. Turner, which they reached about sunrise on Monday morning. Henry, Austin, and Sam went to the still, where they found and killed the overseer, Peebles, Austin shooting him. Then all went to the house. The family saw them coming and shut the door—to no avail, however, as Will with one stroke of his ax opened it and entered to find Mrs. Turner and Mrs. Newsome in the middle of the room almost frightened to death. Will killed Mrs. Turner with one blow of his ax, and after Nat had struck Mrs. Newsome over the head with his sword, Will turned and killed her also. By this time the company amounted to fifteen. Nine went mounted to the home of Mrs. Whitehead and six others went along a byway to the home of Henry Bryant. As they neared the first house Richard Whitehead, the son of the family, was standing in the cotton-patch near the fence. Will killed him with his ax immediately. In the house he killed Mrs. Whitehead, almost severing her head from her body with one blow. Margaret, a daughter, tried to conceal herself and ran, but was killed by Turner with a fence-rail. The men in this first company were now joined by those in the second, the six who had gone to the Bryant home, who informed them that they had done the work assigned, which was to kill Henry Bryant himself, his wife and child, and his wife's mother. By this time the killing had become fast and furious. The company divided again; some would go ahead, and Nat would come up to find work already accomplished. Generally fifteen or twenty of the best mounted were put in front to strike terror and prevent escape, and Nat himself frequently did not get to the houses where killing was done. More and more the Negroes, now about forty in number, were getting drunken and noisy. The alarm was given, and by nine or ten o'clock on Monday morning one Captain Harris and his family had escaped. Prominent among the events of the morning, however, was the killing at the home of Mrs. Waller of ten children who were gathering for school.*

As the men neared the home of James Parker, it was suggested that they call there; but Turner objected, as this man

---

* In "Horrid Massacre," or, to use the more formal title, "Authentic and Impartial Narrative of the Tragical Scene which was Witnessed in Southampton County (Virginia) on Monday the 22d of August Last," the list below of the victims of Nat Turner's insurrection is given. It must be said about this work, however, that it is not altogether impeccable; it seems to have been prepared very hastily after the event, its spelling of names is often arbitrary, and instead of the fifty-five victims noted it appears that at least fifty-seven white persons were killed:

Joseph Travis, wife and three children.	5
Mrs. Elizabeth Turner, Hartwell Peebles, and Sarah Newsum	3
Mrs. Piety Reese and son, William.	2
Trajan Doyal	1
Henry Briant, wife and child, and wife's mother.	4
Mrs. Catherine Whitehead, her son Richard, four daughters and a grandchild.	7
Salathael Francis	1
Nathaniel Francis's overseer and two children.	3
John T. Barrow and George Vaughan.	2
Mrs. Levi Waller and ten children.	11
Mr. William Williams, wife and two boys.	4
Mrs. Caswell Worrell and child.	2
Mrs. Rebacca Vaughan, Ann Eliza Vaughan, and son Arthur	3
Mrs. Jacob Williams and three children and Edwin Drewry	5
	55

had already gone to Jerusalem and he himself wished to reach the county seat as soon as possible. However, he and some of the men remained at the gate while others went to the house half a mile away. This exploit proved to be the turning-point of the events of the day. Uneasy at the delay of those who went to the house, Turner went thither also. On his return he was met by a company of white men who had fired on those Negroes left at the gate and dispersed them. On discovering these men, Turner ordered his own men to halt and form, as now they were beginning to be alarmed. The white men, eighteen in number, approached and fired, but were forced to retreat. Reënforcements for them from Jerusalem were already at hand, however, and now the great pursuit of the Negro insurrectionists began.

Hark's horse was shot under him and five or six of the men were wounded. Turner's force was largely dispersed, but on Monday night he stopped at the home of Major Ridley, and his company again increased to forty. He tried to sleep a little, but a sentinel gave the alarm; all were soon up and the number was again reduced to twenty. Final resistance was offered at the home of Dr. Blunt, but here still more of the men were put to flight and were never again seen by Turner.

A little later, however, the leader found two of his men named Jacob and Nat. These he sent with word to Henry, Hark, Nelson, and Sam to meet him at the place where on Sunday they had taken dinner together. With what thoughts Nat Turner returned alone to this place on Tuesday evening can only be imagined. Throughout the night he remained, but no one joined him and he presumed that his followers had all either been taken or had deserted him. Nor did any one come on Wednesday, or on Thursday. On Thursday night, having supplied himself with provisions from the Travis home, he scratched a hole under a pile of fence-rails, and here he remained for six weeks, leaving only at night to get water. All the while of course he had no means of learning of the fate of his companions or of anything else. Meanwhile not only the vicinity but the whole South was being wrought up to an hysterical state of mind. A reward of $500 for the capture of the man was offered by the Governor, and other rewards were also offered. On September 30 a false account of his capture appeared in the newspapers; on October 7 another; on October 8 still another. By this time Turner had begun to move about a little at night, not speaking to any human being and returning always to his hole before daybreak. Early on October 15 a dog smelt his provisions and led thither two Negroes. Nat appealed to these men for protection, but they at once began to run and excitedly spread the news. Turner fled in another direction and for ten days more hid among the wheat-stacks on the Francis plantation. All the while not less than five hundred men were on the watch for him, and they found the stick that he had notched from day to day. Once he thought of surrendering, and walked within two miles of Jerusalem. Three times he tried to get away, and failed. On October 25 he was discovered by Francis, who discharged at him a load of buckshot, twelve of which passed through his hat, and he was at large for five days more. On October 30 Benjamin Phipps, a member of the patrol, passing a clearing in the woods noticed a motion among the boughs. He paused, and gradually he saw Nat's head emerging from a hole beneath. The fugitive now gave up as he knew that the woods were full of men. He was taken to the nearest house, and the crowd was so great and the excitement so intense that it was with difficulty that he was taken to Jerusalem. For more than two months, from August 25 to October 30, he had eluded his pursuers, remaining all the while in the vicinity of his insurrection.

While Nat Turner was in prison, Thomas C. Gray, his counsel, received from him what are known as his "Confessions." This pamphlet is now almost inaccessible,* but it was in great demand at the time it was printed and it is now the chief source for information about the progress of the insurrection. Turner was tried November 5 and sentenced to be hanged six days later. Asked in court by Gray if he still believed in the providential nature of his mission, he asked, "Was not Christ crucified?" Of his execution itself we read: "Nat Turner was executed according to sentence, on Friday, the 11th of Novem-

---

* The only copy that the author has seen is that in the library of Harvard University.

ber, 1831, at Jerusalem, between the hours of 10 A. M. and 2 P. M. He exhibited the utmost composure throughout the whole ceremony; and, although assured that he might, if he thought proper, address the immense crowd assembled on the occasion, declined availing himself of the privilege; and, being asked if he had any further confessions to make, replied that he had nothing more than he had communicated; and told the sheriff in a firm voice that he was ready. Not a limb or muscle was observed to move. His body, after death, was given over to the surgeons for dissection."

Of fifty-three Negroes arraigned in connection with the insurrection "seventeen were executed and twelve transported. The rest were discharged, except . . . four free Negroes sent on to the Superior Court. Three of the four were executed." * Such figures as these, however, give no conception of the number of those who lost their lives in connection with the insurrection. In general, if slaves were convicted by legal process and executed or transported, or if they escaped before trial, they were paid for by the commonwealth; if killed, they were not paid for, and a man like Phipps might naturally desire to protect his prisoner in order to get his reward. In spite of this, the Negroes were slaughtered without trial and sometimes under circumstances of the greatest barbarity. One man proudly boasted that he had killed between ten and fifteen. A party went from Richmond with the intention of killing every Negro in Southampton County. Approaching the cabin of a free Negro they asked, "Is this Southampton County?" "Yes, sir," came the reply, "you have just crossed the line by yonder tree." They shot him dead and rode on. In general the period was one of terror, with voluntary patrols, frequently drunk, going in all directions. These men tortured, burned, or maimed the Negroes practically at will. Said one old woman † of them: "The patrols were low drunken whites, and in Nat's time, if they heard any of the colored folks prayin' or singin' a hymn, they would fall upon 'em and abuse 'em, and sometimes kill 'em. . . . The brightest and best was

* Drewry, 101.
† Charity Bowery, who gave testimony to L. M. Child, quoted by Higginson.

killed in Nat's time. The whites always suspect such ones. They killed a great many at a place called Duplon. They killed Antonio, a slave of Mr. J. Stanley, whom they shot; then they pointed their guns at him and told him to confess about the insurrection. He told 'em he didn't know anything about any insurrection. They shot several balls through him, quartered him, and put his head on a pole at the fork of the road leading to the court. . . . It was there but a short time. He had no trial. They never do. In Nat's time, the patrols would tie up the free colored people, flog 'em, and try to make 'em lie against one another, and often killed them before anybody could interfere. Mr. James Cole, High Sheriff, said if any of the patrols came on his plantation, he would lose his life in defense of his people. One day he heard a patroller boasting how many Negroes he had killed. Mr. Cole said, 'If you don't pack up, as quick as God Almighty will let you, and get out of this town, and never be seen in it again, I'll put you where dogs won't bark at you.' He went off, and wasn't seen in them parts again."

The immediate panic created by the Nat Turner insurrection in Virginia and the other states of the South it would be impossible to exaggerate. When the news of what was happening at Cross Keys spread, two companies, on horse and foot, came from Murfreesboro as quickly as possible. On the Wednesday after the memorable Sunday night there came from Fortress Monroe three companies and a piece of artillery. These commands were reënforced from various sources until not less than eight hundred men were in arms. Many of the Negroes fled to the Dismal Swamp, and the wildest rumors were afloat. One was that Wilmington had been burned, and in Raleigh and Fayetteville the wildest excitement prevailed. In the latter place scores of white women and children fled to the swamps, coming out two days afterwards muddy, chilled, and half-starved. Slaves were imprisoned wholesale. In Wilmington four men were shot without trial and their heads placed on poles at the four corners of the town. In Macon, Ga., a report was circulated that an armed band of Negroes was only five miles away, and within an hour the women and children were assembled in the largest building in the town, with a military force in front for protection.

The effects on legislation were immediate. Throughout the South the slave codes became more harsh; and while it was clear that the uprising had been one of slaves rather than of free Negroes, as usual special disabilities fell upon the free people of color. Delaware, that only recently had limited the franchise to white men, now forbade the use of firearms by free Negroes and would not suffer any more to come within the state. Tennessee also forbade such immigration, while Maryland passed a law to the effect that all free Negroes must leave the state and be colonized in Africa—a monstrous piece of legislation that it was impossible to put into effect and that showed once for all the futility of attempts at forcible emigration as a solution of the problem. In general, however, the insurrection assisted the colonization scheme and also made more certain the carrying out of the policy of the Jackson administration to remove the Indians of the South to the West. It also focussed the attention of the nation upon the status of the Negro, crystallized opinion in the North, and thus helped with the formation of anti-slavery organizations. By it for the time being the Negro lost; in the long run he gained.

3. The "Amistad" and "Creole" Cases

On June 28, 1839, a schooner, the Amistad, sailed from Havana bound for Guanaja in the vicinity of Puerto Principe. She was under the command of her owner, Don Ramon Ferrer, was laden with merchandise, and had on board fifty-three Negroes, forty-nine of whom supposedly belonged to a Spaniard, Don Jose Ruiz, the other four belonging to Don Pedro Montes. During the night of June 30 the slaves, under the lead of one of their number named Cinque, rose upon the crew, killed the captain, a slave of his, and two sailors, and while they permitted most of the crew to escape, they took into close custody the two owners, Ruiz and Montes. Montes, who had some knowledge of nautical affairs, was ordered to steer the vessel back to Africa. So he did by day, when the

Negroes would watch him, but at night he tried to make his way to some land nearer at hand. Other vessels passed from time to time, and from these the Negroes bought provisions, but Montes and Ruiz were so closely watched that they could not make known their plight. At length, on August 26, the schooner reached Long Island Sound, where it was detained by the American brig-of-war *Washington,* in command of Captain Gedney, who secured the Negroes and took them to New London, Conn. It took a year and a half to dispose of the issue thus raised. The case attracted the greatest amount of attention, led to international complications, and was not really disposed of until a former President had exhaustively argued the case for the Negroes before the Supreme Court of the United States.

In a letter of September 6, 1839, to John Forsyth, the American Secretary of State, Calderon, the Spanish minister, formally made four demands: 1. That the *Amistad* be immediately delivered up to her owner, together with every article on board at the time of her capture; 2. That it be declared that no tribunal in the United States had the right to institute proceedings against, or to impose penalties upon, the subjects of Spain, for crimes committed on board a Spanish vessel, and in the waters of Spanish territory; 3. That the Negroes be conveyed to Havana or otherwise placed at the disposal of the representatives of Spain; and 4. That if, in consequence of the intervention of the authorities in Connecticut, there should be any delay in the desired delivery of the vessel and the slaves, the owners both of the latter and of the former be indemnified for the injury that might accrue to them. In support of his demands Calderon invoked "the law of nations, the stipulations of existing treaties, and those good feelings so necessary in the maintenance of the friendly relations that subsist between the two countries, and are so interesting to both." Forsyth asked for any papers bearing on the question, and Calderon replied that he had none except "the declaration on oath of Montes and Ruiz."

Meanwhile the abolitionists were insisting that protection had *not* been afforded the African strangers cast on American soil and that in no case did the executive arm of the

Government have any authority to interfere with the regular administration of justice. "These Africans," it was said, "are detained in jail, under process of the United States courts, in a free state, after it has been decided by the District Judge, on sufficient proof, that they are recently from Africa, were never the lawful slaves of Ruiz and Montes," and "when it is clear as noonday that there is no law or treaty stipulation that requires the further detention of these Africans or their delivery to Spain or its subjects."

Writing on October 24 to the Spanish representative with reference to the arrest of Ruiz and Montes, Forsyth informed him that the two Spanish subjects had been arrested on process issuing from the superior court of the city of New York upon affidavits of certain men, natives of Africa, "for the purpose of securing their appearance before the proper tribunal, to answer for wrongs alleged to have been inflicted by them upon the persons of said Africans," that, consequently, the occurrence constituted simply a "case of resort by individuals against others to the judicial courts of the country, which are equally open to all without distinction," and that the agency of the Government to obtain the release of Messrs. Ruiz and Montes could not be afforded in the manner requested. Further pressure was brought to bear by the Spanish representative, however, and there was cited the case of Abraham Wendell, captain of the brig *Franklin,* who was prosecuted at first by Spanish officials for maltreatment of his mate, but with reference to whom documents were afterwards sent from Havana to America. Much more correspondence followed, and Felix Grundy, of Tennessee, Attorney General of the United States, at length muddled everything by the following opinion: "These Negroes deny that they are slaves; if they should be delivered to the claimants, no opportunity may be afforded for the assertion of their right to freedom. For these reasons, it seems to me that a delivery to the Spanish minister is the only safe course for this Government to pursue." The fallacy of all this was shown in a letter dated November 18, 1839, from B. F. Butler, United States District Attorney in New York, to Aaron Vail, acting Secretary of State. Said Butler: "It does not appear to me that any question has yet arisen under the treaty with Spain; because, although it is an admitted principle, that neither the courts of this state, nor those of the United States, can take jurisdiction of criminal offenses committed by foreigners within the territory of a foreign state, yet it is equally settled in this country, that our courts will take cognizance of *civil* actions between foreigners transiently within our jurisdiction, founded upon contracts or other transactions made or had in a foreign state." Southern influence was strong, however, and a few weeks afterwards an order was given from the Department of State to have a vessel anchor off New Haven, Conn., January 10, 1840, to receive the Negroes from the United States marshal and take them to Cuba; and on January 7 the President, Van Buren, issued the necessary warrant.

The rights of humanity, however, were not to be handled in this summary fashion. The executive order was stayed, and the case went further on its progress to the highest tribunal in the land. Meanwhile the anti-slavery people were teaching the Africans the rudiments of English in order that they might be better able to tell their own story. From the first a committee had been appointed to look out for their interests and while they were awaiting the final decision in their case they cultivated a garden of fifteen acres.

The appearance of John Quincy Adams in behalf of these Negroes before the Supreme Court of the United States February 24 and March 1, 1841, is in every way one of the most beautiful acts in American history. In the fullness of years, with his own administration as President twelve years behind him, the "Old Man Eloquent" came once more to the tribunal that he knew so well to make a last plea for the needy and oppressed. To the task he brought all his talents—his profound knowledge of law, his unrivaled experience, and his impressive personality; and his argument covers 135 octavo pages. He gave an extended analysis of the demand of the Spanish minister, who asked the President to do what he simply had no constitutional right to do. "The President," said Adams, "has no power to arrest either citizens or foreigners. But even that power is almost insignificant compared with that of sending men beyond seas to deliver them up to a foreign government." The Secretary of State had "degraded the country, in the face of the whole civilized world, not only by allowing these demands to remain unanswered, but by proceeding, throughout the whole transaction, as if the Executive were earnestly desirous to comply with every one of the demands." The Spanish minister had naturally insisted in his demands because he had not been properly met at first. The slave-trade was illegal by international agreement, and the only thing to do under the circumstances was to release the Negroes. Adams closed his plea with a magnificent review of his career and of the labors of the distinguished jurists he had known in the court for nearly forty years, and be it recorded wherever the name of Justice is spoken, he won his case.

Lewis Tappan now accompanied the Africans on a tour through the states to raise money for their passage home. The first meeting was in Boston. Several members of the company interested the audience by their readings from the New Testament or by their descriptions of their own country and of the horrors of the voyage. Cinque gave the impression of great dignity and of extraordinary ability; and Kali, a boy only eleven years of age, also attracted unusual attention. Near the close of 1841, accompanied by five missionaries and teachers, the Africans set sail from New York, to make their way first to Sierra Leone and then to their own homes as well as they could.

While this whole incident of the *Amistad* was still engaging the interest of the public, there occurred another that also occasioned international friction and even more prolonged debate between the slavery and anti-slavery forces. On October 25, 1841, the brig *Creole,* Captain Ensor, of Richmond, Va., sailed from Richmond and on October 27 from Hampton Roads, with a cargo of tobacco and one hundred and thirty slaves bound for New Orleans. On the vessel also, aside from the crew, were the captain's wife and child, and three or four passengers, who were chiefly in charge of the slaves, one man, John R. Hewell, being directly in charge of those belonging to an owner named McCargo. About 9.30 on the night of Sunday, November 7, while out at sea, nineteen of the slaves rose, cowed the others, wounded the captain, and generally took command of the vessel. Madison Washington began the uprising by an attack on Gifford, the first mate, and Ben Blacksmith, one of the most aggressive of his assistants, killed Hewell. The insurgents seized the arms of the vessel, permitted no conversation between members of the crew except in their hearing, demanded and obtained the manifests of slaves, and threatened that if they were not taken to Abaco or some other British port they would throw the officers and crew overboard. The *Creole* reached Nassau, New Providence, on Tuesday, November 9, and the arrival of the vessel at once occasioned intense excitement. Gifford went ashore and reported the matter, and the American consul, John F. Bacon, contended to the English authorities that the slaves on board the brig were as much a part of the cargo as the tobacco and entitled to the same protection from loss to the owners. The governor, Sir Francis Cockburn, however, was uncertain whether to interfere in the business at all. He liberated those slaves who were not concerned in the uprising, spoke of all of the slaves as "passengers," and guaranteed to the nineteen who were shown by an investigation to have been connected with the uprising all the rights of prisoners called before an English court. He told them further that the British Government would be communicated with before their case was finally passed upon, that if they wished copies of the informations these would be furnished them, and that they were privileged to have witnesses examined in refutation of the charges against them. From time to time Negroes who were natives of the island crowded about the brig in small boats and intimidated the American crew, but when on the morning of November 12 the Attorney General questioned them as to their intentions they replied with transparent good humor that they intended no violence and had assembled only for the purpose of conveying to shore such of the persons on the *Creole* as might be permitted to leave and might need their assistance. The Attorney General required, however, that they throw overboard a dozen stout cudgels that they had. Here the whole case really rested. Daniel Webster as Secretary of State aroused the antislavery element by making a strong demand for the return of the slaves, basing his argument on the sacredness of vessels flying the American flag; but the English authorities at Nassau never returned any of them. On March 21, 1842, Joshua R. Giddings, untiring defender of the rights of the Negro, offered in the House of Representatives resolutions to the effect that slavery could exist only by positive law of the different states; that the states had delegated no control over slavery to the Federal Government, which alone had jurisdiction on the high seas, and that, therefore, slaves on the high seas became free and the coastwise trade was unconstitutional. The House, strongly pro-Southern, replied with a vote of censure and Giddings resigned, but he was immediately reëlected by his Ohio constituency.

CHAPTER VIII

It is not the purpose of the present chapter primarily to consider social progress on the part of the Negro. A little later we shall endeavor to treat this interesting subject for the period between the Missouri Compromise and the Civil War. Just now we are concerned with the attitude of the Negro himself toward the problem that seemed to present itself to America and for which such different solutions were proposed. So far as slavery was concerned, we have seen that the remedy suggested by Denmark Vesey and Nat Turner was insurrection. It is only to state an historical fact, however, to say that the great heart of the Negro people in the South did not believe in violence, but rather hoped and prayed for a better day to come by some other means. But what was the attitude of those people, progressive citizens and thinking leaders, who were not satisfied with the condition of the race and who had to take a stand on the issues that confronted them? If we study the matter from this point of view, we shall find an amount of ferment and unrest and honest difference of opinion that is sometimes overlooked or completely forgotten in the questions of a later day.

1. *Walker's "Appeal"*

The most widely discussed book written by a Negro in the period was one that appeared in Boston in 1829. David Walker, the author, had been born in North Carolina in 1785, of a free mother and a slave father, and he was therefore free.* He received a fair education, traveled widely over the United States, and by 1827 was living in Boston as the pro-

---

* Adams: *Neglected Period of Anti-Slavery,* 93.

prietor of a second-hand clothing store on Brattle Street. He felt very strongly on the subject of slavery and actually seems to have contemplated leading an insurrection. In 1828 he addressed various audiences of Negroes in Boston and elsewhere, and in 1829 he published his *Appeal, in four articles; together with a Preamble to the Coloured Citizens of the World, but in particular, and very expressly, to those of the United States of America*. The book was remarkably successful. Appearing in September, by March of the following year it had reached its third edition; and in each successive edition the language was more bold and vigorous. Walker's projected insurrection did not take place, and he himself died in 1830. While there was no real proof of the fact, among the Negro people there was a strong belief that he met with foul play.

Article I Walker headed "Our Wretchedness in Consequence of Slavery." A trip over the United States had convinced him that the Negroes of the country were "the most degraded, wretched and abject set of beings that ever lived since the world began." He quoted a South Carolina paper as saying, "The Turks are the most barbarous people in the world— they treat the Greeks more like brutes than human beings"; and then from the same paper cited an advertisement of the sale of eight Negro men and four women. "Are we men?" he exclaimed. "I ask you, O! my brothers, are we men? . . . Have we any other master but Jesus Christ alone? Is He not their master as well as ours? What right, then, have we to obey and call any man master but Himself? How we could be so submissive to a gang of men, whom we can not tell whether they are as good as ourselves, or not, I never could conceive." "The whites," he asserted, "have always been an unjust, jealous, unmerciful, avaricious and bloodthirsty set of beings, always seeking after power and authority." As heathen the white people had been cruel enough, but as Christians they were ten times more so. As heathen "they were not quite so audacious as to go and take vessel loads of men, women and children, and in cold blood, through devilishness, throw them into the sea, and murder them in all kind of ways. But being Christians, enlightened and sensible, they are completely prepared for such hellish cruelties." Next was considered "Our Wretchedness in Consequence of Ignorance." In general the writer maintained that his people as a whole did not have intelligence enough to realize their own degradation; even if boys studied books they did not master their texts, nor did their information go sufficiently far to enable them actually to meet the problems of life. If one would but go to the South or West, he would see there a son take his mother, who bore almost the pains of death to give him birth, and by the command of a tyrant, strip her as naked as she came into the world and apply the cowhide to her until she fell a victim to death in the road. He would see a husband take his dear wife, not unfrequently in a pregnant state and perhaps far advanced, and beat her for an unmerciful wretch, until her infant fell a lifeless lump at her feet. Moreover, "there have been, and are this day, in Boston, New York, Philadelphia, and Baltimore, colored men who are in league with tyrants and who receive a great portion of their daily bread of the moneys which they acquire from the blood and tears of their more miserable brethren, whom they scandalously deliver into the hands of our natural enemies." In Article III Walker considered "Our Wretchedness in Consequence of the Preachers of the Religion of Jesus Christ." Here was a fertile field, which was only partially developed. Walker evidently did not have at hand the utterances of Furman and others to serve as a definite point of attack. He did point out, however, the general failure of Christian ministers to live up to the teachings of Christ. "Even here in Boston," we are informed, "pride and prejudice have got to such a pitch, that in the very houses erected to the Lord they have built little places for the reception of colored people, where they must sit during meeting, or keep away from the house of God." Hypocrisy could hardly go further than that of preachers who could not see the evils at their door but could "send out missionaries to convert the heathen, notwithstanding." Article IV was headed "Our Wretchedness in Consequence of the Colonizing Plan." This was a bitter arraignment, especially directed against Henry Clay. "I appeal and ask every citizen of these United States," said Walker, "and of the world, both white and black, who has any knowledge of Mr. Clay's public labors for these states—I want you candidly to answer the Lord, who sees the secrets of your hearts, Do you believe that Mr. Henry Clay, late Secretary of State, and now in Kentucky, is a friend to the blacks further than his personal interest extends? . . . Does he care a pinch of snuff about Africa—whether it remains a land of pagans and of blood, or of Christians, so long as he gets enough of her sons and daughters to dig up gold and silver for him? . . . Was he not made by the Creator to sit in the shade, and make the blacks work without remuneration for their services, to support him and his family? I have been for some time taking notice of this man's speeches and public writings, but never to my knowledge have I seen anything in his writings which insisted on the emancipation of slavery, which has almost ruined his country." Walker then paid his compliments to Elias B. Caldwell and John Randolph, the former of whom had said, "The more you improve the condition of these people, the more you cultivate their minds, the more miserable you make them in their present state." "Here," the work continues, "is a demonstrative proof of a plan got up, by a gang of slaveholders, to select the free people of color from among the slaves, that our more miserable brethren may be the better secured in ignorance and wretchedness, to work their farms and dig their mines, and thus go on enriching the Christians with their blood and groans. What our brethren could have been thinking about, who have left their native land and gone away to Africa, I am unable to say. . . . The Americans may say or do as they please, but they have to raise us from the condition of brutes to that of respectable men, and to make a national acknowledgment to us for the wrongs they have inflicted on us. . . . You may doubt it, if you please. I know that thousands will doubt—they think they have us so well secured in wretchedness, to them and their children, that it is impossible for such things to occur. So did the antediluvians doubt Noah, until the day in which the flood came and swept them away. So did the Sodomites doubt, until Lot had got out of the city, and God rained down fire and brimstone from heaven upon them and burnt them up. So did the king of Egypt doubt the very existence of God, saying, 'Who is the Lord, that I should let Israel go?' . . . So did the Romans doubt. . . . But they got dreadfully deceived."

This document created the greatest consternation in the South. The Mayor of Savannah wrote to Mayor Otis of Boston, demanding that Walker be punished. Otis, in a widely published letter, replied expressing his disapproval of the pamphlet, but saying that the author had done nothing that made him "amenable" to the laws. In Virginia the legislature considered passing an "extraordinary bill," not only forbidding the circulation of such seditious publications but forbidding the education of free Negroes. The bill passed the House of Delegates, but failed in the Senate. The *Appeal* even found its way to Louisiana, where there were already rumors of an insurrection, and immediately a law was passed expelling all free Negroes who had come to the state since 1825.

2. *The Convention Movement*

As may be inferred from Walker's attitude, the representative men of the race were almost a unit in their opposition to colonization. They were not always opposed to colonization itself, for some looked favorably upon settlement in Canada, and a few hundred made their way to the West Indies. They did object, however, to the plan offered by the American Colonization Society, which more and more impressed them as a device on the part of slaveholders to get free Negroes out of the country in order that slave labor might be more valuable. Richard Allen, bishop of the African Methodist Episcopal Church, and the foremost Negro of the period, said: "We were stolen from our mother country and brought here. We have tilled the ground and made fortunes for thousands, and still they are not weary of our services. *But they who stay to till the ground must be slaves.* Is there not land enough in America, or 'corn enough in Egypt'? Why should they send us into a far country to die? See the thousands of foreigners emigrating to America every year: and if there be ground sufficient for them to cultivate, and bread for them to eat, why would they wish to send the *first tillers* of the land away? Africans have made fortunes for thousands, who are yet unwilling to part with their services; but the free must be sent away, and those who remain must be slaves. I have no doubt that there are many good men who do not see as I do, and who are sending us to Liberia; but they have not duly considered the subject—they are not men of color. This land which we have watered with our tears and our blood is now our *mother country*, and we are well satisfied to stay where wisdom abounds and the gospel is free." * This point of view received popular expression in a song which bore the cumbersome title, "The Colored Man's Opinion of Colonization," and which was sung to the tune of "Home, Sweet Home." The first stanza was as follows:

> Great God, if the humble and weak are as dear
> To thy love as the proud, to thy children give ear!
> Our brethren would drive us in deserts to roam;
> Forgive them, O Father, and keep us at home.
>   Home, sweet home!
> We have no other; this, this is our home.†

To this sentiment formal expression was given in the measures adopted at various Negro meetings in the North. In 1817 the greatest excitement was occasioned by a report that through the efforts of the newly-formed Colonization Society all free Negroes were forcibly to be deported from the country. Resolutions of protest were adopted, and these were widely circulated.‡ Of special importance was the meeting in Philadelphia in January, presided over by James Forten. Of this the full report is as follows:

At a numerous meeting of the people of color, convened at Bethel Church, to take into consideration the propriety of remonstrating against the contemplated measure that is to exile us from the land of our nativity, James Forten was called to the chair, and Russell Parrott appointed secretary. The intent of the meeting having been stated by the chairman, the following resolutions were adopted without one dissenting voice:

* *Freedom's Journal*, November 2, 1827, quoted by Walker.
† *Anti-Slavery Picknick*, 105-107.
‡ They are fully recorded in Garrison's *Thoughts on African Colonization*.

WHEREAS, Our ancestors (not of choice) were the first successful cultivators of the wilds of America, we their descendants feel ourselves entitled to participate in the blessings of her luxuriant soil, which their blood and sweat manured; and that any measure or system of measures, having a tendency to banish us from her bosom, would not only be cruel, but in direct violation of those principles which have been the boast of this republic,

Resolved, That we view with deep abhorrence the unmerited stigma attempted to be cast upon the reputation of the free people of color, by the promoters of this measure, "that they are a dangerous and useless part of the community," when in the state of disfranchisement in which they live, in the hour of danger they ceased to remember their wrongs, and rallied around the standard of their country.

Resolved, That we never will separate ourselves voluntarily from the slave population of this country; they are our brethren by the ties of consanguinity, of suffering, and of wrong; and we feel that there is more virtue in suffering privations with them, than fancied advantages for a season.

Resolved, That without arts, without science, without a proper knowledge of government to cast upon the savage wilds of Africa the free people of color, seems to us the circuitous route through which they must return to perpetual bondage.

Resolved, That having the strongest confidence in the justice of God, and philanthropy of the free states, we cheerfully submit our destinies to the guidance of Him who suffers not a sparrow to fall without his special providence.

Resolved, That a committee of eleven persons be appointed to open a correspondence with the honorable Joseph Hopkinson, member of Congress from this city, and likewise to inform him of the sentiments of this meeting, and that the following named persons constitute the committee, and that they have power to call a general meeting, when they, in their judgment, may deem it proper: Rev. Absalom Jones, Rev. Richard Allen, James Forten, Robert Douglass, Francis Perkins, Rev. John Gloucester, Robert Gorden, James Johnson, Quamoney Clarkson, John Summersett, Randall Shepherd.

RUSSELL PARROTT, Secretary.   JAMES FORTEN, Chairman.

In 1827, in New York, was begun the publication of *Freedom's Journal,* the first Negro newspaper in the United States. The editors were John B. Russwurm and Samuel E. Cornish. Russwurm was a recent graduate of Bowdoin College and was later to become better known as the governor of Maryland in Africa. By 1830 feeling was acute throughout the country, especially in Ohio and Kentucky, and on the part of Negro men had developed the conviction that the time had come for national organization and protest.

In the spring of 1830 Hezekiah Grice of Baltimore, who had become personally acquainted with the work of Lundy and Garrison, sent a letter to prominent Negroes in the free states bringing in question the general policy of emigration.* He received no immediate response, but in August he received from Richard Allen an urgent request to come at once to Philadelphia. Arriving there he found in session a meeting discussing the wisdom of emigration to Canada, and Allen "showed him a printed circular signed by Peter Williams, rector of St. Philip's Church, New York, Peter Vogelsang and Thomas L. Jennings of the same place, approving the plan of convention." † The Philadelphians now issued a call for a convention of the Negroes of the United States to be held in their city September 15, 1830.

This September meeting was held in Bethel A. M. E. Church. Bishop Richard Allen was chosen president, Dr. Belfast Burton of Philadelphia and Austin Steward of Rochester vice-presidents, Junius C. Morell of Pennsylvania secretary, and Robert Cowley of Maryland assistant secretary. There were accredited delegates from seven states. While this meeting might really be considered the first national convention of Negroes in the United States (aside of course from the gathering of denominational bodies), it seems to have been regarded merely as preliminary to a still more formal assembling, for the minutes of the next year were printed as the "Minutes and Proceedings of the First Annual Convention of the People of Color, held by adjournments in the city of Philadelphia, from the sixth to the eleventh of June, inclusive, 1831. Philadelphia, 1831." The meetings of this convention were held in the Wesleyan Church on Lombard Street. Richard Allen had died earlier in the year and Grice was not present; not long afterwards he emigrated to Hayti, where he became prominent as a contractor. Rev. James W. C. Pennington of New York, however, now for the first time appeared on the larger horizon of race affairs; and John Bowers of Philadel-

* John W. Cromwell: *The Early Negro Convention Movement.*
† *Ibid.,* 5.

phia served as president, Abraham D. Shadd of Delaware and William Duncan of Virginia as vice-presidents, William Whipper of Philadelphia as secretary, and Thomas L. Jennings of New York as assistant secretary. Delegates from five states were present. The gathering was not large, but it brought together some able men; moreover, the meeting had some distinguished visitors, among them Benjamin Lundy, William Lloyd Garrison, Rev. S. S. Jocelyn of New Haven, and Arthur Tappan of New York.

The very first motion of the convention resolved "That a committee be appointed to institute an inquiry into the condition of the free people of color throughout the United States, and report their views upon the subject at a subsequent meeting." As a result of its work this committee recommended that the work of organizations interested in settlement in Canada be continued; that the free people of color be annually called to assemble by delegation; and it submitted "the necessity of deliberate reflection on the dissolute, intemperate, and ignorant condition of a large portion of the colored population of the United States." "And, lastly, your Committee view with unfeigned regret, and respectfully submit to the wisdom of this Convention, the operations and misrepresentations of the American Colonization Society in these United States. . . . We feel sorrowful to see such an immense and wanton waste of lives and property, not doubting the benevolent feelings of some individuals engaged in that cause. But we can not for a moment doubt but that the cause of many of our unconstitutional, unchristian, and unheard-of sufferings emanate from that unhallowed source; and we would call on Christians of every denomination firmly to resist it." The report was unanimously received and adopted.

Jocelyn, Tappan, and Garrison addressed the convention with reference to a proposed industrial college in New Haven, toward the $20,000 expense of which one individual (Tappan himself) had subscribed $1000 with the understanding that the remaining $19,000 be raised within a year; and the convention approved the project, *provided* the Negroes had a majority of at least one on the board of trustees. An illuminating address to the public called attention to the progress of emancipation abroad, to the fact that it was American persecution that led to the calling of the convention, and that it was this also that first induced some members of the race to seek an asylum in Canada, where already there were two hundred log houses, and five hundred acres under cultivation.

In 1832 eight states were represented by a total of thirty delegates. By this time we learn that a total of eight hundred acres had been secured in Canada, that two thousand Negroes had gone thither, but that considerable hostility had been manifested on the part of the Canadians. Hesitant, the convention appointed an agent to investigate the situation. It expressed itself as strongly opposed to any national aid to the American Colonization Society and urged the abolition of slavery in the District of Columbia—all of which activity, it is well to remember, was a year before the American Anti-Slavery Society was organized.

In 1833 there were fifty-eight delegates, and Abraham Shadd, now of Washington, was chosen president. The convention again gave prominence to the questions of Canada and colonization, and expressed itself with reference to the new law in Connecticut prohibiting Negroes from other states from attending schools within the state. The 1834 meeting was held in New York. Prudence Crandall * was commended for her stand in behalf of the race, and July 4 was set apart as a day for prayer and addresses on the condition of the Negro throughout the country. By this time we hear much of societies for temperance and moral reform, especially of the so-called Phœnix Societies "for improvement in general culture —literature, mechanic arts, and morals." Of these organizations Rev. Christopher Rush, of the A. M. E. Zion Church, was general president, and among the directors were Rev. Peter Williams, Boston Crummell, the father of Alexander Crummell, and Rev. William Paul Quinn, afterwards a well-known bishop of the A. M. E. Church. The 1835 and 1836 meetings were held in Philadelphia, and especially were the students of Lane Seminary in Cincinnati commended for their zeal in the cause of abolition. A committee was appointed to

* See Chapter X, Section 3.

look into the dissatisfaction of some emigrants to Liberia and generally to review the work of the Colonization Society.

In the decade 1837-1847 Frederick Douglass was outstanding as a leader, and other men who were now prominent were Dr. James McCune Smith, Rev. James W. C. Pennington, Alexander Crummell, William C. Nell, and Martin R. Delany. These are important names in the history of the period. These were the men who bore the brunt of the contest in the furious days of Texas annexation and the Compromise of 1850. About 1853 and 1854 there was renewed interest in the idea of an industrial college; steps were taken for the registry of Negro mechanics and artisans who were in search of employment, and of the names of persons who were willing to give them work; and there was also a committee on historical records and statistics that was not only to compile studies in Negro biography but also to reply to any assaults of note.*

Immediately after the last of the conventions just mentioned, those who were interested in emigration and had not been able to get a hearing in the regular convention issued a call for a National Emigration Convention of Colored Men to take place in Cleveland, Ohio, August 24-26, 1854. The preliminary announcement said: "No person will be admitted to a seat in the Convention who would introduce the subject of emigration to the Eastern Hemisphere—either to Asia, Africa, or Europe—as our object and determination are to consider our claims to the West Indies, Central and South America, and the Canadas. This restriction has no reference to personal preference, or individual enterprise, but to the great question of national claims to come before the Convention." † Douglass pronounced the call "uncalled for, unwise, unfortunate and premature," and his position led him into a wordy discussion in the press with James M. Whitfield, of Buffalo, prominent at the time as a writer. Delany explained the call

* We can not too much emphasize the fact that the leaders of this period were by no means impractical theorists but men who were scientifically approaching the social problem of their people. They not only anticipated such ideas as those of industrial education and of the National Urban League of the present day, but they also endeavored to lay firmly the foundations of racial self-respect.

† Official Report of the Niger Valley Exploring Party, by M. R. Delany, Chief Commissioner to Africa, New York, 1861.

as follows: "It was a mere policy on the part of the authors of these documents, to confine their scheme to America (including the West Indies), whilst they were the leading advocates of the regeneration of Africa, lest they compromised themselves and their people to the avowed enemies of their race." * At the secret sessions, he informs us, Africa was the topic of greatest interest. In order to account for this position it is important to take note of the changes that had taken place between 1817 and 1854. When James Forten and others in Philadelphia in 1817 protested against the American Colonization Society as the plan of a "gang of slaveholders" to drive free people from their homes, they had abundant ground for the feeling. By 1839, however, not only had the personnel of the organization changed, but, largely through the influence of Garrison, the purpose and aim had also changed, and not Virginia and Maryland, but New York and Pennsylvania were now dominant in influence. Colonization had at first been regarded as a possible solution of the race problem; money was now given, however, "rather as an aid to the establishment of a model Negro republic in Africa, whose effort would be to discourage the slave-trade, and encourage energy and thrift among those free Negroes from the United States who chose to emigrate, and to give native Africans a demonstration of the advantages of civilization." † In view of the changed conditions, Delany and others who disagreed with Douglass felt that for the good of the race in the United States the whole matter of emigration might receive further consideration; at the same time, remembering old discussions, they did not wish to be put in the light of betrayers of their people. The Pittsburgh *Daily Morning Post* of October 18, 1854, sneered at the new plan as follows: "If Dr. Delany drafted this report it certainly does him much credit for learning and ability; and can not fail to establish for him a reputation for vigor and brilliancy of imagination never yet surpassed. It is a vast conception of impossible birth. The Committee seem to have entirely overlooked the strength of the

* Delany, 8.
† Fox: *The American Colonization Society,* 177; also note pp. 12, 120-2.

'powers on earth' that would oppose the Africanization of more than half the Western Hemisphere. We have no motive in noticing this gorgeous dream of 'the Committee' except to show its fallacy—its impracticability, in fact, its absurdity. No sensible man, whatever his color, should be for a moment deceived by such impracticable theories." However, in spite of all opposition, the Emigration Convention met. Upon Delany fell the real brunt of the work of the organization. In 1855 Bishop James Theodore Holly was commissioned to Faustin Soulouque, Emperor of Hayti; and he received in his visit of a month much official attention with some inducement to emigrate. Delany himself planned to go to Africa as the head of a "Niger Valley Exploring Party." Of the misrepresentation and difficulties that he encountered he himself has best told. He did get to Africa, however, and he had some interesting and satisfactory interviews with representative chiefs. The Civil War put an end to his project, he himself accepting a major's commission from President Lincoln. Through the influence of Holly about two thousand persons went to Hayti, but not more than a third of these remained. A plan fostered by Whitfield for a colony in Central America came to naught when this leading spirit died in San Francisco on his way thither.*

3. *Sojourner Truth and Woman Suffrage*

With its challenge to the moral consciousness it was but natural that anti-slavery should soon become allied with temperance, woman suffrage, and other reform movements that were beginning to appeal to the heart of America. Especially were representative women quick to see that the arguments used for their cause were very largely identical with those used for the Negro. When the woman suffrage movement was launched at Seneca Falls, N. Y., in 1848, Lucretia Mott, Elizabeth Cady Stanton, and their co-workers issued a Declaration of Sentiments which like many similar documents copied the phrasing of the Declaration of Independence. This said in

*For the progress of all the plans offered to the convention note important letter written by Holly and given by Cromwell, 20-21.

part: "The history of mankind is a history of repeated injuries and usurpations on the part of man towards woman, having in direct object the establishment of an absolute tyranny over her. . . . He has never permitted her to exercise her inalienable right to the elective franchise. . . . He has made her, if married, in the eye of the law civilly dead. . . . He has denied her the facilities for obtaining a thorough education, all colleges being closed to her." It mattered not at the time that male suffrage was by no means universal, or that amelioration of the condition of woman had already begun; the movement stated its case clearly and strongly in order that it might fully be brought to the attention of the American people. In 1850 the first formal National Woman's Rights Convention assembled in Worcester, Mass. To this meeting came a young Quaker woman who was already listed in the cause of temperance. In fact, wherever she went Susan B. Anthony entered into "causes." She possessed great virtues and abilities, and at the same time was capable of very great devotion. "She not only sympathized with the Negro; when an opportunity offered she drank tea with him, to her own 'unspeakable satisfaction.' "* Lucy Stone, an Oberlin graduate, was representative of those who came into the agitation by the anti-slavery path. Beginning in 1848 to speak as an agent of the Anti-Slavery Society, almost from the first she began to introduce the matter of woman's rights in her speeches.

To the second National Woman's Suffrage Convention, held in Akron, Ohio, in 1852, and presided over by Mrs. Frances D. Gage, came Sojourner Truth.

The "Libyan Sibyl" was then in the fullness of her powers. She had been born of slave parents about 1798 in Ulster County, New York. In her later years she remembered vividly the cold, damp cellar-room in which slept the slaves of the family to which she belonged, and where she was taught by her mother to repeat the Lord's Prayer and to trust in God. When in the course of gradual emancipation she became legally free in 1827, her master refused to comply with the law and

*Ida M. Tarbell: "The American Woman: Her First Declaration of Independence," *American Magazine*, February, 1910.

kept her in bondage. She left, but was pursued and found. Rather than have her go back, a friend paid for her services for the rest of the year. Then came an evening when, searching for one of her children who had been stolen and sold, she found herself a homeless wanderer. A Quaker family gave her lodging for the night. Subsequently she went to New York City, joined a Methodist church, and worked hard to improve her condition. Later, having decided to leave New York for a lecture tour through the East, she made a small bundle of her belongings and informed a friend that her name was no longer *Isabella* but *Sojourner*. She went on her way, speaking to people wherever she found them assembled and being entertained in many aristocratic homes. She was entirely untaught in the schools, but was witty, original, and always suggestive. By her tact and her gift of song she kept down ridicule, and by her fervor and faith she won many friends for the anti-slavery cause. As to her name she said: "And the Lord gave me *Sojourner* because I was to travel up an' down the land showin' the people their sins an' bein' a sign unto them. Afterwards I told the Lord I wanted another name, 'cause everybody else had two names, an' the Lord gave me *Truth*, because I was to declare the truth to the people."

On the second day of the convention in Akron, in a corner, crouched against the wall, sat this woman of care, her elbows resting on her knees, and her chin resting upon her broad, hard palms.* In the intermission she was employed in selling "The Life of Sojourner Truth." From time to time came to the presiding officer the request, "Don't let her speak; it will ruin us. Every newspaper in the land will have our cause mixed with abolition and niggers, and we shall be utterly denounced." Gradually, however, the meeting waxed warm. Baptist, Methodist, Episcopalian, Presbyterian, and Universalist preachers had come to hear and discuss the resolutions presented. One argued the superiority of the male intellect, another the sin of Eve, and the women, most of whom did not "speak in meeting," were becoming filled with dismay. Then

---

* *Reminiscences* of the president, Mrs. Frances D. Gage, cited by Tarbell.

slowly from her seat in the corner rose Sojourner Truth, who till now had scarcely lifted her head. Slowly and solemnly to the front she moved, laid her old bonnet at her feet, and turned her great, speaking eyes upon the chair. Mrs. Gage, quite equal to the occasion, stepped forward and announced "Sojourner Truth," and begged the audience to be silent a few minutes. "The tumult subsided at once, and every eye was fixed on this almost Amazon form, which stood nearly six feet high, head erect, and eye piercing the upper air, like one in a dream." At her first word there was a profound hush. She spoke in deep tones, which, though not loud, reached every ear in the house, and even the throng at the doors and windows. To one man who had ridiculed the general helplessness of woman, her needing to be assisted into carriages and to be given the best place everywhere, she said, "Nobody eber helped me into carriages, or ober mud puddles, or gibs me any best place"; and raising herself to her full height, with a voice pitched like rolling thunder, she asked, "And a'n't I a woman? Look at me. Look at my arm." And she bared her right arm to the shoulder, showing her tremendous muscular power. "I have plowed, and planted, and gathered into barns, and no man could head me—and a'n't I a woman? I could work as much and eat as much as a man, when I could get it, and bear de lash as well—and a'n't I a woman? I have borne five chilern and seen 'em mos' all sold off into slavery, and when I cried out with a mother's grief, none but Jesus heard—and a'n't I a woman? . . . Dey talks 'bout dis ting in de head—what dis dey call it?" "Intellect," said some one near. "Dat's it, honey. What's dat got to do with women's rights or niggers' rights? If my cup won't hold but a pint and yourn holds a quart, wouldn't ye be mean not to let me have my little half-measure full?" And she pointed her significant finger and sent a keen glance at the minister who had made the argument. The cheering was long and loud. "Den dat little man in black dar, he say women can't have as much rights as man, 'cause Christ wa'n't a woman. But whar did Christ come from?" Rolling thunder could not have stilled that crowd as did those deep, wonderful tones as the woman stood there with her outstretched arms and her eyes of fire. Raising her voice she repeated, "Whar did Christ come from? From God and a woman. Man had nothing to do with Him." Turning to another objector, she took up the defense of Eve. She was pointed and witty, solemn and serious at will, and at almost every sentence awoke deafening applause; and she ended by asserting, "If de fust woman God made was strong enough to turn the world upside down, all alone, dese togedder,"—and she glanced over the audience—"ought to be able to turn it back and get it right side up again, and now dey is askin' to do it, de men better let 'em."

"Amid roars of applause," wrote Mrs. Gage, "she returned to her corner, leaving more than one of us with streaming eyes and hearts beating with gratitude." Thus, as so frequently happened, Sojourner Truth turned a difficult situation into splendid victory. She not only made an eloquent plea for the slave, but placing herself upon the broadest principles of humanity, she saved the day for woman suffrage as well.

CHAPTER IX

In a former chapter we have traced the early development of the American Colonization Society, whose efforts culminated in the founding of the colony of Liberia. The recent world war, with Africa as its prize, fixed attention anew upon the little republic. This comparatively small tract of land, just slightly more than one-three hundredth part of the surface of Africa, is now of interest and strategic importance not only because (if we except Abyssinia, which claims slightly different race origin, and Hayti, which is now really under the government of the United States) it represents the one distinctively Negro government in the world, but also because it is the only tract of land on the great West Coast of the continent that has survived, even through the war, the aggression of great European powers. It is just at the bend of the shoulder of Africa, and its history is as romantic as its situation is unique.

Liberia has frequently been referred to as an outstanding example of the incapacity of the Negro for self-government. Such a judgment is not necessarily correct. It is indeed an open question if, in view of the nature of its beginning, the history of the country proves anything one way or the other with reference to the capacity of the race. The early settlers were frequently only recently out of bondage, but upon them were thrust all the problems of maintenance and government, and they brought with them, moreover, the false ideas of life and work that obtained in the Old South. Sometimes they suffered from neglect, sometimes from excessive solicitude; never were they really left alone. In spite of all, however, more than a score of native tribes have been subdued by only a few thousand civilized men, the republic has preserved its integrity, and there has been handed down through the years a tradition of constitutional government.

1. *The Place and the People*

The resources of Liberia are as yet imperfectly known. There is no question, however, about the fertility of the interior, or of its capacity when properly developed. There are no rivers of the first rank, but the longest streams are about three hundred miles in length, and at convenient distances apart flow down to a coastline somewhat more than three hundred miles long. Here in a tract of land only slightly larger than our own state of Ohio are a civilized population between 30,000 and 100,000 in number, and a native population estimated at 2,000,000. Of the civilized population the smaller figure, 30,000, is the more nearly correct if we consider only those persons who are fully civilized, and this number would be about evenly divided between Americo-Liberians and natives. Especially in the towns along the coast, however, there are many people who have received only some degree of civilization, and most of the households in the larger towns have several native children living in them. If all such elements are considered, the total might approach 100,000. The natives in their different tribes fall into three or four large divisions. In general they follow their native customs, and the foremost tribes exhibit remarkable intelligence and skill in industry. Outstanding are the dignified Mandingo, with a Mohammedan tradition, and the Vai, distinguished for skill in the arts and with a culture similar to that of the Mandingo. Also easily recognized are the Kpwessi, skillful in weaving and ironwork; the Kru, intelligent, sea-faring, and eager for learning; the Grebo, ambitious and aggressive, and in language connection close to the Kru; the Bassa, with characteristics somewhat similar to those of the Kru, but in general not quite so ambitious; the Buzi, wild and highly tattooed; and the cannibalistic Mano. By reason of numbers if nothing else, Liberia's chief asset for the future consists in her native population.

2. History

(a) Colonization and Settlement

In pursuance of its plans for the founding of a permanent colony on the coast of Africa, the American Colonization Society in November, 1817, sent out two men, Samuel J. Mills and Ebenezer Burgess, who were authorized to find a suitable place for a settlement. Going by way of England, these men were cordially received by the officers of the African Institution and given letters to responsible persons in Sierra Leone. Arriving at the latter place in March, 1818, they met John Kizell, a native and a man of influence, who had received some training in America and had returned to his people, built a house of worship, and become a preacher. Kizell undertook to accompany them on their journey down the coast and led the way to Sherbro Island, a place long in disputed territory but since included within the limits of Sierra Leone. Here the agents were hospitably received; they fixed upon the island as a permanent site, and in May turned their faces homeward. Mills died on the voyage in June and was buried at sea; but Burgess made a favorable report, though the island was afterwards to prove by no means healthy. The Society was impressed, but efforts might have languished at this important stage if Monroe, now President, had not found it possible to bring the resources of the United States Government to assist in the project. Smuggling, with the accompanying evil of the sale of "recaptured Africans," had by 1818 become a national disgrace, and on March 3, 1819, a bill designed to do away with the practice became a law. This said in part: "The President of the United States is hereby authorized to make such regulations and arrangements as he may deem expedient for the safe-keeping, support, and removal beyond the limits of the United States, of all such Negroes, mulattoes, or persons of color as may be so delivered and brought within their jurisdiction; and to appoint a proper person or persons residing upon the coast of Africa as agent or agents for receiving the Negroes, mulattoes, or persons of color, delivered from on board vessels seized in the prosecution of the slave-trade by commanders of the United States armed vessels." For the carrying out of the purpose of this act $100,000 was appropriated, and Monroe was disposed to construe as broadly as necessary the powers given him under it. In his message of December 20, he informed Congress that he had appointed Rev. Samuel Bacon, of the American Colonization Society, with John Bankson as assistant, to charter a vessel and take the first group of emigrants to Africa, the understanding being that he was to go to the place fixed upon by Mills and Burgess. Thus the National Government and the Colonization Society, while technically separate, began to work in practical coöperation. The ship *Elizabeth* was made ready for the voyage; the Government informed the Society that it would "receive on board such free blacks recommended by the Society as might be required for the purpose of the agency"; $33,000 was placed in the hands of Mr. Bacon; Rev. Samuel A. Crozer was appointed as the Society's official representative; 88 emigrants were brought together (33 men and 18 women, the rest being children); and on February 5, 1820, convoyed by the war-sloop *Cyane,* the expedition set forth.

An interesting record of the voyage—important for the sidelights it gives—was left by Daniel Coker, the respected minister of a large Methodist congregation in Baltimore who was persuaded to accompany the expedition for the sake of the moral influence that he might be able to exert.* There was much bad weather at the start, and it was the icy sea that on February 4 made it impossible to get under way until the next day. On board, moreover, there was much distrust of the agents in charge, with much questioning of their motives; nor were matters made better by a fight between one of the emigrants and the captain of the vessel. It was a restless company, uncertain as to the future, and dissatisfied and peevish from day to day. Kizell afterwards remarked that "some would not be governed by white men, and some would not be governed by black men, and some would not be governed by mulattoes; but the truth was they did not want to

* "Journal of Daniel Coker, a descendant of Africa, from the time of leaving New York, in the ship *Elizabeth,* Capt. Sebor, on a voyage for Sherbro, in Africa. Baltimore, 1820."

be governed by anybody." On March 3, however, the ship sighted the Cape Verde Islands and six days afterwards was anchored at Sierra Leone; and Coker rejoiced that at last he had seen Africa. Kizell, however, whom the agents had counted on seeing, was found to be away at Sherbro; accordingly, six days after their arrival * they too were making efforts to go on to Sherbro, for they were allowed at anchor only fifteen days and time was passing rapidly. Meanwhile Bankson went to find Kizell. Captain Sebor was at first decidedly unwilling to go further; but his reluctance was at length overcome; Bacon purchased for $3,000 a British schooner that had formerly been engaged in the slave-trade; and on March 17 both ship and schooner got under way for Sherbro. The next day they met Bankson, who informed them that he had seen Kizell. This man, although he had not heard from America since the departure of Mills and Burgess, had already erected some temporary houses against the rainy season. He permitted the newcomers to stay in his little town until land could be obtained; sent them twelve fowls and a bushel of rice; but he also, with both dignity and pathos, warned Bankson that if he and his companions came with Christ in their hearts, it was well that they had come; if not, it would have been better if they had stayed in America.

Now followed much fruitless bargaining with the native chiefs, in all of which Coker regretted that the slave-traders had so ruined the people that it seemed impossible to make any progress in a "palaver" without the offering of rum. Meanwhile a report was circulated through the country that a number of Americans had come and turned Kizell out of his own town and put some of his people in the hold of their ship. Disaster followed disaster. The marsh, the bad water, and the malaria played havoc with the colonists, and all three of the responsible agents died. The few persons who remained alive made their way back to Sierra Leone.

Thus the first expedition failed. One year later, in March, 1821, a new company of twenty-one emigrants, in charge of J. B. Winn and Ephraim Bacon, arrived at Freetown in the

* March 15. The narrative, page 26, says February 15, but this is obviously a typographical error.

brig *Nautilus*. It had been the understanding that in return for their passage the members of the first expedition would clear the way for others; but when the agents of the new company saw the plight of those who remained alive, they brought all of the colonists together at Fourah Bay, and Bacon went farther down the coast to seek a more favorable site. A few persons who did not wish to go to Fourah Bay remained in Sierra Leone and became British subjects. Bacon found a promising tract about two hundred and fifty miles down the coast at Cape Montserado; but the natives were not especially eager to sell, as they did not wish to break up the slave traffic. Meanwhile Winn and several more of the colonists died; and Bacon now returned to the United States. The second expedition had thus proved to be little more successful than the first; but the future site of Monrovia had at least been suggested.

In November came Dr. Eli Ayres as agent of the Society, and in December Captain Robert F. Stockton of the *Alligator* with instructions to coöperate. These two men explored the coast and on December 11 arrived at Mesurado Bay. Through the jungle they made their way to a village and engaged in a palaver with King Peter and five of his associates. The negotiations were conducted in the presence of an excited crowd and with imminent danger; but Stockton had great tact and at length, for the equivalent of $300, he and Ayres purchased the mouth of the Mesurado River, Cape Montserado, and the land for some distance in the interior. There was also an understanding (for half a dozen gallons of rum and some trade-cloth and tobacco) with King George, who "resided on the Cape and claimed a sort of jurisdiction over the northern district of the peninsula of Montserado, by virtue of which the settlers were permitted to pass across the river and commence the laborious task of clearing away the heavy forest which covered the site of their intended town." * Then the agent returned to effect the removal of the colonists from Fourah Bay, leaving a very small company as a sort of guard on Perseverance (or Providence) Island at the mouth of the river.

---

* Ashmun: *History of the American Colony in Liberia, from 1821 to 1823*, 8.

Some of the colonists refused to leave, remained, and thus became British subjects. For those who had remained on the island there was trouble at once. A small vessel, the prize of an English cruiser, bound to Sierra Leone with thirty liberated Africans, put into the roads for water, and had the misfortune to part her cable and come ashore. "The natives claim to a prescriptive right, which interest never fails to enforce to its fullest extent, to seize and appropriate the wrecks and cargoes of vessels stranded, under whatever circumstances, on their coast." * The vessel in question drifted to the mainland one mile from the cape, a small distance below George's town, and the natives proceeded to act in accordance with tradition. They were fired on by the prize master and forced to desist, and the captain appealed to the few colonists on the island for assistance. They brought into play a brass field piece, and two of the natives were killed and several more wounded. The English officer, his crew, and the captured Africans escaped, though the small vessel was lost; but the next day the Deys (the natives), feeling outraged, made another attack, in the course of which some of them and one of the colonists were killed. In the course of the operations moreover, through the carelessness of some of the settlers themselves, fire was communicated to the storehouse and $3000 worth of property destroyed, though the powder and some of the provisions were saved. Thus at the very beginning, by accident though it happened, the shadow of England fell across the young colony, involving it in difficulties with the natives. When then Ayres returned with the main crowd of settlers on January 7, 1822—which arrival was the first real landing of settlers on what is now Liberian soil—he found that the Deys wished to annul the agreement previously made and to give back the articles paid. He himself was seized in the course of a palaver, and he was able to arrive at no better understanding than that the colonists might remain only until they could make a new purchase elsewhere. Now appeared on the scene Boatswain, a prominent chief from the interior who sometimes exercised jurisdiction over the coast tribes and who, hearing that there was trouble in

* Ashmun, 9.

the bay, had come hither, bringing with him a sufficient following to enforce his decrees. Through this man shone something of the high moral principle so often to be observed in responsible African chiefs, and to him Ayres appealed. Hearing the story he decided in favor of the colonists, saying to Peter, "Having sold your country and accepted payment, you must take the consequences. Let the Americans have their land immediately." To the agent he said, "I promise you protection. If these people give you further disturbance, send for me; and I swear, if they oblige me to come again to quiet them, I will do it to purpose, by taking their heads from their shoulders, as I did old king George's on my last visit to the coast to settle disputes." Thus on the word of a native chief was the foundation of Liberia assured.

By the end of April all of the colonists who were willing to move had been brought from Sierra Leone to their new home. It was now decided to remove from the low and unhealthy island to the higher land of Cape Montserado only a few hundred feet away; on April 28 there was a ceremony of possession and the American flag was raised. The advantages of the new position were obvious, to the natives as well as the colonists, and the removal was attended with great excitement. By July the island was completely abandoned. Meanwhile, however, things had not been going well. The Deys had been rendered very hostile, and from them there was constant danger of attack. The rainy season moreover had set in, shelter was inadequate, supplies were low, and the fever continually claimed its victims. Ayres at length became discouraged. He proposed that the enterprise be abandoned and that the settlers return to Sierra Leone, and on June 4 he did actually leave with a few of them. It was at this juncture that Elijah Johnson, one of the most heroic of the colonists, stepped forth to fame.

The early life of the man is a blank. In 1789 he was taken to New Jersey. He received some instruction and studied for the Methodist ministry, took part in the War of 1812, and eagerly embraced the opportunity to be among the first to come to the new colony. To the suggestion that the enterprise be abandoned he replied, "Two years long have I sought a home; here I have found it; here I remain." To him the great heart of the colonists responded. Among the natives he was known and respected as a valiant fighter. He lived until March 23, 1849.

Closely associated with Johnson, his colleague in many an effort and the pioneer in mission work, was the Baptist minister, Lott Cary, from Richmond, Va., who also had become one of the first permanent settlers.* He was a man of most unusual versatility and force of character. He died November 8, 1828, as the result of a powder explosion that occurred while he was acting in defense of the colony against the Deys.

July (1822) was a hard month for the settlers. Not only were their supplies almost exhausted, but they were on a rocky cape and the natives would not permit any food to be brought to them. On August 8, however, arrived Jehudi Ashmun, a young man from Vermont who had worked as a teacher and as the editor of a religious publication for some years before coming on this mission. He brought with him a company of liberated Africans and emigrants to the number of fifty-five, and as he did not intend to remain permanently he had yielded to the entreaty of his wife and permitted her to accompany him on the voyage. He held no formal commission from the American Colonization Society, but seeing the situation he felt that it was his duty to do what he could to relieve the distress; and he faced difficulties from the very first. On the day after his arrival his own brig, the *Strong,* was in danger of being lost; the vessel parted its cable, and on the following morning broke it again and drifted until it was landlocked between Cape Montserado and Cape Mount. A small anchor was found, however, and the brig was again moored, but five miles from the settlement. The rainy season was now on in full force; there was no proper place for the storing of provisions; and even with the newcomers it soon developed that there were in the colony only thirty-five men capable of bearing arms, so great had been the number of deaths from the fever. Sometimes almost all of these were sick; on September 10 only two were in condition for any kind of service.

* See Chapter III, Section 5.

Ashmun tried to make terms with the native chiefs, but their malignity was only partially concealed. His wife languished before his eyes and died September 15, just five weeks after her arrival. He himself was incapacitated for several months, nor at the height of his illness was he made better by the ministrations of a French charlatan. He never really recovered from the great inroads made upon his strength at this time.

As a protection from sudden attack a clearing around the settlement was made. Defenses had to be erected without tools, and so great was the anxiety that throughout the months of September and October a nightly watch of twenty men was kept. On Sunday, November 10, the report was circulated that the Deys were crossing the Mesurado River, and at night it became known that seven or eight hundred were on the peninsula only half a mile to the west. The attack came at early dawn on the 11th and the colonists might have been annihilated if they had not brought a field-piece into play. When this was turned against the natives advancing in compact array, it literally tore through masses of living flesh until scores of men were killed. Even so the Deys might have won the engagement if they had not stopped too soon to gather plunder. As it was, they were forced to retreat. Of the settlers three men and one woman were killed, two men and two women injured, and several children taken captive, though these were afterwards returned. At this time the colonists suffered greatly from the lack of any supplies for the treatment of wounds. Only medicines for the fever were on hand, and in the hot climate those whose flesh had been torn by bullets suffered terribly. In this first encounter, as often in these early years, the real burden of conflict fell upon Cary and Johnson. After the battle these men found that they had on hand ammunition sufficient for only one hour's defense. All were placed on a special allowance of provisions and November 23 was observed as a day of prayer. A passing vessel furnished additional supplies and happily delayed for some days the inevitable attack. This came from two sides very early in the morning of December 2. There was a desperate battle. Three bullets passed through Ashmun's clothes, one of the gunners was killed, and repeated attacks were resisted only with the most dogged determination. An accident, or, as the colonists regarded it, a miracle, saved them from destruction. A guard, hearing a noise, discharged a large gun and several muskets. The schooner *Prince Regent* was passing, with Major Laing, Midshipman Gordon, and eleven specially trained men on board. The officers, hearing the sound of guns, came ashore to see what was the trouble. Major Laing offered assistance if ground was given for the erection of a British flag, and generally attempted to bring about an adjustment of difficulties on the basis of submitting these to the governor of Sierra Leone. To these propositions Elijah Johnson replied, "We want no flagstaff put up here that it will cost more to get down than it will to whip the natives." However, Gordon and the men under him were left behind for the protection of the colony until further help could arrive. Within one month he and seven of the eleven were dead. He himself had found a ready place in the hearts of the settlers, and to him and his men Liberia owes much. They came in a needy hour and gave their lives for the cause of freedom.

An American steamer passing in December, 1822, gave some temporary relief. On March 31, 1823, the *Cyane,* with Capt. R. T. Spence in charge, arrived from America with supplies. As many members of his crew became ill after only a few days, Spence soon deemed it advisable to leave. His chief clerk, however, Richard Seaton, heroically volunteered to help with the work, remained behind, and died after only three months. On May 24 came the *Oswego* with sixty-one new colonists and Dr. Ayres, who, already the Society's agent, now returned with the additional authority of Government agent and surgeon. He made a survey and attempted a new allotment of land, only to find that the colony was soon in ferment, because some of those who possessed the best holdings or who had already made the beginnings of homes, were now required to give these up. There was so much rebellion that in December Ayres again deemed it advisable to leave. The year 1823 was in fact chiefly noteworthy for the misunderstandings that arose between the colonists and Ashmun. This man had been placed in a most embarrassing situation by the arrival of Dr. Ayres.* He not only found himself superseded in the government, but had the additional misfortune to learn that his drafts had been dishonored and that no provision had been made to remunerate him for his past services or provide for his present needs. Finding his services undervalued, and even the confidence of the Society withheld, he was naturally indignant, though his attachment to the cause remained steadfast. Seeing the authorized agent leaving the colony, and the settlers themselves in a state of insubordination, with no formal authority behind him he yet resolved to forget his own wrongs and to do what he could to save from destruction that for which he had already suffered so much. He was young and perhaps not always as tactful as he might have been. On the other hand, the colonists had not yet learned fully to appreciate the real greatness of the man with whom they were dealing. As for the Society at home, not even so much can be said. The real reason for the withholding of confidence from Ashmun was that many of the members objected to his persistent attacks on the slave-trade.

By the regulations that governed the colony at the time, each man who received rations was required to contribute to the general welfare two days of labor a week. Early in December twelve men cast off all restraint, and on the 13th Ashmun published a notice in which he said: "There are in the colony more than a dozen healthy persons who will receive no more provisions out of the public store until they earn them." On the 19th, in accordance with this notice, the provisions of the recalcitrants were stopped. The next morning, however, the men went to the storehouse, and while provisions were being issued, each seized a portion and went to his home. Ashmun now issued a circular, reminding the colonists of all of their struggles together and generally pointing out to them how such a breach of discipline struck at the very heart of the settlement. The colonists rallied to his support and the twelve men returned to duty. The trouble, however, was not yet over. On March 19, 1824, Ashmun found it necessary to order a cut in provisions. He had previously declared to the

* Stockwell, 73.

Board that in his opinion the evil was "incurable by any of the remedies which fall within the existing provisions"; and counter remonstrances had been sent by the colonists, who charged him with oppression, neglect of duty, and the seizure of public property. He now, seeing that his latest order was especially unpopular, prepared new despatches, on March 22 reviewed the whole course of his conduct in a strong and lengthy address, and by the last of the month had left the colony.

Meanwhile the Society, having learned that things were not going well with the colony, had appointed its secretary, Rev. R. R. Gurley, to investigate conditions. Gurley met Ashmun at the Cape Verde Islands and urgently requested that he return to Monrovia.* This Ashmun was not unwilling to do, as he desired the fullest possible investigation into his conduct. Gurley was in Liberia from August 13 to August 22, 1824, only; but from the time of his visit conditions improved. Ashmun was fully vindicated and remained for four years more until his strength was all but spent. There was adopted what was known as the Gurley Constitution. According to this the agent in charge was to have supreme charge and preside at all public meetings. He was to be assisted, however, by eleven officers annually chosen, the most important of whom he was to appoint on nomination by the colonists. Among these were a vice-agent, two councilors, two justices of the peace, and two constables. There was to be a guard of twelve privates, two corporals, and one sergeant.

For a long time it was the custom of the American Colonization Society to send out two main shipments of settlers a year, one in the spring and one in the fall. On February 13, 1824, arrived a little more than a hundred emigrants, mainly from Petersburg, Va. These people were unusually intelligent and industrious and received a hearty welcome. Within a month practically all of them were sick with the fever. On

---

* This name, in honor of President Monroe, had recently been adopted by the Society at the suggestion of Robert Goodloe Harper, of Maryland, who also suggested the name *Liberia* for the country. Harper himself was afterwards honored by having the chief town in Maryland in Africa named after him.

this occasion, as on many others, Lott Cary served as physician, and so successful was he that only three of the sufferers died. Another company of unusual interest was that which arrived early in 1826. It brought along a printer, a press with the necessary supplies, and books sent by friends in Boston. Unfortunately the printer was soon disabled by the fever.

Sickness, however, and wars with the natives were not the only handicaps that engaged the attention of the colony in these years. "At this period the slave-trade was carried on extensively within sight of Monrovia. Fifteen vessels were engaged in it at the same time, almost under the guns of the settlement; and in July of this year a contract was existing for eight hundred slaves to be furnished, in the short space of four months, within eight miles of the cape. Four hundred of these were to be purchased for two American traders." * Ashmun attacked the Spaniards engaged in the traffic, and labored generally to break up slave factories. On one occasion he received as many as one hundred and sixteen slaves into the colony as freemen. He also adopted an attitude of justice toward the native Krus. Of special importance was the attack on Trade Town, a stronghold of French and Spanish traders about one hundred miles below Monrovia. Here there were not less than three large factories. On the day of the battle, April 10, there were three hundred and fifty natives on shore under the direction of the traders, but the colonists had the assistance of some American vessels, and a Liberian officer, Captain Barbour, was of outstanding courage and ability. The town was fired after eighty slaves had been surrendered. The flames reached the ammunition of the enemy and over two hundred and fifty casks of gunpowder exploded. By July, however, the traders had built a battery at Trade Town and were prepared to give more trouble. All the same a severe blow had been dealt to their work.

In his report rendered at the close of 1825 Ashmun showed that the settlers were living in neatness and comfort; two chapels had been built, and the militia was well organized,

* Stockwell, 79.

equipped, and disciplined. The need of some place for the temporary housing of immigrants having more and more impressed itself upon the colony, before the end of 1826 a "receptacle" capable of holding one hundred and fifty persons was erected. Ashmun himself served on until 1828, by which time his strength was completely spent. He sailed for America early in the summer and succeeded in reaching New Haven, only to die after a few weeks. No man had given more for the founding of Liberia. The principal street in Monrovia is named after him.

Aside from wars with the natives, the most noteworthy being the Dey-Gola war of 1832, the most important feature of Liberian history in the decade 1828-1838 was the development along the coast of other settlements than Monrovia. These were largely the outgrowth of the activity of local branch organizations of the American Colonization Society, and they were originally supposed to have the oversight of the central organization and of the colony of Monrovia. The circumstances under which they were founded, however, gave them something of a feeling of independence which did much to influence their history. Thus arose, about seventy-five miles farther down the coast, under the auspices especially of the New York and Pennsylvania societies, the Grand Bassa settlements at the mouth of the St. John's River, the town Edina being outstanding. Nearly a hundred miles farther south, at the mouth of the Sino River, another colony developed as its most important town Greenville; and as most of the settlers in this vicinity came from Mississippi, their province became known as Mississippi in Africa. A hundred miles farther, on Cape Palmas, just about twenty miles from the Cavalla River marking the boundary of the French possessions, developed the town of Harper in what became known as Maryland in Africa. This colony was even more aloof than others from the parent settlement of the American Colonization Society. When the first colonists arrived at Monrovia in 1831, they were not very cordially received, there being trouble about the allotment of land. They waited for some months for reënforcements and then sailed down the coast to the vicinity of the Cavalla River, where they secured land for their future home and where their distance from the other colonists from America made it all the more easy for them to cultivate their tradition of independence.* These four ports are now popularly known as Monrovia, Grand Bassa, Sino, and Cape Palmas; and to them for general prominence might now be added Cape Mount, about fifty miles from Monrovia higher up the coast and just a few miles from the Mano River, which now marks the boundary between Sierra Leone and Liberia. In 1838, on a constitution drawn up by Professor Greenleaf, of Harvard College, was organized the "Commonwealth of Liberia," the government of which was vested in a Board of Directors composed of delegates from the state societies, and which included all the settlements except Maryland. This remote colony, whose seaport is Cape Palmas, did not join with the others until 1857, ten years after Liberia had become an independent republic. When a special company of settlers arrived from Baltimore and formally occupied Cape Palmas (1834), Dr. James Hall was governor and he served in this capacity until 1836, when failing health forced him to return to America. He was succeeded by John B. Russwurm, a young Negro who had come to Liberia in 1829 for the purpose of superintending the system of education. The country, however, was not yet ready for the kind of work he wanted to do, and in course of time he went into politics. He served very efficiently as Governor of Maryland from 1836 to 1851, especially exerting himself to standardize the currency and to stabilize the revenues. Five years after his death Maryland suffered greatly from an attack by the Greboes, twenty-six colonists being killed. An appeal to Monrovia for help led to the sending of a company of men and later to the incorporation of the colony in the Republic.

Of the events of the period special interest attaches to the murder of I. F. C. Finley, Governor of Mississippi in Africa, to whose father, Rev. Robert Finley, the organization of the American Colonization Society had been very largely due. In September, 1838, Governor Finley left his colony to go to Monrovia on business, and making a landing at Bassa Cove,

---

*McPherson is especially valuable for his study of the Maryland colony.

he was robbed and killed by the Krus.   This unfortunate murder led to a bitter conflict between the settlers in the vicinity and the natives.   This is sometimes known as the Fish War (from being waged around Fishpoint) and did not really cease for a year.

(b)   *The Commonwealth of Liberia*

The first governor of the newly formed Commonwealth was Thomas H. Buchanan, a man of singular energy who represented the New York and Pennsylvania societies and who had come in 1836 especially to take charge of the Grand Bassa settlements.   Becoming governor in 1838, he found it necessary to proceed vigorously against the slave dealers at Trade Town.   He was also victorious in 1840 in a contest with the Gola tribe led by Chief Gatumba.   The Golas had defeated the Dey tribe so severely that a mere remnant of the latter had taken refuge with the colonists at Millsburg, a station a few miles up the St. Paul's River.   Thus, as happened more than once, a tribal war in time involved the very existence of the new American colonies.   Governor Buchanan's victory greatly increased his prestige and made it possible for him to negotiate more and more favorable treaties with the natives.   A contest of different sort was that with a Methodist missionary, John Seyes, who held that all goods used by missionaries, including those sold to the natives, should be admitted free of duty.   The governor contended that such privilege should be extended only to goods intended for the personal use of missionaries; and the Colonization Society stood behind him in this opinion.   As early as 1840 moreover some shadow of future events was cast by trouble made by English traders on the Mano River, the Sierra Leone boundary.   Buchanan sent an agent to England to represent him in an inquiry into the matter; but in the midst of his vigorous work he died in 1841.   He was the last white man formally under any auspices at the head of Liberian affairs.   Happily his period of service had given opportunity and training to an efficient helper, upon whom now the burden fell and of

whom it is hardly too much to say that he is the foremost
figure in Liberian history.

Joseph Jenkin Roberts was a mulatto born in Virginia in
1809. At the age of twenty, with his widowed mother and
younger brothers, he went to Liberia and engaged in trade.
In course of time he proved to be a man of unusual tact and
graciousness of manner, moving with ease among people of
widely different rank. His abilities soon demanded recognition, and he was at the head of the force that defeated Gatumba. As governor he realized the need of cultivating more
far-reaching diplomacy than the Commonwealth had yet
known. He had the coöperation of the Maryland governor,
Russwurm, in such a matter as that of uniform customs duties;
and he visited the United States, where he made a very good
impression. He soon understood that he had to reckon primarily with the English and the French. England had indeed
assumed an attitude of opposition to the slave-trade; but her
traders did not scruple to sell rum to slave dealers, and especially were they interested in the palm oil of Liberia. When
the Commonwealth sought to impose customs duties, England
took the position that as Liberia was not an independent government, she had no right to do so; and the English attitude
had some show of strength from the fact that the American
Colonization Society, an outside organization, had a veto
power over whatever Liberia might do. When in 1845 the
Liberian Government seized the *Little Ben,* an English trading vessel whose captain acted in defiance of the revenue laws,
the British in turn seized the *John Seyes,* belonging to a Liberian named Benson, and sold the vessel for £8000. Liberia
appealed to the United States; but the Oregon boundary question as well as slavery had given the American Government
problems enough at home; and the Secretary of State, Edward Everett, finally replied to Lord Aberdeen (1845) that
America was not "presuming to settle differences arising between Liberian and British subjects, the Liberians being responsible for their own acts." The Colonization Society,
powerless to act except through its own government,
in January, 1846, resolved that "the time had arrived
when it was expedient for the people of the Commonwealth

of Liberia to take into their own hands the whole work of self-government including the management of all their foreign relations." Forced to act for herself Liberia called a constitutional convention and on July 26, 1847, issued a Declaration of Independence and adopted the Constitution of the Liberian Republic. In October, Joseph Jenkin Roberts, Governor of the Commonwealth, was elected the first President of the Republic.

It may well be questioned if by 1847 Liberia had developed sufficiently internally to be able to assume the duties and responsibilities of an independent power. There were at the time not more than 4,500 civilized people of American origin in the country; these were largely illiterate and scattered along a coastline more than three hundred miles in length. It is not to be supposed, however, that this consummation had been attained without much yearning and heart-beat and high spiritual fervor. There was something pathetic in the effort of this small company, most of whose members had never seen Africa but for the sake of their race had made their way back to the fatherland. The new seal of the Republic bore the motto: THE LOVE OF LIBERTY BROUGHT US HERE. The flag, modeled on that of the United States, had six red and five white stripes for the eleven signers of the Declaration of Independence, and in the upper corner next to the staff a lone white star in a field of blue. The Declaration itself said in part:

We, the people of the Republic of Liberia, were originally inhabitants of the United States of North America.

In some parts of that country we were debarred by law from all the rights and privileges of men; in other parts public sentiment, more powerful than law, frowned us down.

We were everywhere shut out from all civil office.

We were excluded from all participation in the government.

We were taxed without our consent.

We were compelled to contribute to the resources of a country which gave us no protection.

We were made a separate and distinct class, and against us every avenue of improvement was effectually closed. Strangers from all lands of a color different from ours were preferred before us.

We uttered our complaints, but they were unattended to, or met only by alleging the peculiar institution of the country.

All hope of a favorable change in our country was thus wholly extinguished in our bosom, and we looked with anxiety abroad for some asylum from the deep degradation.

The Western coast of Africa was the place selected by American benevolence and philanthropy for our future home. Removed beyond those influences which depressed us in our native land, it was hoped we would be enabled to enjoy those rights and privileges, and exercise and improve those faculties, which the God of nature had given us in common with the rest of mankind.

(c) *The Republic of Liberia*

With the adoption of its constitution the Republic of Liberia formally asked to be considered in the family of nations; and since 1847 the history of the country has naturally been very largely that of international relations. In fact, preoccupation with the questions raised by powerful neighbors has been at least one strong reason for the comparatively slow internal development of the country. The Republic was officially recognized by England in 1848, by France in 1852, but on account of slavery not by the United States until 1862. Continuously there has been an observance of the forms of order, and only one president has been deposed. For a long time the presidential term was two years in length; but by an act of 1907 it was lengthened to four years. From time to time there have been two political parties, but not always has such a division been emphasized.

It is well to pause and note exactly what was the task set before the little country. A company of American Negroes suddenly found themselves placed on an unhealthy and uncultivated coast which was thenceforth to be their home. If we compare them with the Pilgrim Fathers, we find that as the Pilgrims had to subdue the Indians, so they had to hold their own against a score of aggressive tribes. The Pilgrims had the advantage of a thousand years of culture and experience in government; the Negroes, only recently out of bondage, had been deprived of any opportunity for improvement whatsoever. Not only, however, did they have to contend against native tribes and labor to improve their own shortcomings; on every hand they had to meet the designs of nations supposedly more enlightened and Christian. On the coast Spanish traders defied international law; on one side the English, and on the other the French, from the beginning showed a tendency toward arrogance and encroachment. To crown the difficulty, the American Government, under whose auspices the colony had largely been founded, became more and more half-hearted in its efforts for protection and at length abandoned the enterprise altogether. It did not cease, however, to regard the colony as the dumping-ground of its own troubles, and whenever a vessel with slaves from the Congo was captured on the high seas, it did not hesitate to take these people to the Liberian coast and leave them there, nearly dead though they might be from exposure or cramping. It is well for one to remember such facts as these before he is quick to belittle or criticize. To the credit of the "Congo men" be it said that from the first they labored to make themselves a quiet and industrious element in the body politic.

The early administrations of President Roberts (four terms, 1848-1855) were mainly devoted to the quelling of the native tribes that continued to give trouble and to the cultivating of friendly relations with foreign powers. Soon after his inauguration Roberts made a visit to England, the power from which there was most to fear; and on this occasion as on several others England varied her arrogance with a rather excessive friendliness toward the little republic. She presented to Roberts the *Lark,* a ship with four guns, and sent the President home on a war-vessel. Some years afteryards, when the *Lark* was out of repair, England sent instead a schooner, the *Quail.* Roberts made a second visit to England in 1852 to adjust disputes with traders on the western boundary. He also visited France, and Louis Napoleon, not to be outdone by England, presented to him a vessel, the *Hirondelle,* and also guns and uniforms for his soldiers. In general the administrations of Roberts (we might better say his first series of administrations, for he was later to be called again to office) made a period of constructive statesmanship and solid development, and not a little of the respect that the young republic won was due to the personal influence of its first president. Roberts, however, happened to be very fair, and generally successful though his administrations were, the desire on the part of the people that the highest office in the country be held by a black man seems to have been a determining factor in the choice of his successor. There was an interesting campaign toward the close of his last term. "There were about this time two political parties in the country—the old Republicans and the 'True Liberians,' a party which had been formed in opposition to Roberts's foreign policies. But during the canvass the platform of this new party lost ground; the result was in favor of the Republican candidate." *

Stephen Allen Benson (four terms, 1856-1863) was forced to meet in one way or another almost all of the difficulties that have since played a part in the life of the Liberian people. He had come to the country in 1822 at the age of six and had developed into a practical and efficient merchant. To his high office he brought the same principles of sobriety and good sense that had characterized him in business. On February 28, 1857, the independent colony of Maryland formally became a part of the republic. This action followed immediately upon the struggle with the Greboes in the vicinity of Cape Palmas in which assistance was rendered by the Liberians under Ex-President Roberts. In 1858 an incident that threatened complications with France but that was soon happily closed arose from the fact that a French vessel which sought to carry away some Kru laborers to the West Indies was attacked by these men when they had reason to fear that they might be sold into slavery and not have to work simply along the coast, as they at first supposed. The ship was seized and all but one of the crew, the physician, were killed. Trouble meanwhile continued with British smugglers in the West, and to this whole matter we shall have to give further and special attention. In 1858 and a year or two thereafter the numerous arrivals from America, especially of Congo men captured on the high seas, were such as to present a serious social problem. Flagrant violation by the South of the laws against the slave-

* Karnga, 28.

trade led to the seizure by the United States Government of many Africans. Hundreds of these people were detained at a time at such a port as Key West. The Government then adopted the policy of ordering commanders who seized slave-ships at sea to land the Africans directly upon the coast of Liberia without first bringing them to America, and appropriated $250,000 for the removal and care of those at Key West. The suffering of many of these people is one of the most tragic stories in the history of slavery. To Liberia came at one time 619, at another 867, and within two months as many as 4000. There was very naturally consternation on the part of the people at this sudden immigration, especially as many of the Africans arrived cramped or paralyzed or otherwise ill from the conditions under which they had been forced to travel. President Benson stated the problem to the American Government; the United States sent some money to Liberia, the people of the Republic helped in every way they could, and the whole situation was finally adjusted without any permanently bad effects, though it is well for students to remember just what Liberia had to face at this time. Important toward the close of Benson's terms was the completion of the building of the Liberia College, of which Joseph Jenkin Roberts became the first president.

The administrations of Daniel Bashiel Warner (two terms, 1864-1867) and the earlier one of James Spriggs Payne (1868-1869) were comparatively uneventful. Both of these men were Republicans, but Warner represented something of the shifting of political parties at the time. At first a Republican, he went over to the Whig party devoted to the policy of preserving Liberia from white invasion. Moved to distrust of English merchants, who delighted in defrauding the little republic, he established an important Ports-of-Entry Law in 1865, which it is hardly necessary to say was very unpopular with the foreigners. Commerce was restricted to six ports and a circle six miles in diameter around each port. On account of the Civil War and the hopes that emancipation held out to the Negroes in the United States, immigration from America ceased rapidly; but a company of 346 came from Barbadoes at this time. The Liberian Government assisted these people with $4000, set apart for each man an allotment of twenty-five rather than the customary ten acres; the Colonization Society appropriated $10,000, and after a pleasant voyage of thirty-three days they arrived without the loss of a single life. In the company was a little boy, Arthur Barclay, who was later to be known as the President of the Republic. At the semi-centennial of the American Colonization Society held in Washington in January, 1867, it was shown that the Society and its auxiliaries had been directly responsible for the sending of more than 12,000 persons to Africa. Of these 4541 had been born free, 344 had purchased their freedom, 5957 had been emancipated to go to Africa, and 1227 had been settled by the Maryland Society. In addition, 5722 captured Africans had been sent to Liberia. The need of adequate study of the interior having more and more impressed itself, Benjamin Anderson, an adventurous explorer, assisted with funds by a citizen of New York, in 1869 studied the country for two hundred miles from the coast. He found the land constantly rising, and made his way to Musardu, the chief city of the western Mandingoes. He summed up his work in his *Narrative of a Journey to Musardo* and made another journey of exploration in 1874.

Edward James Roye (1870-October 26, 1871), a Whig whose party was formed out of the elements of the old True Liberian party, attracts attention by reason of a notorious British loan to which further reference must be made. Of the whole amount of £100,000 sums were wasted or misappropriated until it has been estimated that the country really reaped the benefit of little more than a quarter of the whole amount. President Roye added to other difficulties by his seizure of a bank building belonging to an Industrial Society of the St. Paul's River settlements, and by attempting by proclamation to lengthen his term of office. Twice a constitutional amendment for lengthening the presidential term from two years to four had been considered and voted down. Roye contested the last vote, insisted that his term ran to January, 1874, and issued a proclamation forbidding the coming biennial election. He was deposed, his house sacked, some of his cabinet officers tried before a court of impeachment,* and he himself was drowned as he was pursued while attempting to escape to a British ship in the harbor. A committee of three was appointed to govern the country until a new election could be held; and in this hour of storm and stress the people turned once more to the guidance of their old leader, Joseph J. Roberts (two terms, 1872-1875). His efforts were mainly devoted to restoring order and confidence, though there was a new war with the Greboes to be waged.† He was succeeded by another trusted leader, James S. Payne (1876-1877), whose second administration was as devoid as the first of striking incident. In fact, the whole generation succeeding the loan of 1871 was a period of depression. The country not only suffered financially, but faith in it was shaken both at home and abroad. Coffee grown in Liberia fell as that produced at Brazil grew in favor, the farmer witnessing a drop in value from 24 to 4 cents a pound. Farms were abandoned, immigration from the United States ceased, and the country entered upon a period of stagnation from which it has not yet fully recovered.

Within just a few years after 1871, however, conditions in the United States led to an interesting revival of the whole idea of colonization, and to noteworthy effort on the part of the Negroes themselves to better their condition. The withdrawal of Federal troops from the South, and all the evils of the aftermath of reconstruction, led to such a terrorizing of the Negroes and such a denial of civil rights that there set in the movement that culminated in the great exodus from the South in 1879. The movement extended all the way from North Carolina to Louisiana and Arkansas. Insofar as it led to migration to Kansas and other states in the West, it belongs to American history. However, there was also interest in going to Africa. Applications by the thousands poured in upon the American Colonization Society, and one organization in Arkansas sent hundreds of its members to seek the

* But not Hilary R. W. Johnson, the efficient Secretary of State, later President.

† President Roberts died February 21, 1876, barely two months after giving up office. He was caught in the rain while attending a funeral, took a severe chill, and was not able to recover.

help of the New York State Colonization Society. In all such endeavor Negro Baptists and Methodists joined hands, and especially prominent was Bishop H. M. Turner, of the African Methodist Episcopal Church. By 1877 there was organized in South Carolina the Liberian Exodus and Joint Stock Company; in North Carolina there was the Freedmen's Emigration Aid Society; and there were similar organizations in other states. The South Carolina organization had the three-fold purpose of emigration, missionary activity, and commercial enterprise, and to these ends it purchased a vessel, the *Azor*, at a cost of $7000. The white people of Charleston unfortunately embarrassed the enterprise in every possible way, among other things insisting when the *Azor* was ready to sail that it was not seaworthy and needed a new copper bottom (to cost $2000). The vessel at length made one or two trips, however, on one voyage carrying as many as 274 emigrants. It was then stolen and sold in Liverpool, and one gets an interesting sidelight on Southern conditions in the period when he knows that even the United States Circuit Court in South Carolina refused to entertain the suit brought by the Negroes.

In the administration of Anthony W. Gardiner (three terms, 1878-1883) difficulties with England and Germany reached a crisis. Territory in the northwest was seized; the British made a formal show of force at Monrovia; and the looting of a German vessel along the Kru Coast and personal indignities inflicted by the natives upon the shipwrecked Germans, led to the bombardment of Nana Kru by a German warship and the presentation at Monrovia of a claim for damages, payment of which was forced by the threat of the bombardment of the capital. To the Liberian people the outlook was seldom darker than in this period of calamities. President Gardiner, very ill, resigned office in January of his last year of service, being succeeded by the vice-president, Alfred F. Russell. More and more was pressure brought to bear upon Liberian officials for the granting of monopolies and concessions, especially to Englishmen; and in his message of 1883 President Russell said, "Recent events admonish us as to the serious responsibility of claims held against us by foreigners, and we cannot tell what complications may arise." In the midst of all this, however, Russell did not forget the natives and the need of guarding them against liquor and exploitation.

Hilary Richard Wright Johnson (four terms, 1884-1891), the next president, was a son of the distinguished Elijah Johnson and the first man born in Liberia who had risen to the highest place in the republic. Whigs and Republicans united in his election. Much of his time had necessarily to be given to complications arising from the loan of 1871; but the western boundary was adjusted (with great loss) with Great Britain at the Mano River, though new difficulties arose with the French, who were pressing their claim to territory as far as the Cavalla River. In the course of the last term of President Johnson there was an interesting grant (by act approved January 21, 1890) to F. F. Whittekin, of Pennsylvania, of the right to "construct, maintain, and operate a system of railroads, telegraph and telephone lines." Whittekin bought up in England stock to the value of half a million dollars, but died on the way to Liberia to fulfil his contract. His nephew, F. F. Whittekin, asked for an extension of time, which was granted, but after a while the whole project languished.*

Joseph James Cheeseman (1892-November 15, 1896) was a Whig. He conducted what was known as the third Grebo War and labored especially for a sound currency. He was a man of unusual ability and his devotion to his task undoubtedly contributed toward his death in office near the middle of his third term. As up to this time there had been no internal improvement and little agricultural or industrial development in the country, O. F. Cook, the agent of the New York State Colonization Society, in 1894 signified to the legislature a desire to establish a station where experiments could be made as to the best means of introducing, receiving, and propagating beasts of burden, commercial plants, etc. His request was approved and one thousand acres of land granted for the purpose by act of January 20, 1894. Results, however, were neither permanent nor far-reaching. In fact, by the close of the century immigration had practically ceased and the activi-

* See *Liberia*, Bulletin No. 5, November, 1894.

ties of the American Colonization Society had also ceased, many of the state organizations having gone out of existence. In 1893 Julius C. Stevens, of Goldsboro, N. C., went to Liberia and served for a nominal salary as agent of the American Colonization Society, becoming also a teacher in the Liberia College and in time Commissioner of Education, in connection with which post he edited his *Liberian School Reader;* but he died in 1903.*

William D. Coleman as vice-president finished the incomplete term of President Cheeseman (to the end of 1897) and later was elected for two terms in his own right. In the course of his last administration, however, his interior policy became very unpopular, as he was thought to be harsh in his dealing with the natives, and he resigned in December, 1900. As there was at the time no vice-president, he was succeeded by the Secretary of State, Garretson W. Gibson, a man of scholarly attainments, who was afterwards elected for a whole term (1902-1903). The feature of this term was the discussion that arose over the proposal to grant a concession to an English concern known as the West African Gold Concessions, Ltd. This offered to the legislators a bonus of £1500, and for this bribe it asked for the sole right to prospect for and obtain gold, precious stones, and all other minerals over more than half of Liberia. Specifically it asked for the right to acquire freehold land and to take up leases for eighty years, in blocks of from ten to a thousand acres; to import all mining machinery and all other things necessary free of duty; to establish banks in connection with the mining enterprises, these to have the power to issue notes; to construct telegraphs and telephones; to organize auxiliary syndicates; and to establish its own police. It would seem that English impudence could hardly go further, though time was to prove that there were still other things to be borne. The proposal was indignantly rejected.

---

* Interest in Liberia by no means completely died. Contributions for education were sometimes made by the representative organizations, and individual students came to America from time to time. When, however, the important commission representing the Government came to America in 1908, the public was slightly startled as having heard from something half-forgotten.

Arthur Barclay (1904-1911) had already served in three cabinet positions before coming to the presidency; he had also been a professor in the Liberia College and for some years had been known as the leader of the bar in Monrovia. It was near the close of his second term that the president's term of office was lengthened from two to four years, and he was the first incumbent to serve for the longer period. In his first inaugural address President Barclay emphasized the need of developing the resources of the hinterland and of attaching the native tribes to the interests of the state. In his foreign policy he was generally enlightened and broad-minded, but he had to deal with the arrogance of England. In 1906 a new British loan was negotiated. This also was for £100,000, more than two-thirds of which amount was to be turned over to the Liberian Development Company, an English scheme for the development of the interior. The Company was to work in coöperation with the Liberian Government, and as security for the loan British officials were to have charge of the customs revenue, the chief inspector acting as financial adviser to the Republic. It afterwards developed that the Company never had any resources except those it had raised on the credit of the Republic, and the country was forced to realize that it had been cheated a second time. Meanwhile the English officials who, on various pretexts of reform, had taken charge of the barracks and the customs in Monrovia, were carrying things with a high hand. The Liberian force appeared with English insignia on the uniforms, and in various other ways the commander sought to overawe the populace. At the climax of the difficulties, on February 13, 1909, a British warship *happened* to appear in the waters of Monrovia, and a calamity was averted only by the skillful diplomacy of the Liberians. Already, however, in 1908, Liberia had sent a special commission to ask the aid of the United States. This consisted of Garretson W. Gibson, former president; J. J. Dossen, vice-president at the time, and Charles B. Dunbar. The commission was received by President Roosevelt and by Secretary Taft just before the latter was nominated for the presidency. On May 8, 1909, a return commission consisting of Roland P. Falkner, George Sale, and Emmett J. Scott, arrived in Monrovia. The work of this commission must receive further and special attention.

President Barclay was succeeded by Daniel Edward Howard (two long terms, 1912-1919), who at his inauguration began the policy of giving prominence to the native chiefs. The feature of President Howard's administrations was of course Liberia's connection with the Great War in Europe. War against Germany having been declared, on the morning of April 10, 1918, a submarine came to Monrovia and demanded that the French wireless station be torn down. The request being refused, the town was bombarded. The excitement of the day was such as has never been duplicated in the history of Liberia. In one house two young girls were instantly killed and an elderly woman and a little boy fatally wounded; but except in this one home the actual damage was comparatively slight, though there might have been more if a passing British steamer had not put the submarine to flight. Suffering of another and more far-reaching sort was that due to the economic situation. The comparative scarcity of food in the world and the profiteering of foreign merchants in Liberia by the summer of 1919 brought about a condition that threatened starvation; nor was the situation better early in 1920, when butter retailed at $1.25 a pound, sugar at 72 cents a pound, and oil at $1.00 a gallon.

President Howard was succeeded by Charles Dunbar Burgess King, who as president-elect had visited Europe and America, and who was inaugurated January 5, 1920. His address on this occasion was a comprehensive presentation of the needs of Liberia, especially along the lines of agriculture and education. He made a plea also for an enlightened native policy. Said he: "We cannot afford to destroy the native institutions of the country. Our true mission lies not in the building here in Africa of a Negro state based solely on Western ideas, but rather a Negro nationality indigenous to the soil, having its foundation rooted in the institutions of Africa and purified by Western thought and development."

3. International Relations

Our study of the history of Liberia has suggested two or three matters that call for special attention. Of prime importance is the country's connection with world politics. Any consideration of Liberia's international relations falls into three divisions: first, that of titles to land; second, that of foreign loans; and third, that of so-called internal reform.

In the very early years of the colony the raids of slave-traders gave some excuse for the first aggression on the part of a European power. "Driven from the Pongo Regions northwest of Sierra Leone, Pedro Blanco settled in the Gallinhas territory northwest of the Liberian frontier, and established elaborate headquarters for his mammoth slave-trading operations in West Africa, with slave-trading sub-stations at Cape Mount, St. Paul River, Bassa, and at other points of the Liberian coast, employing numerous police, watchers, spies, and servants. To obtain jurisdiction the colony of Liberia began to purchase from the lords of the soil as early as 1824 the lands of the St. Paul Basin and the Grain Coast from the Mafa River on the west to the Grand Sesters River on the east; so that by 1845, twenty-four years after the establishment of the colony, Liberia with the aid of Great Britain had destroyed throughout these regions the baneful traffic in slaves and the slave barracoons, and had driven the slave-trading leaders from the Liberian coast." * The trade continued to flourish, however, in the Gallinhas territory, and in course of time, as we have seen, the colony had also to reckon with British merchants in this section, the Declaration of Independence in 1847 being very largely a result of the defiance of Liberian revenue-laws by Englishmen. While President Roberts was in England not long after his inauguration, Lord Ashley, moved by motives of philanthropy, undertook to raise £2000 with which he (Roberts) might purchase the Gallinhas territory; and by 1856 Roberts had secured the title and deeds to all of this territory from the Mafa River to Sherbro Island. The whole transaction was thoroughly honorable,

* Ellis in *Journal of Race Development*, January, 1911.

Roberts informed England of his acquisition, and his right
to the territory was not then called in question. Trouble, however, developed out of the attitude of John M. Harris, a
British merchant, and in 1862, while President Benson was
in England, he was officially informed that the right of Liberia
was recognized *only* to the land "east of Turner's Peninsula
to the River San Pedro." Harris now worked up a native
war against the Vais; the Liberians defended themselves; and
in the end the British Government demanded £8878.9.3 as
damages for losses sustained by Harris, and arbitrarily extended its territory from Sherbro Island to Cape Mount. In
the course of the discussion claims mounted up to £18,000.
Great Britain promised to submit this boundary question to
the arbitration of the United States, but when the time arrived at the meeting of one of the commissions in Sierra Leone
she firmly declined to do so. After this, whenever she was
ready to take more land she made a plausible pretext and was
ready to back up her demands with force. On March 20,
1882, four British men-of-war came to Monrovia and Sir
A. E. Havelock, Governor of Sierra Leone, came ashore;
and President Gardiner was forced to submit to an agreement by which, in exchange for £4750 and the abandonment
of all further claims, the Liberian Government gave up all
right to the Gallinhas territory from Sherbro Island to the
Mafa River. This agreement was repudiated by the Liberian
Senate, but when Havelock was so informed he replied, "Her
Majesty's Government can not in any case recognize any
rights on the part of Liberia to any portions of the territories
in dispute." Liberia now issued a protest to other great
powers; but this was without avail, even the United States
counseling acquiescence, though through the offices of
America the agreement was slightly modified and the boundary fixed at the Mano River. Trouble next arose on the
east. In 1846 the Maryland Colonization Society purchased
the lands of the Ivory Coast east of Cape Palmas as far as the
San Pedro River. These lands were formally transferred to
Liberia in 1857, and remained in the undisputed possession
of the Republic for forty years. France now, not to be outdone by England, on the pretext of title deeds obtained by

French naval commanders who visited the coast in 1890, in 1891 put forth a claim not only to the Ivory Coast, but to land as far away as Grand Bassa and Cape Mount. The next year, under threat of force, she compelled Liberia to accept a treaty which, for 25,000 francs and the relinquishment of all other claims, permitted her to take all the territory east of the Cavalla River. In 1904 Great Britain asked permission to advance her troops into Liberian territory to suppress a native war threatening her interests. She occupied at this time what is known as the Kaure-Lahun section, which is very fertile and of easy access to the Sierra Leone railway. This land she never gave up; instead she offered Liberia £6000 or some poorer land for it. France after 1892 made no endeavor to delimit her boundary, and, roused by the action of Great Britain, she made great advances in the hinterland, claiming tracts of Maryland and Sino; and now France and England each threatened to take more land if the other was not stopped. President Barclay visited both countries; but by a treaty of 1907 his commission was forced to permit France to occupy all the territory seized by force; and as soon as this agreement was reached France began to move on to other land in the basin of the St. Paul's and St. John's rivers. This is all then simply one more story of the oppression of the weak by the strong. For eighty years England has not ceased to intermeddle in Liberian affairs, cajoling or browbeating as at the moment seemed advisable; and France has been only less bad. Certainly no country on earth now has better reason than Liberia to know that "they should get who have the power, and they should keep who can."

The international loans and the attempts at reform must be considered together. In 1871, at the rate of 7 per cent, there was authorized a British loan of £100,000. *For their services* the British negotiators retained £30,000, and £20,000 more was deducted as the interest for three years. President Roye ordered Mr. Chinery, a British subject and the Liberian consul general in London, to supply the Liberian Secretary of Treasury with goods and merchandise to the value of £10,000; and other sums were misappropriated until the country itself actually received the benefit of not more than £27,000, if so much. This whole unfortunate matter was an embarrassment to Liberia for years; but in 1899 the Republic assumed responsibility for £80,000, the interest being made a first charge on the customs revenue. In 1906, not yet having learned the lesson of "Cavete Graecos dona ferentes," and moved by the representations of Sir Harry H. Johnston, the country negotiated a new loan of £100,000. £30,000 of this amount was to satisfy pressing obligations; but the greater portion was to be turned over to the Liberian Development Company, a great scheme by which the Government and the company were to work hand in hand for the development of the country. As security for the loan, British officials were to have charge of the customs revenue, the chief inspector acting as financial adviser to the Republic. When the Company had made a road of fifteen miles in one district and made one or two other slight improvements, it represented to the Liberian Government that its funds were exhausted. When President Barclay asked for an accounting the managing director expressed surprise that such a demand should be made upon him. The Liberian people were chagrined, and at length they realized that they had been cheated a second time, with all the bitter experiences of the past to guide them. Meanwhile the English representatives in the country were demanding that the judiciary be reformed, that the frontier force be under British officers, and that Inspector Lamont as financial adviser have a seat in the Liberian cabinet and a veto power over all expenditures; and the independence of the country was threatened if these demands were not complied with. Meanwhile also the construction of barracks went forward under Major Cadell, a British officer, and the organization of the frontier force was begun. Not less than a third of this force was brought from Sierra Leone, and the whole Cadell fitted out with suits and caps stamped with the emblems of His Britannic Majesty's service. He also persuaded the Monrovia city government to let him act without compensation as chief of police, and he likewise became street commissioner, tax collector, and city treasurer. The Liberian people naturally objected to the usurping of all these prerogatives, but Cadell refused to resign and presented a large bill for his services. He also threatened violence to the President if his demands were not met within twenty-four hours. Then it was that the British warship, the *Mutiny*, suddenly appeared at Monrovia (February 12, 1909). Happily the Liberians rose to the emergency. They requested that any British soldiers at the barracks be withdrawn in order that they might be free to deal with the insurrectionary movement said to be there on the part of Liberian soldiers; and thus tactfully they brought about the withdrawal of Major Cadell.

By this time, however, the Liberian commission to the United States had done its work, and just three months after Cadell's retirement the return American commission came. After studying the situation it made the following recommendations: That the United States extend its aid to Liberia in the prompt settlement of pending boundary disputes; that the United States enable Liberia to refund its debt by assuming as a guarantee for the payment of obligations under such arrangement the control and collection of the Liberian customs; that the United States lend its assistance to the Liberian Government in the reform of its internal finances; that the United States lend its aid to Liberia in organizing and drilling an adequate constabulary or frontier police force; that the United States establish and maintain a research station at Liberia; and that the United States reopen the question of establishing a coaling-station in Liberia. Under the fourth of these recommendations Major (now Colonel) Charles Young went to Liberia, where from time to time since he has rendered most efficient service. Arrangements were also made for a new loan, one of $1,700,000, which was to be floated by banking institutions in the United States, Germany, France, and England; and in 1912 an American General Receiver of Customs and Financial Adviser to the Republic of Liberia (with an assistant from each of the other three countries mentioned) opened his office in Monrovia. It will be observed that a complicated and expensive receivership was imposed on the Liberian people when an arrangement much more simple would have served. The loan of $1,700,000 soon proving inadequate for any large development of the country, negotiations were begun in 1918 for a new loan, one of

$5,000,000. Among the things proposed were improvements on the harbor of Monrovia, some good roads through the country, a hospital, and the broadening of the work of education. About the loan two facts were outstanding: first, any money to be spent would be spent wholly under American and not under Liberian auspices; and, second, to the Liberians acceptance of the terms suggested meant practically a surrender of their sovereignty, as American appointees were to be in most of the important positions in the country, at the same time that upon themselves would fall the ultimate burden of the interest of the loan. By the spring of 1920 (in Liberia, the commencement of the rainy season) it was interesting to note that although the necessary measures of approval had not yet been passed by the Liberian Congress, perhaps as many as fifteen American officials had come out to the country to begin work in education, engineering, and sanitation. Just a little later in the year President King called an extra session of the legislature to consider amendments. While it was in session a cablegram from the United States was received saying that no amendments to the plan would be accepted and that it must be accepted as submitted, "or the friendly interest which has heretofore existed would become lessened." The Liberians were not frightened, however, and stood firm. Meanwhile a new presidential election took place in the United States; there was to be a radical change in the government; and the Liberians were disposed to try further to see if some changes could not be made in the proposed arrangements. Most watchfully from month to month, let it be remembered, England and France were waiting; and in any case it could easily be seen that as the Republic approached its centennial it was face to face with political problems of the very first magnitude.*

4. *Economic and Social Conditions*

From what has been said, it is evident that there is still much to be done in Liberia along economic lines. There has

* Early in 1921 President King headed a new commission to the United States to take up the whole matter of Liberia with the incoming Republican administration.

been some beginning in coöperative effort; thus the Bassa Trading Association is an organization for mutual betterment of perhaps as many as fifty responsible merchants and farmers. The country has as yet (1921), however, no railroads, no street cars, no public schools, and no genuine newspapers; nor are there any manufacturing or other enterprises for the employment of young men on a large scale. The most promising youth accordingly look too largely to an outlet in politics; some come to America to be educated and not always do they return. A few become clerks in the stores, and a very few assistants in the customs offices. There is some excellent agriculture in the interior, but as yet no means of getting produce to market on a large scale. In 1919 the total customs revenue at Monrovia, the largest port, amounted to $196,-913.21. For the whole country the figure has recently been just about half a million dollars a year. Much of this amount goes to the maintenance of the frontier force. Within the last few years also the annual income for the city of Monrovia— for the payment of the mayor, the police, and all other city officers—has averaged $6000.

In any consideration of social conditions the first question of all of course is that of the character of the people themselves. Unfortunately Liberia was begun with faulty ideals of life and work. The early settlers, frequently only recently out of bondage, too often felt that in a state of freedom they did not have to work, and accordingly they imitated the habits of the old master class of the South. The real burden of life then fell upon the native. There is still considerable feeling between the native and the Americo-Liberian; but more and more the wisest men of the country realize that the good of one is the good of all, and they are endeavoring to make the native chiefs work for the common welfare. From time to time the people of Liberia have given to visitors an impression of arrogance, and perhaps no one thing had led to more unfriendly criticism of this country than this. The fact is that the Liberians, knowing that their country has various shortcomings according to Western standards, are quick to assume the defensive, and one method of protecting themselves is by erecting a barrier of dignity and reserve. One has only to go beyond this, however, to find the real heartbeat of the people. The comparative isolation of the Republic moreover, and the general stress of living conditions have together given to the everyday life an undue seriousness of tone, with a rather excessive emphasis on the church, on politics, and on secret societies. In such an atmosphere boys and girls too soon became mature, and for them especially one might wish to see a little more wholesome outdoor amusement. In school or college catalogues one still sees much of jurisprudence and moral philosophy, but little of physics or biology. Interestingly enough, this whole system of education and life has not been without some elements of very genuine culture. Literature has been mainly in the diction of Shakespeare and Milton; but Shakespeare and Milton, though not of the twentieth century, are still good models, and because the officials have had to compose many state documents and deliver many formal addresses, there has been developed in the country a tradition of good English speech. A service in any one of the representative churches is dignified and impressive.

The churches and schools of Liberia have been most largely in the hands of the Methodists and the Episcopalians, though the Baptists, the Presbyterians, and the Lutherans are well represented. The Lutherans have penetrated to a point in the interior beyond that attained by any other denomination. The Episcopalians have excelled others, even the Methodists, by having more constant and efficient oversight of their work. The Episcopalians have in Liberia a little more than 40 schools, nearly half of these being boarding-schools, with a total attendance of 2000. The Methodists have slightly more than 30 schools, with 2500 pupils. The Lutherans in their five mission stations have 20 American workers and 300 pupils. While it seems from these figures that the number of those reached is small in proportion to the outlay, it must be remembered that a mission school becomes a center from which influence radiates in all directions.

While the enterprise of the denominational institutions can not be doubted, it may well be asked if, in so largely relieving the people of the burden of the education of their children, they are not unduly cultivating a spirit of dependence rather than of self-help. Something of this point of view was emphasized by the Secretary of Public Instruction, Mr. Walter F. Walker, in an address, "Liberia and Her Educational Problems," delivered in Chicago in 1916. Said he of the day schools maintained by the churches: "These day schools did invaluable service in the days of the Colony and Commonwealth, and, indeed, in the early days of the Republic; but to their continuation must undoubtedly be ascribed the tardy recognition of the government and people of the fact that no agency for the education of the masses is as effective as the public school. . . . There is not one public school building owned by the government or by any city or township."

It might further be said that just now in Liberia there is no institution that is primarily doing college work. Two schools in Monrovia, however, call for special remark. The College of West Africa, formerly Monrovia Seminary, was founded by the Methodist Church in 1839. The institution does elementary and lower high school work, though some years ago it placed a little more emphasis on college work than it has been able to do within recent years. It was of this college that the late Bishop A. P. Camphor served so ably as president for twelve years. Within recent years it has recognized the importance of industrial work and has had in all departments an average annual enrollment of 300. Not quite so prominent within the last few years, but with more tradition and theoretically at the head of the educational system of the Republic is the Liberia College. In 1848 Simon Greenleaf of Boston, received from John Payne, a missionary at Cape Palmas, a request for his assistance in building a theological school. Out of this suggestion grew the Board of Trustees of Donations for Education in Liberia incorporated in Massachusetts in March, 1850. The next year the Liberia legislature incorporated the Liberia College, it being understood that the institution would emphasize academic as well as theological subjects. In 1857 Ex-President J. J. Roberts was elected president; he superintended the erection of a large building; and in 1862 the college was opened for work. Since then it has had a very uneven existence, sometimes enrolling, aside from its preparatory department, twenty or thirty college students, then again having no college students at all. Within the last few years, as the old building was completely out of repair, the school has had to seek temporary quarters. It is too vital to the country to be allowed to languish, however, and it is to be hoped that it may soon be well started upon a new career of usefulness. In the course of its history the Liberia College has had connected with it some very distinguished men. Famous as teacher and lecturer, and president from 1881 to 1885, was Edward Wilmot Blyden, generally regarded as the foremost scholar that Western Africa has given to the world. Closely associated with him in the early years, and well known in America as in Africa, was Alexander Crummell, who brought to his teaching the richness of English university training. A trustee for a number of years was Samuel David Ferguson, of the Protestant Episcopal Church, who served with great dignity and resource as missionary bishop of the country from 1884 until his death in 1916. A new president of the college, Rev. Nathaniel H. B. Cassell, was elected in 1918, and it is expected that under his efficient direction the school will go forward to still greater years of service.

Important in connection with the study of the social conditions in Liberia is that of health and living conditions. One who lives in America and knows that Africa is a land of unbounded riches can hardly understand the extent to which the West Coast has been exploited, or the suffering that is there just now. The distress is most acute in the English colonies, and as Liberia is so close to Sierra Leone and the Gold Coast, much of the same situation prevails there. In Monrovia the only bank is the branch of the Bank of British West Africa. In the branches of this great institution all along the coast, as a result of the war, gold disappeared, silver became very scarce, and the common form of currency became paper notes, issued in denominations as low as one and two shillings. These the natives have refused to accept. They go even further: rather than bring their produce to the towns and receive paper for it they will not come at all. In Monrovia an effort was made to introduce the British West African paper currency, and while this failed, more and more the merchants insisted on being paid in silver, nor in an ordinary purchase would silver be given in change on an English ten-shilling note. Prices accordingly became exorbitant; children were not properly nourished and the infant mortality grew to astonishing proportions. Nor were conditions made better by the lack of sanitation and by the prevalence of disease. Happily relief for these conditions—for some of them at least—seems to be in sight, and it is expected that before very long a hospital will be erected in Monrovia.

One or two reflections suggest themselves. It has been said that the circumstances under which Liberia was founded led to a despising of industrial effort. The country is now quite awake, however, to the advantages of industrial and agricultural enterprise. A matter of supreme importance is that of the relation of the Americo-Liberian to the native; this will work itself out, for the native is the country's chief asset for the future. In general the Republic needs a few visible evidences of twentieth century standards of progress; two or three high schools and hospitals built on the American plan would work wonders. Finally let it not be forgotten that upon the American Negro rests the obligation to do whatever he can to help to develop the country. If he will but firmly clasp hands with his brother across the sea, a new day will dawn for American Negro and Liberian alike.

CHAPTER X

1. *Current Tendencies*

It is evident from what has been said already that the idea of the Negro current about 1830 in the United States was not very exalted. It was seriously questioned if he was really a human being, and doctors of divinity learnedly expounded the "Cursed be Canaan" passage as applying to him. A prominent physician of Mobile * gave it as his opinion that "the brain of the Negro, when compared with the Caucasian, is smaller by a tenth . . . and the intellect is wanting in the same proportion," and finally asserted that Negroes could not live in the North because "a cold climate so freezes their brains as to make them insane." About mulattoes, like many others, he stretched his imagination marvelously. They were incapable of undergoing fatigue; the women were very delicate and subject to all sorts of diseases, and they did not beget children as readily as either black women or white women. In fact, said Nott, between the ages of twenty-five and forty mulattoes died ten times as fast as either white or black people; between forty and fifty-five fifty times as fast, and between fifty-five and seventy one hundred times as fast.

To such opinions was now added one of the greatest misfortunes that have befallen the Negro race in its entire history in America—burlesque on the stage. When in 1696 Thomas Southerne adapted *Oroonoko* from the novel of Mrs. Aphra Behn and presented in London the story of the African prince who was stolen from his native Angola, no one saw any reason why the Negro should not be a subject for

* See "Two Lectures on the Natural History of the Caucasian and Negro Races. By Josiah C. Nott, M.D., Mobile, 1844."

serious treatment on the stage, and the play was a great success, lasting for decades. In 1768, however, was presented at Drury Lane a comic opera, *The Padlock,* and a very prominent character was Mungo, the slave of a West Indian planter, who got drunk in the second act and was profane throughout the performance. In the course of the evening Mungo entertained the audience with such lines as the following:

> Dear heart, what a terrible life I am led!
> A dog has a better, that's sheltered and fed.
>> Night and day 'tis the same;
>> My pain is deir game:
> Me wish to de Lord me was dead!
>> Whate'er's to be done,
>> Poor black must run.
>> Mungo here, Mungo dere,
>> Mungo everywhere:
>> Above and below,
>> Sirrah, come; sirrah, go;
>> Do so, and do so,
>>> Oh! oh!
> Me wish to de Lord me was dead!

The depreciation of the race that Mungo started continued, and when in 1781 *Robinson Crusoe* was given as a pantomime at Drury Lane, Friday was represented as a Negro. The exact origins of Negro minstrelsy are not altogether clear; there have been many claimants, and it is interesting to note in passing that there was an "African Company" playing in New York in the early twenties, though this was probably nothing more than a small group of amateurs. Whatever may have been the beginning, it was Thomas D. Rice who brought the form to genuine popularity. In Louisville in the summer of 1828, looking from one of the back windows of a theater, he was attracted by an old and decrepit slave who did odd jobs about a livery stable. The slave's master was named Crow and he called himself Jim Crow. His right shoulder was drawn up high and his left leg was stiff at the knee, but he took his deformity lightly, singing as he worked. He had one favorite tune to which he had fitted words of his own, and at the end of each verse he made a ludicrous step which in time came to be known as "rocking the heel." His refrain consisted of the words:

> Wheel about, turn about,
>   Do jis so,
> An' ebery time I wheel about
>   I jump Jim Crow.

Rice, who was a clever and versatile performer, caught the air, made up like the Negro, and in the course of the next season introduced Jim Crow and his step to the stage, and so successful was he in his performance that on his first night in the part he was encored twenty times.* Rice had many imitators among the white comedians of the country, some of whom indeed claimed priority in opening up the new field, and along with their burlesque these men actually touched upon the possibilities of plaintive Negro melodies, which they of course capitalized. In New York late in 1842 four men— "Dan" Emmett, Frank Brower, "Billy" Whitlock, and "Dick" Pelham—practiced together with fiddle and banjo, "bones" and tambourine, and thus was born the first company, the "Virginia Minstrels," which made its formal debut in New York February 17, 1843. Its members produced in connection with their work all sorts of popular songs, one of Emmett's being "Dixie," which, introduced by Mrs. John Wood in a burlesque in New Orleans at the outbreak of the Civil War, leaped into popularity and became the war-song of the Confederacy. Companies multipled apace. "Christy's Minstrels" claimed priority to the company already mentioned, but did not actually enter upon its New York career until 1846. "Bryant's Minstrels" and Buckley's "New Orleans Serenaders" were only two others of the most popular aggregations featuring and burlesquing the Negro. In a social history of the Negro in America, however, it is important to observe in passing that already, even in burlesque, the Negro element was beginning to enthrall the popular mind. About the same time as minstrelsy also developed the habit of belittling the race by making the name of

* See Laurence Hutton: "The Negro on the Stage," in *Harper's Magazine*, 79:137 (June, 1889), referring to article by Edmon S. Conner in *New York Times*, June 5, 1881.

some prominent and worthy Negro a term of contempt; thus "cuffy" (corrupted from Paul Cuffe) now came into widespread use.

This was not all. It was now that the sinister crime of lynching raised its head in defiance of all law. At first used as a form of punishment for outlaws and gamblers, it soon came to be applied especially to Negroes. One was burned alive near Greenville, S. C., in 1825; in May, 1835, two were burned near Mobile for the murder of two children; and for the years between 1823 and 1860 not less than fifty-six cases of the lynching of Negroes have been ascertained, though no one will ever know how many lost their lives without leaving any record. Certainly more men were executed illegally than legally; thus of forty-six recorded murders by Negroes of owners or overseers between 1850 and 1860 twenty resulted in legal execution and twenty-six in lynching. Violent crimes against white women were not relatively any more numerous than now; but those that occurred or were attempted received swift punishment; thus of seventeen cases of rape in the ten years last mentioned Negroes were legally executed in five and lynched in twelve.*

Extraordinary attention was attracted by the burning in St. Louis in 1835 of a man named McIntosh, who had killed an officer who was trying to arrest him.† This event came in the midst of a period of great agitation, and it was for denouncing this lynching that Elijah P. Lovejoy had his printing-office destroyed in St. Louis and was forced to remove to Alton, Ill., where his press was three times destroyed and where he finally met death at the hands of a mob while trying to protect his property November 7, 1837. Judge Lawless defended the lynching and even William Ellery Channing took a compromising view. Abraham Lincoln, however, then a very young man, in an address on "The Perpetuation of Our Political Institutions" at Springfield, January 27, 1837, said: "Accounts of outrages committed by mobs form the everyday news of the times. They have pervaded the country from New Eng-

---

* See Hart: *Slavery and Abolition*, 11 and 117, citing Cutler: *Lynch Law*, 98-100 and 126-128.
† Cutler: *Lynch Law*, 109, citing Niles's *Register*, June 4, 1836.

land to Louisiana; they are neither peculiar to the eternal snows of the former nor the burning suns of the latter; they are not the creatures of climate, neither are they confined to the slaveholding or the nonslaveholding states. . . . Turn to that horror-striking scene at St. Louis. A single victim only was sacrificed there. This story is very short, and is perhaps the most highly tragic of anything that has ever been witnessed in real life. A mulatto man by the name of McIntosh was seized in the street, dragged to the suburbs of the city, chained to a tree, and actually burned to death; and all within a single hour from the time he had been a free man attending to his own business and at peace with the world. . . . Such are the effects of mob law, and such are the scenes becoming more and more frequent in this land so lately famed for love of law and order, and the stories of which have even now grown too familiar to attract anything more than an idle remark."

All the while flagrant crimes were committed against Negro women and girls, and free men in the border states were constantly being dragged into slavery by kidnapers. Two typical cases will serve for illustration. George Jones, a respectable man of New York, was in 1836 arrested on Broadway on the pretext that he had committed assault and battery. He refused to go with his captors, for he knew that he had done nothing to warrant such a charge; but he finally yielded on the assurance of his employer that everything possible would be done for him. He was placed in the Bridewell and a few minutes afterwards taken before a magistrate, to whose satisfaction he was proved to be a slave. Thus, in less than two hours after his arrest he was hurried away by the kidnapers, whose word had been accepted as sufficient evidence, and he had not been permitted to secure a single friendly witness. Solomon Northrup, who afterwards wrote an account of his experiences, was a free man who lived in Saratoga and made his living by working about the hotels, where in the evenings he often played the violin at parties. One day two men, supposedly managers of a traveling circus company, met him and offered him good pay if he would go with them as a violinist to Washington. He consented, and some mornings afterwards awoke to find himself in a slave pen in the capital. How he got there was ever a mystery to him, but evidently he had been drugged. He was taken South and sold to a hard master, with whom he remained twelve years before he was able to effect his release.* In the South any free Negro who entertained a runaway might himself become a slave; thus in South Carolina in 1827 a free woman with her three children suffered this penalty because she gave succor to two homeless and fugitive children six and nine years old.

Day by day, moreover, from the capital of the nation went on the internal slave-trade. "When by one means and another a dealer had gathered twenty or more likely young Negro men and girls, he would bring them forth from their cells; would huddle the women and young children into a cart or wagon; would handcuff the men in pairs, the right hand of one to the left hand of another; make the handcuffs fast to a long chain which passed between each pair of slaves, and would start his procession southward." † It is not strange that several of the unfortunate people committed suicide. One distracted mother, about to be separated from her loved ones, dumbfounded the nation by hurling herself from the window of a prison in the capital on the Sabbath day and dying in the street below.

Meanwhile even in the free states the disabilities of the Negro continued. In general he was denied the elective franchise, the right of petition, the right to enter public conveyances or places of amusement, and he was driven into a status of contempt by being shut out from the army and the militia. He had to face all sorts of impediments in getting education or in pursuing honest industry; he had nothing whatever to do with the administration of justice; and generally he was subject to insult and outrage.

One might have supposed that on all this proscription and denial of the ordinary rights of human beings the Christian Church would have taken a positive stand. Unfortunately, as so often happens, it was on the side of property and vested interest rather than on that of the oppressed. We have already

* McDougall: *Fugitive Slaves*, 36-37.
† McMaster, V, 219-220.

seen that Southern divines held slaves and countenanced the system; and by 1840 James G. Birney had abundant material for his indictment, "The American Churches the Bulwarks of American Slavery." He showed among other things that while in 1780 the Methodist Episcopal Church had opposed slavery and in 1784 had given a slaveholder one month to repent or withdraw from its conferences, by 1836 it had so drifted away from its original position as to disclaim "any right, wish, or intention to interfere in the civil and political relation between master and slave, as it existed in the slaveholding states of the union." Meanwhile in the churches of the North there was the most insulting discrimination; in the Baptist Church in Hartford the pews for Negroes were boarded up in front, and in Stonington, Conn., the floor was cut out of a Negro's pew by order of the church authorities. In Boston, in a church that did not welcome and that made little provision for Negroes, a consecrated deacon invited into his own pew some Negro people, whereupon he lost the right to hold a pew in his church. He decided that there should be some place where there might be more freedom of thought and genuine Christianity, he brought others into the plan, and the effort that he put forth resulted in what has since become the Tremont Temple Baptist Church.

Into all this proscription, burlesque, and crime, and denial of the fundamental principles of Christianity, suddenly came the program of the Abolitionists; and it spoke with tongues of fire, and had all the vigor and force of a crusade.

2. The Challenge of the Abolitionists

The great difference between the early abolition societies which resulted in the American Convention and the later anti-slavery movement of which Garrison was the representative figure was the difference between a humanitarian impulse tempered by expediency and one that had all the power of a direct challenge. Before 1831 "in the South the societies were more numerous, the members no less earnest, and the hatred of slavery no less bitter, . . . yet the conciliation and persuasion so noticeable in the earlier period in twenty years accomplished practically nothing either in legislation or in the education of public sentiment; while gradual changes in economic conditions at the South caused the question to grow more difficult." * Moreover, "the evidence of open-mindedness can not stand against the many instances of absolute refusal to permit argument against slavery. In the Colonial Congress, in the Confederation, in the Constitutional Convention, in the state ratifying conventions, in the early Congresses, there were many vehement denunciations of anything which seemed to have an anti-slavery tendency, and wholesale suspicion of the North at all times when the subject was opened." † One can not forget the effort of James G. Birney, or that Benjamin Lundy's work was most largely done in what we should now call the South, or that between 1815 and 1828 at least four journals which avowed the extinction of slavery as one, if not the chief one, of their objects were published in the Southern states.‡ Only gradual emancipation, however, found any real support in the South; and, as compared with the work of Garrison, even that of Lundy appears in the distance with something of the mildness of "sweetness and light." Even before the rise of Garrison, Robert James Turnbull of South Carolina, under the name of "Brutus," wrote a virulent attack on anti-slavery; and Representative Drayton of the same state, speaking in Congress in 1828, said, "Much as we love our country, we would rather see our cities in flames, our plains drenched in blood—rather endure all the calamities of civil war, than parley for an instant upon the right of any power than our own to interfere with the regulation of our slaves." § More and more this was to be the real sentiment of the South, and in the face of this kind of eloquence and passion mere academic discussion was powerless.

The *Liberator* was begun January 1, 1831. The next year Garrison was the leading spirit in the formation of the New England Anti-Slavery Society; and in December, 1833, in

* Adams: *The Neglected Period of Anti-Slavery, 1808-1831,* 250-251.
  † *Ibid.,* 110.
  ‡ William Birney: *James G. Birney and His Times,* 85-86.
  § Register of Debates, 4,975, cited by Adams, 112-3.

Philadelphia, the American Anti-Slavery Society was organized. In large measure these organizations were an outgrowth
of the great liberal and humanitarian spirit that by 1830 had
become manifest in both Europe and America. Hugo and
Mazzini, Byron and Macaulay had all now appeared upon
the scene, and romanticism was regnant. James Montgomery
and William Faber wrote their hymns, and Reginald Heber
went as a missionary bishop to India. Forty years afterwards
the French Revolution was bearing fruit. France herself had
a new revolution in 1830, and in this same year the kingdom
of Belgium was born. In England there was the remarkable
reign of William IV, which within the short space of seven
years summed up in legislation reforms that had been agitated
for decades. In 1832 came the great Reform Bill, in 1833 the
abolition of slavery in English dominions, and in 1834 a revision of factory legislation and the poor law. Charles Dickens
and Elizabeth Barrett Browning began to be heard, and in
1834 came to America George Thompson, a powerful and refined speaker who had had much to do with the English agitation against slavery. The young republic of the United States,
lusty and self-confident, was seething with new thought. In
New England the humanitarian movement that so largely began with the Unitarianism of Channing "ran through its later
phase in transcendentalism, and spent its last strength in the
anti-slavery agitation and the enthusiasms of the Civil War." *
The movement was contemporary with the preaching of many
novel gospels in religion, in sociology, in science, education,
and medicine. New sects were formed, like the Universalists,
the Spiritualists, the Second Adventists, the Mormons, and the
Shakers, some of which believed in trances and miracles, others
in the quick coming of Christ, and still others in the reorgani-
zation of society; and the pseudo-sciences, like mesmerism and
phrenology, had numerous followers. The ferment has long
since subsided, and much that was then seething has since
gone off in vapor; but when all that was spurious has been
rejected, we find that the general impulse was but a new baptism of the old Puritan spirit. Transcendentalism appealed to

* Henry A. Beers: *Initial Studies in American Letters,* 95-98 passim.

the private consciousness as the sole standard of truth and right. With kindred movements it served to quicken the ethical sense of a nation that was fast becoming materialistic and to nerve it for the conflict that sooner or later had to come.

In his salutatory editorial Garrison said with reference to his position: "In Park Street Church, on the Fourth of July, 1829, in an address on slavery, I unreflectingly assented to the popular but pernicious doctrine of gradual abolition. I seize this opportunity to make a full and unequivocal recantation, and thus publicly to ask pardon of my God, of my country, and of my brethren, the poor slaves, for having uttered a sentiment so full of timidity, injustice, and absurdity. . . . I am aware that many object to the severity of my language; but is there not cause for severity? I will be as harsh as truth, and as uncompromising as justice. On this subject, I do not wish to think, or speak, or write, with moderation. No! no! Tell a man whose house is on fire, to give a moderate alarm; tell him to moderately rescue his wife from the hands of the ravisher; tell the mother to gradually extricate her babe from the fire into which it has fallen; but urge me not to use moderation in a cause like the present! I am in earnest. I will not equivocate—I will not excuse—I will not retreat a single inch—AND I WILL BE HEARD." With something of the egotism that comes of courage in a holy cause, he said: "On this question my influence, humble as it is, is felt at this moment to a considerable extent, and shall be felt in coming years—not perniciously, but beneficially—not as a curse, but as a blessing; and POSTERITY WILL BEAR TESTIMONY THAT I WAS RIGHT."

All the while, in speaking to the Negro people themselves, Garrison endeavored to beckon them to the highest possible ground of personal and racial self-respect. Especially did he advise them to seek the virtues of education and coöperation. Said he to them: * "Support each other. . . . When I say 'support each other,' I mean, sell to each other, and buy of each other, in preference to the whites. This is a duty: the

---

* "An Address delivered before the Free People of Color in Philadelphia, New York, and other cities, during the month of June, 1831, by Wm. Lloyd Garrison. Boston, 1831," pp. 14-18.

whites do not trade with you; why should you give them your patronage? If one of your number opens a little shop, do not pass it by to give your money to a white shopkeeper. If any has a trade, employ him as often as possible. If any is a good teacher, send your children to him, and be proud that he is one of your color. . . . Maintain your rights, in all cases, and at whatever expense. . . . Wherever you are allowed to vote, see that your names are put on the lists of voters, and go to the polls. If you are not strong enough to choose a man of your own color, give your votes to those who are friendly to your cause; but, if possible, elect intelligent and respectable colored men. I do not despair of seeing the time when our State and National Assemblies will contain a fair proportion of colored representatives—especially if the proposed college at New Haven goes into successful operation. Will you despair now so many champions are coming to your help, and the trump of jubilee is sounding long and loud; when is heard a voice from the East, a voice from the West, a voice from the North, a voice from the South, crying, *Liberty and Equality now, Liberty and Equality forever!* Will you despair, seeing Truth, and Justice, and Mercy, and God, and Christ, and the Holy Ghost, are on your side? Oh, no—never, never despair of the complete attainment of your rights!"

To second such sentiments rose a remarkable group of men and women, among them Elijah P. Lovejoy, Wendell Phillips, Theodore Parker, John Greenleaf Whittier, Lydia Maria Child, Samuel J. May, William Jay, Charles Sumner, Henry Ward Beecher, Harriet Beecher Stowe, and John Brown. Phillips, the "Plumed Knight" of the cause, closed his law office because he was not willing to swear that he would support the Constitution; he relinquished the franchise because he did not wish to have any responsibility for a government that countenanced slavery; and he lost sympathy with the Christian Church because of its compromising attitude. Garrison himself termed the Constitution "a covenant with death and an agreement with hell." Lydia Maria Child in 1833 published an *Appeal in Favor of That Class of Americans Called Africans,* and wrote or edited numerous other books for the cause, while the anti-slavery poems of Whittier are now a part of the main stream of American literature. The Abolitionists repelled many conservative men by their refusal to countenance any laws that recognized slavery; but they gained force when Congress denied them the right of petition and when President Jackson refused them the use of the mails.

There could be no question as to the directness of their attack. They held up the slaveholder to scorn. They gave thousands of examples of the inhumanity of the system of slavery, publishing scores and even hundreds of tracts and pamphlets. They called the attention of America to the slave who for running away was for five days buried in the ground up to his chin with his arms tied behind him; to women who were whipped because they did not breed fast enough or would not yield to the lust of planters or overseers; to men who were tied to be whipped and then left bleeding, or who were branded with hot irons, or forced to wear iron yokes and clogs and bells; to the Presbyterian preacher in Georgia who tortured a slave until he died; to a woman in New Jersey who was "bound to a log, and scored with a knife, in a shocking manner, across her back, and the gashes stuffed with salt, after which she was tied to a post in a cellar, where, after suffering three days, death kindly terminated her misery"; and finally to the fact that even when slaves were dead they were not left in peace, as the South Carolina Medical College in Charleston advertised that the bodies were used for dissection.* In the face of such an indictment the South appeared more injured and innocent than ever, and said that evils had been greatly exaggerated. Perhaps in some instances they were; but the South and everybody also knew that no pen could nearly do justice to some of the things that were possible under the iniquitous and abominable system of American slavery.

The Abolitionists, however, did not stop with a mere attack on slavery. Not satisfied with the mere enumeration of examples of Negro achievement, they made even higher claims in behalf of the people now oppressed. Said Alexander H.

* See "American Slavery as it is: Testimony of a Thousand Witnesses. By Theodore Dwight Weld. Published by the American Anti-Slavery Society, New York, 1839"; but the account of the New Jersey woman is from "A Portraiture of Domestic Slavery in the United States, by Jesse Torrey, Ballston Spa, Penn., 1917," p. 67.

Everett:* "We are sometimes told that all these efforts will be unavailing—that the African is a degraded member of the human family—that a man with a dark skin and curled hair is necessarily, as such, incapable of improvement and civilization, and condemned by the vice of his physical conformation to vegetate forever in a state of hopeless barbarism. I reject with contempt and indignation this miserable heresy. In replying to it the friends of truth and humanity have not hitherto done justice to the argument. In order to prove that the blacks were capable of intellectual efforts, they have painfully collected a few specimens of what some of them have done in this way, even in the degraded condition which they occupy at present in Christendom. This is not the way to treat the subject. Go back to an earlier period in the history of our race. See what the blacks were and what they did three thousand years ago, in the period of their greatness and glory, when they occupied the forefront in the march of civilization —when they constituted in fact the whole civilized world of their time. Trace this very civilization, of which we are so proud, to its origin, and see where you will find it. We received it from our European ancestors: they had it from the Greeks and Romans, and the Jews. But, sir, where did the Greeks and the Romans and the Jews get it? They derived it from Ethiopia and Egypt—in one word, from Africa.† . . . The ruins of the Egyptian temples laugh to scorn the architectural monuments of any other part of the world. They will be what they are now, the delight and admiration of travelers from all quarters, when the grass is growing on the sites of St. Peter's and St. Paul's, the present pride of Rome and London. . . . It seems, therefore, that for this very civilization of which we are so proud, and which is the only ground of our present claim of superiority, we are indebted to the ances-

---

* See "The Anti-Slavery Picknick: a collection of Speeches, Poems, Dialogues, and Songs, intended for use in schools and anti-slavery meetings. By John A. Collins, Boston, 1842," 10-12.

† It is worthy of note that this argument, which was long thought to be fallacious, · is more and more coming to be substantiated by the researches of scholars, and that not only as affecting Northern but also Negro Africa. Note Lady Lugard (Flora L. Shaw): *A Tropical Dependency*, London, 1906, pp. 16-18.

tors of these very blacks, whom we are pleased to consider as naturally incapable of civilization."

In adherence to their convictions the Abolitionists were now to give a demonstration of faith in humanity such as has never been surpassed except by Jesus Christ himself. They believed in the Negro even before the Negro had learned to believe in himself. Acting on their doctrine of equal rights, they traveled with their Negro friends, "sat upon the same platforms with them, ate with them, and one enthusiastic abolitionist white couple adopted a Negro child." *

Garrison appealed to posterity. He has most certainly been justified by time. Compared with his high stand for the right, the opportunism of such a man as Clay shrivels into nothingness. Within recent years a distinguished American scholar,† writing of the principles for which he and his co-workers stood, has said: "The race question transcends any academic inquiry as to what ought to have been done in 1866. It affects the North as well as the South; it touches the daily life of all of our citizens, individually, politically, humanly. It molds the child's conception of democracy. It tests the faith of the adult. It is by no means an American problem only. What is going on in our states, North and South, is only a local phase of a world-problem. . . . Now, Whittier's opinions upon that world-problem are unmistakable. He believed, quite literally, that all men are brothers; that oppression of one man or one race degrades the whole human family; and that there should be the fullest equality of opportunity. That a mere difference in color should close the door of civil, industrial, and political hope upon any individual was a hateful thing to the Quaker poet. The whole body of his verse is a protest against the assertion of race pride, against the emphasis upon racial differences. To Whittier there was no such thing as a 'white man's civilization.' The only distinction was between civilization and barbarism. He had faith in education, in equality before the law, in freedom of opportunity, and in the ultimate triumph of brotherhood.

* Hart: *Slavery and Abolition*, 245-6.
† Bliss Perry: "Whittier for To-Day," *Atlantic Monthly*, Vol. 100, 851-859 (December, 1907).

'They are rising,—
All are rising,
The black and white together.'

This faith is at once too sentimental and too dogmatic to suit those persons who have exalted economic efficiency into a fetish and who have talked loudly at times—though rather less loudly since the Russo-Japanese War—about the white man's task of governing the backward races. *But whatever progress has been made by the American Negro since the Civil War, in self-respect, in moral and intellectual development, and —for that matter—in economic efficiency, has been due to fidelity to those principles which Whittier and other like-minded men and women long ago enunciated.** The immense tasks which still remain, alike for 'higher' as for 'lower' races, can be worked out by following Whittier's program, if they can be worked out at all."

3. The Contest

Even before the Abolitionists became aggressive a test law had been passed, the discussion of which did much to prepare for their coming. Immediately after the Denmark Vesey insurrection the South Carolina legislature voted that the moment that a vessel entered a port in the state with a free Negro or person of color on board he should be seized, even if he was the cook, the steward, or a mariner, or if he was a citizen of another state or country.† The sheriff was to board the vessel, take the Negro to jail and detain him there until the vessel was actually ready to leave. The master of the ship was then to pay for the detention of the Negro and take him away, or pay a fine of $1,000 and see the Negro sold as a slave. Within a short time after this enactment was passed, as many as forty-one vessels were deprived of one or more hands, from one British trading vessel almost the entire crew being taken. The captains appealed to the judge of the United

* The italics are our own.
† Note McMaster, V, 200-204.

States District Court, who with alacrity turned the matter over to the state courts. Now followed much legal proceeding, with an appeal to higher authorities, in the course of which both Canning and Adams were forced to consider the question, and it was generally recognized that the act violated both the treaty with Great Britain and the power of Congress to regulate trade. To all of this South Carolina replied that as a sovereign state she had the right to interdict the entry of foreigners, that in fact she had been a sovereign state at the time of her entrance into the Union and that she never had surrendered the right to exclude free Negroes. Finally she asserted that if a dissolution of the Union must be the alternative she was quite prepared to abide by the result. Unusual excitement arose soon afterwards when four free Negroes on a British ship were seized by the sheriff and dragged from the deck. The captain had to go to heavy expense to have these men released, and on reaching Liverpool he appealed to the Board of Trade. The British minister now sent a more vigorous protest, Adams referred the same to Wirt, the Attorney General, and Wirt was forced to declare South Carolina's act unconstitutional and void. His opinion with a copy of the British protest Adams sent to the Governor of the state, who immediately transmitted the same to the legislature. Each branch of the legislature passed resolutions which the other would not accept, but neither voted to repeal the law. In fact, it remained technically in force until the Civil War. In 1844 Massachusetts sent Samuel Hoar as a commissioner to Charleston to make a test case of a Negro who had been deprived of his rights. Hoar cited Article II, Section 2, of the National Constitution ("The citizens of each state shall be entitled to all the privileges and immunities of citizens in the several states"), intending ultimately to bring a case before the United States Supreme Court. When he appeared, however, the South Carolina legislature voted that "this agent comes here not as a citizen of the United States, but as an emissary of a foreign Government hostile to our domestic institutions and with the sole purpose of subverting our internal police." Hoar was at length notified that his life was in danger and he was forced to leave the state. Meanwhile Southern sentiment against the

American Colonization Society had crystallized, and the excitement raised by David Walker's *Appeal* was exceeded only by that occasioned by Nat Turner's insurrection.

When, then, the Abolitionists began their campaign the country was already ripe for a struggle, and in the North as well as the South there was plenty of sentiment unfavorable to the Negro. In July, 1831, when an attempt was made to start a manual training school for Negro youth in New Haven, the citizens at a public meeting declared that "the founding of colleges for educating colored people is an unwarrantable and dangerous interference with the internal concerns of other states, and ought to be discouraged"; and they ultimately forced the project to be abandoned. At Canterbury in the same state Prudence Crandall, a young Quaker woman twenty-nine years of age, was brought face to face with the problem when she admitted a Negro girl, Sarah Harris, to her school.* When she was boycotted she announced that she would receive Negro girls only if no others would attend, and she advertised accordingly in the *Liberator*. She was subjected to various indignities and efforts were made to arrest her pupils as vagrants. As she was still undaunted, her opponents, on May 24, 1833, procured a special act of the legislature forbidding, under severe penalties, the instruction of any Negro from outside the state without the consent of the town authorities. Under this act Miss Crandall was arrested and imprisoned, being confined to a cell which had just been vacated by a murderer. The Abolitionists came to her defense, but she was convicted, and though the higher courts quashed the proceedings on technicalities, the village shopkeepers refused to sell her food, manure was thrown into her well, her house was pelted with rotten eggs and at last demolished, and even the meeting-house in the town was closed to her. The attempt to continue the school was then abandoned. In 1834 an academy was built by subscription in Canaan, N. H.; it was granted a charter by the legislature, and the proprietors determined to admit all applicants having "suitable moral and intellectual recommen-

* Note especially "Connecticut's Canterbury Tale; its Heroine, Prudence Crandall, and its Moral for To-Day, by John C. Kimball," Hartford (1886).

dations, without other distinctions." The town-meeting "viewed with abhorrence" the attempt to establish the school, but when it was opened twenty-eight white and fourteen Negro scholars attended. The town-meeting then ordered that the academy be forcibly removed and appointed a committee to execute the mandate. Accordingly on August 10 three hundred men with two hundred oxen assembled, took the edifice from its place, dragged it for some distance and left it a ruin. From 1834 to 1836, in fact, throughout the country, from east to west, swept a wave of violence. Not less than twenty-five attempts were made to break up anti-slavery meetings. In New York in October, 1833, there was a riot in Clinton Hall, and from July 7 to 11 of the next year a succession of riots led to the sacking of the house of Lewis Tappan and the destruction of other houses and churches. When George Thompson arrived from England in September, 1834, his meetings were constantly disturbed, and Garrison himself was mobbed in Boston in 1835, being dragged through the streets with a rope around his body.

In general the Abolitionists were charged by the South with promoting both insurrection and the amalgamation of the races. There was no clear proof of these charges; nevertheless, May said, "If we do not emancipate our slaves by our own moral energy, they will emancipate themselves and that by a process too horrible to contemplate"; * and Channing said, "Allowing that amalgamation is to be anticipated, then, I maintain, we have no right to resist it. Then it is not unnatural." † While the South grew hysterical at the thought, it was, as Hart remarks, a fair inquiry, which the Abolitionists did not hesitate to put—Who was responsible for the only amalgamation that had so far taken place? After a few years there was a cleavage among the Abolitionists. Some of the more practical men, like Birney, Gerrit Smith, and the Tappans, who believed in fighting through governmental machinery, in 1838 broke away from the others and prepared to take a part in Federal politics. This was the beginning of the Liberty party, which nominated Birney for the presidency in 1840

* Hart, 221, citing *Liberator*, V, 59.
† Hart, 216, citing Channing, *Works*, V. 57.

and again in 1844. In 1848 it became merged in the Free Soil party and ultimately in the Republican party.

With the forties came division in the Church—a sort of prelude to the great events that were to thunder through the country within the next two decades. Could the Church really countenance slavery? Could a bishop hold a slave? These were to become burning questions. In 1844-5 the Baptists of the North and East refused to approve the sending out of missionaries who owned slaves, and the Southern Baptist Convention resulted. In 1844, when James O. Andrew came into the possession of slaves by his marriage to a widow who had these as a legacy from her former husband, the Northern Methodists refused to grant that one of their bishops might hold a slave, and the Methodist Episcopal Church, South, was formally organized in Louisville the following year. The Presbyterians and the Episcopalians, more aristocratic in tone, did not divide.

The great events of the annexation of Texas, with the Mexican War that resulted, the Compromise of 1850, with the Fugitive Slave Law, the Kansas-Nebraska Bill of 1854, and the Dred Scott decision of 1857 were all regarded in the North as successive steps in the campaign of slavery, though now in the perspective they appear as vain efforts to beat back a resistless tide. In the Mexican War it was freely urged by the Mexicans that, should the American line break, their host would soon find itself among the rich cities of the South, where perhaps it could not only exact money, but free two million slaves as well, call to its assistance the Indians, and even draw aid from the Abolitionists in the North.* Nothing of all this was to be. Out of the academic shades of Harvard, however, at last came a tongue of flame. In "The Present Crisis" James Russell Lowell produced lines whose tremendous beat was like a stern call of the whole country to duty:

Once to every man and nation comes the moment to decide,
In the strife of Truth with Falsehood, for the good or evil side;
Some great cause, God's new Messiah, offering each the bloom or
    blight,

* Justin H. Smith: *The War with Mexico*, I, 107.

Parts the goats upon the left hand, and the sheep upon the right,
And the choice goes by forever 'twixt that darkness and that light.

. . . .

Then to side with Truth is noble when we share her wretched crust,
Ere her cause bring fame and profit and 'tis prosperous to be just;
Then it is the brave man chooses, while the coward stands aside,
Doubting in his abject spirit, till his Lord is crucified,
And the multitude make virtue of the faith they had denied.

. . . .

New occasions teach new duties; Time makes ancient good uncouth;
They must upward still and onward, who would keep abreast of
    Truth;
Lo, before us gleam her camp-fires! we ourselves must Pilgrims be,
Launch our *Mayflower,* and steer boldly through the desperate winter
    sea,
Nor attempt the Future's portal with the Past's blood-rusted key.

As "The Present Crisis" came after the Mexican War, so after the new Fugitive Slave Law appeared *Uncle Tom's Cabin* (1852). "When despairing Hungarian fugitives make their way, against all the search-warrants and authorities of their lawful governments, to America, press and political cabinet ring with applause and welcome. When despairing African fugitives do the same thing—it is—what *is* it?" asked Harriet Beecher Stowe; and in her remarkable book she proceeded to show the injustice of the national position. *Uncle Tom's Cabin* has frequently been termed a piece of propaganda that gave an overdrawn picture of Southern conditions. The author, however, had abundant proof for her incidents, and she was quite aware of the fact that the problem of the Negro, North as well as South, transcended the question of slavery. Said St. Clair to Ophelia: "If we emancipate, are you willing to educate? How many families of your town would take in a Negro man or woman, teach them, bear with them, and seek to make them Christians? How many merchants would take Adolph, if I wanted to make him a clerk; or mechanics, if I wanted to teach him a trade? If I wanted to put Jane and Rosa to school, how many schools are there in the Northern states that would take them in? . . . We are in a bad position. We are the more *obvious* oppressors of the Negro; but the unchristian prejudice of the North is an oppressor almost equally severe."

Meanwhile the thrilling work of the Underground Railroad was answered by a practical reopening of the slave-trade. From 1820 to 1840, as the result of the repressive measure of 1819, the traffic had declined; between 1850 and 1860, however, it was greatly revived, and Southern conventions resolved that all laws, state or Federal, prohibiting the slave-trade, should be repealed. The traffic became more and more open and defiant until, as Stephen A. Douglas computed, as many as 15,000 slaves were brought into the country in 1859. It was not until the Lincoln government in 1862 hanged the first trader who ever suffered the extreme penalty of the law, and made with Great Britain a treaty embodying the principle of international right of search, that the trade was effectually checked. By the end of the war it was entirely suppressed, though as late as 1866 a squadron of ships patrolled the slave coast.

The Kansas-Nebraska Bill, repealing the Missouri Compromise and providing for "squatter sovereignty" in the territories in question, outraged the North and led immediately to the forming of the Republican party. It was not long before public sentiment began to make itself felt, and the first demonstration took place in Boston. Anthony Burns was a slave who escaped from Virginia and made his way to Boston, where he was at work in the winter of 1853-4. He was discovered by a United States marshal who presented a writ for his arrest just at the time of the repeal of the Missouri Compromise in May, 1854. Public feeling became greatly aroused. Wendell Phillips and Theodore Parker delivered strong addresses at a meeting in Faneuil Hall while an unsuccessful attempt to rescue Burns from the Court House was made under the leadership of Thomas Wentworth Higginson, who with others of the attacking party was wounded. It was finally decided in court that Burns must be returned to his master. The law was obeyed; but Boston had been made very angry, and generally her feeling had counted for something in the history of the country. The people draped their houses in mourning, hissed the procession that took Burns to his ship and at the wharf a riot was averted only by a minister's call to prayer. This incident did more to crystallize Northern sentiment against slavery than any other except the exploit of John Brown, and this was the last time that a fugitive slave was taken out of Boston. Burns himself was afterwards bought by popular subscription, and ultimately became a Baptist minister in Canada.

In 1834 Dr. Emerson, an army officer stationed in Missouri, removed to Illinois, taking with him his slave, Dred Scott. Two years later, again accompanied by Scott, he went to Minnesota. In Illinois slavery was prohibited by state law and Minnesota was a free territory. In 1838 Emerson returned with Scott to Missouri. After a while the slave raised the important question: Had not his residence outside of a slave state made him a free man? Beaten by his master in 1848, with the aid of anti-slavery lawyers Scott brought a suit against him for assault and battery, the circuit court of St. Louis rendering a decision in his favor. Emerson appealed and in 1852 the Supreme Court of the state reversed the decision of the lower court. Not long after this Emerson sold Scott to a citizen of New York named Sandford. Scott now brought suit against Sandford, on the ground that they were citizens of different states. The case finally reached the Supreme Court of the United States, which in 1857 handed down the decision that Scott was not a citizen of Missouri and had no standing in the Federal courts, that a slave was only a piece of property, and that a master might take his property with impunity to any place within the jurisdiction of the United States. The ownership of Scott and his family soon passed to a Massachusetts family by whom they were liberated; but the important decision that the case had called forth aroused the most intense excitement throughout the country, and somehow out of it all people remembered more than anything else the amazing declaration of Chief Justice Taney that "the Negroes were so far inferior that they had no rights which the white man was bound to respect." The extra-legal character and the general fallacy of his position were exposed by Justice Curtis in a masterly dissenting opinion.

No one incident of the period showed more clearly the tension under which the country was laboring than the assault on Charles Sumner by Preston S. Brooks, a congressional representative from South Carolina. As a result of this regrettable occurrence splendid canes with such inscriptions as "Hit him again" and "Use knock-down arguments" were sent to Brooks from different parts of the South and he was triumphantly reëlected by his constituency, while on the other hand resolutions denouncing him were passed all over the North, in Canada, and even in Europe. More than ever the South was thrown on the defensive, and in impassioned speeches Robert Toombs now glorified his state and his section. Speaking at Emory College in 1853 he had already made an extended apology for slavery; * speaking in the Georgia legislature on the eve of secession he contended that the South had been driven to bay by the Abolitionists and must now "expand or perish." A writer in the *Southern Literary Messenger,*† in an article "The Black Race in North America," made the astonishing statement that "the slavery of the black race on this continent is the price America has paid for her liberty, civil and religious, and, humanly speaking, these blessings would have been unattainable without their aid." Benjamin M. Palmer, a distinguished minister of New Orleans, in a widely quoted sermon in 1860 spoke of the peculiar trust that had been given to the South—to be the guardians of the slaves, the conservers of the world's industry, and the defenders of the cause of religion.‡ "The blooms upon Southern fields gathered by black hands have fed the spindles and looms of Manchester and Birmingham not less than of Lawrence and Lowell. Strike now a blow at this system of labor and the world itself totters at the stroke. Shall we permit that blow to fall? Do we not owe it to civilized man to stand in the breach and stay the uplifted arm? . . . This trust we will discharge in the face of the worst possible peril. Though war be the aggregation of all evils, yet, should the madness

* See "An Oration delivered before the Few and Phi Gamma Societies of Emory College: Slavery in the United States; its consistency with republican institutions, and its effects upon the slave and society. Augusta, Ga., 1853."
† November, 1855.
‡ "The Rights of the South defended in the Pulpits, by B. M. Palmer, D.D., and W. T. Leacock, D.D., Mobile, 1860."

of the hour appeal to the arbitration of the sword, we will not shrink even from the baptism of fire. . . . The position of the South is at this moment sublime. If she has grace given her to know her hour, she will save herself, the country, and the world."

All of this was very earnest and very eloquent, but also very mistaken, and the general fallacy of the South's position was shown by no less a man than he who afterwards became vice-president of the Confederacy. Speaking in the Georgia legislature in opposition to the motion for secession, Stephens said that the South had no reason to feel aggrieved, for all along she had received more than her share of the nation's privileges, and had almost always won in the main that which was demanded. She had had sixty years of presidents to the North's twenty-four; two-thirds of the clerkships and other appointments although the white population in the section was only one-third that of the country; fourteen attorneys general to the North's five; and eighteen Supreme Court judges to the North's eleven, although four-fifths of the business of the court originated in the free states. "This," said Stephens in an astonishing declaration, "we have required so as to guard against any interpretation of the Constitution unfavorable to us."

Still another voice from the South, in a slightly different key, attacked the tendencies in the section. *The Impending Crisis* (1857), by Hinton Rowan Helper, of North Carolina, was surpassed in sensational interest by no other book of the period except *Uncle Tom's Cabin.* The author did not place himself upon the broadest principles of humanity and statesmanship; he had no concern for the Negro, and the great planters of the South were to him simply the "whelps" and "curs" of slavery. He spoke merely as the voice of the non-slaveholding white men in the South. He set forth such unpleasant truths as that the personal and real property, including slaves, of Virginia, North Carolina, Tennessee, Missouri, Arkansas, Florida, and Texas, taken all together, was less than the real and personal estate in the single state of New York; that representation in Southern legislatures was unfair; that in Congress a Southern planter was twice as powerful as a

Northern man; that slavery was to blame for the migration from the South to the West; and that in short the system was in every way harmful to the man of limited means. All of this was decidedly unpleasant to the ears of the property owners of the South; Helper's book was proscribed, and the author himself found it more advisable to live in New York than in his native state. *The Impending Crisis* was eagerly read, however, and it succeeded as a book because it attempted to attack with some degree of honesty a great economic problem.

The time for speeches and books, however, was over, and the time for action had come. For years the slave had chanted, "I've been listenin' all the night long"; and his prayer had reached the throne. On October 16, 1859, John Brown made his raid on Harper's Ferry and took his place with the immortals. In the long and bitter contest on American slavery the Abolitionists had won.

CHAPTER XI

So far in our study we have seen the Negro as the object of interest on the part of the American people. Some were disposed to give him a helping hand, some to keep him in bondage, and some thought that it might be possible to dispose of any problem by sending him out of the country. In all this period of agitation and ferment, aside from the efforts of friends in his behalf, just what was the Negro doing to work out his own salvation? If for the time being we can look primarily at constructive effort rather than disabilities, just what do we find that on his own account he was doing to rise to the full stature of manhood?

Naturally in the answer to such a question we shall have to be concerned with those people who had already attained unto nominal freedom. We shall indeed find many examples of industrious slaves who, working in agreement with their owners, managed sometimes to purchase themselves and even to secure ownership of their families. Such cases, while considerable in the aggregate, were after all exceptional, and for the ordinary slave on the plantation the outlook was hopeless enough. In 1860 the free persons formed just one-ninth of the total Negro population in the country, there being 487,970 of them to 3,953,760 slaves. It is a commonplace to remark the progress that the race has made since emancipation. A study of the facts, however, will show that with all their disadvantages less than half a million people had before 1860 not only made such progress as amasses a surprising total, but that they had already entered every large field of endeavor in which the race is engaged to-day.

---

* This chapter follows closely upon Chapter III, Section 5, and is largely complementary to Chapter VIII.

When in course of time the status of the Negro in the American body politic became a live issue, the possibility and the danger of an *imperium in imperio* were perceived; and Rev. James W. C. Pennington, undoubtedly a leader, said in his lectures in London and Glasgow: "The colored population of the United States have no destiny separate from that of the nation in which they form an integral part. Our destiny is bound up with that of America. Her ship is ours; her pilot is ours; her storms are ours; her calms are ours. If she breaks upon any rock, we break with her. If we, born in America, can not live upon the same soil upon terms of equality with the descendants of Scotchmen, Englishmen, Irishmen, Frenchmen, Germans, Hungarians, Greeks, and Poles, then the fundamental theory of America fails and falls to the ground." * While everybody was practically agreed upon this fundamental matter of the relation of the race to the Federal Government, more and more there developed two lines of thought, equally honest, as to the means by which the race itself was to attain unto the highest things that American civilization had to offer. The leader of one school of thought was Richard Allen, founder of the African Methodist Episcopal Church. When this man and his friends found that in white churches they were not treated with courtesy, they said, We shall have our own church; we shall have our own bishop; we shall build up our own enterprises in any line whatsoever; and even to-day the church that Allen founded remains as the greatest single effort of the race in organization. The foremost representative of the opposing line of thought was undoubtedly Frederick Douglass, who in a speech in Rochester in 1848 said: "I am well aware of the anti-Christian prejudices which have excluded many colored persons from white churches, and the consequent necessity for erecting their own places of worship. This evil I would charge upon its originators, and not the colored people. But such a necessity does not now exist to the extent of former years. There are societies where color is not regarded as a test of membership, and such places I deem more appropriate for colored persons than

* Nell: *Colored Patriots of the American Revolution,* 356.

exclusive or isolated organizations." There is much more difference between these two positions than can be accounted for by the mere lapse of forty years between the height of the work of Allen and that of Douglass. Allen certainly did not sanction segregation under the law, and no man worked harder than he to relieve his people from proscription. Douglass moreover, who did not formally approve of organizations that represented any such distinction as that of race, again and again presided over gatherings of Negro men. In the last analysis, however, it was Allen who was foremost in laying the basis of distinctively Negro enterprise, and Douglass who felt that the real solution of any difficulty was for the race to lose itself as quickly as possible in the general body politic.

We have seen that the Church was from the first the race's foremost form of social organization, and that sometimes in very close touch with it developed the early lodges of such a body as the Masons. By 1800 emancipation was well under way; then began emigration from the South to the central West; emigration brought into being the Underground Railroad; and finally all forces worked together for the development of Negro business, the press, conventions, and other forms of activity. It was natural that states so close to the border as Pennsylvania and Ohio should be important in this early development.

The Church continued the growth that it had begun several decades before. The A. M. E. denomination advanced rapidly from 7 churches and 400 members in 1816 to 286 churches and 73,000 members by the close of the Civil War. Naturally such a distinctively Negro organization could make little progress in the South before the war, but there were small congregations in Charleston and New Orleans, and William Paul Quinn blazed a path in the West, going from Pittsburgh to St. Louis.

In 1847 the Prince Hall Lodge of the Masons in Massachusetts, the First Independent African Grand Lodge in Pennsylvania, and the Hiram Grand Lodge of Pennsylvania formed a National Grand Lodge, and from one or another of these all other Grand Lodges among Negroes have descended. In

1842 the members of the Philomathean Institute of New York and of the Philadelphia Library Company and Debating Society applied for admission to the International Order of Odd Fellows. They were refused on account of their race. Thereupon Peter Ogden, a Negro, who had already joined the Grand United Order of Odd Fellows of England, secured a charter for the first Negro American lodge, Philomathean, No. 646, of New York, which was set up March 1, 1843. It was followed within the next two years by lodges in New York, Philadelphia, Albany, and Poughkeepsie. The Knights of Pythias were not organized until 1864 in Washington; but the Grand Order of Galilean Fishermen started on its career in Baltimore in 1856.

The benefit societies developed apace. At first they were small and confined to a group of persons well known to each other, thus being genuinely fraternal. Simple in form, they imposed an initiation fee of hardly less than $2.50 or more than $5.00, a monthly fee of about 50 cents, and gave sick dues ranging from $1.50 to $5.00 a month, with guarantee of payment of one's funeral expenses and subsequent help to the widow. By 1838 there were in Philadelphia alone 100 such groups with 7,448 members. As bringing together spirits supposedly congenial, these organizations largely took the place of clubs, and the meetings were relished accordingly. Some drifted into secret societies, and after the Civil War some that had not cultivated the idea of insurance were forced to add this feature to their work.

In the sphere of civil rights the Negroes, in spite of circumstances, were making progress, and that by their own efforts as well as those of their friends the Abolitionists. Their papers helped decidedly. The *Journal of Freedom* (commonly known as *Freedom's Journal*), begun March 30, 1827, ran for three years. It had numerous successors, but no one of outstanding strength before the *North Star* (later known as *Frederick Douglass' Paper*) began publication in 1847, continuing until the Civil War. Largely through the effort of Paul Cuffe for the franchise, New Bedford, Mass., was generally prominent in all that made for racial prosperity. Here even by 1850 the Negro voters held the balance of power

and accordingly exerted a potent influence on Election day.*
Under date March 6, 1840, there was brought up for repeal
so much of the Massachusetts Statutes as forbade intermarriage between white persons and Negroes, mulattoes, or Indians, as "contrary to the principles of Christianity and republicanism." The committee said that it did not recommend
a repeal in the expectation that the number of connections,
legal or illegal, between the races would be thereupon increased; but its object rather was that wherever such connections were found the usual civil liabilities and obligations
should not fail to attach to the contracting parties. The enactment was repealed. In the same state, by January, 1843,
an act forbidding discrimination on railroads was passed.
This grew out of separate petitions or remonstrances from
Francis Jackson and Joseph Nunn, each man being supported
by friends, and the petitioners based their request "not on the
supposition that the colored man is not as well treated as his
white fellow-citizen, but on the broad principle that the constitution allows no distinction in public privileges among the
different classes of citizens in this commonwealth." † In
New York City an interesting case arose over the question of
public conveyances. When about 1852 horse-cars began to
supersede omnibuses on the streets, the Negro was excluded
from the use of them, and he continued to be excluded until
1855, when a decision of Judge Rockwell gave him the right
to enter them. The decision was ignored and the Negro continued to be excluded as before. One Sunday in May, however, Rev. James W. C. Pennington, after service, reminded
his hearers of Judge Rockwell's decision, urged them to stand
up for their rights, and especially to inform any friends who
might visit the city during the coming anniversary week that
Negroes were no longer excluded from the street cars. He
himself then boarded a car on Sixth Avenue, refused to leave
when requested to do so, and was forcibly ejected. He brought
suit against the company and won his case; and thus the Negro
made further advance toward full citizenship in New York.‡

* Nell, 111.
† Senate document 63 of 1842.
‡ McMaster, VIII, 74.

Thus was the Negro developing in religious organization, in his benefit societies, and toward his rights as a citizen. When we look at the economic life upon which so much depended, we find that rather amazing progress had been made. Doors were so often closed to the Negro, competing white artisans were so often openly hostile, and he himself labored under so many disadvantages generally that it has often been thought that his economic advance before 1860 was negligible; but nothing could be farther from the truth. It must not be forgotten that for decades the South had depended upon Negro men for whatever was to be done in all ordinary trades; some brick-masons, carpenters, and shoemakers had served a long apprenticeship and were thoroughly accomplished; and when some of the more enterprising of these men removed to the North or West they took their training with them. Very few persons became paupers. Certainly many were destitute, especially those who had most recently made their way from slavery; and in general the colored people cared for their own poor. In 1852, of 3500 Negroes in Cincinnati, 200 were holders of property who paid taxes on their real estate.* In 1855 the Negro per capita ownership of property compared most favorably with that of the white people. Altogether the Negroes owned $800,000 worth of property in the city and $5,000,000 worth in the state. In the city there were among other workers three bank tellers, a landscape artist who had visited Rome to complete his education, and nine daguerreotypists, one of whom was the best in the entire West.† Of 1696 Negroes at work in Philadelphia in 1856, some of the more important occupations numbered workers as follows: tailors, dressmakers, and shirtmakers, 615; barbers, 248; shoemakers, 66; brickmakers, 53; carpenters, 49; milliners, 45; tanners, 24; cake-bakers, pastry-cooks, or confectioners, 22; blacksmiths, 22. There were also 15 musicians or music-teachers, 6 physicians, and 16 school-teachers.‡ The foremost and the most wealthy man of business of the race in the country about 1850 was Stephen Smith, of the firm of Smith and Whipper,

* Clarke: *Condition of the Free Colored People of the United States.*
† Nell, 285.
‡ Bacon: *Statistics,* 13.

of Columbia, Pa.* He and his partner were lumber merchants. Smith was a man of wide interests. He invested his capital judiciously, engaging in real estate and spending much of his time in Philadelphia, where he owned more than fifty brick houses, while Whipper, a relative, attended to the business of the firm. Together these men gave employment to a large number of persons. Of similar quality was Samuel T. Wilcox, of Cincinnati, the owner of a large grocery business who also engaged in real estate. Henry Boyd, of Cincinnati, was the proprietor of a bedstead manufactory that filled numerous orders from the South and West and that sometimes employed as many as twenty-five men, half of whom were white. Sometimes through an humble occupation a Negro rose to competence; thus one of the eighteen hucksters in Cincinnati became the owner of $20,000 worth of property. Here and there several caterers and tailors became known as having the best places in their line of business in their respective towns. John Julius, of Pittsburgh, was the proprietor of a brilliant place known as Concert Hall. When President-elect William Henry Harrison in 1840 visited the city it was here that his chief reception was held. Cordovell became widely known as the name of the leading tailor and originator of fashions in New Orleans. After several years of success in business this merchant removed to France, where he enjoyed the fortune that he had accumulated.

Cordovell was representative of the advance of the people of mixed blood in the South. The general status of these people was better in Louisiana than anywhere else in the country, North or South; at the same time their situation was such as to call for special consideration. In Louisiana the "F. M. C." (Free Man of Color) formed a distinct and anomalous class in society.† As a free man he had certain rights, and sometimes his property holdings were very large.‡ In fact, in New Orleans a few years before the Civil War not less than one-

---

* Delany.

† See "The F. M. C.'s of Louisiana," by P. F. de Gournay, *Lippincott's Magazine*, April, 1894; and "Black Masters," by Calvin Dill Wilson, *North American Review*, November, 1905.

‡ See Stone: "The Negro in the South," in *The South in the Building of the Nation*, X, 180.

fifth of the taxable property was in the hands of free people of color. At the same time the lot of these people was one of endless humiliation. Among some of them irregular household establishments were regularly maintained by white men, and there were held the "quadroon balls" which in course of time gave the city a distinct notoriety. Above the people of this group, however, was a genuine aristocracy of free people of color who had a long tradition of freedom, being descended from the early colonists, and whose family life was most exemplary. In general they lived to themselves. In fact, it was difficult for them to do otherwise. They were often compelled to have papers filled out by white guardians, and they were not allowed to be visited by slaves or to have companionship with them, even when attending church or walking along the roads. Sometimes free colored men owned their women and children in order that the latter might escape the invidious law against Negroes recently emancipated; or the situation was sometimes turned around, as in Norfolk, Va., where several women owned their husbands. When the name of a free man of color had to appear on any formal document—a deed of conveyance, a marriage-license, a certificate of birth or death, or even in a newspaper report—the initials F. M. C. had to be appended. In Louisiana these people petitioned in vain for the suffrage, and at the outbreak of the Civil War organized and splendidly equipped for the Confederacy two battalions of five hundred men. For these they chose two distinguished white commanders, and the governor accepted their services, only to have to inform them later that the Confederacy objected to the enrolling of Negro soldiers. In Charleston thirty-seven men in a remarkable petition also formally offered their services to the Confederacy.* What most readily found illustration in New Orleans or Charleston was also true to some extent of other centers of free people of color such as Mobile and Baltimore. In general the F. M. C.'s were industrious and they almost monopolized one or two avenues of employment; but as a group they had not yet learned to place themselves upon the broad basis of racial aspiration.

* Note broadside (Charleston, 1861) accessible in Special Library of Boston Public Library as Document No. 9 in *20th Cab. 3.7.

Whatever may have been the situation of special groups, however, it can readily be seen that there were at least some Negroes in the country—a good many in the aggregate—who by 1860 were maintaining a high standard in their ordinary social life. It must not be forgotten that we are dealing with a period when the general standard of American culture was by no means what it is to-day. "Four-fifths of the people of the United States of 1860 lived in the country, and it is perhaps fair to say that half of these dwelt in log houses of one or two rooms. Comforts such as most of us enjoy daily were as good as unknown. . . . For the workaday world shirt-sleeves, heavy brogan boots and shoes, and rough wool hats were the rule." * In Philadelphia, a fairly representative city, there were at this time a considerable number of Negroes of means or professional standing. These people were regularly hospitable; they visited frequently; and they entertained in well furnished parlors with music and refreshments. In a day when many of their people had not yet learned to get beyond showiness in dress, they were temperate and self-restrained, they lived within their incomes, and they retired at a seasonable hour.†

In spite moreover of all the laws and disadvantages that they had to meet the Negroes also made general advance in education. In the South efforts were of course sporadic, but Negroes received some teaching through private or clandestine sources.‡ More than one slave learned the alphabet while entertaining the son of his master. In Charleston for a long time before the Civil War free Negroes could attend schools especially designed for their benefit and kept by white people or other Negroes. The course of study not infrequently embraced such subjects as physiology, physics, and plane geometry. After John Brown's raid the order went forth that no longer should any colored person teach Negroes. This resulted in a white person's being brought to sit in the classroom, though at the outbreak of the war schools were closed

* W. E. Dodd: *Expansion and Conflict*, Volume 3 of "Riverside History of the United States," Houghton Mifflin Co., Boston, 1915, p. 208.
† Turner: *The Negro in Pennsylvania*, 140.
‡ For interesting examples see C. G. Woodson: *The Education of the Negro prior to 1861.*

altogether. In the North, in spite of all proscription, conditions were somewhat better. As early as 1850 there were in the public schools in New York 3,393 Negro children, these sustaining about the same proportion to the Negro population that white children sustained to the total white population. Two institutions for the higher education of the Negro were established before the Civil War, Lincoln University in Pennsylvania (1854) and Wilberforce University in Ohio (1856). Oberlin moreover was founded in 1833. In 1835 Professor Asa Mahan, of Lane Seminary, was offered the presidency. As he was an Abolitionist he said that he would accept only if Negroes were admitted on equal terms with other students. After a warm session of the trustees the vote was in his favor. Though, before this, individual Negroes had found their way into Northern institutions, it was here at Oberlin that they first received a real welcome. By the outbreak of the war nearly one-third of the students were of the Negro race, and one of the graduates, John M. Langston, was soon to be generally prominent in the affairs of the country.

It has been maintained that in their emphasis on education and on the highest culture possible for the Negro the Abolitionists were mere visionaries who had no practical knowledge whatever of the race's real needs. This was neither true nor just. It was absolutely necessary first of all to establish the Negro's right to enter any field occupied by any other man, and time has vindicated this position. Even in 1850, however, the needs of the majority of the Negro people for advance in their economic life were not overlooked either by the Abolitionists or the Negroes themselves. Said Martin V. Delany: "Our elevation must be the result of *self-efforts,* and work of our *own hands.* No other human power can accomplish it. . . . Let our young men and young women prepare themselves for usefulness and business; that the men may enter into merchandise, trading, and other things of importance; the young women may become teachers of various kinds, and otherwise fill places of usefulness. Parents must turn their attention more to the education of their children. We mean, to educate them for useful practical business purposes. Educate them for the store and counting-house—to do everyday practical business. Consult the children's propensities, and direct their education according to their inclinations. It may be that there is too great a desire on the part of parents to give their children a professional education, before the body of the people are ready for it. A people must be a business people and have more to depend upon than mere help in people's houses and hotels, before they are either able to support or capable of properly appreciating the services of professional men among them. This has been one of our great mistakes— we have gone in advance of ourselves. We have commenced at the superstructure of the building, instead of the foundation—at the top instead of the bottom. We should first be mechanics and common tradesmen, and professions as a matter of course would grow out of the wealth made thereby." *

In professional life the Negro had by 1860 made a noteworthy beginning. Already he had been forced to give attention to the law, though as yet little by way of actual practice had been done. In this field Robert Morris, Jr., of Boston, was probably foremost. William C. Nell, of Rochester and Boston, at the time prominent in newspaper work and politics, is now best remembered for his study of the Negro in the early wars of the country. About the middle of the century Samuel Ringgold Ward, author of the *Autobiography of a Fugitive Negro,* and one of the most eloquent men of the time, was for several years pastor of a white Congregational church in Courtlandville, N. Y.; and Henry Highland Garnet was the pastor of a white congregation in Troy, and well known as a public-spirited citizen as well. Upon James W. C. Pennington the degree of Doctor of Divinity was conferred by Heidelberg, and generally this man had a reputation in England and on the continent of Europe as well as in America. About the same time Bishops Daniel A. Payne and William Paul Quinn were adding to the dignity of the African Methodist Episcopal Church.

Special interest attaches to the Negro physician. Even in colonial times, though there was much emphasis on the control

* *The Condition, Elevation, Emigration, and Destiny of the Colored People of the United States, Politically Considered,* Philadelphia, 1852, p. 45.

of diseases by roots or charms, there was at least a beginning
in work genuinely scientific. As early as 1792 a Negro named
Cæsar had gained such distinction by his knowledge of cura-
tive herbs that the Assembly of South Carolina purchased his
freedom and gave him an annuity. In the earlier years of the
last century James Derham, of New Orleans, became the first
regularly recognized Negro physician of whom there is a complete record. Born in Philadelphia in 1762, as a boy he was
transferred to a physician for whom he learned to perform
minor duties. Afterwards he was sold to a physician in New
Orleans who used him as an assistant. Two or three years
later he won his freedom, he became familiar with French
and Spanish as well as English, and he soon commanded general respect by his learning and skill. About the middle of
the century, in New York, James McCune Smith, a graduate of the University of Glasgow, was prominent. He was the
author of several scientific papers, a man of wide interests,
and universally held in high esteem. "The first real impetus
to bring Negroes in considerable numbers into the professional
world came from the American Colonization Society, which
in the early years flourished in the South as well as the North
. . . and undertook to prepare professional leaders of their
race for the Liberian colony. To execute this scheme, leaders
of the colonization movement endeavored to educate Negroes
in mechanic arts, agriculture, science, and Biblical literature.
Especially bright or promising youths were to be given special
training as catechists, teachers, preachers, and physicians.
Not much was said about what they were doing, but now and
then appeared notices of Negroes who had been prepared privately in the South or publicly in the North for service in
Liberia. Dr. William Taylor and Dr. Fleet were thus educated in the District of Columbia. In the same way John V.
De Grasse, of New York, and Thomas J. White, of Brooklyn,
were allowed to complete the medical course at Bowdoin in
1849. In 1854 Dr. De Grasse was admitted as a member of
the Massachusetts Medical Society.' " *   Martin V. Delany,

* Kelly Miller: "The Background of the Negro Physician," *Journal
of Negro History*, April, 1916, quoting in part Woodson: *The Education
of the Negro prior to 1861.*

more than once referred to in these pages, after being refused admission at a number of institutions, was admitted to the medical school at Harvard. He became distinguished for his work in a cholera epidemic in Pittsburgh in 1854. It was of course not until after the Civil War that medical departments were established in connection with some of the new higher institutions of learning for Negro students.

Before 1860 a situation that arose more than once took from Negroes the real credit for inventions. If a slave made an invention he was not permitted to take out a patent, for no slave could make a contract. At the same time the slave's master could not take out a patent for him, for the Government would not recognize the slave as having the legal right to make the assignment to his master. It is certain that Negroes, who did most of the mechanical work in the South before the Civil War, made more than one suggestion for the improvement of machinery. We have already referred to the strong claim put forth by a member of the race for the real credit of the cotton-gin. The honor of being the first Negro to be granted a patent belongs to Henry Blair, of Maryland, who in 1834 received official protection for a corn harvester.

Throughout the century there were numerous attempts at poetical composition, and several booklets were published. Perhaps the most promising was George Horton's *The Hope of Liberty*, which appeared in 1829. Unfortunately, Horton could not get the encouragement that he needed and in course of time settled down to the life of a janitor at the University of North Carolina.* Six years before the war Frances Ellen Watkins (later Mrs. Harper) struck the popular note by readings from her *Miscellaneous Poems*, which ran through several editions. About the same time William Wells Brown was prominent, though he also worked for several years after the war. He was a man of decided talent and had traveled considerably. He wrote several books dealing with Negro history and biography; and he also treated racial subjects in a novel, *Clotel*, and in a drama, *The Escape*. The latter suffers from an excess of moralizing, but several times it

---

* See "George Moses Horton: Slave Poet," by Stephen B. Weeks, *Southern Workman*, October, 1914.

flashes out with the quality of genuine drama, especially when it deals with the jealousy of a mistress for a favorite slave and the escape of the latter with her husband. In 1841 the first Negro magazine began to appear, this being issued by the A. M. E. Church. There were numerous autobiographies, that of Frederick Douglass, first appearing in 1845, running through edition after edition. On the stage there was the astonishing success of Ira Aldridge, a tragedian who in his earlier years went to Europe, where he had the advantage of association with Edmund Kean. About 1857 he was commonly regarded as one of the two or three greatest actors in the world. He became a member of several of the continental academies of arts and science, and received many decorations of crosses and medals, the Emperors of Russia and Austria and the King of Prussia being among those who honored him. In the great field of music there was much excellent work both in composition and in the performance on different instruments. Among the free people of color in Louisiana there were several distinguished musicians, some of whom removed to Europe for the sake of greater freedom.* The highest individual achievement was that of Elizabeth Taylor Greenfield, of Philadelphia. This singer was of the very first rank. Her voice was of remarkable sweetness and had a compass of twenty-seven notes. She sang before many distinguished audiences in both Europe and America and was frequently compared with Jenny Lind, than at the height of her fame.

It is thus evident that honorable achievement on the part of Negroes and general advance in social welfare by no means began with the Emancipation Proclamation. In 1860 eight-ninths of the members of the race were still slaves, but in the face of every possible handicap the one-ninth that was free had entered practically every great field of human endeavor. Many were respected citizens in their communities, and a few had even laid the foundations of wealth. While there was as yet no book of unquestioned genius or scholarship, there was considerable intellectual activity, and only time and a little more freedom from economic pressure were needed for the production of works of the first order of merit.

* See Washington: *The Story of the Negro*, II, 276-7.

CHAPTER XII

THE CIVIL WAR AND EMANCIPATION

At the outbreak of the Civil War two great questions affecting the Negro overshadowed all others—his freedom and his employment as a soldier. The North as a whole had no special enthusiasm about the Negro and responded only to Lincoln's call to the duty of saving the Union. Among both officers and men moreover there was great prejudice against the use of the Negro as a soldier, the feeling being that he was disqualified by slavery and ignorance. Privates objected to meeting black men on the same footing as themselves and also felt that the arming of slaves to fight for their former masters would increase the bitterness of the conflict. If many men in the North felt thus, the South was furious at the thought of the Negro as a possible opponent in arms.

The human problem, however, was not long in presenting itself and forcing attention. As soon as the Northern soldiers appeared in the South, thousands of Negroes—men, women, and children—flocked to their camps, feeling only that they were going to their friends. In May, 1861, while in command at Fortress Monroe, Major-General Benjamin F. Butler came into national prominence by his policy of putting to work the men who came within his lines and justifying their retention on the ground that, being of service to the enemy for purposes of war, they were like guns, powder, etc., "contraband of war," and could not be reclaimed. On August 30th of this same year Major-General John C. Fremont, in command in Missouri, placed the state under martial law and declared the slaves there emancipated. The administration was embarrassed, Fremont's order was annulled, and he was relieved of his command. On May 9, 1862, Major-General David Hunter, in charge of the Department of the South (South

Carolina, Georgia, and Florida) issued his famous order freeing the slaves in his department, and thus brought to general
attention the matter of the employment of Negro soldiers in
the Union armies.   The Confederate government outlawed
Hunter, Lincoln annulled his order, and the grace of the nation
was again saved; but in the meantime a new situation had
arisen.   While Brigadier-General John W. Phelps was taking part in the expedition against New Orleans, a large sugar-
planter near the city, disgusted with Federal interference with
affairs on his plantation, drove all his slaves away, telling them
to go to their friends, the Yankees.   The Negroes came to
Phelps in great numbers, and for the sake of discipline he
attempted to organize them into troops.   Accordingly he, too,
was outlawed by the Confederates, and his act was disavowed
by the Union, that was not ready to take this step.

Meanwhile President Lincoln was debating the Emancipation Proclamation.   Pressure from radical anti-slavery sources
was constantly being brought to bear upon him, and Horace
Greeley in his famous editorial, "The Prayer of Twenty Millions," was only one of those who criticized what seemed to
be his lack of strength in handling the situation.   After Mc-
Clellan's unsuccessful campaign against Richmond, however,
he felt that the freedom of the slaves was a military and moral
necessity for its effects upon both the North and the South;
and Lee's defeat at Antietam, September 17, 1862, furnished
the opportunity for which he had been waiting.   Accordingly
on September 22nd he issued a preliminary declaration giving
notice that on January 1, 1865, he would free all slaves in the
states still in rebellion, and asserting as before that the object
of the war was the preservation of the Union.

The Proclamation as finally issued January 1st is one of
the most important public documents in the history of the
United States, ranking only below the Declaration of Independence and the Constitution itself.   It full text is as follows:

Whereas, on the twenty-second day of September, in the year of
our Lord one thousand eight hundred and sixty-two, a proclamation
was issued by the President of the United States containing among
other things the following, to-wit:

That on the first day of January, in the year of our Lord one thousand eight hundred and sixty-three, all persons held as slaves within any state or designated part of a state, the people whereof shall then be in rebellion against the United States, shall be then, thenceforward, and forever free; and the executive government of the United States, including the military and naval authority thereof, will recognize and maintain the freedom of such persons, and will do no act or acts to repress such persons, or any of them, in any efforts they may make for their actual freedom.

That the Executive will, on the first day of January aforesaid, by proclamation, designate the states and parts of states, if any, in which the people thereof shall then be in rebellion against the United States; and the fact that any state, or the people thereof, shall on that day be in good faith represented in the Congress of the United States, by members chosen thereto at elections wherein a majority of the qualified voters of such state shall have participated, shall, in the absence of strong countervailing testimony, be deemed conclusive evidence that such state, and the people thereof, are not then in rebellion against the United States.

Now, therefore, I, Abraham Lincoln, President of the United States, by virtue of the power in me vested as Commander-in-Chief of the Army and Navy of the United States, in time of actual armed rebellion against the authority and government of the United States, and as a fit and necessary war measure for suppressing said rebellion, do on this first day of January, in the year of our Lord one thousand eight hundred and sixty-three, and in accordance with my purpose so to do, publicly proclaimed for the full period of one hundred days from the date first above mentioned, order and designate as the states and parts of states wherein the people thereof respectively are this day in rebellion against the United States, the following to-wit:

Arkansas, Texas, Louisiana (except the parishes of St. Bernard, Plaquemine, Jefferson, St. John, St. Charles, St. James, Ascension, Assumption, Terre Bonne, Lafourche, Ste. Marie, St. Martin, and Orleans, including the city of New Orleans), Mississippi, Alabama, Florida, Georgia, South Carolina, North Carolina, and Virginia (except the forty-eight counties designated as West Virginia, and also the counties of Berkeley, Accomac, Northampton, Elizabeth City, York, Princess Anne, and Norfolk, including the cities of Norfolk and Portsmouth), and which excepted parts are, for the present, left precisely as if this proclamation were not issued.

And by virtue of the power and for the purpose aforesaid, I do order and declare that all persons held as slaves within said designated states and parts of states are and henceforward shall be free, and that the executive government of the United States, including the military and naval authorities thereof, will recognize and maintain the freedom of said persons.

And I hereby enjoin upon the people so declared to be free to abstain from all violence, unless in necessary self-defense; and I recommend to them that, in all cases when allowed, they labor faithfully for reasonable wages.

And I further declare and make known that such persons, of suitable condition, will be received into the armed service of the United States to garrison forts, positions, stations, and other places, and to man vessels of all sorts in said service.

And upon this act, sincerely believed to be an act of justice, warranted by the Constitution upon military necessity, I invoke the considerate judgment of mankind, and the gracious favor of Almighty God.

In testimony whereof, I have hereunto set my name, and caused the seal of the United States to be affixed.

Done at the City of Washington, this first day of January, in the year of our Lord one thousand eight hundred and sixty-three, and of the independence of the United States the eighty-seventh.

By the President,
ABRAHAM LINCOLN.

WILLIAM H. SEWARD,
Secretary of State.

It will be observed that the Proclamation was merely a war measure resting on the constitutional power of the President. Its effects on the legal status of the slaves gave rise to much discussion; and it is to be noted that it did not apply to what is now West Virginia, to seven counties in Virginia, and to thirteen parishes in Louisiana, which districts had already come under Federal jurisdiction. All questions raised by the measure, however, were finally settled by the Thirteenth Amendment to the Constitution, and as a matter of fact freedom actually followed the progress of the Union arms from 1863 to 1865.

Meanwhile from the very beginning of the war Negroes were used by the Confederates in making redoubts and in doing other rough work, and even before the Emancipation Proclamation there were many Northern officers who said that definite enlistment was advisable. They felt that such a course would help to destroy slavery and that as the Negroes had so much at stake they should have some share in the overthrow of the rebellion. They said also that the men would be proud to wear the national uniform. Individuals moreover as officers' servants saw much of fighting and won confidence in their ability; and as the war advanced and more and more men were killed the conviction grew that a Negro could stop a bullet as well as a white man and that in any case the use of Negroes for fatigue work would release numbers of other men for the actual fighting.

At last—after a great many men had been killed and the Emancipation Proclamation had changed the status of the Negro—enlistment was decided on. The policy was that Negroes might be non-commissioned men while white men who had seen service would be field and line officers. In general it was expected that only those who had kindly feeling toward the Negro would be used as officers, but in the pressure of military routine this distinction was not always observed. Opinion for the race gained force after the Draft Riot in New York (July, 1863), when Negroes in the city were persecuted by the opponents of conscription. Soon a distinct bureau was established in Washington for the recording of all matters pertaining to Negro troops, a board was organized for the examination of candidates, and recruiting stations were set up in Maryland, Missouri, and Tennessee. The Confederates were indignant at the thought of having to meet black men on equal footing, and refused to exchange Negro soldiers for white men. How such action was met by Stanton, Secretary of War, may be seen from the fact that when he learned that three Negro prisoners had been placed in close confinement, he ordered three South Carolina men to be treated likewise, and the Confederate leaders to be informed of his policy.

The economic advantage of enlistment was apparent. It gave work to 187,000 men who had been cast adrift by the war and who had found no place of independent labor. It gave them food, clothing, wages, and protection, but most of all the feeling of self-respect that comes from profitable employment. To the men themselves the year of jubilee had come. At one great step they had crossed the gulf that separates chattels from men and they now had a chance to vindicate their manhood. A common poster of the day represented a Negro soldier bearing the flag, the shackles of a slave being broken, a young Negro boy reading a newspaper, and several children going into a public school. Over all were the words: "All

Slaves were made Freemen by Abraham Lincoln, President of the United States, January 1st, 1863. Come, then, able-bodied Colored Men, to the nearest United States Camp, and fight for the Stars and Stripes."

To the credit of the men be it said that in their new position they acted with dignity and sobriety. When they picketed lines through which Southern citizens passed, they acted with courtesy at the same time that they did their duty. They captured Southern men without insulting them, and by their own self-respect won the respect of others. Meanwhile their brothers in the South went about the day's work, caring for the widow and the orphan; and a nation that still lynches the Negro has to remember that in all these troublous years deeds of violence against white women and girls were absolutely unknown.

Throughout the country the behavior of the black men under fire was watched with the most intense interest. More and more in the baptism of blood they justified the faith for which their friends had fought for years. At Port Hudson, Fort Wagner, Fort Pillow, and Petersburg their courage was most distinguished. Said the New York *Times* of the battle at Port Hudson (1863): "General Dwight, at least, must have had the idea not only that they (the Negro troops) were men, but something more than men, from the terrific test to which he put their valor. . . . Their colors are torn to pieces by shot, and literally bespattered by blood and brains." This was the occasion on which Color-Sergeant Anselmas Planciancois said before a shell blew off his head, "Colonel, I will bring back these colors to you on honor, or report to God the reason why." On June 6 the Negroes again distinguished themselves and won friends by their bravery at Milliken's Bend. The Fifty-fourth Massachusetts, commanded by Robert Gould Shaw, was conspicuous in the attempt to take Fort Wagner, on Morris Island near Charleston, July 18, 1863. The regiment had marched two days and two nights through swamps and drenching rains in order to be in time for the assault. In the engagement nearly all the officers of the regiment were killed, among them Colonel Shaw. The picturesque deed was that of Sergeant William H. Carney, who seized the regiment's colors from the hands of a falling comrade, planted the flag on the works, and said when borne bleeding and mangled from the field, "Boys, the old flag never touched the ground." Fort Pillow, a position on the Mississippi, about fifty miles above Memphis, was garrisoned by 557 men, 262 of whom were Negroes, when it was attacked April 13, 1864. The fort was finally taken by the Confederates, but the feature of the engagement was the stubborn resistance offered by the Union troops in the face of great odds. In the Mississippi Valley, and in the Department of the South, the Negro had now done excellent work as a soldier. In the spring of 1864 he made his appearance in the Army of the Potomac. In July there was around Richmond and Petersburg considerable skirmishing between the Federal and the Confederate forces. Burnside, commanding a corps composed partly of Negroes, dug under a Confederate fort a trench a hundred and fifty yards long. This was filled with explosives, and on July 30 the match was applied and the famous crater formed. Just before the explosion the Negroes had figured in a gallant charge on the Confederates. The plan was to follow the eruption by a still more formidable assault, in which Burnside wanted to give his Negro troops the lead. A dispute about this and a settlement by lot resulted in the awarding of precedence to a New Hampshire regiment. Said General Grant later of the whole unfortunate episode: "General Burnside wanted to put his colored division in front; I believe if he had done so it would have been a success." After the men of a Negro regiment had charged and taken a battery at Decatur, Ala., in October, 1864, and shown exceptional gallantry under fire, they received an ovation from their white comrades "who by thousands sprang upon the parapets and cheered the regiment as it reëntered the lines." *

When all was over there was in the North a spontaneous recognition of the right of such men to honorable and generous

* General Thomas J. Morgan: "The Negroes in the Civil War," in the *Baptist Home Mission Monthly*, quoted in *Liberia*, Bulletin 12, February, 1898. General Morgan in October, 1863, became a major in the Fourteenth United States Colored Infantry. He organized the regiment and became its colonel. He also organized the Forty-second and Forty-fourth regiments of colored infantry.

treatment at the hands of the nation, and in Congress there was the feeling that if the South could come back to the Union with its autonomy unimpaired, certainly the Negro soldier should have the rights of citizenship. Before the war closed, however, there was held in Syracuse, N. Y., a convention of Negro men that threw interesting light on the problems and the feeling of the period.* At this gathering John Mercer Langston was temporary chairman, Frederick Douglass, president, and Henry Highland Garnet, of Washington; James W. C. Pennington, of New York; George L. Ruffin, of Boston, and Ebenezer D. Bassett, of Philadelphia, were among the more prominent delegates. There was at the meeting a fear that some of the things that seemed to have been gained by the war might not actually be realized; and as Congress had not yet altered the Constitution so as to abolish slavery, grave question was raised by a recent speech in which no less a man than Seward, Secretary of State, had said: "When the insurgents shall have abandoned their armies and laid down their arms, the war will instantly cease; and all the war measures then existing, including those which affect slavery, will cease also." The convention thanked the President and the Thirty-Seventh Congress for revoking a prohibitory law in regard to the carrying of mails by Negroes, for abolishing slavery in the District of Columbia, for recognizing Hayti and Liberia, and for the military order retaliating for the unmilitary treatment accorded Negro soldiers by the Confederate officers; and especially it thanked Senator Sumner "for his noble efforts to cleanse the statute-books of the nation from every stain of inequality against colored men," and General Butler for the stand he had taken early in the war. At the same time it resolved to send a petition to Congress to ask that the rights of the country's Negro patriots in the field be respected, and that the Government cease to set an example to those in arms against it by making invidious distinctions, based upon color, as to pay, labor, and promotion. It begged especially to be

* See Proceedings of the National Convention of Colored Men, held in the city of Syracuse, N. Y., October 4, 5, 6, and 7, 1864, with the Bill of Wrongs and Rights, and the Address to the American People. Boston, 1864.

saved from supposed friends: "When the *Anti-Slavery Standard*, representing the American Anti-Slavery Society, denies that the society asks for the enfranchisement of colored men, and the *Liberator* apologizes for excluding the colored men of Louisiana from the ballot-box, they injure us more vitally than all the ribald jests of the whole pro-slavery press." Finally the convention insisted that any such things as the right to own real estate, to testify in courts of law, and to sue and be sued, were mere privileges so long as general political liberty was withheld, and asked frankly not only for the formal and complete abolition of slavery in the United States, but also for the elective franchise in all the states then in the Union and in all that might come into the Union thereafter. On the whole this representative gathering showed a very clear conception of the problems facing the Negro and the country in 1864. Its reference to well-known anti-slavery publications shows not only the increasing race consciousness that came through this as through all other wars in which the country has engaged, but also the great drift toward conservatism that had taken place in the North within thirty years.

Whatever might be the questions of the moment, however, about the supreme blessing of freedom there could at last be no doubt. It had been long delayed and had finally come merely as an incident to the war; nevertheless a whole race of people had passed from death unto life. Then, as before and since, they found a parallel for their experiences in the story of the Jews in the Old Testament. They, too, had sojourned in Egypt and crossed the Red Sea. What they could not then see, or only dimly realize, was that they needed faith—faith in God and faith in themselves—for the forty years in the wilderness. They did not yet fully know that He who guided the children of Israel and drove out before them the Amorite and the Hittite, would bring them also to the Promised Land.

.   .   .   .

To those who led the Negro in these wonderful years—to Robert Gould Shaw, the young colonel of the Fifty-Fourth Massachusetts, who died leading his men at Fort Wagner; to Norwood Penrose Hallowell, lieutenant-colonel of the Fifty-Fourth and then colonel of the Fifty-Fifth; to his brother,

Edward N. Hallowell, who succeeded Shaw when he fell; and to Thomas Wentworth Higginson, who commanded the first regiment of freed slaves—no ordinary eulogy can apply. Their names are written in letters of flame and their deeds live after them. On the Shaw Monument in Boston are written these words:

THE WHITE OFFICERS

Taking Life and Honor in their Hands—Cast their lot with Men of a Despised Race Unproved in War—and Risked Death as Inciters of a Servile Insurrection if Taken Prisoners, Besides Encountering all the Common Perils of Camp, March, and Battle.

THE BLACK RANK AND FILE

Volunteered when Disaster Clouded the Union Cause —Served without Pay for Eighteen Months till Given that of White Troops—Faced Threatened Enslavement if Captured—Were Brave in Action—Patient under Dangerous and Heavy Labors and Cheerful amid Hardships and Privations.

TOGETHER

They Gave to the Nation Undying Proof that Americans of African Descent Possess the Pride, Courage, and Devotion of the Patriot Soldier—One Hundred and Eighty Thousand Such Americans Enlisted under the Union Flag in MDCCCLXIII-MDCCCLXV.

CHAPTER XIII

1. *The Problem*

At the close of the Civil War the United States found it-self face to face with one of the gravest social problems of modern times. More and more it became apparent that it was not only the technical question of the restoration of the states to the Union that had to be considered, but the whole adjustment for the future of the lives of three and a half million Negroes and five and a half million white people in the South. In its final analysis the question was one of race, and to add to the difficulties of this problem it is to be regretted that there should have been actually upon the scene politicians and specu-lators who sought to capitalize for their own gain the public distress.

The South was thoroughly demoralized, and the women who had borne the burden of the war at home were especially bit-ter. Slave property to the amount of two billions of dollars had been swept away; several of the chief cities had suffered bombardment; the railroads had largely run down; and the confiscation of property was such as to lead to the indemnifica-tion of thousands of claimants afterwards. The Negro was not yet settled in new places of abode, and his death rate was appalling. Throughout the first winter after the war the whole South was on the verge of starvation.

Here undoubtedly was a difficult situation—one calling for the highest quality of statesmanship, and of sportsmanship on the part of the vanquished. Many Negroes, freed from the tradition of two hundred and fifty years of slavery, took a holiday; some resolved not to work any more as long as they lived, and some even appropriated to their own use the produce of their neighbors. If they remained on the old plantations, they feared that they might still be considered slaves; on the other hand, if they took to the high road, they might be considered vagrants. If one returned from a Federal camp to claim his wife and children, he might be driven away. "Freedom cried out," and undoubtedly some individuals did foolish things; but serious crime was noticeably absent. On the whole the race bore the blessing of emancipation with remarkable good sense and temper. Returning soldiers paraded, there were some meetings and processions, sometimes a little regalia—and even a little noise; then everybody went home. Unfortunately even so much the white South regarded as insolence.

The example of how the South *might* have met the situation was afforded by no less a man than Robert E. Lee, about whose unselfishness and standard of conduct as a gentleman there could be no question. One day in Richmond a Negro from the street, intent on asserting his rights, entered a representative church, pushed his way to the communion altar and knelt. The congregation paused, and all fully realized the factors that entered into the situation. Then General Lee rose and knelt beside the Negro; the congregation did likewise, and the tension was over. Furthermore, every one went home spiritually uplifted.

Could the handling of this incident have been multipled a thousand times—could men have realized that mere accidents are fleeting but that principles are eternal—both races would have been spared years of agony, and our Southland would be a far different place to-day. The Negro was at the heart of the problem, but to that problem the South undoubtedly held the key. Of course the cry of "social equality" might have been raised; *anything* might have been said to keep the right thing from being done. In this instance, as in many others, the final question was not what somebody else did, but how one himself could act most nobly.

Unfortunately Lee's method of approach was not to prevail. Passion and prejudice and demagoguery were to have their day, and conservative and broadly patriotic men were to be made to follow leaders whom they could not possibly approve. Sixty years afterwards we still suffer from the KuKlux solution of the problem.

2. Meeting the Problem

The story of reconstruction has been many times told, and it is not our intention to tell that story again. We must content ourselves by touching upon some of the salient points in the discussion.

Even before the close of the war the National Government had undertaken to handle officially the thousands of Negroes who had crowded to the Federal lines and not less than a million of whom were in the spring of 1865 dependent upon the National Government for support. The Bureau of Refugee Freedmen and Abandoned Lands, created in connection with the War Department by an act of March 3, 1865, was to remain in existence throughout the war and for one year thereafter. Its powers were enlarged July 16, 1866, and its chief work did not end until January 1, 1869, its educational work continuing for a year and a half longer. The Freedmen's Bureau was to have "the supervision and management of all abandoned lands, and the control of all subjects relating to refugees and freedmen." Of special importance was the provision in the creating act that gave the freedmen to understand that each male refugee was to be given forty acres with the guarantee of possession for three years. Throughout the existence of the Bureau its chief commissioner was General O. O. Howard. While the principal officers were undoubtedly men of noble purpose, many of the minor officials were just as undoubtedly corrupt and self-seeking. In the winter of 1865-6 one-third of its aid was given to the white people of the South. For Negro pupils the Bureau established altogether 4,239 schools, and these had 9,307 teachers and 247,333 students. Its real achievement has been thus ably summed up: "The greatest success of the Freedmen's Bureau lay in the planting of the free school among Negroes, and the idea of free elementary education among all classes in the South. . . . For some fifteen million dollars, beside the sum spent before

1865, and the dole of benevolent societies, this bureau set going a system of free labor, established a beginning of peasant proprietorship, secured the recognition of black freedmen before courts of law, and founded the free common school in the South. On the other hand, it failed to begin the establishment of good will between ex-masters and freedmen, to guard its work wholly from paternalistic methods, which discouraged self-reliance, and to carry out to any considerable extent its implied promises to furnish the freedmen with land." * To this tale of its shortcomings must be added also the management of the Freedmen's Bank, which "was morally and practically part of the Freedmen's Bureau, although it had no legal connection with it." This institution made a really remarkable start in the development of thrift among the Negroes, and its failure, involving the loss of the first savings of hundreds of ex-slaves, was as disastrous in its moral as in its immediate financial consequences.

When the Freedmen's Bureau came to an end, it turned its educational interests and some money over to the religious and benevolent societies which had coöperated with it, especially to the American Missionary Association. This society had been organized before the Civil War on an interdenominational and strong anti-slavery basis; but with the withdrawal of general interest the body passed in 1881 into the hands of the Congregational Church. Other prominent agencies were the American Baptist Home Mission Society (also the American Baptist Publication Society), the Freedmen's Aid Society (representing the Northern Methodists), and the Presbyterian Board of Missions. Actual work was begun by the American Missionary Association. In 1861 Lewis Tappan, treasurer of the organization, wrote to General Butler to ask just what aid could be given. The result of the correspondence was that on September 3 of this year Rev. L. C. Lockwood reached Hampton and on September 17 opened the first day school among the freedmen. This school was taught by Mrs. Mary S. Peake, a woman of the race who had had the advantage of a free mother, and whose devotion to the work

* DuBois: *The Souls of Black Folk,* 32-37.

was such that she soon died. However, she had helped to lay the foundations of Hampton Institute. Soon there was a school at Norfolk, there were two at Newport News, and by January schools at Hilton Head and Beaufort, S. C. Then came the Emancipation Proclamation, throwing wide open the door of the great need. Rev. John Eaton, army chaplain from Ohio, afterwards United States Commissioner of Education, was placed in charge of the instruction of the Negroes, and in one way or another by the close of the war probably as many as one million in the South had learned to read and write. The 83 missionaries and teachers of the Association in 1863 increased to 250 in 1864. At the first day session of the school in Norfolk after the Proclamation there were 350 scholars, with 300 others in the evening. On the third day there were 550 in the day school and 500 others in the evening. The school had to be divided, a part going to another church; the assistants increased in number, and soon the day attendance was 1,200. For such schools the houses on abandoned plantations were used, and even public buildings were called into commission. Afterwards arose the higher institutions, Atlanta, Berea, Fisk, Talladega, Straight, with numerous secondary schools. Similarly the Baptists founded the colleges which, with some changes of name, have become Virginia Union, Hartshorn, Shaw, Benedict, Morehouse, Spelman, Jackson, and Bishop, with numerous affiliated institutions. The Methodists began to operate Clark (in South Atlanta), Claflin, Rust, Wiley, and others; and the Presbyterians, having already founded Lincoln in 1854, now founded Biddle and several seminaries for young women; while the United Presbyterians founded Knoxville. In course of time the distinctively Negro denominations—the A. M. E., the A. M. E. Z., and the C. M. E. (which last represented a withdrawal from the Southern Methodists in 1870)—also helped in the work, and thus, in addition to Wilberforce in Ohio, arose such institutions as Morris Brown University, Livingstone College, and Lane College. In 1867, moreover, the Federal Government crowned its work for the education of the Negro by the establishment at Washington of Howard University.

As these institutions have grown they have naturally developed some differences or special emphasis. Hampton and Atlanta University are now independent; and Berea has had a peculiar history, legislation in Kentucky in 1903 restricting the privileges of the institution to white students. Hampton, in the hands of General Armstrong, placed emphasis on the idea of industrial and practical education which has since become world-famous. In 1871 the Fisk Jubilee Singers began their memorable progress through America and Europe, meeting at first with scorn and sneers, but before long touching the heart of the world with their strange music. Their later success was as remarkable as their mission was unique. Meanwhile Spelman Seminary, in the record of her graduates who have gone as missionaries to Africa, has also developed a glorious tradition.

To those heroic men and women who represented this idea of education at its best, too much credit can not be given. Cravath at Fisk, Ware at Atlanta, Armstrong at Hampton, Graves at Morehouse, Tupper at Shaw, and Packard and Giles at Spelman, are names that should ever be recalled with thanksgiving. These people had no enviable task. They were ostracized and persecuted, and some of their co-workers even killed. It is true that their idea of education founded on the New England college was not very elastic; but their theory was that the young men and women whom they taught, before they were Negroes, were human beings. They had the key to the eternal verities, and time will more and more justify their position.

To the Freedmen's Bureau the South objected because of the political activity of some of its officials. To the schools founded by missionary endeavor it objected primarily on the score of social equality. To both the provisional Southern governments of 1865 replied with the so-called Black Codes. The theory of these remarkable ordinances—most harsh in Mississippi, South Carolina, and Louisiana—was that even if the Negro was nominally free he was by no means able to take care of himself and needed the tutelage and oversight of the white man. Hence developed what was to be known as a system of "apprenticeship." South Carolina in her act of

December 21, 1865, said, "A child, over the age of two years, born of a colored parent, may be bound by the father if he be living in the district, or in case of his death or absence from the district, by the mother, as an apprentice to any respectable white or colored person who is competent to make a contract; a male until he shall attain the age of twenty-one years, and a female until she shall attain the age of eighteen. . . . Males of the age of twelve years, and females of the age of ten years, shall sign the indenture of apprenticeship, and be bound thereby. . . . The master shall receive to his own use the profits of the labor of his apprentice." To this Mississippi added: "If any apprentice shall leave the employment of his or her master or mistress, said master or mistress may pursue and recapture said apprentice, and bring him or her before any justice of peace of the county, whose duty it shall be to remand said apprentice to the service of his or her master or mistress; and in the event of a refusal on the part of said apprentice so to return, then said justice shall commit said apprentice to the jail of said county," etc., etc. In general by such legislation the Negro was given the right to sue and be sued, to testify in court concerning Negroes, and to have marriage and the responsibility for children recognized. On the other hand, he could not serve on juries, could not serve in the militia, and could not vote or hold office. He was virtually forbidden to assemble, and his freedom of movement was restricted. Within recent years the Black Codes have been more than once defended as an honest effort to meet a difficult situation, but the old slavery attitude peered through them and gave the impression that those who framed them did not yet know that the old order had passed away.

Meanwhile the South was in a state of panic, and the provisional governor of Mississippi asked of President Johnson permission to organize the local militia. The request was granted and the patrols immediately began to show their hostility to Northern people and the freedmen. In the spring of 1866 there was a serious race riot in Memphis. On July 30, while some Negroes were marching to a political convention in New Orleans, they became engaged in brawls with the white spectators. Shots were exchanged; the police, assisted by the spectators, undertook to arrest the Negroes; the Negroes took refuge in the convention hall; and their pursuers stormed the building and shot down without mercy the Negroes and their white supporters. Altogether not less than forty were killed and not less than one hundred wounded; but not more than a dozen men were killed on the side of the police and the white citizens. General Sheridan, who was in command at New Orleans, characterized the affair as "an absolute massacre . . . a murder which the mayor and police of the city perpetrated without the shadow of a necessity."

In the face of such events and tendencies, and influenced to some extent by a careful and illuminating but much criticized report of Carl Schurz, Congress, led by Charles Sumner and Thaddeus Stevens, proceeded to pass legislation designed to protect the freedmen and to guarantee to the country the fruits of the war. The Thirteenth Amendment to the Constitution formally abolishing slavery was passed December 18, 1865. In the following March Congress passed over the President's veto the first Civil Rights Bill, guaranteeing to the freedmen all the ordinary rights of citizenship, and it was about the same time that it enlarged the powers of the Freedmen's Bureau. The Fourteenth Amendment (July 28, 1868) denied to the states the power to abridge the privileges or immunities of citizens of the United States; and the Fifteenth Amendment (March 30, 1870) sought to protect the Negro by giving to him the right of suffrage instead of military protection. In 1875 was passed the second Civil Rights act, designed to give Negroes equality of treatment in theaters, railway cars, hotels, etc.; but this the Supreme Court declared unconstitutional in 1883.

As a result of this legislation the Negro was placed in positions of responsibility; within the next few years the race sent two senators and thirteen representatives to Congress, and in some of the state legislatures, as in South Carolina, Negroes were decidedly in the majority. The attainments of some of these men were undoubtedly remarkable; the two United States senators, Hiram R. Revels and Blanche K. Bruce, both from Mississippi, were of unquestioned intelligence and ability, and Robert B. Elliott, one of the representatives from South Carolina, attracted unusual attention by his speech in reply to Alexander Stephens on the constitutionality of the Civil Rights bill. At the same time among the Negro legislators there was also considerable ignorance, and there set in an era of extravagance and corruption from which the "carpet-baggers" and the "scalawags" rather than the Negroes themselves reaped the benefit. Accordingly within recent years it has become more and more the fashion to lament the ills of the period, and no representative American historian can now write of reconstruction without a tone of apology. A few points, however, are to be observed. In the first place the ignorance was by no means so vast as has been supposed. Within the four years from 1861 to 1865, thanks to the army schools and missionary agencies, not less than half a million Negroes in the South had learned to read and write. Furthermore, the suffrage was not immediately given to the emancipated Negroes; this was the last rather than the first step in reconstruction. The provisional legislatures formed at the close of the war were composed of white men only; but the experiment failed because of the short-sighted laws that were enacted. If the fruit of the Civil War was not to be lost, if all the sacrifice was not to prove in vain, it became necessary for Congress to see that the overthrow of slavery was final and complete. By the Fourteenth Amendment the Negro was invested with the ordinary rights and dignity of a citizen of the United States. He was not enfranchised, but he could no longer be made the victim of state laws designed merely to keep him in servile subjection. If the Southern states had accepted this amendment, they might undoubtedly have reëntered the Union without further conditions. They refused to do so; they refused to help the National Government in any way whatsoever in its effort to guarantee to the Negro the rights of manhood. Achilles sulked in his tent, and whenever he sulks the world moves on—without him. The alternative finally presented to Congress, if it was not to make an absolute surrender, was either to hold the South indefinitely under military subjection or to place the ballot in the hands of the Negro. The former course was impossible; the latter was chosen, and the Union was really restored—was really saved—by the force of the ballot in the hands of black men.

It has been held that the Negro was primarily to blame for the corruption of the day. Here again it is well to recall the tendencies of the period. The decade succeeding the war was throughout the country one of unparalleled political corruption. The Tweed ring, the Crédit Mobilier, and the "salary grab" were only some of the more outstanding signs of the times. In the South the Negroes were not the real leaders in corruption; they simply followed the men who they supposed were their friends. Surely in the face of such facts as these it is not just to fix upon a people groping to the light the peculiar odium of the corruption that followed in the wake of the war.

And we shall have to leave it to those better informed than we to say to just what extent city and state politics in the South have been cleaned up since the Negro ceased to be a factor. Many of the constitutions framed by the reconstruction governments were really excellent models, and the fact that they were overthrown seems to indicate that some other spoilsmen were abroad. Take North Carolina, for example. In this state in 1868 the reconstruction government by its new constitution introduced the township system so favorably known in the North and West. When in 1875 the South regained control, with all the corruption it found as excellent a form of republican state government as was to be found in any state in the Union. "Every provision which any state enjoyed for the protection of public society from its bad members and bad impulses was either provided or easily procurable under the Constitution of the state." * Yet within a year, in order to annul the power of their opponents in every county in the state, the new party so amended the Constitution as to take away from every county the power of self-government and centralize everything in the legislature. Now was realized an extent of power over elections and election returns so great that no party could wholly clear itself of the idea of corrupt intentions.

* George W. Cable: *The Southern Struggle for Pure Government: An Address.* Boston, 1890, included in *The Negro Question*, New York, 1890.

At the heart of the whole question of course was race. As a matter of fact much work of genuine statesmanship was accomplished or attempted by the reconstruction governments. For one thing the idea of common school education for all people was now for the first time fully impressed upon the South. The Charleston *News and Courier* of July 11, 1876, formally granted that in the administration of Governor Chamberlain of South Carolina the abuse of the pardoning power had been corrected; the character of the officers appointed by the Executive had improved; the floating indebtedness of the state had been provided for in such a way that the rejection of fraudulent claims was assured and that valid claims were scaled one-half; the tax laws had been so amended as to secure substantial equality in the assessment of property; taxes had been reduced to eleven mills on the dollar; the contingent fund of the executive department had been reduced at a saving in two years of $101,200; legislative expenses had also been reduced so as to save in two years $350,000; legislative contingent expenses had also been handled so as to save $355,000; and the public printing reduced from $300,000 to $50,000 a year. There were, undoubtedly, at first, many corrupt officials, white and black. Before they were through, however, after only a few years of experimenting, the reconstruction governments began to show signs of being quite able to handle the situation; and it seems to have been primarily the fear on the part of the white South *that they might not fail* that prompted the determination to regain power at whatever cost. Just how this was done we are now to see.

3. *Reaction: The KuKlux Klan*

Even before the Civil War a secret organization, the Knights of the Golden Circle, had been formed to advance Southern interests. After the war there were various organizations—Men of Justice, Home Guards, Pale Faces, White Brotherhood, White Boys, Council of Safety, etc., and, with headquarters at New Orleans, the thoroughly organized Knights of the White Camelia. All of these had for their general aim the restoration of power to the white men of the South, which aim they endeavored to accomplish by regulating the conduct of the Negroes and their leaders in the Republican organization, the Union League, especially by playing upon the fears and superstitions of the Negroes. In general, especially in the Southeast, everything else was surpassed or superseded by the KuKlux Klan, which originated in Tennessee in the fall of 1865 as an association of young men for amusement, but which soon developed into a union for the purpose of whipping, banishing, terrorizing, and murdering Negroes and Northern white men who encouraged them in the exercise of their political rights. No Republican, no member of the Union League, and no G. A. R. man could become a member. The costume of the Klan was especially designed to strike terror in the uneducated Negroes. Loose-flowing sleeves, hoods in which were apertures for the eyes, nose, and mouth trimmed with red material, horns made of cotton-stuff standing out on the front and sides, high cardboard hats covered with white cloth decorated with stars or pictures of animals, long tongues of red flannel, were all used as occasion demanded. The KuKlux Klan finally extended over the whole South and greatly increased its operations on the cessation of martial law in 1870. As it worked generally at night, with its members in disguise, it was difficult for a grand jury to get evidence on which to frame a bill, and almost impossible to get a jury that would return a verdict for the state. Repeated measures against the order were of little effect until an act of 1870 extended the jurisdiction of the United States courts to all KuKlux cases. Even then for some time the organization continued active.

Naturally there were serious clashes before government was restored to the white South, especially as the KuKlux Klan grew bolder. At Colfax, Grant Parish, Louisiana, in April, 1873, there was a pitched battle in which several white men and more than fifty Negroes were killed; and violence increased as the "red shirt" campaign of 1876 approached.

In connection with the events of this fateful year, and with reference to South Carolina, where the Negro seemed most solidly in power, we recall one episode, that of the Hamburg

Massacre. We desire to give this as fully as possible in all its incidents, because we know of nothing that better illustrates the temper of the times, and because a most important matter is regularly ignored or minimized by historians.*

In South Carolina an act providing for the enrollment of the male citizens of the state, who were by the terms of the said act made subject to the performance of militia duty, was passed by the General Assembly and approved by the Governor March 16, 1869. By virtue of this act Negro citizens were regularly enrolled as a part of the National Guard of the State of South Carolina, and as the white men, with very few exceptions, failed or refused to become a part of the said force, the active militia was composed almost wholly of Negro men. The County of Edgefield, of which Hamburg was a part, was one of the military districts of the state under the apportionment of the Adjutant-General, one regiment being allotted to the district. One company of this regiment was in Hamburg. In 1876 it had recently been reorganized with Doc Adams as captain, Lewis Cartledge as first lieutenant, and A. T. Attaway as second lieutenant. The ranks were recruited to the requisite number of men, to whom arms and equipment were duly issued.

On Tuesday, July 4, the militia company assembled for drill and while thus engaged paraded through one of the least fre-

* Fleming, in his latest and most mature account of reconstruction, *The Sequel of Appomattox*, has not one word to say about the matter. Dunning, in *Reconstruction Political and Economic* (306), speaks as follows: "July 6, 1876, an armed collision between whites and blacks at Hamburg, Aiken County, resulted in the usual slaughter of the blacks. Whether the original cause of the trouble was the insolence and threats of a Negro militia company, or the aggressiveness and violence of some young white men, was much discussed throughout the state, and, indeed, the country at large. Chamberlain took frankly and strongly the ground that the whites were at fault." Such a statement we believe simply does not do justice to the facts. The account given herewith is based upon the report of the matter in a letter published in a Washington paper and submitted in connection with the debate in the United States House of Representatives, July 15th and 18th, 1876, on the Massacre of Six Colored Citizens at Hamburg, S. C., July 4, 1876; and on "An Address to the People of the United States, adopted at a Conference of Colored Citizens, held at Columbia, S. C., July 20th and 21st, 1876" (Republican Printing Co., Columbia, S. C., 1876). The Address, a document most important for the Negro's side of the story, was signed by no less than sixty representative men, among them R. B. Elliott, R. H. Gleaves, F. L. Cardozo, D. A. Straker, T. McC. Stewart, and H. N. Bouey.

quented streets of the town. This street was unusually wide,
but while marching four abreast the men were interrupted by
a horse and buggy driven *into their ranks* by Thomas Butler
and Henry Getzen, white men who resided about two miles
from the town. At the time of this interference the company
was occupying a space covering a width of not more than
eight feet, so that on either side there was abundant room for
vehicles. At the interruption Captain Adams commanded a
halt and, stepping to the head of his column, said, "Mr. Getzen, I did not think that you would treat me this way; I would
not so act towards you." To this Getzen replied with curses,
and after a few more remarks on either side, Adams, in order
to avoid further trouble, commanded his men to break ranks
and permit the buggy to pass through. The company was then
marched to the drill rooms and dismissed.

On Wednesday, July 5, Robert J. Butler, father of Thomas
Butler and father-in-law of Getzen, appeared before P. R.
Rivers, colored trial justice, and made complaint that the militia company had on the previous day obstructed one of the
public streets of Hamburg and prevented his son and son-in-
law from passing through. Rivers accordingly issued a sum-
mons for the officers to appear the next day, July 6. When
Adams and his two lieutenants appeared on Thursday, they
found present Robert J. Butler and several other white men
heavily armed with revolvers. On the calling of the case it
was announced that the defendants were present and that
Henry Sparnick, a member of the circuit bar of the county,
had been retained to represent them. Butler angrily protested
against such representation and demanded that the hearing be
postponed until he could procure counsel from the city of
Augusta; whereupon Adams and his lieutenants, after consul-
tation with their attorney, who informed them that there were
no legal grounds on which the case could be decided against
them, waived their constitutional right to be represented by
counsel and consented to go to trial. On this basis the case
was opened and proceeded with for some time, when on account of some disturbance its progress was arrested, and it
was adjourned for further hearing on the following Saturday,
July 8, at four o'clock in the afternoon.

On Saturday, between two and three o'clock, General M. C. Butler, of Edgefield, formerly an officer in the Confederate army, arrived in Hamburg, and he was followed by mounted men in squads of ten or fifteen until the number was more than two hundred, the last to arrive being Colonel A. P. Butler at the head of threescore men. Immediately after his arrival General Butler sent for Attorney Sparnick, who was charged with the request to Rivers and the officers of the militia company to confer with him at once. There was more passing of messengers back and forth, and it was at length deemed best for the men to confer with Butler. To this two of the officers objected on the ground that the whole plan was nothing more than a plot for their assassination. They sent to ask if General Butler would meet them without the presence of his armed force. He replied Yes, but before arrangements could be made for the interview another messenger came to say that the hour for the trial had arrived, that General Butler was at the court, and that he requested the presence of the trial justice, Rivers. Rivers proceeded to court alone and found Butler there waiting for him. He was about to proceed with the case when Butler asked for more time, which request was granted. He went away and never returned to the court. Instead he went to the council chamber, being surrounded now by greater and greater numbers of armed men, and he sent a committee to the officers asking that they come to the council chamber to see him. The men again declined for the same reason as before. Butler now sent an ultimatum demanding that the officers apologize for what took place on July 4 and that they surrender to him their arms, threatening that if the surrender was not made at once he would take their guns and officers by force. Adams and his men now awoke to a full sense of their danger, and they asked Rivers, who was not only trial justice but also Major General of the division of the militia to which they belonged, if he demanded their arms of them. Rivers replied that he did not. Thereupon the officers refused the request of Butler on the ground that he had no legal right to demand their arms or to receive them if surrendered. At this point Butler let it be known that he demanded the surrender of the arms within half an hour and that if he did not receive them he would "lay the d—— town in ashes." Asked in an interview whether, if his terms were complied with, he would guarantee protection to the people of the town he answered that he did not know and that that would depend altogether upon how they behaved themselves.

Butler now went with a companion to Augusta, returning in about thirty minutes. A committee called upon him as soon as he got back. He had only to say that he demanded the arms immediately. Asked if he would accept the boxing up of the arms and the sending of them to the Governor, he said, "D—— the Governor. I am not here to consult him, but am here as Colonel Butler, and this won't stop until after November." Asked again if he would guarantee general protection if the arms were surrendered, he said, "I guarantee nothing."

All the while scores of mounted men were about the streets. Such members of the militia company as were in town and their friends to the number of thirty-eight repaired to their armory—a large brick building about two hundred yards from the river—and barricaded themselves for protection. Firing upon the armory was begun by the mounted men, and after half an hour there were occasional shots from within. After a while the men in the building heard an order to bring cannon from Augusta, and they began to leave the building from the rear, concealing themselves as well as they could in a cornfield. The cannon was brought and discharged three or four times, those firing it not knowing that the building had been evacuated. When they realized their mistake they made a general search through lots and yards for the members of the company and finally captured twenty-seven of them, after two had been killed. The men, none of whom now had arms, were marched to a place near the railroad station, where the sergeant of the company was ordered to call the roll. Allan T. Attaway, whose name was first, was called out and shot in cold blood. Twelve men fired upon him and he was killed instantly. The men whose names were second, third, and fourth on the list were called out and treated likewise. The fifth man made a dash for liberty and escaped with a slight wound in the leg. All the others were then required to hold up their right hands and swear that they would never bear arms against the white people or give in court any testimony whatsoever regarding the occurrence. They were then marched off two by two and dispersed, but stray shots were fired after them as they went away. In another portion of the town the chief of police, James Cook, was taken from his home and brutally murdered. A marshal of the town was shot through the body and mortally wounded. One of the men killed was found with his tongue cut out. The members of Butler's party finally entered the homes of most of the prominent Negroes in the town, smashed the furniture, tore books to pieces, and cut pictures from their frames, all amid the most heartrending distress on the part of the women and children. That night the town was desolate, for all who could do so fled to Aiken or Columbia.

Upon all of which our only comment is that while such a process might seem for a time to give the white man power, it makes no progress whatever toward the ultimate solution of the problem.

4. *Counter-Reaction: The Negro Exodus*

The Negro Exodus of 1879 was partially considered in connection with our study of Liberia; but a few facts are in place here.

After the withdrawal of Federal troops conditions in the South were changed so much that, especially in South Carolina, Mississippi, Louisiana, and Texas, the state of affairs was no longer tolerable. Between 1866 and 1879 more than three thousand Negroes were summarily killed.[*] The race began to feel that a new slavery in the horrible form of peonage was approaching, and that the disposition of the men in power was to reduce the laborer to the minimum of advantages as a free man and to none at all as a citizen. The fear, which soon developed into a panic, rose especially in conse-

[*] Emmett J. Scott: Negro Migration during the War (in Preliminary Economic Studies of the War—Carnegie Endowment for International Peace: Division of Economics and History). Oxford University Press, American Branch, New York, 1920.

quence of the work of political mobs in 1874 and 1875, and it soon developed organization. About this the outstanding fact was that the political leaders of the last few years were regularly distrusted and ignored, the movement being secret in its origin and committed either to the plantation laborers themselves or their direct representatives. In North Carolina circulars about Nebraska were distributed. In Tennessee Benjamin ("Pap") Singleton began about 1869 to induce Negroes to go to Kansas, and he really founded two colonies with a total of 7432 Negroes from his state, paying of his own money over $600 for circulars. In Louisiana alone 70,000 names were taken of those who wished to better their condition by removal; and by 1878 98,000 persons in Louisiana, Mississippi, Alabama, and Texas were ready to go elsewhere. A convention to consider the whole matter of migration was held in Nashville in 1879. At this the politician managed to put in an appearance and there was much wordy discussion. At the same time much of the difference of opinion was honest; the meeting was on the whole constructive; and it expressed itself as favorable to "reasonable migration." Already, however, thousands of Negroes were leaving their homes in the South and going in greatest numbers to Kansas, Missouri, and Indiana. Within twenty months Kansas alone received in this way an addition to her population of 40,000 persons. Many of these people arrived at their destination practically penniless and without prospect of immediate employment; but help was afforded by relief agencies in the North, and they themselves showed remarkable sturdiness in adapting themselves to the new conditions.

Many of the stories that the Negroes told were pathetic.* Sometimes boats would not take them on, and they suffered from long exposure on the river banks. Sometimes, while they were thus waiting, agents of their own people employed by the planters tried to induce them to remain. Frequently they were clubbed or whipped. Said one: "I saw nine put in one pile, that had been killed, and the colored people had to bury them; eight others were found killed in the woods. . . . It is

* See *Negro Exodus* (Report of Colonel Frank H. Fletcher).

done this way: they arrest them for breach of contract and carry them to jail. Their money is taken from them by the jailer and it is not returned when they are let go." Said another: "If a colored man stays away from the polls and does not vote, they spot him and make him vote. If he votes their way, they treat him no better in business. They hire the colored people to vote, and then take their pay away. I know a man to whom they gave a cow and a calf for voting their ticket. After election they came and told him that if he kept the cow he must pay for it; and they took the cow and calf away." Another: "One man shook his fist in my face and said, 'D—— you, sir, you are my property.' He said that I owed him. He could not show it and then said, 'You sha'n't go anyhow.' All we want is a living chance." Another: "There is a general talk among the whites and colored people that Jeff Davis will run for president of the Southern states, and the colored people are afraid they will be made slaves again. They are already trying to prevent them from going from one plantation to another without a pass." Another: "The deputy sheriff came and took away from me a pair of mules. He had a constable and twenty-five men with guns to back him." Another: "Last year, after settling with my landlord, my share was four bales of cotton. I shipped it to Richardson and May, 38 and 40 Perdido Street, New Orleans, through W. E. Ringo & Co., merchants, at Mound Landing, Miss. I lived four miles back of this landing. I received from Ringo a ticket showing that my cotton was sold at nine and three-eighths cents, but I could never get a settlement. He kept putting me off by saying that the bill of lading had not come. Those bales averaged over four hundred pounds. I did not owe him over twenty-five dollars. A man may work there from Monday morning to Saturday night, and be as economical as he pleases, and he will come out in debt. I am a close man, and I work hard. I want to be honest in getting through the world. I came away and left a crop of corn and cotton growing up. I left it because I did not want to work twelve months for nothing. I have been trying it for fifteen years, thinking every year that it would get better, and it gets worse." Said still another: "I learned about Kansas from the newspapers that I got hold of. They were Southern papers. I got a map, and found out where Kansas was; and I got a History of the United States, and read about it."

Query: Was it genuine statesmanship that permitted these people to feel that they must leave the South?

---

5. *A Postscript on the War and Reconstruction*

Of all of the stories of these epoch-making years we have chosen one—an idyl of a woman with an alabaster box, of one who had a clear conception of the human problem presented and who gave her life in the endeavor to meet it.

In the fall of 1862 a young woman who was destined to be a great missionary entered the Seminary at Rockford, Illinois. There was little to distinguish her from the other students except that she was very plainly dressed and seemed forced to spend most of her spare time at work. Yes, there was one other difference. She was older than most of the girls—already thirty, and rich in experience. When not yet fifteen she had taught a country school in Pennsylvania. At twenty she was considered capable of managing an unusually turbulent crowd of boys and girls. When she was twenty-seven her father died, leaving upon her very largely the care of her mother. At twenty-eight she already looked back upon fourteen years as a teacher, upon some work for Christ incidentally accomplished, but also upon a fading youth of wasted hopes and unfulfilled desires.

Then came a great decision—not the first, not the last, but one of the most important that marked her long career. Her education was by no means complete, and, at whatever cost, she would go to school. That she had no money, that her clothes were shabby, that her mother needed her, made no difference; now or never she would realize her ambition. She would do anything, however menial, if it was honest and would give her food while she continued her studies. For one long day she walked the streets of Belvidere looking for a home. Could any one use a young woman who wanted to work for her board? Always the same reply. Nightfall brought her to a farmhouse in the suburbs of the town. She timidly knocked on the door. "No, we do not need any one," said the woman who greeted her, "but wait until I see my husband." The man of the house was very unwilling, but decided to give shelter for the night. The next morning he thought differently about the matter, and a few days afterwards the young woman entered school. The work was hard; fires had to be made, breakfasts on cold mornings had to be prepared, and sometimes the washing was heavy. Naturally the time for lessons was frequently cut short or extended far into the night. But the woman of the house was kind, and her daughter a helpful fellow-student.

The next summer came another season at school-teaching, and then the term at Rockford. 1862! a great year that in American history, one more famous for the defeat of the Union arms than for their success. But in September came Antietam, and the heart of the North took courage. Then with the new year came the Emancipation Proclamation.

The girls at Rockford, like the people everywhere, were interested in the tremendous events that were shaking the nation. A new note of seriousness crept into their work. Embroidery was laid aside; instead, socks were knit and bandages prepared. On the night of January 1 a jubilee meeting was held in the town.

To Joanna P. Moore, however, the news of freedom brought a strange undertone of sadness. She could not help thinking of the spiritual and intellectual condition of the millions now emancipated. Strange that she should be possessed by this problem! She had thought of work in China, or India, or even in Africa—but of this, never!

In February a man who had been on Island No. 10 came to the Seminary and told the girls of the distress of the women and children there. Cabins and tents were everywhere. As many as three families, with eight or ten children each, cooked their food in the same pot on the same fire. Sometimes the women were peevish or quarrelsome; always the children were dirty. "What can a man do to help such a suffering mass of humanity?" asked the speaker. "Nothing. A woman is needed;

nobody else will do." For the student listening so intently the cheery schoolrooms with their sweet associations faded; the vision of foreign missions also vanished; and in their stead stood only a pitiful black woman with a baby in her arms.

She reached Island No. 10 in November. The outlook was dismal enough. The Sunday school at Belvidere had pledged four dollars a month toward her support, and this was all the money in sight, though the Government provided transportation and soldiers' rations. That was in 1863, sixty years ago; but every year since then, until 1916, in summer and winter, in sunshine and rain, in the home and the church, with teaching and praying, feeding and clothing, nursing and hoping and loving, Joanna P. Moore in one way or another ministered to the Negro people of the South.

In April, 1864, her whole colony was removed to Helena, Arkansas. The Home Farm was three miles from Helena. Here was gathered a great crowd of women and children and helpless old men, all under the guard of a company of soldiers in a fort nearby. Thither went the missionary alone, except for her faith in God. She made an arbor with some rude seats, nailed a blackboard to a tree, divided the people into four groups, and began to teach school. In the twilight every evening a great crowd gathered around her cabin for prayers. A verse of the Bible was read and explained, petitions were offered, one of the sorrow-songs was chanted, and then the service was over.

Some Quaker workers were her friends in Helena, and in 1868 she went to Lauderdale, Mississippi, to help the Friends in an orphan asylum. Six weeks after her arrival the superintendent's daughter died, and the parents left to take their child back to their Indiana home to rest. The lone woman was left in charge of the asylum. Cholera broke out. Eleven children died within one week. Still she stood by her post. Often, she said, those who were well and happy when they retired, ere daylight came were in the grave, for they were buried the same hour they died. Night after night she prayed to God in the dark, and at length the fury of the plague was abated.

From time to time the failing health of her mother called her home, and from 1870 to 1873 she once more taught school near Belvidere. The first winter the school was in the country. "You can never have a Sunday school in the winter," they told her. But she did; in spite of the snow, the house was crowded every Sunday, whole families coming in sleighs. Even at that the real work of the teacher was with the Negroes of the South. In her prayers and public addresses they were always with her, and in 1873 friends in Chicago made it possible for her to return to the work of her choice. In 1877 the Woman's Baptist Home Mission Society honored itself by giving to her its first commission.

Nine years she spent in the vicinity of New Orleans. Near Leland University she found a small, one-room house. After buying a bed, a table, two chairs, and a few cooking utensils, she began housekeeping. Often she started out at six in the morning, not to return until dark. Most frequently she read the Bible to those who could not read. Sometimes she gave cheer to mothers busy over the washtub. Sometimes she would teach the children to read or to sew. Often she would write letters for those who had been separated from friends or kindred in the dark days. She wrote hundreds and hundreds of such letters; and once in a while, a very long while, came a response.

Most pitiful of all the objects she found in New Orleans were the old women worn out with years of slavery. They were usually rag-pickers who ate at night the scraps for which they had begged during the day. There was in the city an Old Ladies' Home; but this was not for Negroes. A house was secured and the women taken in, Joanna Moore and her associates moving into the second story. Sometimes, very often, there was real need; but sometimes, too, provisions came when it was not known who sent them; money or boxes came from Northern friends who had never seen the workers; and the little Negro children in the Sunday schools in the city gave their pennies.

In 1878 the laborer in the Southwest started on a journey of exploration. In Atlanta Dr. Robert at Atlanta Baptist Seminary (now Morehouse College) gave her cheer; so did President Ware at Atlanta University. At Benedict in Columbia she saw Dr. Goodspeed, President Tupper at Shaw in Raleigh,

and Dr. Corey in Richmond. In May she appeared at the
Baptist anniversaries, with fifteen years of missionary achievement already behind her.

But each year brought its own sorrows and disappointments.
She wanted the Society to establish a training school for
women; but to this objection was raised. In Louisiana also
it was not without danger that a white woman attended a
Negro association in 1877; and there were always sneers and
jeers. At length, however, a training school for mothers was
opened in Baton Rouge. All went well for two years; and
then a notice with skull and crossbones was placed on the gate.
The woman who had worked through the cholera still stood
firm; but the students had gone. Sick at heart and worn out
with waiting, she at last left Baton Rouge and the state in
which so many of her best years had been spent.

"Bible Band" work was started in 1884, and *Hope* in 1885.
The little paper, beginning with a circulation of five hundred,
has now reached a monthly issue of twenty thousand copies,
and daily it brings its lesson of cheer to thousands of mothers
and children in the South. In connection with it all has developed the Fireside School, than which few agencies have been
more potent in the salvation and uplift of the humble Negro
home.

What wisdom was gathered from the passing of fourscore
years! On almost every page of her tracts, her letters, her
account of her life, one finds quotations of proverbial pith:

The love of God gave me courage for myself and the rest of mankind; therefore I concluded to invest in human souls. They surely
are worth more than anything else in the world.

Beloved friends, be hopeful, be courageous. God can not use discouraged people.

The good news spread, not by telling what we were going to do
but by praising God for what had been done.

So much singing in all our churches leaves too little time for the
Bible lesson. Do not misunderstand me. I do love music that im-
presses the meaning of words. But no one climbs to heaven on
musical scales.

I thoroughly believe that the only way to succeed with any vocation
is to make it a part of your very self and weave it into your every
thought and prayer.

You must love before you can comfort and help.

There is no place too lowly or dark for our feet to enter, and no place so high and bright but it needs the touch of the light that we carry from the Cross.

How shall we measure such a life? Who can weigh love and hope and service, and the joy of answered prayer? "An annual report of what?" she once asked the secretary of her organization. "Report of tears shed, prayers offered, smiles scattered, lessons taught, steps taken, cheering words, warning words—tender, patient words for the little ones, stern but loving tones for the wayward—songs of hope and songs of sorrow, wounded hearts healed, light and love poured into dark sad homes? Oh, Miss Burdette, you might as well ask me to gather up the raindrops of last year or the petals that fall from the flowers that bloomed. It is true that I can send you a little stagnant water from the cistern, and a few dried flowers; but if you want to know the freshness, the sweetness, the glory, the grandeur, of our God-given work, then you must come and keep step with us from early morn to night for three hundred and sixty-five days in the year."

Until the very last she was on the roll of the active workers of the Woman's American Baptist Home Mission Society. In the fall of 1915 she decided that she must once more see the schools in the South that meant so much to her. In December she came again to her beloved Spelman. While in Atlanta she met with an accident that still further weakened her. After a few weeks, however, she went on to Jacksonville, and then to Selma. There she passed.

. . . .

When the Son of Man shall come in his glory, and all the holy angels with him, then shall he sit upon the throne of his glory. . . . Then shall the righteous answer him, saying, Lord, when saw we thee an hungered, and fed thee? or thirsty, and gave thee drink? When saw we thee a stranger, and took thee in? or naked, and clothed thee? Or when saw we thee sick, or in prison, and came unto thee? And the King shall answer and say unto them, Verily I say unto you, Inasmuch as ye have done it unto one of the least of these my brethren, you have done it unto me.

CHAPTER XIV

THE NEGRO IN THE NEW SOUTH

1. *Political Life: Disfranchisement*

By 1876 the reconstruction governments had all but passed.
A few days after his inauguration in 1877 President Hayes
sent to Louisiana a commission to investigate the claims of
rival governments there. The decision was in favor of the
Democrats. On April 9 the President ordered the removal of
Federal troops from public buildings in the South; and in
Columbia, S. C., within a few days the Democratic administration of Governor Wade Hampton was formally recognized. The new governments at once set about the abrogation
of the election laws that had protected the Negro in the exercise of suffrage, and, having by 1877 obtained a majority in
the national House of Representatives, the Democrats resorted
to the practice of attaching their repeal measures to appropriation bills in the hope of compelling the President to sign them.
Men who had been prominently connected with the Confederacy were being returned to Congress in increasing numbers,
but in general the Democrats were not able to carry their measures over the President's veto. From the Supreme Court,
however, they received practical assistance, for while this body
did not formally grant that the states had full powers over
elections, it nevertheless nullified many of the most objection-
able sections of the laws. Before the close of the decade, by
intimidation, the theft, suppression or exchange of the ballot
boxes, the removal of the polls to unknown places, false certi-
fications, and illegal arrests on the day before an election, the
Negro vote had been rendered ineffectual in every state of the
South.

When Cleveland was elected in 1884 the Negroes of the
South naturally felt that the darkest hour of their political

fortunes had come. It had, for among many other things this election said that after twenty years of discussion and tumult the Negro question was to be relegated to the rear, and that the country was now to give main attention to other problems. For the Negro the new era was signalized by one of the most effective speeches ever delivered in this or any other country, all the more forceful because the orator was a man of unusual nobility of spirit. In 1886 Henry W. Grady, of Georgia, addressed the New England Club in New York on "The New South." He spoke to practical men and he knew his ground. He asked his hearers to bring their "full faith in American fairness and frankness" to judgment upon what he had to say. He pictured in brilliant language the Confederate soldier, "ragged, half-starved, heavy-hearted, who wended his way homeward to find his house in ruins and his farm devastated." He also spoke kindly of the Negro: "Whenever he struck a blow for his own liberty he fought in open battle, and when at last he raised his black and humble hands that the shackles might be struck off, those hands were innocent of wrong against his helpless charges." But Grady also implied that the Negro had received too much attention and sympathy from the North. Said he: "To liberty and enfranchisement is as far as law can carry the Negro. The rest must be left to conscience and common sense." Hence on this occasion and others he asked that the South be left alone in the handling of her grave problem. The North, a little tired of the Negro question, a little uncertain also as to the wisdom of the reconstruction policy that it had forced on the South, and if concerned with this section at all, interested primarily in such investments as it had there, assented to this request; and in general the South now felt that it might order its political life in its own way.

As yet, however, the Negro was not technically disfranchised, and at any moment a sudden turn of events might call him into prominence. Formal legislation really followed the rise of the Populist party, which about 1890 in many places in the South waged an even contest with the Democrats. It was evident that in such a struggle the Negro might still hold the balance of power, and within the next few years a fusion of the Republicans and the Populists in North Carolina sent a Negro, George H. White, to Congress. This event finally served only to strengthen the movement for disfranchisement which had already begun. In 1890 the constitution of Mississippi was so amended as to exclude from the suffrage any person who had not paid his poll-tax or who was unable to read any section of the constitution, or understand it when read to him, or to give a reasonable interpretation of it. The effect of the administration of this provision was that in 1890 only 8615 Negroes out of 147,000 of voting age became registered. South Carolina amended her constitution with similar effect in 1895. In this state the population was almost three-fifths Negro and two-fifths white. The franchise of the Negro was already in practical abeyance; but the problem now was to devise a means for the perpetuity of a government of white men. Education was not popular as a test, for by it many white illiterates would be disfranchised and in any case it would only postpone the race issue. For some years the dominant party had been engaged in factional controversies, with the populist wing led by Benjamin R. Tillman prevailing over the conservatives. It was understood, however, that each side would be given half of the membership of the convention, which would exclude all Negro and Republican representation, and that the constitution would go into effect without being submitted to the people. Said the most important provision: "Any person who shall apply for registration after January 1, 1898, if otherwise qualified, shall be registered; provided that he can both read and write any section of this constitution submitted to him by the registration officer or can show that he owns and has paid all taxes collectible during the previous year on property in this state assessed at three hundred dollars or more"—clauses which it is hardly necessary to say the registrars regularly interpreted in favor of white men and against the Negro. In 1898 Louisiana passed an amendment inventing the so-called "grandfather clause." This excused from the operation of her disfranchising act all descendants of men who had voted before the Civil War, thus admitting to the suffrage all white men who were illiterate and without property. North Carolina in 1900, Virginia and Alabama in 1901, Georgia in 1907, and Oklahoma in 1910 in one way or another practically disfranchised the Negro, care being taken in every instance to avoid any definite clash with the Fifteenth Amendment. In Maryland there have been several attempts to disfranchise the Negro by constitutional amendments, one in 1905, another in 1909, and still another in 1911, but all have failed. About the intention of its disfranchising legislation the South, as represented by more than one spokesman, was very frank. Unfortunately the new order called forth a group of leaders—represented by Tillman in South Carolina, Hoke Smith in Georgia, and James K. Vardaman in Mississippi—who made a direct appeal to prejudice and thus capitalized the racial feeling that already had been brought to too high tension.

Naturally all such legislation as that suggested had ultimately to be brought before the highest tribunal in the country. The test came over the following section from the Oklahoma law: "No person shall be registered as an elector of this state or be allowed to vote in any election herein unless he shall be able to read and write any section of the Constitution of the State of Oklahoma; but no person who was on January 1, 1866, or at any time prior thereto, entitled to vote under any form of government, or who at any time resided in some foreign nation, and no lineal descendant of such person shall be denied the right to register and vote because of his inability to so read and write sections of such Constitution." This enactment the Supreme Court declared unconstitutional in 1915. The decision exerted no great and immediate effect on political conditions in the South; nevertheless as the official recognition by the nation of the fact that the Negro was not accorded his full political rights, it was destined to have far-reaching effect on the whole political fabric of the section.

When the era of disfranchisement began it was in large measure expected by the South that with the practical elimination of the Negro from politics this section would become wider in its outlook and divide on national issues. Such has not proved to be the case. Except for the noteworthy deflection of Tennessee in the presidential election of 1920, and Republican gains in some counties in other states, this section remains just as "solid" as it was forty years ago, largely of course because the Negro, through education and the acquisition of property, is becoming more and more a potential factor in politics. Meanwhile it is to be observed that the Negro is not wholly without a vote, even in the South, and sometimes his power is used with telling effect, as in the city of Atlanta in the spring of 1919, when he decided in the negative the question of a bond issue. In the North moreover—especially in Indiana, Ohio, New Jersey, Illinois, Pennsylvania, and New York—he has on more than one occasion proved the deciding factor in political affairs. Even when not voting, however, he involuntarily wields tremendous influence on the destinies of the nation, for even though men may be disfranchised, all are nevertheless counted in the allotment of congressmen to Southern states. This anomalous situation means that in actual practice the vote of one white man in the South is four or six or even eight times as strong as that of a man in the North;* and it directly accounted for the victory of President Wilson and the Democrats over the Republicans led by Charles E. Hughes in 1916. For remedying it by the enforcement of the Fourteenth Amendment bills have been frequently presented in Congress, but on these no action has been taken.

2. *Economic Life: Peonage*

Within fifteen years after the close of the war it was clear that the Emancipation Proclamation was a blessing to the poor white man of the South as well as to the Negro. The break-up of the great plantation system was ultimately to prove good for all men whose slender means had given them little chance before the war. At the same time came also the development of cotton-mills throughout the South, in which as early as 1880 not less than 16,000 white people were employed. With the decay of the old system the average acreage of hold-

---

* In 1914 Kansas and Mississippi each elected eight members of the House of Representatives, but Kansas cast 483,683 votes for her members, while Mississippi cast only 37,185 for hers, less than one-twelfth as many.

ings in the South Atlantic states decreased from 352.8 in 1860 to 108.4 in 1900. It was still not easy for an independent Negro to own land on his own account; nevertheless by as early a year as 1874 the Negro farmers had acquired 338,769 acres. After the war the planters first tried the wage system for the Negroes. This was not satisfactory—from the planter's standpoint because the Negro had not yet developed stability as a laborer; from the Negro's standpoint because while the planter might advance rations, he frequently postponed the payment of wages and sometimes did not pay at all. Then land came to be rented; but frequently the rental was from 80 to 100 pounds of lint cotton an acre for land that produced only 200 to 400 pounds. In course of time the share system came to be most widely used. Under this the tenant frequently took his whole family into the cotton-field, and when the crop was gathered and he and the landlord rode together to the nearest town to sell it, he received one-third, one-half, or two-thirds of the money according as he had or had not furnished his own food, implements, and horses or mules. This system might have proved successful if he had not had to pay exorbitant prices for his rations. As it was, if the landlord did not directly furnish foodstuffs he might have an understanding with the keeper of the country store, who frequently charged for a commodity twice what it was worth in the open market. At the close of the summer there was regularly a huge bill waiting for the Negro at the store; this had to be disposed of first, *and he always came out just a few dollars behind.* However, the landlord did not mind such a small matter and in the joy of the harvest might even advance a few dollars; but the understanding was always that the tenant was to remain on the land the next year. Thus were the chains of peonage forged about him.

At the same time there developed a still more vicious system. Immediately after the war legislation enacted in the South made severe provision with reference to vagrancy. Negroes were arrested on the slightest pretexts and their labor as that of convicts leased to landowners or other business men. When, a few years later, Negroes, dissatisfied with the returns from their labor on the farms, began a movement to the cities, there arose a tendency to make the vagrancy legislation still more harsh, so that at last a man could not stop work without technically committing a crime. Thus in all its hideousness developed the convict lease system.

This institution and the accompanying chain-gang were at variance with all the humanitarian impulses of the nineteenth century. Sometimes prisoners were worked in remote parts of a state altogether away from the oversight of responsible officials; if they stayed in a prison the department for women was frequently in plain view and hearing of the male convicts, and the number of cubic feet in a cell was only one-fourth of what a scientific test would have required. Sometimes there was no place for the dressing of the dead except in the presence of the living. The system was worst when the lessee was given the entire charge of the custody and discipline of the convicts, and even of their medical or surgical care. Of real attention there frequently was none, and reports had numerous blank spaces to indicate deaths from unknown causes. The sturdiest man could hardly survive such conditions for more than ten years. In Alabama in 1880 only three of the convicts had been in confinement for eight years, and only one for nine. In Texas, from 1875 to 1880, the total number of prisoners discharged was 1651, while the number of deaths and escapes for the same period totalled 1608. In North Carolina the mortality was eight times as great as in Sing Sing.

At last the conscience of the nation began to be heard, and after 1883 there were remedial measures. However, the care of the prisoner still left much to be desired; and as the Negro is greatly in the majority among prisoners in the South, and as he is still sometimes arrested illegally or on flimsy pretexts, the whole matter of judicial and penal procedure becomes one of the first points of consideration in any final settlement of the Negro Problem.*

* Within recent years it has been thought that the convict lease system and peonage had practically passed in the South. That this was by no means the case was shown by the astonishing revelations from Jasper County, Georgia, early in 1921, it being demonstrated in court that a white farmer, John S. Williams, who had "bought out" Negroes from the prisons of Atlanta and Macon, had not only held these people in

3. *Social Life: Proscription, Lynching*

Meanwhile proscription went forward. Separate and inferior traveling accommodations, meager provision for the education of Negro children, inadequate street, lighting and water facilities in most cities and towns, and the general lack of protection of life and property, made living increasingly harder for a struggling people. For the Negro of aspiration or culture every day became a long train of indignities and insults. On street cars he was crowded into a few seats, generally in the rear; he entered a railway station by a side door; in a theater he might occupy only a side, or more commonly the extreme rear, of the second balcony; a house of ill fame might flourish next to his own little home; and from public libraries he was shut out altogether, except where a little branch was sometimes provided. Every opportunity for such self-improvement as a city might be expected to afford him was either denied him, or given on such terms as his self-respect forced him to refuse.

Meanwhile—and worst of all—he failed to get justice in the courts. Formally called before the bar he knew beforehand that the case was probably already decided against him. A white boy might insult and pick a quarrel with his son, but if the case reached the court room the white boy would be freed and the Negro boy fined $25 or sent to jail for three months. Some trivial incident involving no moral responsibility whatever on the Negro's part might yet cost him his life.

Lynching grew apace. Generally this was said to be for

peonage, but had been directly responsible for the killing of not less than eleven of them.

However, as the present work passes through the press, word comes of the remarkable efforts of Governor Hugh M. Dorsey for a more enlightened public conscience in his state. In addition to special endeavor for justice in the Williams case, he has issued a booklet citing with detail one hundred and thirty-five cases in which Negroes have suffered grave wrong. He divides his cases into four divisions: (1) The Negro lynched, (2) The Negro held in peonage, (3) The Negro driven out by organized lawlessness, and (4) The Negro subject to individual acts of cruelty. "In some counties," he says, "the Negro is being driven out as though he were a wild beast. In others he is being held as a slave. In others no Negroes remain. . . . In only two of the 135 cases cited is crime against white women involved."

For the more recent history of peonage see pp. 306, 329, 344, 360-363.

the protection of white womanhood; but statistics certainly did not give rape the prominence that it held in the popular mind. Any cause of controversy, however slight, that forced a Negro to defend himself against a white man might result in a lynching, and possibly in a burning. In the period of 1871-73 the number of Negroes lynched in the South is said to have been not more than 11 a year. Between 1885 and 1915, however, the number of persons lynched in the country amounted to 3500, the great majority being Negroes in the South. For the year 1892 alone the figure was 235.

One fact was outstanding: astonishing progress was being made by the Negro people, but in the face of increasing education and culture on their part, there was no diminution of race feeling. Most Southerners preferred still to deal with a Negro of the old type rather than with one who was neatly dressed, simple and unaffected in manner, and ambitious to have a good home. In any case, however, it was clear that since the white man held the power, upon him rested primarily the responsibility of any adjustment. Old schemes for deportation or colonization in a separate state having proved ineffective or chimerical, it was necessary to find a new platform on which both races could stand. The Negro was still the outstanding factor in agriculture and industry; in large numbers he had to live, and will live, in Georgia and South Carolina, Mississippi and Texas; and there should have been some plane on which he could reside in the South not only serviceably but with justice to his self-respect. The wealth of the New South, it is to be remembered, was won not only by the labor of black hands but also that of little white boys and girls. As laborers and citizens, real or potential, both of these groups deserved the most earnest solicitude of the state, for it is not upon the riches of the few but the happiness of the many that a nation's greatness depends. Moreover no state can build permanently or surely by denying to a half or a third of those governed any voice whatever in the government. If the Negro was ignorant, he was also economically defenseless; and it is neither just nor wise to deny to any man, however humble, any real power for his legal protection. If these principles hold—and we think they are in line with enlightened conceptions of society—the prosperity of the New South was by no means as genuine as it appeared to be, and the disfranchisement of the Negro, morally and politically, was nothing less than a crime.

CHAPTER XV

"THE VALE OF TEARS," 1890-1910

1. *Current Opinion and Tendencies*

In the two decades that we are now to consider we find the working out of all the large forces mentioned in our last chapter. After a generation of striving the white South was once more thoroughly in control, and the new program well under way. Predictions for both a broader outlook for the section as a whole and greater care for the Negro's moral and intellectual advancement were destined not to be fulfilled; and the period became one of bitter social and economic antagonism.

All of this was primarily due to the one great fallacy on which the prosperity of the New South was built, and that was that the labor of the Negro existed only for the good of the white man. To this one source may be traced most of the ills borne by both white man and Negro during the period. If the Negro's labor was to be exploited, it was necessary that he be without the protection of political power and that he be denied justice in court. If he was to be reduced to a peon, certainly socially he must be given a peon's place. Accordingly there developed everywhere—in schools, in places of public accommodation, in the facilities of city life—the idea of inferior service for Negroes; and an unenlightened prison system flourished in all its hideousness. Furthermore, as a result of the vicious economic system, arose the sinister form of the Negro criminal. Here again the South begged the question, representative writers lamenting the passing of the dear dead days of slavery, and pointing cynically to the effects of freedom on the Negro. They failed to remember in the case of the Negro criminal that from childhood to manhood—in education, in economic chance, in legal power—they had by their own system deprived a human being of every privilege that was due him, ruining him body and soul; and then they stood aghast at the thing their hands had made. More than that, they blamed the race itself for the character that now sometimes appeared, and called upon thrifty, aspiring Negroes to find the criminal and give him up to the law. Thrifty, aspiring Negroes wondered what was the business of the police.

It was this pitiful failure to get down to fundamentals that characterized the period and that made life all the more hard for those Negroes who strove to advance. Every effort was made to brutalize a man, and then he was blamed for not being a St. Bernard. Fortunately before the period was over there arose not only clear-thinking men of the race but also a few white men who realized that such a social order could not last forever.

Early in the nineties, however, the pendulum had swung fully backward, and the years from 1890 to 1895 were in some ways the darkest that the race has experienced since emancipation. When in 1892 Cleveland was elected for a second term and the Democrats were once more in power, it seemed to the Southern rural Negro that the conditions of slavery had all but come again. More and more the South formulated its creed; it glorified the old aristocracy that had flourished and departed, and definitely it began to ask the North if it had not been right after all. It followed of course that if the Old South had the real key to the problem, the proper place of the Negro was that of a slave.

Within two or three years there were so many important articles on the Negro in prominent magazines and these were by such representative men that taken together they formed a symposium. In December, 1891, James Bryce wrote in the *North American Review,* pointing out that the situation in the South was a standing breach of the Constitution, that it suspended the growth of political parties and accustomed the section to fraudulent evasions, and he emphasized education as a possible remedy; he had quite made up his mind that the Negro had little or no place in politics. In January, 1892, a distinguished classical scholar, Basil L. Gildersleeve, turned aside from linguistics to write in the *Atlantic* "The Creed

of the Old South," which article he afterwards published as
a special brochure, saying that it had been more widely read
than anything else he had ever written. In April, Thomas
Nelson Page in the *North American* contended that in spite
of the $5,000,000 spent on the education of the Negro in
Virginia between 1870 and 1890 the race had retrograded or
not greatly improved, and in fact that the Negro "did not
possess the qualities to raise himself above slavery." Later
in the same year he published *The Old South.* In the same
month Frederick L. Hoffman, writing in the *Arena,* contended
that in view of its mortality statistics the Negro race would
soon die out.* Also in April, 1892, Henry Watterson wrote
of the Negro in the *Chautauquan,* recalling the facts that the
era of political turmoil had been succeeded by one of reaction
and violence, and that by one of exhaustion and peace; but
with all his insight he ventured no constructive suggestion,
thinking it best for everybody "simply to be quiet for a time."
Early in 1893 John C. Wycliffe, a prominent lawyer of New
Orleans, writing in the *Forum,* voiced the desires of many in
asking for a repeal of the Fifteenth Amendment; and in October, Bishop Atticus G. Haygood, writing in the same periodical of a recent and notorious lynching, said, "It was horrible
to torture the guilty wretch; the burning was an act of insanity. But had the dismembered form of his victim been the
dishonored body of my baby, I might also have gone into
an insanity that might have ended never." Again and again
was there the lament that the Negroes of forty years after
were both morally and intellectually inferior to their antebellum ancestors; and if college professors and lawyers and
ministers of the Gospel wrote in this fashion one could not
wonder that the politician made capital of choice propaganda.

In this chorus of dispraise truth struggled for a hearing,
but then as now traveled more slowly than error. In the

---

* In 1896 this paper entered into an elaborate study, *Race Traits and
Tendencies of the American Negro,* a publication of the American
Economic Association. In this Hoffman contended at length that the
race was not only not holding its own in population, but that it was also
astonishingly criminal and was steadily losing economically. His work
was critically studied and its fallacies exposed in the *Nation,* April 1,
1897.

North American for July, 1892, Frederick Douglass wrote
vigorously of "Lynch Law in the South." In the same month
George W. Cable answered affirmatively and with emphasis
the question, "Does the Negro pay for his education?" He
showed that in Georgia in 1889-90 the colored schools did not
really cost the white citizens a cent, and that in the other
Southern states the Negro was also contributing his full share
to the maintenance of the schools. In June of the same year
William T. Harris, Commissioner of Education, wrote in
truly statesmanlike fashion in the *Atlantic* of "The Education
of the Negro." Said he: "With the colored people all educated
in schools and become a reading people interested in the daily
newspaper; with all forms of industrial training accessible to
them, and the opportunity so improved that every form of
mechanical and manufacturing skill has its quota of colored
working men and women; with a colored ministry educated in
a Christian theology interpreted in a missionary spirit, and
finding its auxiliaries in modern science and modern literature;
with these educational essentials the Negro problem for the
South will be solved without recourse to violent measures of
any kind, whether migration, or disfranchisement, or ostra-
cism." In December, 1893, Walter H. Page, writing in the
Forum of lynching under the title, "The Last Hold of the
Southern Bully," said that "the great danger is not in the first
violation of law, nor in the crime itself, but in the danger that
Southern public sentiment under the stress of this phase of
the race problem will lose the true perspective of civilization";
and L. E. Bleckley, Chief Justice of Georgia, spoke in similar
vein. On the whole, however, the country, while occasionally
indignant at some atrocity, had quite decided not to touch the
Negro question for a while; and when in the spring of 1892
some representative Negroes protested without avail to President Harrison against the work of mobs, the *Review of Reviews* but voiced the drift of current opinion when it said:
"As for the colored men themselves, their wisest course would
be to cultivate the best possible relations with the most upright
and intelligent of their white neighbors, and for some time

to come to forget all about politics and to strive mightily for industrial and educational progress." *

It is not strange that under the circumstances we have now to record such discrimination, crime, and mob violence as can hardly be paralleled in the whole of American history. The Negro was already down; he was now to be trampled upon. When in the spring of 1892 some members of the race in the lowlands of Mississippi lost all they had by the floods and the Federal Government was disposed to send relief, the state government protested against such action on the ground that it would keep the Negroes from accepting the terms offered by the white planters. In Louisiana in 1895 a Negro presiding elder reported to the *Southwestern Christian Advocate* that he had lost a membership of a hundred souls, the people being compelled to leave their crops and move away within ten days.

In 1891 the jail at Omaha was entered and a Negro taken out and hanged to a lamp-post. On February 27, 1892, at Jackson, La., where there was a pound party for the minister at the Negro Baptist church, a crowd of white men gathered, shooting revolvers and halting the Negroes as they passed. Most of the people were allowed to go on, but after a while the sport became furious and two men were fatally shot. About the same time, and in the same state, at Rayville, a Negro girl of fifteen was taken from a jail by a mob and hanged to a tree. In Texarkana, Ark., a Negro who had outraged a farmer's wife was captured and burned alive, the injured woman herself being compelled to light the fire. Just a few days later, in March, a constable in Memphis in attempting to arrest a Negro was killed. Numerous arrests followed, and at night a mob went to the jail, gained easy access, and, having seized three well-known Negroes who were thought to have been leaders in the killing, lynched them, the whole proceeding being such a flagrant violation of law that it has not yet been forgotten by the older Negro citizens of this important city. On February 1, 1893, at Paris, Texas, after one of the most brutal crimes occurred one of the most horrible lynch-

* June, 1892, p. 526.

ings on record. Henry Smith, the Negro, who seems to have harbored a resentment against a policeman of the town because of ill-treatment that he had received, seized the officer's three-year-old child, outraged her, and then tore her body to pieces. He was tortured by the child's father, her uncles, and her fifteen-year-old brother, his eyes being put out with hot irons before he was burned. His stepson, who had refused to tell where he could be found, was hanged and his body riddled with bullets. Thus the lynchings went on, the victims sometimes being guilty of the gravest crimes, but often also perfectly innocent people. In February, 1893, the average was very nearly one a day. At the same time injuries inflicted on the Negro were commonly disregarded altogether. Thus at Dickson, Tenn., a young white man lost forty dollars. A fortune-teller told him that the money had been taken by a woman and gave a description that seemed to fit a young colored woman who had worked in the home of a relative. Half a dozen men then went to the home of the young woman and outraged her, her mother, and also another woman who was in the house. At the very close of 1894, in Brooks County, Ga., after a Negro named Pike had killed a white man with whom he had a quarrel, seven Negroes were lynched after the real murderer had escaped. Any relative or other Negro who, questioned, refused to tell of the whereabouts of Pike, whether he knew of the same or not, was shot in his tracks, one man being shot before he had chance to say anything at all. Meanwhile the White Caps or "Regulators" took charge of the neighboring counties, terrifying the Negroes everywhere; and in the trials that resulted the state courts broke down altogether, one judge in despair giving up the holding of court as useless.

Meanwhile discrimination of all sorts went forward. On May 29, 1895, moved by the situation at the Orange Park Academy, the state of Florida approved "An Act to Prohibit White and Colored Youth from being Taught in the same Schools." Said one section: "It shall be a penal offense for any individual body of inhabitants, corporation, or association to conduct within this State any school of any grade, public, private, or parochial, wherein white persons and Negroes shall be instructed or boarded within the same building, or taught in the same class or at the same time by the same teacher." Religious organizations were not to be left behind in such action; and when before the meeting of the Baptist Young People's Union in Baltimore a letter was sent to the secretary of the organization and the editor of the *Baptist Union,* in behalf of the Negroes, who the year before had not been well treated at Toronto, he sent back an evasive answer, saying that the policy of his society was to encourage local unions to affiliate with their own churches.

More grave than anything else was the formal denial of the Negro's political rights. As we have seen, South Carolina in 1895 followed Mississippi in the disfranchising program and within the next fifteen years most of the other Southern states did likewise. With the Negro thus deprived of any genuine political voice, all sorts of social and economic injustice found greater license.

2. *Industrial Education: Booker T. Washington*

Such were the tendencies of life in the South as affecting the Negro thirty years after emancipation. In September, 1895, a rising educator of the race attracted national attention by a remarkable speech that he made at the Cotton States Exposition in Atlanta. Said Booker T. Washington: "To those of my race who depend on bettering their condition in a foreign land, or who underestimate the importance of cultivating friendly relations with the Southern white man who is their next door neighbor, I would say, 'Cast down your bucket where you are'—cast it down in making friends in every manly way of the people of all races by whom we are surrounded. . . . To those of the white race who look to the incoming of those of foreign birth and strange tongue and habits for the prosperity of the South, were I permitted I would repeat what I say to my own race, 'Cast down your bucket where you are.' Cast it down among 8,000,000 Negroes whose habits you know, whose fidelity and love you have tested in days when to have proved treacherous meant the ruin of your firesides. . . . In all things that are purely social we can be as separate as the fingers, yet one as the hand in all things essential to mutual progress."

The message that Dr. Washington thus enunciated he had already given in substance the previous spring in an address at Fisk University, and even before then his work at Tuskegee Institute had attracted attention.* The Atlanta Exposition simply gave him the great occasion that he needed; and he was now to proclaim the new word throughout the length and breadth of the land. Among the hundreds of addresses that he afterwards delivered, especially important were those at Harvard University in 1896, at the Chicago Peace Jubilee in 1898, and before the National Education Association in St. Louis in 1904. Again and again in these speeches one comes upon such striking sentences as the following: "Freedom can never be given. It must be purchased." † "The race, like the individual, that makes itself indispensable, has solved most of its problems." † "As a race there are two things we must learn to do—one is to put brains into the common occupations of life, and the other is to dignify common labor." ‡ "Ignorant and inexperienced, it is not strange that in the first years of our new life we began at the top instead of at the bottom; that a seat in Congress or the State Legislature was worth more than real estate or industrial skill." § "The opportunity to earn a dollar in a factory just now is worth infinitely more than the opportunity to spend a dollar in an opera house." § One of the most vital questions that touch our American life is how to bring the strong, wealthy, and learned into helpful contact with the poorest, most ignorant, and humblest, and at the same time make the one appreciate the vitalizing, strengthening influence of the other." ‖ "There is no defense or security for any of us except in the highest intelligence and development of all." §

The time was ripe for a new leader. Frederick Douglass

---

* See article by Albert Shaw, "Negro Progress on the Tuskegee Plan," in *Review of Reviews*, April, 1894.
† Speech before N. E. A., in St. Louis, June 30, 1904.
‡ Speech at Fisk University, 1895.
§ Speech at Atlanta Exposition, September 18, 1895.
‖ Speech at Harvard University, June 24, 1896.

had died in February, 1895. In his later years he had more than once lost hold on the heart of his people, as when he opposed the Negro Exodus or seemed not fully in sympathy with the religious convictions of those who looked to him. At his passing, however, the race remembered only his early service and his old magnificence, and to a striving people his death seemed to make still darker the gathering gloom. Coming when he did, Booker T. Washington was thoroughly in line with the materialism of his age; he answered both an economic and an educational crisis. He also satisfied the South of the new day by what he had to say about social equality.

The story of his work reads like a romance, and he himself has told it better than any one else ever can. He did not claim the credit for the original idea of industrial education; that he gave to General Armstrong, and it was at Hampton that he himself had been nurtured. What was needed, however, was for some one to take the Hampton idea down to the cotton belt, interpret the lesson for the men and women digging in the ground, and generally to put the race in line with the country's industrial development. This was what Booker T. Washington undertook to do.

He reached Tuskegee early in June, 1881. July 4 was the date set for the opening of the school in the little shanty and church which had been secured for its accommodation. On the morning of this day thirty students reported for admission. The greater number were school-teachers and some were nearly forty years of age. Just about three months after the opening of the school there was offered for sale an old and abandoned plantation a mile from Tuskegee on which the mansion had been burned. All told the place seemed to be just the location needed to make the work effective and permanent. The price asked was five hundred dollars, the owner requiring the immediate payment of two hundred and fifty dollars, the remaining two hundred and fifty to be paid within a year. In his difficulty Mr. Washington wrote to General J. F. B. Marshall, treasurer of Hampton Institute, placing the matter before him and asking for the loan of two hundred and fifty dollars. General Marshall replied that he had no authority to lend money belonging to Hampton Institute, but that he would gladly advance the amount needed from his personal funds. Toward the paying of this sum the assisting teacher, Olivia A. Davidson (afterwards Mrs. Washington), helped heroically. Her first effort was made by holding festivals and suppers, but she also canvassed the families in the town of Tuskegee, and the white people as well as the Negroes helped her. "It was often pathetic," said the principal, "to note the gifts of the older colored people, many of whom had spent their best days in slavery. Sometimes they would give five cents, sometimes twenty-five cents. Sometimes the contribution was a quilt, or a quantity of sugarcane. I recall one old colored woman, who was about seventy years of age, who came to see me when we were raising money to pay for the farm. She hobbled into the room where I was, leaning on a cane. She was clad in rags, but they were clean. She said, 'Mr. Washington, God knows I spent de bes' days of my life in slavery. God knows I's ignorant an' poor; but I knows what you an' Miss Davidson is tryin' to do. I knows you is tryin' to make better men an' better women for de colored race. I ain't got no money, but I wants you to take dese six eggs, what I's been savin' up, an' I wants you to put dese six eggs into de eddication of dese boys an' gals.' Since the work at Tuskegee started," added the speaker, "it has been my privilege to receive many gifts for the benefit of the institution, but never any, I think, that touched me as deeply as this one."

It was early in the history of the school that Mr. Washington conceived the idea of extension work. The Tuskegee Conferences began in February, 1892. To the first meeting came five hundred men, mainly farmers, and many woman. Outstanding was the discussion of the actual terms on which most of the men were living from year to year. A mortgage was given on the cotton crop before it was planted, and to the mortgage was attached a note which waived all right to exemptions under the constitution and laws of the state of Alabama or of any other state to which the tenant might move. Said one: "The mortgage ties you tighter than any rope and a waive note is a consuming fire." Said another: "The waive note is good for twenty years and when you sign one you must either pay out or die out." Another: "When you sign a waive note you just cross your hands behind you and go to the merchant and say, 'Here, tie me and take all I've got.' " All agreed that the people mortgaged more than was necessary, to buy sewing machines (which sometimes were not used), expensive clocks, great family Bibles, or other things easily dispensed with. Said one man: "My people want all they can get on credit, not thinking of the day of settlement. We must learn to bore with a small augur first. The black man totes a heavy bundle, and when he puts it down there is a plow, a hoe, and ignorance."

It was to people such as these that Booker T. Washington brought hope, and serving them he passed on to fame. Within a few years schools on the plan of Tuskegee began to spring up all over the South, at Denmark, at Snow Hill, at Utica, and elsewhere. In 1900 the National Negro Business League began its sessions, giving great impetus to the establishment of banks, stores, and industrial enterprises throughout the country, and especially in the South. Much of this progress would certainly have been realized if the Business League had never been organized; but every one granted that in all the development the genius of the leader at Tuskegee was the chief force. About his greatness and his very definite contribution there could be no question.

3. *Individual Achievement: The Spanish-American War*

It happened that just at the time that Booker T. Washington was advancing to great distinction, three or four other individuals were reflecting special credit on the race. One of these was a young scholar, W. E. Burghardt DuBois, who after a college career at Fisk continued his studies at Harvard and Berlin and finally took the Ph.D. degree at Harvard in 1895. There had been sound scholars in the race before DuBois, but generally these had rested on attainment in the languages or mathematics, and most frequently they had expressed themselves in rather philosophical disquisition. Here, however, was a thorough student of economics, and one who was able to attack the problems of his people and meet opponents on the basis of modern science. He was destined to do great good, and the race was proud of him.

In 1896 also an authentic young poet who had wrestled with poverty and doubt at last gained a hearing. After completing the course at a high school in Dayton, Paul Laurence Dunbar ran an elevator for four dollars a week, and then he peddled from door to door two little volumes of verse that had been privately printed. William Dean Howells at length gave him a helping hand, and Dodd, Mead & Co. published *Lyrics of Lowly Life*. Dunbar wrote both in classic English and in the dialect that voiced the humor and the pathos of the life of those for whom he spoke. What was not at the time especially observed was that in numerous poems he suggested the discontent with the age in which he lived and thus struck what later years were to prove an important keynote. After he had waited and struggled so long, his success was so great that it became a vogue, and imitators sprang up everywhere. He touched the heart of his people and the race loved him.

By 1896 also word began to come of a Negro American painter, Henry O. Tanner, who was winning laurels in Paris. At the same time a beautiful singer, Mme. Sissieretta Jones, on the concert stage was giving new proof of the possibilities of the Negro as an artist in song. In the previous decade Mme. Marie Selika, a cultured vocalist of the first rank, had delighted audiences in both America and Europe, and in 1887 had appeared Flora Batson, a ballad singer whose work at its best was of the sort that sends an audience into the wildest enthusiasm. In 1894, moreover, Harry T. Burleigh, competing against sixty candidates, became baritone soloist at St. George's Episcopal Church, New York, and just a few years later he was to be employed also at Temple Emanu-El, the Fifth Avenue Jewish synagogue. From abroad also came word of a brilliant musician, Samuel Coleridge-Taylor, who by his "Hiawatha's Wedding-Feast" in 1898 leaped into the rank of the foremost living English composers. On the more popular stage appeared light musical comedy, intermediate between the old Negro minstrelsy and a genuine Negro drama, the representative companies becoming within the next few years those of Cole and Johnson, and Williams and Walker.

Especially outstanding in the course of the decade, however, was the work of the Negro soldier in the Spanish-American War. There were at the time four regiments of colored regulars in the Army of the United States, the Twenty-fourth Infantry, the Twenty-fifth Infantry, the Ninth Cavalry, and the Tenth Cavalry. When the war broke out President McKinley sent to Congress a message recommending the enlistment of more regiments of Negroes. Congress failed to act; nevertheless colored troops enlisted in the volunteer service in Massachusetts, Indiana, Illinois, Kansas, Ohio, North Carolina, Tennessee, and Virginia. The Eighth Illinois was officered throughout by Negroes, J. R. Marshall commanding; and Major Charles E. Young, a West Point graduate, was in charge of the Ohio battalion. The very first regiment ordered to the front when the war broke out was the Twenty-fourth Infantry; and Negro troops were conspicuous in the fighting around Santiago. They figured in a brilliant charge at Las Quasimas on June 24, and in an attack on July 1 upon a garrison at El Caney (a position of importance for securing possession of a line of hills along the San Juan River, a mile and a half from Santiago) the First Volunteer Cavalry (Colonel Roosevelt's "Rough Riders") was practically saved from annihilation by the gallant work of the men of the Tenth Cavalry. Fully as patriotic, though in another way, was a deed of the Twenty-fourth Infantry. Learning that General Miles desired a regiment for the cleaning of a yellow fever hospital and the nursing of some victims of the disease, the Twenty-fourth volunteered its services and by one day's work so cleared away the rubbish and cleaned the camp that the number of cases was greatly reduced. Said the *Review of Reviews* in editorial comment: * "One of the most gratifying incidents of the Spanish War has been the enthusiasm that the colored regiments of the regular army have aroused throughout the whole country. Their fighting at Santiago was magnificent. The Negro soldiers showed excellent discipline, the highest qualities of personal bravery, very superior physical endurance, unfailing good temper, and the most generous disposition toward all

* October, 1898, p. 387.

comrades in arms, whether white or black. Roosevelt's Rough Riders have come back singing the praises of the colored troops. There is not a dissenting voice in the chorus of praise. . . . Men who can fight for their country as did these colored troops ought to have their full share of gratitude and honor."

4. *Mob Violence; Election Troubles; The Atlanta Massacre*

After two or three years of comparative quiet—but only *comparative* quiet—mob violence burst forth about the turn of the century with redoubled intensity. In a large way this was simply a result of the campaigns for disfranchisement that in some of the Southern states were just now getting under way; but charges of assault and questions of labor also played a part. In some places people who were innocent of any charge whatever were attacked, and so many were killed that sometimes it seemed that the law had broken down altogether. Not the least interesting development of these troublous years was that in some cases as never before Negroes began to fight with their backs to the wall, and thus at the very close of the century—at the end of a bitter decade and the beginning of one still more bitter—a new factor entered into the problem, one that was destined more and more to demand consideration.

On one Sunday toward the close of October, 1898, the country recorded two race wars, one lynching, two murders, one of which was expected to lead to a lynching, with a total of ten Negroes killed and four wounded and four white men killed and seven wounded. The most serious outbreak was in the state of Mississippi, and it is worthy of note that in not one single case was there any question of rape.

November was made red by election troubles in both North and South Carolina. In the latter state, at Phœnix, in Greenwood County, on November 8 and for some days thereafter, the Tolberts, a well-known family of white Republicans, were attacked by mobs and barely escaped alive. R. R. Tolbert was a candidate for Congress and also chairman of the Republican state committee. John R. Tolbert, his father, collector of the port of Charleston, had come home to vote and was at one of the polling-places in the county. Thomas Tolbert at Phœnix was taking the affidavits of the Negroes who were not permitted to vote for his brother in order that later there might be ground on which to contest the election. While thus engaged he was attacked by Etheridge, the Democratic manager of another precinct. The Negroes came to Tolbert's defense, and in the fight that followed Etheridge was killed and Tolbert wounded. John Tolbert, coming up, was filled with buckshot, and a younger member of the family was also hurt. The Negroes were at length overpowered and the Tolberts forced to flee. All told it appears that two white men and about twelve Negroes lost their lives in connection with the trouble, six of the latter being lynched on account of the death of Etheridge.

In North Carolina in 1894 the Republicans by combining with the Populists had secured control of the state legislature. In 1896 the Democrats were again outvoted, Governor Russell being elected by a plurality of 9000. A considerable number of local offices was in the hands of Negroes, who had the backing of the Governor, the legislature, and the Supreme Court as well. Before the November elections in 1898 the Democrats in Wilmington announced their determination to prevent Negroes from holding office in the city. Especially had they been made angry by an editorial in a local Negro paper, the *Record,* in which, under date August 18, the editor, Alex. L. Manly, starting with a reference to a speaker from Georgia, who at the Agricultural Society meeting at Tybee had advocated lynching as an extreme measure, said that she "lost sight of the basic principle of the religion of Christ in her plea for one class of people as against another," and continued: "The papers are filled with reports of rapes of white women, and the subsequent lynching of the alleged rapists. The editors pour forth volleys of aspersions against all Negroes because of the few who may be guilty. If the papers and speakers of the other race would condemn the commission of crime because it is crime and not try to make it appear that the Negroes were the only criminals, they would find their strongest allies in the intelligent Negroes themselves, and together the whites and blacks would root the evil out of both races. . . . Our experience among poor white people in the country teaches us that the women of that race are not any more particular in the matter of clandestine meetings with colored men than are the white men with colored women. Meetings of this kind go on for some time until the woman's infatuation or the man's boldness brings attention to them and the man is lynched for rape." In reply to this the speaker quoted in a signed statement said: "When the Negro Manly attributed the crime of rape to intimacy between Negro men and white women of the South, the slanderer should be made to fear a lyncher's rope rather than occupy a place in New York newspapers"—a method of argument that was unfortunately all too common in the South. As election day approached the Democrats sought generally to intimidate the Negroes, the streets and roads being patrolled by men wearing red shirts. Election day, however, passed without any disturbance; but on the next day there was a mass meeting of white citizens, at which there were adopted resolutions to employ white labor instead of Negro, to banish the editor of the *Record,* and to send away from the city the printing-press in the office of that paper; and a committee of twenty-five was appointed to see that these resolutions were carried into effect within twenty-four hours. In the course of the terrible day that followed the printing office was destroyed, several white Republicans were driven from the city, and nine Negroes were killed at once, though no one could say with accuracy just how many more lost their lives or were seriously wounded before the trouble was over.

Charles W. Chesnutt, in *The Marrow of Tradition,* has given a faithful portrayal of these disgraceful events, the Wellington of the story being Wilmington. Perhaps the best commentary on those who thus sought power was afforded by their apologist, a Presbyterian minister and editor, A. J. Mc-Kelway, who on this occasion and others wrote articles in the *Independent* and the *Outlook* justifying the proceedings. Said he: "It is difficult to speak of the Red Shirts without a smile. They victimized the Negroes with a huge practical joke. . . . A dozen men would meet at a crossroad, on horseback, clad in red shirts or calico, flannel or silk, according to the taste of the owner and the enthusiasm of his womankind. They would gallop through the country, and the Negro would quietly make up his mind that his interest in political affairs was not a large one, anyhow. It would be wise not to vote, and wiser not to register to prevent being dragooned into voting on election day." It thus appears that the forcible seizure of the political rights of people, the killing and wounding of many, and the compelling of scores to leave their homes amount in the end to not more than a "practical joke."

One part of the new program was the most intense opposition to Federal Negro appointees anywhere in the South. On the morning of February 22, 1898, Frazer B. Baker, the colored postmaster at Lake City, S. C., awoke to find his house in flames. Attempting to escape, he and his baby boy were shot and killed and their bodies consumed in the burning house. His wife and the other children were wounded but escaped. The Postmaster-General was quite disposed to see that justice was done in this case; but the men charged with the crime gave the most trivial alibis, and on Saturday, April 22, 1899, the jury in the United States Circuit Court at Charleston reported its failure to agree on a verdict. Three years later the whole problem was presented strongly to President Roosevelt. When Mrs. Minne Cox, who was serving efficiently as postmistress at Indianola, Miss., was forced to resign because of threats, he closed the office; and when there was protest against the appointment of Dr. William D. Crum as collector of the port of Charleston, he said, "I do not intend to appoint any unfit man to office. So far as I legitimately can, I shall always endeavor to pay regard to the wishes and feelings of the people of each locality; but I can not consent to take the position that the door of hope—the door of opportunity—is to be shut upon any man, no matter how worthy, purely upon the grounds of race or color. Such an attitude would, according to my convictions, be fundamentally wrong." These memorable words, coming in a day of compromise and expediency in high places, greatly cheered the heart of the race. Just the year before, the importance of the incident of Booker T. Washington's taking lunch with President Roosevelt was rather unnecessarily magnified by the South into all sorts of discussion of social equality.

On Tuesday, January 24, 1899, a fire in the center of the

town of Palmetto, Ga., destroyed a hotel, two stores, and a storehouse, on which property there was little insurance. The next Saturday there was another fire and this destroyed a considerable part of the town. For some weeks there was no clue as to the origin of these fires; but about the middle of March something overheard by a white citizen led to the implicating of nine Negroes. These men were arrested and confined for the night of March 15 in a warehouse to await trial the next morning, a dummy guard of six men being placed before the door. About midnight a mob came, pushed open the door, and fired two volleys at the Negroes, killing four immediately and fatally wounding four more. The circumstances of this atrocious crime oppressed the Negro people of the state as few things had done since the Civil War. That it did no good was evident, for in its underlying psychology it was closely associated with a double crime that was now to be committed. In April, Sam Hose, a Negro who had brooded on the happenings at Palmetto, not many miles from the scene killed a farmer, Alfred Cranford, who had been a leader of the mob, and outraged his wife. For two weeks he was hunted like an animal, the white people of the state meanwhile being almost unnerved and the Negroes sickened by the pursuit. At last, however, he was found, and on Sunday, April 23, at Newnan, Ga., he was burned, his execution being accompanied by unspeakable mutilation; and on the same day Lige Strickland, a Negro preacher whom Hose had accused of complicity in his crime, was hanged near Palmetto. The nation stood aghast, for the recent events in Georgia had shaken the very foundations of American civilization. Said the Charleston *News and Courier:* "The chains which bound the citizen, Sam Hose, to the stake at Newnan mean more for us and for his race than the chains or bonds of slavery, which they supplanted. The flames that lit the scene of his torture shed their baleful light throughout every corner of our land, and exposed a state of things, actual and potential, among us that should rouse the dullest mind to a sharp sense of our true condition, and of our unchanged and unchangeable relations to the whole race whom the tortured wretch represented."

Violence breeds violence, and two or three outstanding

events are yet to be recorded. On August 23, 1899, at Darien, Ga., hundreds of Negroes, who for days had been aroused by rumors of a threatened lynching, assembled at the ringing of the bell of a church opposite the jail and by their presence prevented the removal of a prisoner. They were later tried for insurrection and twenty-one sent to the convict farms for a year. The general circumstances of the uprising excited great interest throughout the country. In May, 1900, in Augusta, Ga., an unfortunate street car incident resulted in the death of the aggressor, a young white man named Whitney, and in the lynching of the colored man, Wilson, who killed him. In this instance the victim was tortured and mutilated, parts of his body and of the rope by which he was hanged being passed around as souvenirs. A Negro organization at length recovered the body, and so great was the excitement at the funeral that the coffin was not allowed to be opened. Two months later, in New Orleans, there was a most extraordinary occurrence, the same being important because the leading figure was very frankly regarded by the Negroes as a hero and his fight in his own defense a sign that the men of the race would not always be shot down without some effort to protect themselves.

One night in July, an hour before midnight, two Negroes Robert Charles and Leonard Pierce, who had recently come into the city from Mississippi and whose movements had interested the police, were found by three officers on the front steps of a house in Dryades Street. Being questioned they replied that they had been in the town two or three days and had secured work. In the course of the questioning the larger of the Negroes, Charles, rose to his feet; he was seized by one of the officers, Mora, who began to use his billet; and in the struggle that resulted Charles escaped and Mora was wounded in each hand and the hip. Charles now took refuge in a small house on Fourth Street, and when he was surrounded, with deadly aim he shot and instantly killed the first two officers who appeared.* The other men advancing, retreated and waited

* From this time forth the wildest rumors were afloat and the number of men that Charles had killed was greatly exaggerated. Some reports said scores or even hundreds, and it is quite possible that any figures given herewith are an understatement.

until daylight for reënforcement, and Charles himself withdrew to other quarters, and for some days his whereabouts were unknown. With the new day, however, the city was wild with excitement and thousands of men joined in the search, the newspapers all the while stirring the crowd to greater fury. Mobs rushed up and down the streets assaulting Negroes wherever they could be found, no effort to check them being made by the police. On the second night a crowd of nearly a thousand was addressed at the Lee Monument by a man from Kenner, a town a few miles above the city. Said he: "Gentlemen, I am from Kenner, and I have come down here to-night to assist you in teaching the blacks a lesson. I have killed a Negro before and in revenge of the wrong wrought upon you and yours I am willing to kill again. The only way you can teach these niggers a lesson and put them in their place is to go out and lynch a few of them as an object lesson. String up a few of them. That is the only thing to do—kill them, string them up, lynch them. I will lead you. On to the parish prison and lynch Pierce." The mob now rushed to the prison, stores and pawnshops being plundered on the way. Within the next few hours a Negro was taken from a street car on Canal Street, killed, and his body thrown into the gutter. An old man of seventy going to work in the morning was fatally shot. On Rousseau Street the mob fired into a little cabin; the inmates were asleep and an old woman was killed in bed. Another old woman who looked out from her home was beaten into insensibility. A man sitting at his door was shot, beaten, and left for dead. Such were the scenes that were enacted almost hourly from Monday until Friday evening. One night the excellent school building given by Thomy Lafon, a member of the race and a philanthropist, was burned.

About three o'clock on Friday afternoon Charles was found to be in a two-story house at the corner of Saratoga and Clio Streets. Two officers, Porteus and Lally, entered a lower room. The first fell dead at the first shot, and the second was mortally wounded by the next. A third, Bloomfield, waiting with gun in hand, was wounded at the first shot and killed at the second. The crowd retreated, but bullets rained upon the house, Charles all the while keeping watch in every direction from four different windows. Every now and then he thrust his rifle through one of the shattered windowpanes and fired, working with incredible rapidity. He succeeded in killing two more of his assailants and wounding two. At last he realized that the house was on fire, and knowing that the end had come he rushed forth upon his foes, fired one shot more and fell dead. He had killed eight men and mortally wounded two or three more. His body was mutilated. In his room there was afterwards found a copy of a religious publication, and it was known that he had resented disfranchisement in Louisiana and had distributed pamphlets to further a colonization scheme. No incriminating evidence, however, was found.

In the same memorable year, 1900, on the night of Wednesday, August 15, there were serious riots in the city of New York. On the preceding Sunday a policeman named Thorpe in attempting to arrest a colored woman was stabbed by a Negro, Arthur Harris, so fatally that he died on Monday. On Wednesday evening Negroes were dragged from the street cars and beaten, and by midnight there were thousands of rioters between 25th and 35th Streets. On the next night the trouble was resumed. These events were followed almost immediately by riots in Akron, Ohio. On the last Sunday in October, 1901, while some Negroes were holding their usual fall camp-meeting in a grove in Washington Parish, Louisiana, they were attacked, and a number of people, not less than ten and perhaps several more, were killed; and hundreds of men, women, and children felt forced to move away from the vicinity. In the first week of March, 1904, there was in Mississippi a lynching that exceeded even others of the period in its horror and that became notorious for its use of a corkscrew. A white planter of Doddsville was murdered, and a Negro, Luther Holbert, was charged with the crime. Holbert fled, and his innocent wife went with him. Further report we read in the Democratic *Evening Post* of Vicksburg as follows: "When the two Negroes were captured, they were tied to trees, and while the funeral pyres were being prepared they were forced to suffer the most fiendish tortures. The blacks were forced to hold out their hands while one finger at a time was chopped off. The fingers were distributed as souvenirs. The ears of the murderers were cut off. Holbert was beaten severely, his skull was fractured, and one of his eyes, knocked out with a stick, hung by a shred from the socket. . . . The most excruciating form of punishment consisted in the use of a large corkscrew in the hands of some of the mob. This instrument was bored into the flesh of the man and the woman, in the arms, legs, and body, and then pulled out, the spirals tearing out big pieces of raw, quivering flesh every time it was withdrawn." In the summer of this same year Georgia was once more the scene of a horrible lynching, two Negroes, Paul Reed and Will Cato—because of the murder of the Hodges family six miles from the town on July 20—being burned at the stake at Statesville under unusually depressing circumstances. In August, 1908, there were in Springfield, Illinois, race riots of such a serious nature that a force of six thousand soldiers was required to quell them. These riots were significant not only because of the attitude of Northern laborers toward Negro competition, but also because of the indiscriminate killing of Negroes by people in the North, this indicating a genuine nationalization of the Negro Problem. The real climax of violence within the period, however, was the Atlanta Massacre of Saturday, September 22, 1906.

Throughout the summer the heated campaign of Hoke Smith for the governorship capitalized the gathering sentiment for the disfranchisement of the Negro in the state and at length raised the race issue to such a high pitch that it leaped into flame. The feeling was intensified by the report of assaults and attempted assaults by Negroes, particularly as these were detailed and magnified or even invented by an evening paper, the *Atlanta News*, against which the Fulton County Grand Jury afterwards brought in an indictment as largely responsible for the riot, and which was forced to suspend publication when the business men of the city withdrew their support. Just how much foundation there was to the rumors may be seen from the following report of the investigator: "Three, charged to white men, attracted comparatively little attention in the newspapers, although one, the offense of a man named Turnadge, was shocking in its details. Of twelve such charges against Negroes in the six months preceding the

riot, two were cases of rape, horrible in their details, three were aggravated attempts at rape, three may have been attempts, three were pure cases of fright on the part of white women, and in one the white woman, first asserting that a Negro had assaulted her, finally confessed attempted suicide." *
On Friday, September 21, while a Negro was on trial, the father of the girl concerned asked the recorder for permission to deal with the Negro with his own hand, and an outbreak was barely averted in the open court. On Saturday evening, however, some elements in the city and from neighboring towns, heated by liquor and newspaper extras, became openly riotous and until midnight defied all law and authority. Negroes were assaulted wherever they appeared, for the most part being found unsuspecting, as in the case of those who happened to be going home from work and were on street cars passing through the heart of the city. In one barber shop two workers were beaten to death and their bodies mangled. A lame bootblack, innocent and industrious, was dragged from his work and kicked and beaten to death. Another young Negro was stabbed with jack-knives. Altogether very nearly a score of persons lost their lives and two or three times as many were injured. After some time Governor Terrell mobilized the militia, but the crowd did not take this move seriously, and the real feeling of the Mayor, who turned on the hose of the fire department, was shown by his statement that just so long as the Negroes committed certain crimes just so long would they be unceremoniously dealt with. Sunday dawned upon a city of astounded white people and outraged and sullen Negroes. Throughout Monday and Tuesday the tension continued, the Negroes endeavoring to defend themselves as well as they could. On Monday night the union of some citizens with policemen who were advancing in a suburb in which most of the homes were those of Negroes, resulted in the death of James Heard, an officer, and in the wounding of some of those who accompanied him. More Negroes were also killed, and a white woman to whose front porch two men were chased died of fright at seeing them shot to death. It was the disposition,

* R. S. Baker: *Following the Colour Line*, 3.

however, on the part of the Negroes to make armed resistance that really put an end to the massacre. Now followed a procedure that is best described in the words of the prominent apologist for such outbreaks. Said A. J. McKelway: "Tuesday every house in the town (i. e., the suburb referred to above) was entered by the soldiers, and some two hundred and fifty Negroes temporarily held, while the search was proceeding and inquiries being made. They were all disarmed, and those with concealed weapons, or under suspicion of having been in the party firing on the police, were sent to jail." * It is thus evident that in this case, as in many others, the Negroes who had suffered most, not the white men who killed a score of them, were disarmed, and that for the time being their terrified women and children were left defenseless. McKelway also says in this general connection: "Any Southern man would protect an innocent Negro who appealed to him for help, with his own life if necessary." This sounds like chivalry, but it is really the survival of the old slavery attitude that begs the whole question. The Negro does not feel that he should ask any other man to protect him. He has quite made up his mind that he will defend his own home himself. He stands as a man before the bar, and the one thing he wants to know is if the law and the courts of America are able to give him justice—simple justice, nothing more.

5. *The Question of Labor*

From time to time, in connection with cases of violence, we have referred to the matter of labor. Riots such as we have described are primarily social in character, the call of race invariably being the final appeal. The economic motive has accompanied this, however, and has been found to be of increasing importance. Says DuBois: "The fatal campaign in Georgia which culminated in the Atlanta Massacre was an attempt, fathered by conscienceless politicians, to arouse the prejudices of the rank and file of white laborers and farmers against the growing competition of black men, so that black

* *Outlook,* November 3, 1906, p. 561.

men by law could be forced back to subserviency and serf-
dom." * The question was indeed constantly recurrent, but
even by the end of the period policies had not yet been definitely decided upon, and for the time being there were frequent armed clashes between the Negro and the white laborer.
Both capital and common sense were making it clear, however, that the Negro was undoubtedly a labor asset and would
have to be given place accordingly.

In March, 1895, there were bloody riots in New Orleans,
these growing out of the fact that white laborers who were
beginning to be organized objected to the employment of
Negro workers by the shipowners for the unloading of vessels. When the trouble was at its height volley after volley
was poured upon the Negroes, and in turn two white men
were killed and several wounded. The commercial bodies of
the city met, blamed the Governor and the Mayor for the
series of outbreaks, and demanded that the outrages cease.
Said they: "Forbearance has ceased to be a virtue. We can no
longer treat with men who, with arms in their hands, are shooting down an inoffensive people because they will not think and
act with them. For these reasons we say to these people that,
cost what it may, we are determined that the commerce of
this city must and shall be protected; that every man who desires to perform honest labor must and shall be permitted to
do so regardless of race, color, or previous condition." About
August 1 of this same year, 1895, there were sharp conflicts
between the white and the black miners at Birmingham, a
number being killed on both sides before military authority
could intervene. Three years later, moreover, the invasion of
the North by Negro labor had begun, and about November 17,
1898, there was serious trouble in the mines at Pana and Vir-
den, Illinois. In the same month the convention of railroad
brotherhoods in Norfolk expressed strong hostility to Negro
labor, Grand Master Frank P. Sargent of the Brotherhood of
Locomotive Firemen saying that one of the chief purposes of
the meeting of the brotherhoods was "to begin a campaign
in advocacy of white supremacy in the railway service." This

* *The Negro in the South,* 115.

November, it will be recalled, was the fateful month of the election riots in North and South Carolina. *The People,* the Socialist-Labor publication, commenting upon a Negro indignation meeting at Cooper Union and upon the problem in general, said that the Negro was essentially a wage-slave, that it was the capitalism of the North and not humanity that in the first place had demanded the freedom of the slave, that in the new day capital demanded the subjugation of the working class—Negro or otherwise; and it blamed the Negroes for not seeing the real issues at stake. It continued with emphasis: "It is not the *Negro* that was massacred in the Carolinas; it was Carolina *workingmen,* Carolina *wage-slaves* who happened to be colored men. Not as Negroes must the race rise; . . . it is as *workingmen,* as a branch of the *working class,* that the Negro must denounce the Carolina felonies. Only by touching that chord can he denounce to a purpose, because only then does he place himself upon that elevation that will enable him to perceive the source of the specific wrong complained of now." This point of view was destined more and more to stimulate those interested in the problem, whether they accepted it in its entirety or not. Another opinion, very different and also important, was that given in 1899 by the editor of *Dixie,* a magazine published in Atlanta and devoted to Southern industrial interests. Said he: "The manufacturing center of the United States will one day be located in the South; and this will come about, strange as it may seem, for the reason that the Negro is a fixture here. . . . Organized labor, as it exists to-day, is a menace to industry. The Negro stands as a permanent and positive barrier against labor organization in the South. . . . So the Negro, all unwittingly, is playing an important part in the drama of Southern industrial development. His good nature defies the Socialist." At the time this opinion seemed plausible, and yet the very next two decades were to raise the question if it was not founded on fallacious assumptions.

The real climax of labor trouble as of mob violence within the period came in Georgia and in Atlanta, a city that now assumed outstanding importance as a battleground of the problems of the New South. In April, 1909, it happened that ten white workers on the Georgia Railroad who had been placed on the "extra list" were replaced by Negroes at lower wages. Against this there was violent protest all along the route. A little more than a month later the white Firemen's Union started a strike that was intended to be the beginning of an effort to drive all Negro firemen from Southern roads, and it was soon apparent that the real contest was one occasioned by the progress in the South of organized labor on the one hand and the progress of the Negro in efficiency on the other. The essential motives that entered into the struggle were in fact the same as those that characterized the trouble in New Orleans in 1895. Said E. A. Ball, second vice-president of the Firemen's Union, in an address to the public: "It will be up to you to determine whether the white firemen now employed on the Georgia Railroad shall be accorded rights and privileges over the Negro, or whether he shall be placed on the same equality with the Negro. Also, it will be for you to determine whether or not white firemen, supporting families in and around Atlanta on a pay of $1.75 a day, shall be compelled to vacate their positions in Atlanta joint terminals for Negroes, who are willing to do the same work for $1.25." Some papers, like the Augusta *Herald,* said that it was a mistaken policy to give preference to Negroes when white men would ultimately have to be put in charge of trains and engines; but others, like the Baltimore *News,* said, "If the Negro can be driven from one skilled employment, he can be driven from another; but a country that tries to do it is flying in the face of every economic law, and must feel the evil effects of its policy if it could be carried out." At any rate feeling ran very high; for a whole week about June 1 there were very few trains between Atlanta and Augusta, and there were some acts of violence; but in the face of the capital at stake and the fundamental issues involved it was simply impossible for the railroad to give way. The matter was at length referred to a board of arbitration which decided that the Georgia Railroad was still to employ Negroes whenever they were found qualified and that they were to receive the same wages as white workers. Some thought that this decision would ultimately tell against the Negro, but such was not the immediate effect at least, and to all intents and purposes the white firemen had lost in the strike. The whole matter was in fact fundamentally one of the most pathetic that we have had to record. Humble white workers, desirous of improving the economic condition of themselves and their families, instead of assuming a statesmanlike and truly patriotic attitude toward their problem, turned aside into the wilderness of racial hatred and were lost.

This review naturally prompts reflection as to the whole function of the Negro laborer in the South. In the first place, what is he worth, and especially what is he worth in honest Southern opinion? It was said after the Civil War that he would not work except under compulsion; just how had he come to be regarded in the industry of the New South? In 1894 a number of large employers were asked about this point. 50 per cent said that in skilled labor they considered the Negro inferior to the white worker, 46 per cent said that he was fairly equal, and 4 per cent said that, all things considered, he was superior. As to common labor 54 per cent said that he was equal, 29 per cent superior, and 17 per cent inferior to the white worker. At the time it appeared that wages paid Negroes averaged 80 per cent of those paid white men. A similar investigation by the Chattanooga *Tradesman* in 1902 brought forth five hundred replies. These were summarized as follows: "We find the Negro more useful and skilled in the cotton-seed oil-mills, the lumber-mills, the foundries, brick kilns, mines, and blast-furnaces. He is superior to white labor and possibly superior to any other labor in these establishments, but not in the capacity of skillful and ingenious artisans." In this opinion, it is to be remembered, the Negro was subjected to a severe test in which nothing whatever was given to him, and at least it appears that in many lines of labor he is not less than indispensable to the progress of the South. The question then arises: Just what is the relation that he is finally to sustain to other workingmen? It would seem that white worker and black worker would long ago have realized their identity of interest and have come together. The unions, however, have been slow to admit Negroes and give them the same footing and backing as white men. Under the circum-

stances accordingly there remained nothing else for the Negro
to do except to work wherever his services were desired and
on the best terms that he was able to obtain.

6. *Defamation: Brownsville*

Crime demands justification, and it is not surprising that
after such violence as that which we have described, and after
several states had passed disfranchising acts, there appeared
in the first years of the new century several publications especially defamatory of the race. Some books unfortunately
descended to a coarseness in vilification such as had not been
reached since the Civil War. From a Bible House in St. Louis
in 1902 came *The Negro a Beast, or In the Image of God,*
a book that was destined to have an enormous circulation
among the white people of the poorer class in the South, and
that of course promoted the mob spirit.* Contemporary and
of the same general tenor were R. W. Shufeldt's *The Negro*
and W. B. Smith's *The Color Line,* while a member of the
race itself, William Hannibal Thomas, published a book, *The
American Negro,* that was without either faith or ideal and
as a denunciation of the Negro in America unparalleled in
its vindictiveness and exaggeration.†

In January, 1904, the new governor of Mississippi, J. K.
Vardaman, in his inaugural address went to the extreme of
voicing the opinion of those who were now contending that
the education of the Negro was only complicating the problem and intensifying its dangerous features. Said he of the
Negro people: "As a race, they are deteriorating morally every

* Its fundamental assumptions were ably refuted by Edward Atkinson
in the *North American Review,* August, 1905.

† It was reviewed in the *Dial,* April 16, 1901, by W. E. B. DuBois,
who said in part: "Mr. Thomas's book is a sinister symptom—a growth
and development under American conditions of life which illustrates
peculiarly the anomalous position of black men, and the terrific stress
under which they struggle. And the struggle and the fight of human
beings against hard conditions of life always tends to develop the
criminal or the hypocrite, the cynic or the radical. Wherever among a
hard-pressed people these types begin to appear, it is a visible sign of a
burden that is threatening to overtax their strength, and the foreshadow-
ing of the age of revolt."

day. Time has demonstrated that they are more criminal as freemen than as slaves; that they are increasing in criminality with frightful rapidity, being one-third more criminal in 1890 than in 1880." A few weeks later Bishop Brown of Arkansas in a widely quoted address contended that the Southern Negro was going backward both morally and intellectually and could never be expected to take a helpful part in the Government; and he also justified lynching. In the same year one of the more advanced thinkers of the South, Edgar Gardner Murphy, in *Problems of the Present South* was not yet quite willing to receive the Negro on the basis of citizenship; and Thomas Nelson Page, who had belittled the Negro in such a collection of stories as *In Ole Virginia* and in such a novel as *Red Rock,** formally stated his theories in *The Negro: The Southerner's Problem*. The worst, however—if there could be a worst in such an array—was yet to appear. In 1905 Thomas Dixon added to a series of high-keyed novels *The Clansman,* a glorification of the KuKlux Klan that gave a malignant portrayal of the Negro and that was of such a quality as to arouse the most intense prejudice and hatred. Within a few months the work was put on the stage and again and again it threw audiences into the wildest excitement. The production was to some extent held to blame for the Atlanta Massacre. In several cities it was proscribed. In Philadelphia on October 23, 1906, after the Negro people had made an unavailing protest, three thousand of them made a demonstration before the Walnut Street theater where the performance was given, while the conduct of some within the playhouse almost precipitated a riot; and in this city the play was suppressed the next day. Throughout the South, however, and sometimes elsewhere it continued to do its deadly work, and it was later to furnish

* For a general treatment of the matter of the Negro as dealt with in American Literature, especially fiction, note "The Negro in American Fiction," in the *Dial,* May 11, 1916, a paper included in *The Negro in Literature and Art.* The thesis there is that imaginative treatment of the Negro is still governed by outworn antebellum types, or that in the search for burlesque some types of young and uncultured Negroes of the present day are deliberately overdrawn, but that there is not an honest or a serious facing of the characters and the situations in the life of the Negro people in the United States to-day. Since the paper first appeared it has received much further point; witness the stories by E. K. Means and Octavius Roy Cohen.

the basis of "The Birth of a Nation," an elaborate motion picture of the same general tendency.

Still another line of attack was now to attempt to deprive the Negro of any credit for initiative or for any independent achievement whatsoever. In May, 1903, Alfred H. Stone contributed to the *Atlantic* a paper, "The Mulatto in the Negro Problem," which contended at the same time that whatever meritorious work the race had accomplished was due to the infusion of white blood and that it was the mulatto that was constantly poisoning the mind of the Negro with "radical teachings and destructive doctrines." These points found frequent iteration throughout the period, and years afterwards, in 1917, the first found formal statement in the *American Journal of Sociology* in an article by Edward Byron Reuter, "The Superiority of the Mulatto," which the next year was elaborated into a volume, *The Mulatto in the United States.* To argue the superiority of the mulatto of course is simply to argue once more the inferiority of the Negro to the white man.

All of this dispraise together presented a formidable case and one from which the race suffered immeasurably; nor was it entirely offset in the same years by the appearance even of DuBois's remarkable book, *The Souls of Black Folk,* or by the several uplift publications of Booker T. Washington. In passing we wish to refer to three points: (1) The effect of education on the Negro; (2) the matter of the Negro criminal (and of mortality), and (3) the quality and function of the mulatto.

Education could certainly not be blamed for the difficulties of the problem in the new day until it had been properly tried. In no one of the Southern states within the period did the Negro child receive a fair chance. He was frequently subjected to inferior teaching, dilapidated accommodations, and short terms. In the representative city of Atlanta in 1903 the white school population numbered 14,465 and the colored 8,118. The Negroes, however, while numbering 35 per cent of the whole, received but 12 per cent of the school funds. The average white teacher received $745 a year, and the Negro teacher $450. In the great reduction of the percentage of illiteracy in the race from 70 in 1880 to 30.4 in 1910 the missionary colleges—those of the American Missionary Association, the American Baptist Home Mission Society, and the Freedmen's Aid Society—played a much larger part than they are ordinarily given credit for; and it is a very, very rare occurrence that a graduate of one of the institutions sustained by these agencies, or even one who has attended them for any length of time, has to be summoned before the courts. Their influence has most decidedly been on the side of law and order. Undoubtedly some of those who have gone forth from these schools have not been very practical, and some have not gained a very firm sense of relative values in life—it would be a miracle if all had; but as a group the young people who have attended the colleges have most abundantly justified the expenditures made in their behalf, expenditures for which their respective states were not responsible but of which they reaped the benefit. From one standpoint, however, the so-called higher education did most undoubtedly complicate the problem. Those critics of the race who felt that the only function of Negroes in life was that of hewers of wood and drawers of water quite fully realized that Negroes who had been to college did not care to work longer as field laborers. Some were to prove scientific students of agriculture, but as a group they were out of the class of peons. In this they were just like white people and all other people. No one who has once seen the light chooses to live always on the plane of the "man with the hoe." Nor need it be thought that these students are unduly crowding into professional pursuits. While, for instance, the number of Negro physicians and dentists has greatly increased within recent years, the number would still have to be four or five times as great to sustain to the total Negro population the same proportion as that borne by the whole number of white physicians and dentists to the total white population.

The subjects of the criminality and the mortality of the race are in their ultimate reaches closely related, both being mainly due, as we have suggested, to the conditions under which Negroes have been forced to live. In the country districts, until 1900 at least, there was little provision for improvements in methods of cooking or in sanitation, while in cities the effects of inferior housing, poor and unlighted streets, and

of the segregation of vice in Negro neighborhoods could not
be otherwise than obvious. Thus it happened in such a year
as 1898 that in Baltimore the Negro death rate was somewhat
more and in Nashville just a little less than twice that of the
white people. Legal procedure, moreover, emphasized a vicious
circle; living conditions sent the Negroes to the courts in increasing numbers, and the courts sent them still farther down
in the scale. There were undoubtedly some Negro thieves,
some Negro murderers, and some Negroes who were incon-
tinent; no race has yet appeared on the face of the earth that
did not contain members having such propensities, and all such
people should be dealt with justly by law. Our present contention is that throughout the period of which we are now
speaking the dominant social system was not only such as to
accentuate criminal elements but also such as even sought
to discourage aspiring men. A few illustrations, drawn from
widely different phases of life, must suffice. In the spring of
1903, and again in 1904, Jackson W. Giles, of Montgomery
County, Alabama, contended before the Supreme Court of
the United States that he and other Negroes in his county
were wrongfully excluded from the franchise by the new Alabama constitution. Twice was his case thrown out on technicalities, the first time it was said because he was petitioning
for the right to vote under a constitution whose validity he
denied, and the second time because the Federal right that he
claimed had not been passed on in the state court from whose
decision he appealed. Thus the supreme tribunal in the United
States evaded at the time any formal judgment as to the real
validity of the new suffrage provisions. In 1903, moreover, in
Alabama, Negroes charged with petty offenses and sometimes
with no offense at all were still sent to convict farms or turned
over to contractors. They were sometimes compelled to work
as peons for a length of time; and they were flogged, starved,
hunted with bloodhounds, and sold from one contractor to
another in direct violation of law. One Joseph Patterson bor-
rowed $1 on a Saturday, promising to pay the amount on the
following Tuesday morning. He did not get to town at the
appointed time, and he was arrested and carried before a justice of the peace, who found him guilty of obtaining money

under false pretenses. No time whatever was given to the Negro to get witnesses or a lawyer, or to get money with which to pay his fine and the costs of court. He was sold for $25 to a man named Hardy, who worked him for a year and then sold him for $40 to another man named Pace. Patterson tried to escape, but was recaptured and given a sentence of six months more. He was then required to serve for an additional year to pay a doctor's bill. When the case at last attracted attention, it appeared that for $1 borrowed in 1903 he was not finally to be released before 1906. Another case of interest and importance was set in New York. In the spring of 1909 a pullman porter was arrested on the charge of stealing a card-case containing $20. The next day he was discharged as innocent. He then entered against his accuser a suit for $10,000 damages. The jury awarded him $2,500, which amount the court reduced to $300, Justice P. H. Dugro saying that a Negro when falsely imprisoned did not suffer the same amount of injury that a white man would suffer— an opinion which the New York *Age* very naturally characterized as "one of the basest and most offensive ever handed down by a New York judge."

In the history of the question of the mulatto two facts are outstanding. One is that before the Civil War, as was very natural under the circumstances, mulattoes became free much faster than pure Negroes; thus the census of 1850 showed that 581 of every 1000 free Negroes were mulattoes and only 83 of every 1000 slaves. Since the Civil War, moreover, the mulatto element has rapidly increased, advancing from 11.2 per cent of the Negro population in 1850 to 20.9 per cent in 1910, or from 126 to 264 per 1000. On the whole question of the function of this mixed element the elaborate study, that of Reuter, is immediately thrown out of court by its lack of accuracy. The fundamental facts on which it rests its case are not always true, and if premises are false conclusions are worthless. No work on the Negro that calls Toussaint L'Ouverture and Sojourner Truth mulattoes and that will not give the race credit for several well-known pure Negroes of the present day, can long command the attention of scholars. This whole argument on the mulatto goes back to the fallacy of degrading human beings by slavery for two hundred years and then arguing that they have not the capacity or the inclination to rise. In a country predominantly white the quadroon has frequently been given some advantage that his black friend did not have, from the time that one was a house-servant and the other a field-hand; but no scientific test has ever demonstrated that the black boy is intellectually inferior to the fair one. In America, however, it is the fashion to place upon the Negro any blame or deficiency and to claim for the white race any merit that an individual may show. Furthermore—and this is a point not often remarked in discussions of the problem—the element of genius that distinguishes the Negro artist of mixed blood is most frequently one characteristically Negro rather than Anglo-Saxon. Much has been made of the fact that within the society of the race itself there have been lines of cleavage, a comparatively few people, very fair in color, sometimes drawing off to themselves. This is a fact, and it is simply one more heritage from slavery, most tenacious in some conservative cities along the coast. Even there, however, old lines are vanishing and the fusion of different groups within the race rapidly going forward. Undoubtedly there has been some snobbery, as there always is, and a few quadroons and octoroons have crossed the color line and been lost to the race; but these cases are after all comparatively few in number, and the younger generation is more and more emphasizing the ideals of racial solidarity. In the future there may continue to be lines of cleavage in society within the race, but the standards governing these will primarily be character and merit. On the whole, then, the mulatto has placed himself squarely on the side of the difficulties, aspirations, and achievements of the Negro people and it is simply an accident and not inherent quality that accounts for the fact that he has been so prominent in the leadership of the race.

The final refutation of defamation, however, is to be found in the actual achievement of members of the race themselves. The progress in spite of handicaps continued to be amazing. Said the New York *Sun* early in 1907 (copied by the *Times*) of "Negroes Who Have Made Good": "Junius C. Groves of

Kansas produces 75,000 bushels of potatoes every year, the world's record. Alfred Smith received the blue ribbon at the World's Fair and first prize in England for his Oklahoma-raised cotton. Some of the thirty-five patented devices of Granville T. Woods, the electrician, form part of the systems of the New York elevated railways and the Bell Telephone Company. W. Sidney Pittman drew the design of the Collis P. Huntington memorial building, the largest and finest at Tuskegee. Daniel H. Williams, M. D., of Chicago, was the first surgeon to sew up and heal a wounded human heart. Mary Church Terrell addressed in three languages at Berlin recently the International Association for the Advancement of Women. Edward H. Morris won his suit between Cook County and the city of Chicago, and has a law practice worth $20,000 a year."

In one department of effort, that of sport, the Negro was especially prominent. In pugilism, a diversion that has always been noteworthy for its popular appeal, Peter Jackson was well known as a contemporary of John L. Sullivan. George Dixon was, with the exception of one year, either bantam-weight or featherweight champion for the whole of the period from 1890 to 1900; and Joe Gans was lightweight champion from 1902 to 1908. Joe Walcott was welterweight champion from 1901 to 1904, and was succeeded by Dixie Kid, who held his place from 1904 to 1908. In 1908, to the chagrin of thousands and with a victory that occasioned a score of racial conflicts throughout the South and West and that resulted in several deaths, Jack Johnson became the heavyweight champion of America, a position that he was destined to hold for seven years. In professional baseball the Negro was proscribed, though occasionally a member of the race played on teams of the second group. Of semi-professional teams the American Giants and the Leland Giants of Chicago, and the Lincoln Giants of New York, were popular favorites, and frequently numbered on their rolls players of the first order of ability. In intercollegiate baseball W. C. Matthews of Harvard was outstanding for several years about 1904. In intercollegiate football Lewis at Harvard in the earlier nineties and Bullock at Dartmouth a decade later were unusually prominent, while

Marshall of Minnesota in 1905 became an All-American end. Pollard of Brown, a half-back, in 1916, and Robeson of Rutgers, an end, in 1918, also won All-American honors. About the turn of the century Major Taylor was a champion bicycle rider, and John B. Taylor of Pennsylvania was an intercollegiate champion in track athletics. Similarly fifteen years later Binga Dismond of Howard and Chicago, Sol Butler of Dubuque, and Howard P. Drew of Southern California were destined to win national and even international honors in track work. Drew broke numerous records as a runner and Butler was the winner in the broad jump at the Inter-Allied Games in the Pershing Stadium in Paris. In 1920 E. Gourdin of Harvard came prominently forward as one of the best track athletes that institution had ever had.

In the face, then, of the Negro's unquestionable physical ability and prowess the supreme criticism that he was called on to face within the period was all the more hard to bear. In all nations and in all ages courage under fire as a soldier has been regarded as the sterling test of manhood, and by this standard we have seen that in war the Negro had more than vindicated himself. His very honor as a soldier was now to be attacked.

In August, 1906, Companies B, C, and D of the Twenty-fifth Regiment, United States Infantry, were stationed at Fort Brown, Brownsville, Texas, where they were forced to exercise very great self-restraint in the face of daily insults from the citizens. On the night of the 13th occurred a riot in which one citizen of the town was killed, another wounded, and the chief of police injured. The people of the town accused the soldiers of causing the riot and demanded their removal. Brigadier-General E. A. Garlington, Inspector General, was sent to find the guilty men, and, failing in his mission, he recommended dishonorable discharge for the regiment. On this recommendation President Roosevelt on November 9 dismissed "without honor" the entire battalion, disqualifying its members for service thereafter in either the military or the civil employ of the United States. When Congress met in December Senator J. B. Foraker of Ohio placed himself at the head of the critics of the President's action, and in a ringing speech said of the discharged men that "they asked no favors because they were Negroes, but only justice because they were men." On January 22 the Senate authorized a general investigation of the whole matter, a special message from the President on the 14th having revoked the civil disability of the discharged soldiers. The case was finally disposed of by a congressional act approved March 3, 1909, which appointed a court of inquiry before which any discharged man who wished to reënlist had the burden of establishing his innocence —a procedure which clearly violated the fundamental principle in law that a man is to be accounted innocent until he is proved guilty.

In connection with the dishonored soldier of Brownsville, and indeed with reference to the Negro throughout the period, we recall Edwin Markham's poem, "Dreyfus," * written for a far different occasion but with fundamental principles of justice that are eternal:

I

A man stood stained; France was one Alp of hate,
Pressing upon him with the whole world's weight;
In all the circle of the ancient sun
There was no voice to speak for him—not one;
In all the world of men there was no sound
But of a sword flung broken to the ground.

Hell laughed its little hour; and then behold
How one by one the guarded gates unfold!
Swiftly a sword by Unseen Forces hurled,
And now a man rising against the world!

II

Oh, import deep as life is, deep as time!
There is a Something sacred and sublime
Moving behind the worlds, beyond our ken,
Weighing the stars, weighing the deeds of men.

* It is here quoted with the permission of the author and in the form in which it originally appeared in *McClure's Magazine*, September, 1899.

Take heart, O soul of sorrow, and be strong!
There is one greater than the whole world's wrong.
Be hushed before the high Benignant Power
That moves wool-shod through sepulcher and tower!
No truth so low but He will give it crown;
No wrong so high but He will hurl it down.
O men that forge the fetter, it is vain;
There is a Still Hand stronger than your chain.
'Tis no avail to bargain, sneer, and nod,
And shrug the shoulder for reply to God.

7. The Dawn of a To-morrow

The bitter period that we have been considering was not
wholly without its bright features, and with the new century
new voices began to be articulate. In May, 1900, there was
in Montgomery a conference in which Southern men undertook as never before to make a study of their problems. That
some who came had yet no real conception of the task and its
difficulties may be seen from the suggestion of one man that
the Negroes be deported to the West or to the islands of the
sea. Several men advocated the repeal of the Fifteenth Amendment. The position outstanding for its statesmanship was that
of ex-Governor William A. McCorkle of West Virginia, who
asserted that the right of franchise was the vital and underlying principle of the life of the people of the United States
and must not be violated, that the remedy for present conditions was an "honest and inflexible educational and property
basis, administered fairly for black and white," and finally
that the Negro Problem was not a local problem but one to
be settled by the hearty coöperation of all of the people of
the United States.

Meanwhile the Southern Educational Congress continued
its sittings from year to year, and about 1901 there developed
new and great interest in education, the Southern Education
Board acting in close coöperation with the General Education
Board, the medium of the philanthropy of John D. Rockefeller,

and frequently also with the Peabody and Slater funds.* In 1907 came the announcement of the Jeanes Fund, established by Anna T. Jeanes, a Quaker of Philadelphia, for the education of the Negro in the rural districts of the South; and in 1911 that of the Phelps-Stokes Fund, established by Caroline Phelps-Stokes with emphasis on the education of the Negro in Africa and America. More and more these agencies were to work in harmony and coöperation with the officials in the different states concerned. In 1900 J. L. M. Curry, a Southern man of great breadth of culture, was still in charge of the Peabody and Slater funds, but he was soon to pass from the scene and in the work now to be done were prominent Robert C. Ogden, Hollis B. Frissell, Wallace Buttrick, George Foster Peabody, and James H. Dillard.

Along with the mob violence, moreover, that disgraced the opening years of the century was an increasing number of officers who were disposed to do their duty even under trying circumstances. Less than two months after his notorious inaugural Governor Vardaman of Mississippi interested the reading public by ordering out a company of militia when a lynching was practically announced to take place, and by boarding a special train to the scene to save the Negro. In this same state in 1909, when the legislature passed a law levying a tax for the establishment of agricultural schools for white students, and levied this on the property of white people and Negroes alike, though only the white people were to have schools, a Jasper County Negro contested the matter before the Chancery Court, which declared the law unconstitutional, and he was further supported by the Supreme Court of the state. Such a decision was inspiring, but it was not the rule, and already the problems of another decade were being foreshadowed. Already also under the stress of conditions in the South many Negroes were seeking a haven in the North. By 1900 there were as many Negroes in Pennsylvania as in Mis-

* In 1867 George Peabody, an American merchant and patriot, established the Peabody Educational Fund for the purpose of promoting "intellectual, moral, and industrial education in the most destitute portion of the Southern states." The John F. Slater Fund was established in 1882 especially for the encouragement of the industrial education of Negroes.

souri, whereas twenty years before there had been twice as many in the latter state. There were in Massachusetts more than in Delaware, whereas twenty years before Delaware had had 50 per cent more than Massachusetts. Within twenty years Virginia gained 312,000 white people and only 29,000 Negroes, the latter having begun a steady movement to New York. North Carolina gained 400,000 white people and only 93,000 Negroes. South Carolina and Mississippi, however, were not yet affected in large measure by the movement.

The race indeed was beginning to be possessed by a new consciousness. After 1895 Booker T. Washington was a very genuine leader. From the first, however, there was a distinct group of Negro men who honestly questioned the ultimate wisdom of the so-called Atlanta Compromise, and who felt that in seeming to be willing temporarily to accept proscription and to waive political rights Dr. Washington had given up too much. Sometimes also there was something in his illustrations of the effects of current methods of education that provoked reply. Those who were of the opposition, however, were not at first united and constructive, and in their utterances they sometimes offended by harshness of tone. Dr. Washington himself said of the extremists in this group that they frequently understood theories but not things; that in college they gave little thought to preparing for any definite task in the world, but started out with the idea of preparing themselves to solve the race problem; and that many of them made a business of keeping the troubles, wrongs, and hardships of the Negro race before the public.* There was ample ground for this criticism. More and more, however, the opposition gained force; the *Guardian,* a weekly paper edited in Boston by Monroe Trotter, was particularly outspoken, and in Boston the real climax came in 1903 in an endeavor to break up a meeting at which Dr. Washington was to speak. Then, beginning in January, 1904, the *Voice of the Negro,* a magazine published in Atlanta for three years, definitely helped toward the cultivation of racial ideals. Publication of the periodical became irregular after the Atlanta Massacre, and

---

* See chapter "The Intellectuals," in *My Larger Education.*

it finally expired in 1907. Some of the articles dealt with older and more philosophical themes, but there were also bright and illuminating studies in education and other social topics, as well as a strong stand on political issues. The *Colored American,* published in Boston just a few years before the *Voice* began to appear, also did inspiring work. Various local or state organizations, moreover, from time to time showed the virtue of coöperation; thus the Georgia Equal Rights Convention, assembled in Macon in February, 1906, at the call of William J. White, the veteran editor of the *Georgia Baptist,* brought together representative men from all over the state and considered such topics as the unequal division of school taxes, the deprivation of the jury rights of Negroes, the peonage system, and the penal system. In 1905 twenty-nine men of the race launched what was known as the Niagara Movement. The aims of this organization were freedom of speech and criticism, an unlettered and unsubsidized press, manhood suffrage, the abolition of all caste distinctions based simply on race and color, the recognition of the principle of human brotherhood as a practical present creed, the recognition of the highest and best training as the monopoly of no class or race, a belief in the dignity of labor, and united effort to realize these ideals under wise and courageous leadership. The time was not yet quite propitious, and the Niagara Movement as such died after three or four years. Its principles lived on, however, and it greatly helped toward the formation of a stronger and more permanent organization.

In 1909 a number of people who were interested in the general effect of the Negro Problem on democracy in America organized in New York the National Association for the Advancement of Colored People.* It was felt that the situation had become so bad that the time had come for a simple declaration of human rights. In 1910 Moorfield Storey, a distinguished lawyer of Boston, became national president, and W. E. Burghardt DuBois director of publicity and research, and editor of the *Crisis,* which periodical began publication

---

* For detailed statement of origin see pamphlet, "How the National Association for the Advancement of Colored People Began," by Mary White Ovington, published by the Association.

in November of this year. The organization was successful from the first, and local branches were formed all over the country, some years elapsing, however, before the South was penetrated. Said the Director: "Of two things we Negroes have dreamed for many years: An organization so effective and so powerful that when discrimination and injustice touched one Negro, it would touch 12,000,000. We have not got this yet, but we have taken a great step toward it. We have dreamed, too, of an organization that would work ceaselessly to make Americans know that the so-called 'Negro problem' is simply one phase of the vaster problem of democracy in America, and that those who wish freedom and justice for their country must wish it for every black citizen. This is the great and insistent message of the National Association for the Advancement of Colored People."

This organization is outstanding as an effort in coöperation between the races for the improvement of the condition of the Negro. Of special interest along the line of economic betterment has been the National League on Urban Conditions among Negroes, now known as the National Urban League, which also has numerous branches with headquarters in New York and through whose offices thousands of Negroes have been placed in honorable employment. The National Urban League was also formally organized in 1910; it represented a merging of the different agencies working in New York City in behalf of the social betterment of the Negro population, especially of the National League for the Protection of Colored Women and of the Committee for Improving the Industrial Conditions among Negroes in New York, both of which agencies had been organized in 1906. As we shall see, the work of the League was to be greatly expanded within the next decade by the conditions brought about by the war; and under the direction of the executive secretary, Eugene Kinckle Jones, with the assistance of alert and patriotic officers, its work was to prove one of genuinely national service.

Interesting also was a new concern on the part of the young Southern college man about the problems at his door. Within just a few years after the close of the period now considered, Phelps-Stokes fellowships for the study of problems relating to the Negro were founded at the Universities of Virginia and Georgia; it was expected that similar fellowships would be founded in other institutions; and there was interest in the annual meetings of the Southern Sociological Congress and the University Commission on Southern Race Questions.

Thus from one direction and another at length broke upon a "vale of tears" a new day of effort and of hope. For the real contest the forces were gathering. The next decade was to be one of unending bitterness and violence, but also one in which the Negro was to rise as never before to the dignity of self-reliant and courageous manhood.

CHAPTER XVI

THE NEGRO IN THE NEW AGE

1. *Character of the Period*

The decade 1910-1920, momentous in the history of the world, in the history of the Negro race in America must finally be regarded as the period of a great spiritual uprising against the proscription, the defamation, and the violence of the preceding twenty years. As never before the Negro began to realize that the ultimate burden of his salvation rested upon himself, and he learned to respect and to depend upon himself accordingly.

The decade naturally divides into two parts, that before and that after the beginning of the Great War in Europe. Even in the earlier years, however, the tendencies that later were dominant were beginning to be manifest. The greater part of the ten years was consumed by the two administrations of President Woodrow Wilson; and not only did the National Government in the course of these administrations discriminate openly against persons of Negro descent in the Federal service and fail to protect those who happened to live in the capital, but its policy also gave encouragement to outrage in places technically said to be beyond its jurisdiction. A great war was to give new occasion and new opportunity for discrimination, defamatory propaganda was to be circulated on a scale undreamed of before, and the close of the war was to witness attempts for a new reign of terror in the South. Even beyond the bounds of continental America the race was now to suffer by reason of the national policy, and the little republic of Hayti to lift its bleeding hands to the calm judgment of the world.

Both a cause and a result of the struggle through which the race was now to pass was its astonishing progress. The fiftieth anniversary of the Emancipation Proclamation—January 1, 1913—called to mind as did nothing else the proscription and the mistakes, but also the successes and the hopes of the Negro people in America. Throughout the South disfranchisement seemed almost complete; and yet, after many attempts, the movement finally failed in Maryland in 1911 and in Arkansas in 1912. In 1915, moreover, the disfranchising act of Oklahoma was declared unconstitutional by the United States Supreme Court, and henceforth the Negro could feel that the highest legal authority was no longer on the side of those who sought to deprive him of all political voice. Eleven years before, the Court had taken refuge in technicalities. The year 1911 was also marked by the appointment of the first Negro policeman in New York, by the election of the first Negro legislator in Pennsylvania, and by the appointment of a man of the race, William H. Lewis, as Assistant Attorney General of the United States; and several civil rights suits were won in Massachusetts, New York, and New Jersey. Banks, insurance companies, and commercial and industrial enterprises were constantly being capitalized; churches erected more and more stately edifices; and fraternal organizations constantly increased in membership and wealth. By 1913 the Odd Fellows numbered very nearly half a million members and owned property worth two and a half million dollars; in 1920 the Dunbar Amusement Corporation of Philadelphia erected a theater costing $400,000; and the foremost business woman of the race in the decade, Mme. C. J. Walker, on the simple business of toilet articles and hair preparations built up an enterprise of national scope and conducted in accordance with the principles regularly governing great American commercial organizations. Fifty years after emancipation, moreover, very nearly one-fourth of all the Negroes in the Southern states were living in homes that they themselves owned; thus 430,449 of 1,917,391 houses occupied in these states were reported in 1910 as owned, and 314,340 were free of all encumbrance. The percentage of illiteracy decreased from 70 in 1880 to 30.4 in 1910, and movements were under way for the still more rapid spread of elementary knowledge. Excellent high schools, such as those in St. Louis, Washington, Kansas City (both cities of this name), Louisville, Baltimore, and other cities and towns in the border states and sometimes as far away as Texas, were setting a standard such as was in accord with the best in the country; and in one year, 1917, 455 young people of the race received the degree of bachelor of arts, while throughout the decade different ones received honors and took the highest graduate degrees at the foremost institutions of learning in the country. Early in the decade the General Education Board began actively to assist in the work of the higher educational institutions, and an outstanding gift was that of half a million dollars to Fisk University in 1920. Meanwhile, through the National Urban League and hundreds of local clubs and welfare organizations, social betterment went forward, much impetus being given to the work by the National Association of Colored Women's Clubs organized in 1896.

Along with its progress, throughout the decade the race had to meet increasing bitterness and opposition, and this was intensified by the motion picture, "The Birth of a Nation," built on lines similar to those of *The Clansman*. Negro men standing high on civil service lists were sometimes set aside; in 1913 the white railway mail clerks of the South began an open campaign against Negroes in the service in direct violation of the rules; and a little later in the same year segregation in the different departments became notorious. In 1911 the American Bar Association raised the question of the color-line; and efforts for the restriction of Negroes to certain neighborhoods in different prominent cities sometimes resulted in violence, as in the dynamiting of the homes of Negroes in Kansas City, Missouri, in 1911. When the Progressive party was organized in 1912 the Negro was given to understand that his support was not sought, and in 1911 a strike of firemen on the Queen and Crescent Railroad was in its main outlines similar to the trouble on the Georgia Railroad two years before. Meanwhile in the South the race received only 18 per cent of the total expenditures for education, although it constituted more than 30 per cent of the population.

Worse than anything else, however, was the matter of lynching. In each year the total number of victims of illegal execution continued to number three- or fourscore; but no one could ever be sure that every instance had been recorded. Between the opening of the decade and the time of the entrance of the United States into the war, five cases were attended by such unusual circumstances that the public could not soon forget them. At Coatesville, Pennsylvania, not far from Philadelphia, on August 12, 1911, a Negro laborer, Zach Walker, while drunk, fatally shot a night watchman. He was pursued and attempted suicide. Wounded, he was brought to town and placed in the hospital. From this place he was taken chained to his cot, dragged for some miles, and then tortured and burned to death in the presence of a great crowd of people, including many women, and his bones and the links of the chain which bound him distributed as souvenirs. At Monticello, Georgia, in January, 1915, when a Negro family resisted an officer who was making an arrest, the father, Dan Barbour, his young son, and his two daughters were all hanged to a tree and their bodies riddled with bullets. Before the close of the year there was serious trouble in the southwestern portion of the state, and behind this lay all the evils of the system of peonage in the black belt. Driven to desperation by the mistreatment accorded them in the raising of cotton, the Negroes at last killed an overseer who had whipped a Negro boy. A reign of terror was then instituted; churches, society halls, and homes were burnt, and several individuals shot. On December 30 there was a wholesale lynching of six Negroes in Early County. Less than three weeks afterwards a sheriff who attempted to arrest some more Negroes and who was accompanied by a mob was killed. Then (January 20, 1916) five Negroes who had been taken from the jail in Worth County were rushed in automobiles into Lee County adjoining, and hanged and shot. On May 15, 1916, at Waco, Texas, Jesse Washington, a sullen and overgrown boy of seventeen, who worked for a white farmer named Fryar at the town of Robinson, six miles away, and who one week before had criminally assaulted and killed Mrs. Fryar, after unspeakable mutilation was burned in the heart of the town. A part of the torture consisted in stabbing with knives and the cutting off of the boy's fingers as he grabbed the chain by which he was bound. Finally, on October 21, 1916, Anthony Crawford, a Negro farmer of Abbeville, South Carolina, who owned four hundred and twenty-seven acres of the best cotton land in his county and who was reported to be worth $20,000, was lynched. He had come to town to the store of W. D. Barksdale to sell a load of cotton-seed, and the two men had quarreled about the price, although no blow was struck on either side. A little later, however, Crawford was arrested by a local policeman and a crowd of idlers from the public square rushed to give him a whipping for his "impudence." He promptly knocked down the ringleader with a hammer. The mob then set upon him, nearly killed him, and at length threw him into the jail. A few hours later, fearing that the sheriff would secretly remove the prisoner, it returned, dragged the wounded man forth, and then hanged and shot him, after which proceedings warning was sent to his family to leave the county by the middle of the next month.

It will be observed that in these five noteworthy occurrences, in only one case was there any question of criminal assault. On the other hand, in one case two young women were included among the victims; another was really a series of lynchings emphasizing the lot of some Negroes under a vicious economic system; and the last simply grew out of the jealousy and hatred aroused by a Negro of independent means who knew how to stand up for his rights.

Such was the progress, such also the violence that the Negro witnessed during the decade. Along with his problems at home he now began to have a new interest in those of his kin across the sea, and this feeling was intensified by the world war. It raises questions of such far-reaching importance, however, that it must receive separate and distinct treatment.

2. *Migration; East St. Louis*

Very soon after the beginning of the Great War in Europe there began what will ultimately be known as the most remarkable migratory movement in the history of the Negro in America. Migration had indeed at no time ceased since the great movement of 1879, but for the most part it had been merely personal and not in response to any great emergency. The sudden ceasing of the stream of immigration from Europe, however, created an unprecedented demand for labor in the great industrial centers of the North, and business men were not long in realizing the possibilities of a source that had as yet been used in only the slightest degree. Special agents undoubtedly worked in some measure; but the outstanding feature of the new migration was that it was primarily a mass movement and not one organized or encouraged by any special group of leaders. Labor was needed in railroad construction, in the steel mills, in the tobacco farms of Connecticut, and in the packing-houses, foundries, and automobile plants. In 1915 the New England tobacco growers hastily got together in New York two hundred girls; but these proved to be unsatisfactory, and it was realized that the labor supply would have to be more carefully supervised. In January, 1916, the management of the Continental Tobacco Corporation definitely decided on the policy of importing workers from the South, and within the next year not less than three thousand Negroes came to Hartford, several hundred being students from the schools and colleges who went North to work for the summer. In the same summer came also train-loads of Negroes from Jacksonville and other points to work for the Erie and Pennsylvania Railroads.

Those who left their homes in the South to find new ones in the North thus worked first of all in response to a new economic demand. Prominent in their thought to urge them on, however, were the generally unsatisfactory conditions in the South from which they had so long suffered and from which all too often there had seemed to be no escape. As it was, they were sometimes greatly embarrassed in leaving. In Jacksonville the city council passed an ordinance requiring that agents who wished to recruit labor to be sent out of the state should pay $1,000 for a license or suffer a fine of $600 and spend sixty days in jail. Macon, Ga., raised the license fee to $25,000. In Savannah the excitement was intense. When two trains did not move as it was expected that they would, three hundred Negroes paid their own fares and went North. Later, when the leaders of the movement could not be found, the police arrested one hundred of the Negroes and sent them to the police barracks, charging them with loitering. Similar scenes were enacted elsewhere, the South being then as ever unwilling to be deprived of its labor supply. Meanwhile wages for some men in such an industrial center as Birmingham leaped to $9 and $10 a day. All told, hardly less than three-fourths of a million Negroes went North within the four years 1915-1918.

Naturally such a great shifting of population did not take place without some inconvenience and hardship. Among the thousands who changed their place of residence were many ignorant and improvident persons; but sometimes it was the most skilled artisans and the most substantial owners of homes in different communities who sold their property and moved away. In the North they at once met congestion in housing facilities. In Philadelphia and Pittsburgh this condition became so bad as to demand immediate attention. In more than one place there were outbreaks in which lives were lost. In East St. Louis, Ill., all of the social problems raised by the movement were seen in their baldest guise. The original population of this city had come for the most part from Georgia, Mississippi, Kentucky, and Tennessee. It had long been an important industrial center. It was also a very rough place, the scene of prize-fights and cock-fights and a haven for escaped prisoners; and there was very close connection between the saloons and politics. For years the managers of the industrial plants had recruited their labor supply from Ellis Island. When this failed they turned to the Negroes of the South; and difficulties were aggravated by a series of strikes on the part of the white workers. By the spring of 1917 not less than ten thousand Negroes had recently arrived in the city, and the housing situation was so acute that these people were more and more being forced into the white localities. Sometimes Negroes who had recently arrived wandered aimlessly about the streets, where they met the rougher elements of the city; there were frequent fights and also much trouble on the street cars. The Negroes interested themselves in politics and even succeeded in placing in office several men of their choice. In February, 1917, there was a strike of the white workers at the Aluminum Ore Works. This was adjusted at the time, but the settlement was not permanent, and meanwhile there were almost daily arrivals from the South, and the East St. Louis *Journal* was demanding: "Make East St. Louis a Lily White Town." There were preliminary riots on May 27-30. On the night of July 1 men in automobiles rode through the Negro section and began firing promiscuously. The next day the massacre broke forth in all its fury, and before it was over hundreds of thousands of dollars in property had been destroyed, six thousand Negroes had been driven from their homes, and about one hundred and fifty shot, burned, hanged, or maimed for life. Officers of the law failed to do their duty, and the testimony of victims as to the torture inflicted upon them was such as to send a thrill of horror through the heart of the American people. Later there was a congressional investigation, but from this nothing very material resulted. In the last week of this same month, July, 1917, there were also serious outbreaks in both Chester and Philadelphia, Penn., the fundamental issues being the same as in East St. Louis.

Meanwhile welfare organizations earnestly labored to adjust the Negro in his new environment. In Chicago the different state clubs helped nobly. Greater than any other one agency, however, was the National Urban League, whose work now witnessed an unprecedented expansion. Representative was the work of the Detroit branch, which was not content merely with finding vacant positions, but approached manufacturers of all kinds through distribution of literature and by personal visits, and within twelve months was successful in placing not less than one thousand Negroes in employment other than unskilled labor. It also established a bureau of investigation and information regarding housing conditions, and generally aimed at the proper moral and social care of those who needed its service. The whole problem of the Negro was of such commanding importance after the United States entered the war as to lead to the creation of a special Division of Negro Economics in the office of the

Secretary of Labor, to the directorship of which Dr. George E. Haynes was called.

In January, 1918, a Conference of Migration was called in New York under the auspices of the National Urban League, and this placed before the American Federation of Labor resolutions asking that Negro labor be considered on the same basis as white. The Federation had long been debating the whole question of the Negro, and it had not seemed to be able to arrive at a clearcut policy though its general attitude was unfavorable. In 1919, however, it voted to take steps to recognize and admit Negro unions. At last it seemed to realize the necessity of making allies of Negro workers, and of course any such change of front on the part of white workmen would menace some of the foundations of racial strife in the South and indeed in the country at large. Just how effective the new decision was to be in actual practice remained to be seen, especially as the whole labor movement was thrown on the defensive by the end of 1920. However, special interest attached to the events in Bogalusa, La., in November, 1919. Here were the headquarters of the Great Southern Lumber Company, whose sawmill in the place was said to be the largest in the world. For some time it had made use of unorganized Negro labor as against the white labor unions. The forces of labor, however, began to organize the Negroes in the employ of the Company, which held political as well as capitalistic control in the community. The Company then began to have Negroes arrested on charges of vagrancy, taking them before the city court and having them fined and turned over to the Company to work out the fines under the guard of gunmen. In the troubles that came to a head on November 22, three white men were shot and killed, one of them being the district president of the American Federation of Labor, who was helping to give protection to a colored organizer. The full significance of this incident remained also to be seen; but it is quite possible that in the final history of the Negro problem the skirmish at Bogalusa will mark the beginning of the end of the exploiting of Negro labor and the first recognition of the identity of interest between white and black workmen in the South.

3. *The Great War*

Just on the eve of America's entrance into the war in Europe occurred an incident that from the standpoint of the Negro at least must finally appear simply as the prelude to the great contest to come. Once more, at an unexpected moment, ten years after Brownsville, the loyalty and heroism of the Negro soldier impressed the American people. The expedition of the American forces into Mexico in 1916, with the political events attending this, is a long story. The outstanding incident, however, was that in which two troops of the Tenth Cavalry engaged. About eighty men had been sent a long distance from the main line of the American army, their errand being supposedly the pursuit of a deserter. At or near the town of Carrizal the Americans seem to have chosen to go through the town rather than around it, and the result was a clash in which Captain Boyd, who commanded the detachment, and some twenty of his men were killed, twenty-two others being captured by the Mexicans. Under the circumstances the whole venture was rather imprudent in the first place. As to the engagement itself, the Mexicans said that the American troops made the attack, while the latter said that the Mexicans themselves first opened fire. However this may have been, all other phases of the Mexican problem seemed for the moment to be forgotten at Washington in the demand for the release of the twenty-two men who had been taken. There was no reason for holding them, and they were brought up to El Paso within a few days and sent across the line. Thus, though "some one had blundered," these Negro soldiers did their duty; "theirs not to make reply; theirs but to do and die." So in the face of odds they fought like heroes and twenty died beneath the Mexican stars.

When the United States entered the war in Europe in April, 1917, the question of overwhelming importance to the Negro people was naturally that of their relation to the great conflict in which their country had become engaged. Their response to the draft call set a noteworthy example of loyalty to all other elements in the country. At the very outset the race faced a terrible dilemma: If there were to be special training camps for officers, and if the National Government would make no provision otherwise, did it wish to have a special camp for Negroes, such as would give formal approval to a policy of segregation, or did it wish to have no camp at all on such terms and thus lose the opportunity to have any men of the race specially trained as officers? The camp was secured—Camp Dodge, near Des Moines, Iowa; and throughout the summer of 1917 the work of training went forward, the heart of a harassed and burdened people responding more and more with pride to the work of their men. On October 15, 625 became commissioned officers, and all told 1200 received commissions. To the fighting forces of the United States the race furnished altogether very nearly 400,000 men, of whom just a little more than half actually saw service in Europe.

Negro men served in all branches of the military establishment and also as surveyors and draftsmen. For the handling of many of the questions relating to them Emmett J. Scott was on October 1, 1917, appointed Special Assistant to the Secretary of War. Mr. Scott had for a number of years assisted Dr. Booker T. Washington as secretary at Tuskegee Institute, and in 1909 he was one of the three members of the special commission appointed by President Taft for the investigation of Liberian affairs. Negro nurses were authorized by the War Department for service in base hospitals at six army camps, and women served also as canteen workers in France and in charge of hostess houses in the United States. Sixty Negro men served as chaplains; 350 as Y. M. C. A. secretaries; and others in special capacities. Service of exceptional value was rendered by Negro women in industry, and very largely also they maintained and promoted the food supply through agriculture at the same time that they released men for service at the front. Meanwhile the race invested millions of dollars in Liberty Bonds and War Savings stamps and contributed generously to the Red Cross, Y. M. C. A., and other relief agencies. In the summer of 1918 interest naturally centered upon the actual performance of Negro soldiers in France and upon the establishment of units of the Students' Army Training Corps in twenty leading educational institutions. When these units were demobilized in December, 1918, provision was made in a number of the schools for the formation of units of the Reserve Officers' Training Corps.

The remarkable record made by the Negro in the previous wars of the country was fully equaled by that in the Great War. Negro soldiers fought with special distinction in the Argonne Forest, at Château-Thierry, in Belleau Wood, in the St. Mihiel district, in the Champagne sector, at Vosges and Metz, winning often very high praise from their commanders. Entire regiments of Negro troops were cited for exceptional valor and decorated with the Croix de Guerre— the 369th, the 371st, and the 372nd; while groups of officers and men of the 365th, the 366th, the 368th, the 370th, and the first battalion of the 367th were also decorated. At the close of the war the highest Negro officers in the army were Lieutenant Colonel Otis B. Duncan, commander of the third battalion of the 370th, formerly the Eighth Illinois, and the highest ranking Negro officer in the American Expeditionary Forces; Colonel Charles Young (retired), on special duty at Camp Grant, Ill.; Colonel Franklin A. Dennison, of the 370th Infantry, and Lieutenant Colonel Benjamin O. Davis, of the Ninth Cavalry. The 370th was the first American regiment stationed in the St. Mihiel sector; it was one of the three that occupied a sector at Verdun when a penetration there would have been disastrous to the Allied cause; and it went direct from the training camp to the firing-line. Noteworthy also was the record of the 369th infantry, formerly the Fifteenth Regiment, New York National Guard. This organization was under shellfire for 191 days, and it held one trench for 91 days without relief. It was the first unit of Allied fighters to reach the Rhine, going down as an advance guard of the French army of occupation. A prominent hero in this regiment was Sergeant Henry Johnson, who returned with the Croix de Guerre with one star and one palm. He is credited with routing a party of Germans at Bois-Hanzey in the Argonne on May 5, 1918, with singularly heavy losses to the enemy. Many other men acted with

similar bravery.   Hardly less heroic was the service of
the stevedore regiments, or the thousands of men in the
army who did not go to France but who did their duty as
they were commanded at home.   General Vincenden said of
the men of the 370th: "Fired by a noble ardor, they go at
times even beyond the objectives given them by the higher
command; they have always wished to be in the front line";
and General Coybet said of the 371st and 372nd: "The most
powerful defenses, the most strongly organized machine gun
nests, the heaviest artillery barrages—nothing could stop them.
These crack regiments overcame every obstacle with a most
complete contempt for danger. . . . They have shown us the
way to victory."

In spite of his noble record—perhaps in some measure because of it—and in the face of his loyal response to the call
to duty, the Negro unhappily became in the course of the war
the victim of proscription and propaganda probably without
parallel in the history of the country.   No effort seems to
have been spared to discredit him both as a man and as a
soldier.   In both France and America the apparent object of
the forces working against him was the intention to prevent
any feeling that the war would make any change in the condition of the race at home.   In the South Negroes were sometimes forced into peonage and restrained in their efforts to
go North; and generally they had no representation on local
boards, the draft was frequently operated so as to be unfair
to them, and every man who registered found special provision for the indication of his race in the corner of his card.
Accordingly in many localities Negroes contributed more than
their quota, this being the result of favoritism shown to white
draftees.   The first report of the Provost-Marshal General
showed that of every 100 Negroes called 36 were certified
for service, while of every 100 white men called only 25 were
certified.   Of those summoned in Class 1 Negroes contributed
51.65 per cent of their registrants as against 32.53 per cent
of the white.   In France the work of defamation was manifest and flagrant.   Slanders about the Negro soldiers were
deliberately circulated among the French people, sometimes
on very high authority, much of this propaganda growing out

of a jealous fear of any acquaintance whatsoever of the Negro men with the French women. Especially insolent and sometimes brutal were the men of the military police, who at times shot and killed on the slightest provocation. Proprietors who sold to Negro soldiers were sometimes boycotted, and offenses were magnified which in the case of white men never saw publication. Negro officers were discriminated against in hotel and traveling accommodations, while upon the ordinary men in the service fell unduly any specially unpleasant duty such as that of re-burying the dead. White women engaged in "Y" work, especially Southern women, showed a disposition not to serve Negroes, though the Red Cross and Salvation Army organizations were much better in this respect; and finally the Negro soldier was not given any place in the great victory parade in Paris. About the close of the war moreover a great picture, or series of pictures, the "Pantheon de la Guerre," that was on a mammoth scale and that attracted extraordinary attention, was noteworthy as giving representation to all of the forces and divisions of the Allied armies except the Negroes in the forces from the United States.* Not unnaturally the Germans endeavored—though without success—to capitalize the situation by circulating among the Negroes insidious literature that sometimes made very strong points. All of these things are to be considered by those people in the United States who think that the Negro suffers unduly from a grievance.

While the Negro soldier abroad was thus facing unusual pressure in addition to the ordinary hardships of war, at home occurred an incident that was doubly depressing coming as it did just a few weeks after the massacre at East St. Louis. In August, 1917, a battalion of the Twenty-fourth Infantry, stationed at Houston, Texas, to assist in the work of concentrating soldiers for the war in Europe, encountered the ill-will of the town, and between the city police and the Negro

---

* On the whole subject of the actual life of the Negro soldier unusual interest attaches to the forthcoming and authoritative "Sidelights on Negro Soldiers," by Charles H. Williams, who as a special and official investigator had unequaled opportunity to study the Negro in camp and on the battle-line both in the United States and in France.

military police there was constant friction. At last when one of the Negroes had been beaten, word was circulated among his comrades that he had been shot, and a number of them set out for revenge. In the riot that followed (August 23) two of the Negroes and seventeen white people of the town were killed, the latter number including five policemen. As a result of this encounter sixty-three members of the battalion were court-martialed at Fort Sam Houston. Thirteen were hanged on December 11, 1917, five more were executed on September 13, 1918, fifty-one were sentenced to life imprisonment and five to briefer terms; and the Negro people of the country felt very keenly the fact that the condemned men were hanged like common criminals rather than given the death of soldiers. Thus for one reason or another the whole matter of the war and the incidents connected therewith simply made the Negro question more bitterly than ever the real disposition toward him of the government under which he lived and which he had striven so long to serve.

4. High Tension: Washington, Chicago, Elaine

Such incidents abroad and such feeling at home as we have recorded not only agitated the Negro people, but gave thousands of other citizens concern, and when the armistice suddenly came on November 11, 1918, not only in the South but in localities elsewhere in the country racial feeling had been raised to the highest point. About the same time there began to be spread abroad sinister rumors that the old KuKlux were riding again; and within a few months parades at night in representative cities in Alabama and Georgia left no doubt that the rumors were well founded. The Negro people fully realized the significance of the new movement, and they felt full well the pressure being brought to bear upon them in view of the shortage of domestic servants in the South. Still more did they sense the situation that would face their sons and brothers when they returned from France. But they were not afraid; and in all of the riots of the period the noteworthy fact stands out that in some of the cities in which the situation was most tense—notably Atlanta and Birmingham—no great race trouble was permitted to start.

In general, however, the violence that had characterized the year 1917 continued through 1918 and 1919. In the one state of Tennessee, within less than a year and on separate occasions, three Negroes were burned at the stake. On May 22, 1917, near Memphis, Ell T. Person, nearly fifty years of age, was burned for the alleged assault and murder of a young woman; and in this case the word "alleged" is used advisedly, for the whole matter of the fixing of the blame for the crime and the fact that the man was denied a legal trial left grave doubt as to the extent of his guilt. On Sunday, December 2, 1917, at Dyersburg, immediately after the adjournment of services in the churches of the town, Lation Scott, guilty of criminal assault, was burned; his eyes were put out with red-hot irons, a hot poker was rammed down his throat, and he was mutilated in unmentionable ways. Two months later, on February 12, 1918, at Estill Springs, Jim McIlheron, who had shot and killed two young white men, was also burned at the stake. In Estill Springs it had for some time been the sport of young white men in the community to throw rocks at single Negroes and make them run. Late one afternoon McIlheron went into a store to buy some candy. As he passed out, a remark was made by one of three young men about his eating his candy. The rest of the story is obvious.

As horrible as these burnings were, it is certain that they did not grind the iron into the Negro's soul any more surely than the three stories that follow. Hampton Smith was known as one of the harshest employers of Negro labor in Brooks County, Ga. As it was difficult for him to get help otherwise, he would go into the courts and whenever a Negro was convicted and was unable to pay his fine or was sentenced to a term on the chain-gang, he would pay the fine and secure the man for work on his plantation. He thus secured the services of Sidney Johnson, fined thirty dollars for gambling. After Johnson had more than worked out the thirty dollars he asked pay for the additional time he served. Smith refused to give this and a quarrel resulted. A few mornings later, when Johnson, sick, did not come to work, Smith found him in his cabin and beat him. A few evenings later, while Smith was sitting in his home, he was shot through a window and killed instantly, and his wife was wounded. As a result of this occurrence the Negroes of both Brooks and Lowndes counties were terrorized for the week May 17-24, 1918, and not less than eleven of them lynched. Into the bodies of two men lynched together not less than seven hundred bullets are said to have been fired. Johnson himself had been shot dead when he was found; but his body was mutilated, dragged through the streets of Valdosta, and burned. Mary Turner, the wife of one of the victims, said that her husband had been unjustly treated and that if she knew who had killed him she would have warrants sworn out against them. For saying this she too was lynched, although she was in an advanced state of pregnancy. Her ankles were tied together and she was hung to a tree, head downward. Gasoline and oil from the automobiles near were thrown on her clothing and a match applied. While she was yet alive her abdomen was cut open with a large knife and her unborn babe fell to the ground. It gave two feeble cries and then its head was crushed by a member of the mob with his heel. Hundreds of bullets were then fired into the woman's body. As a result of these events not less than five hundred Negroes left the immediate vicinity of Valdosta immediately, and hundreds of others prepared to leave as soon as they could dispose of their land, and this they proceeded to do in the face of the threat that any Negro who attempted to leave would be regarded as implicated in the murder of Smith and dealt with accordingly. At the end of this same year—on December 20, 1918—four young Negroes—Major Clark, aged twenty; Andrew Clark, aged fifteen; Maggie Howze, aged twenty, and Alma Howze, aged sixteen—were taken from the little jail at Shubuta, Mississippi, and lynched on a bridge near the town. They were accused of the murder of E. L. Johnston, a white dentist, though all protested their innocence. The situation that preceded the lynching was significant. Major Clark was in love with Maggie Howze and planned to marry her. This thought enraged Johnston, who was soon to become the father of a child by the young woman, and who told Clark to leave her alone. As the two sisters were about to be killed,

Maggie screamed and fought, crying, "I ain't guilty of killing the doctor and you oughtn't to kill me"; and to silence her cries one member of the mob struck her in the mouth with a monkey wrench, knocking her teeth out. On May 24, 1919, at Milan, Telfair County, Georgia, two young white men, Jim Dowdy and Lewis Evans, went drunk late at night to the Negro section of the town and to the home of a widow who had two daughters. They were refused admittance and then fired into the house. The girls, frightened, ran to another home. They were pursued, and Berry Washington, a respectable Negro seventy-two years of age, seized a shotgun, intending to give them protection; and in the course of the shooting that followed Dowdy was killed. The next night, Saturday the 25th, Washington was taken to the place where Dowdy was killed and his body shot to pieces.

It remained for the capital of the nation, however, largely to show the real situation of the race in the aftermath of a great war conducted by a Democratic administration. Heretofore the Federal Government had declared itself powerless to act in the case of lawlessness in an individual state; but it was now to have an opportunity to deal with violence in Washington itself. On July 19, 1919, a series of lurid and exaggerated stories in the daily papers of attempted assaults of Negroes on white women resulted in an outbreak that was intended to terrorize the popular Northwest section, in which lived a large proportion of the Negroes in the District of Columbia. For three days the violence continued intermittently, and as the constituted police authority did practically nothing for the defense of the Negro citizens, the loss of life might have been infinitely greater than it was if the colored men of the city had not assumed their own defense. As it was they saved the capital and earned the gratitude of the race and the nation. It appeared that Negroes—educated, law-abiding Negroes—would not now run when their lives and their homes were at stake, and before such determination the mob retreated ingloriously.

Just a week afterwards—before the country had really caught its breath after the events in Washington—there burst into flame in Chicago a race war of the greatest bitterness and fierceness. For a number of years the Western metropolis had been known as that city offering to the Negro the best industrial and political opportunity in the country. When the migration caused by the war was at its height, tens of thousands of Negroes from the South passed through the city going elsewhere, but thousands also remained to work in the stockyards or other places. With all of the coming and going, the Negroes in the city must at any time in 1918 or 1919 have numbered not less than 150,000; and banks, coöperative societies, and race newspapers flourished. There were also abundant social problems awakened by the saloons and gambling dens, and by the seamy side of politics. Those who had been longest in the city, however, rallied to the needs of the newcomers, and in their homes, their churches, and their places of work endeavored to get them adjusted in their environment. The housing situation, in spite of all such effort, became more and more acute, and when some Negroes were forced beyond the bounds of the old "black belt" there were attempts to dynamite their new residences. Meanwhile hundreds of young men who had gone to France or to cantonments—1850 from the district of one draft board at State and 35th Streets—returned to find again a place in the life of Chicago; and daily from Washington or from the South came the great waves of social unrest. Said Arnold Hill, secretary of the Chicago branch of the National Urban League: "Every time a lynching takes place in a community down South you can depend on it that colored people from that community will arrive in Chicago inside of two weeks; we have seen it happen so often that whenever we read newspaper dispatches of a public hanging or burning in a Texas or a Mississippi town, we get ready to extend greetings to the people from the immediate vicinity of the lynching." Before the armistice was signed the League was each month finding work for 1700 or 1800 men and women; in the following April the number fell to 500, but with the coming of summer it rapidly rose again. Unskilled work was plentiful, and jobs in foundries and steel mills, in building and construction work, and in light factories and packing-houses kept up a steady demand for laborers.

Meanwhile trouble was brewing, and on the streets there were occasional encounters.

Such was the situation when on a Sunday at the end of July a Negro boy at a bathing beach near Twenty-sixth Street swam across an imaginary segregation line. White boys threw rocks at him, knocked him off a raft, and he was drowned. Colored people rushed to a policeman and asked him to arrest the boys who threw the stones. He refused to do so, and as the dead body of the Negro boy was being handled, more rocks were thrown on both sides. The trouble thus engendered spread through the Negro district on the South Side, and for a week it was impossible or dangerous for people to go to work. Some employed at the stockyards could not get to their work for some days further. At the end of three days twenty Negroes were reported as dead, fourteen white men were dead, scores of people were injured, and a number of houses of Negroes burned.

In the face of this disaster the great soul of Chicago rose above its materialism. There were many conferences between representative people; out of all the effort grew the determination to work for a nobler city; and the sincerity was such as to give one hope not only for Chicago but also for a new and better America.

The riots in Washington and Chicago were followed within a few weeks by outbreaks in Knoxville and Omaha. In the latter place the fundamental cause of the trouble was social and political corruption, and because he strongly opposed the lynching of William Brown, the Negro, the mayor of the city, Edward P. Smith, very nearly lost his life. As it was, the county court house was burned, one man more was killed, and perhaps as many as forty injured. More important even than this, however—and indeed one of the two or three most far-reaching instances of racial trouble in the history of the Negro in America—was the reign of terror in and near Elaine, Phillips County, Arkansas, in the first week of October, 1919. The causes of this were fundamental and reached the very heart of the race problem and of the daily life of tens of thousands of Negroes.

Many Negro tenants in eastern Arkansas, as in other states,

were still living under a share system by which the owner
furnished the land and the Negro the labor, and by which at
the end of the year the two supposedly got equal parts of
the crop. Meanwhile throughout the year the tenant would
get his food, clothing, and other supplies at exorbitant prices
from a "commissary" operated by the planter or his agent;
and in actual practice the landowner and the tenant did not
go together to a city to dispose of the crop when it was gathered, as was sometimes done elsewhere, but the landowner
alone sold the crop and settled with the tenant whenever and
however he pleased; nor at the time of settlement was any
itemized statement of supplies given, only the total amount
owed being stated. Obviously the planter could regularly pad
his accounts, keep the Negro in debt, and be assured of his
labor supply from year to year.

In 1918 the price of cotton was constantly rising and at
length reached forty cents a pound. Even with the cheating
to which the Negroes were subjected, it became difficult to
keep them in debt, and they became more and more insistent
in their demands for itemized statements. Nevertheless some
of those whose cotton was sold in October, 1918, did not get
any statement of any sort before July of the next year.

Seeing no other way out of their difficulty, sixty-eight of
the Negroes got together and decided to hire a lawyer who
would help them to get statements of their accounts and settlement at the right figures. Feeling that the life of any Negro
lawyer who took such a case would be endangered, they employed the firm of Bratton and Bratton, of Little Rock. They
made contracts with this firm to handle the sixty-eight cases
at fifty dollars each in cash and a percentage of the moneys
collected from the white planters. Some of the Negroes also
planned to go before the Federal Grand Jury and charge certain planters with peonage. They had secret meetings from
time to time in order to collect the money to be paid in advance
and to collect the evidence which would enable them success-
fully to prosecute their cases. Some Negro cotton-pickers
about the same time organized a union; and at Elaine many
Negroes who worked in the sawmills and who desired to pro-

tect their wives and daughters from insult, refused to allow them to pick cotton or to work for a white man at any price.

Such was the sentiment out of which developed the Progressive Farmers and Household Union of America, which was an effort by legal means to secure protection from unscrupulous landlords, but which did use the form of a fraternal order with passwords and grips and insignia so as the more forcefully to appeal to some of its members. About the first of October the report was spread abroad in Phillips County that the Negroes were plotting an insurrection and that they were rapidly preparing to massacre the white people on a great scale. When the situation had become tense, one Sunday John Clem, a white man from Helena, drunk, came to Elaine and proceeded to terrorize the Negro population by gun play. The colored people kept off the streets in order to avoid trouble and telephoned the sheriff at Helena. This man failed to act. The next day Clem was abroad again, but the Negroes still avoided trouble, thinking that his acts were simply designed to start a race riot. On Tuesday evening, October 1, however, W. D. Adkins, a special agent of the Missouri Pacific Railroad, in company with Charles Pratt, a deputy sheriff, was riding past a Negro church near Hoop Spur, a small community just a few miles from Elaine. According to Pratt, persons in the church fired without cause on the party, killing Adkins and wounding himself. According to the Negroes, Adkins and Pratt fired into the church, evidently to frighten the people there assembled. At any rate word spread through the county that the massacre had started, and for days there was murder and rioting, in the course of which not less than five white men and twenty-five Negroes were killed, though some estimates placed the number of fatalities a great deal higher. Negroes were arrested and disarmed; some were shot on the highways; homes were fired into; and at one time hundreds of men and women were in a stockade under heavy guard and under the most unwholesome conditions, while hundreds of white men, armed to the teeth, rushed to the vicinity from neighboring cities and towns. Governor Charles H. Brough telegraphed to Camp Pike for Federal troops, and five hundred were mobilized at once "to repel the attack of the black army." Worse than any other feature was the wanton slaying of the four Johnston brothers, whose father had been a prominent Presbyterian minister and whose mother was formerly a school-teacher. Dr. D. A. E. Johnston was a successful dentist and owned a three-story building in Helena. Dr. Louis Johnston was a physician who lived in Oklahoma and who had come home on a visit. A third brother had served in France and been wounded and gassed at Château-Thierry.

Altogether one thousand Negroes were arrested and one hundred and twenty-two indicted. A special committee of seven gathered evidence and is charged with having used electric connections on the witness chair in order to frighten the Negroes. Twelve men were sentenced to death (though up to the end of 1920 execution had been stayed), and fifty-four to penitentiary terms. The trials lasted from five to ten minutes each. No witnesses for the defense were called; no Negroes were on the juries; no change of venue was given. Meanwhile lawyers at Helena were preparing to reap further harvest from Negroes who would be indicted and against whom there was no evidence, but who had saved money and Liberty Bonds.

Governor Brough in a statement to the press blamed the *Crisis* and the Chicago *Defender* for the trouble. He had served for a number of years as a professor of economics before becoming governor and had even identified himself with the forward-looking University Commission on Southern Race Questions; and it is true that he postponed the executions in order to allow appeals to be filed in behalf of the condemned men. That he should thus attempt to shift the burden of blame and overlook the facts when in a position of grave responsibility was a keen disappointment to the lovers of progress.

Reference to the monthly periodical and the weekly paper just mentioned, however, brings us to still another matter—the feeling on the part of the Negro that, in addition to the outrages visited on the race, the Government was now, under the cloak of wartime legislation, formally to attempt to curtail its freedom of speech. For some days the issue of the *Crisis* for May, 1919, was held up in the mail; a South Carolina

representative in Congress quoted by way of denunciation
from the editorial "Returning Soldiers" in the same number
of the periodical; and a little later in the year the Department
of Justice devoted twenty-seven pages of the report of the
investigation against "Persons Advising Anarchy, Sedition,
and the Forcible Overthrow of the Government" to a report
on "Radicalism and Sedition among the Negroes as Reflected
in Their Publications." Among other periodicals and papers
mentioned were the *Messenger* and the *Negro World* of New
York; and by the *Messenger* indeed, frankly radical in its
attitude not only on the race question but also on fundamental
economic principles, even the *Crisis* was regarded as conservative in tone. There could be no doubt that a great spiritual
change had come over the Negro people of the United States.
At the very time that their sons and brothers were making the
supreme sacrifice in France they were witnessing such events
as those at East St. Louis or Houston, or reading of three
burnings within a year in Tennessee. A new determination
closely akin to consecration possessed them. Fully to understand the new spirit one would read not only such publications as those that have been mentioned, but also those issued
in the heart of the South. "Good-by, Black Mammy," said
the *Southwestern Christian Advocate,* taking as its theme the
story of four Southern white men who acted as honorary pall-
bearers at an old Negro woman's funeral, but who under no
circumstances would thus have served for a thrifty, intelligent,
well-educated man of the race. Said the Houston *Informer,*
voicing the feeling of thousands, "The black man fought to
make the world safe for democracy; he now demands that
America be made and maintained safe for black Americans."
With hypocrisy in the practice of the Christian religion there
ceased to be any patience whatsoever, as was shown by the
treatment accorded a Y. M. C. A. "Call on behalf of the young
men and boys of the two great sister Anglo-Saxon nations."
"Read! Read! Read!" said the *Challenge Magazine,* "then
when the mob comes, whether with torch or with gun, let us
stand at Armageddon and battle for the Lord." "Protect your
home," said the gentle *Christian Recorder,* "protect your wife
and children, with your life if necessary. If a man crosses

your threshold after you and your family, the law allows you
to protect your home even if you have to kill the intruder."
Perhaps nothing, however, better summed up the new spirit
than the following sonnet by Claude McKay:

> If we must die, let it not be like hogs
>   Hunted and penned in an inglorious spot,
> While round us bark the mad and hungry dogs,
>   Making their mock at our accursed lot.
> If we must die, let it not be like hogs
>   So that our precious blood may not be shed
> In vain; then even the monsters we defy
>   Shall be constrained to honor us, though dead!
> Oh, kinsman! We must meet the common foe;
>   Though far outnumbered, let us still be brave,
> And for their thousand blows deal one deathblow!
>   What though before us lies the open grave?
> Like men we'll face the murderous, cowardly pack
>   Pressed to the wall, dying, but—fighting back!

5. The Widening Problem

In view of the world war and the important part taken in
it by French colonial troops, especially those from Senegal, it
is not surprising that the heart of the Negro people in the
United States broadened in a new sympathy with the problems of their brothers the world over. Even early in the decade
that we are now considering, however, there was some indication of this tendency, and the First Universal Races Congress in London in 1911 attracted wide attention. In February, 1919, largely through the personal effort of Dr. DuBois,
a Pan-African Congress was held in Paris, the chief aims of
which were the hearing of statements on the condition of
Negroes throughout the world, the obtaining of authoritative
statements of policy toward the Negro race from the Great
Powers, the making of strong representations to the Peace
Conference then sitting in Paris in behalf of the Negroes
throughout the world, and the laying down of principles on
which the future development of the race must take place.
Meanwhile the cession of the Virgin Islands had fixed atten-

tion upon an interesting colored population at the very door of the United States; and the American occupation of Hayti culminating in the killing of many of the people in the course of President Wilson's second administration gave a new feeling of kinship for the land of Toussaint L'Ouverture. Among other things the evidence showed that on June 12, 1918, under military pressure a new constitution was forced on the Haytian people, one favoring the white man and the foreigner; that by force and brutality innocent men and women, including native preachers and members of their churches, had been taken, roped together, and marched as slave-gangs to prison; and that in large numbers Haytians had been taken from their homes and farms and made to work on new roads for twenty cents a week, without being properly furnished with food—all of this being done under the pretense of improving the social and political condition of the country. The whole world now realized that the Negro problem was no longer local in the United States or South Africa, or the West Indies, but international in its scope and possibilities.

Very early in the course of the conflict in Europe it was pointed out that Africa was the real prize of the war, and it is now simply a commonplace to say that the bases of the struggle were economic. Nothing did Germany regret more than the forcible seizure of her African possessions. One can not fail to observe, moreover, a tendency of discussion of problems resultant from the war to shift the consideration from that of pure politics to that of racial relations, and early in the conflict students of society the world over realized that it was nothing less than suicide on the part of the white race. After the close of the war many books dealing with the issues at stake were written, and in the year 1920 alone several of these appeared in the United States. Of all of these publications, because of their different points of view, four might call for special consideration—*The Republic of Liberia,* by R. C. F. Maugham; *The Rising Tide of Color,* by Lothrop Stoddard; *Darkwater,* by W. E. Burghardt DuBois, and *Empire and Commerce in Africa: A Study in Economic Imperialism,* by Leonard Woolf. The position of each of these books is clear and all bear directly upon the central theme.

The Republic of Liberia was written by one who some years ago was the English consul at Monrovia and who afterwards was appointed to Dakar. The supplementary preface also gives the information that the book was really written two years before it appeared, publication being delayed on account of the difficulties of printing at the time. Even up to 1918, however, the account is incomplete, and the failure to touch upon recent developments becomes serious; but it is of course impossible to record the history of Liberia from 1847 to the present and reflect credit upon England. There are some pages of value in the book, especially those in which the author speaks of the labor situation in the little African republic; but these are obviously intended primarily for consumption by business men in London. "Liberians," we are informed, "tell you that, whatever may be said to the contrary, the republic's most uncomfortable neighbor has always been France." This is hardly true. France has indeed on more than one occasion tried to equal her great rival in aggrandizement, but she has never quite succeeded in so doing. As we have already shown in connection with Liberia in the present work, from the very first the shadow of Great Britain fell across the country. In more recent years, by loans that were no more than clever plans for thievery, by the forceful occupation of large tracts of land, and by interference in the internal affairs of the country, England has again and again proved herself the arch-enemy of the republic. The book so recently written in the last analysis appears to be little more than the basis of effort toward still further exploitation.

The very merit of *The Rising Tide of Color* depends on its bias, and it is significant that the book closes with a quotation from Kipling's "The Heritage." To Dr. Stoddard the most disquieting feature of the recent situation was not the war but the peace. Says he, "The white world's inability to frame a constructive settlement, the perpetuation of intestine hatreds and the menace of fresh civil wars complicated by the specter of social revolution, evoke the dread thought that the late war may be merely the first stage in a cycle of ruin." As for the war itself, "As colored men realized the significance of it all, they looked into each other's eyes and there saw the light of undreamed-of hopes. The white world was tearing itself to pieces. White solidarity was riven and shattered. And—fear of white power and respect for white civilization together dropped away like garments outworn. Through the bazaars of Asia ran the sibilant whisper: 'The East will see the West to bed.' " At last comes the inevitable conclusion pleading for a better understanding between England and Germany and for everything else that would make for racial solidarity. The pitiful thing about this book is that it is so thoroughly representative of the thing for which it pleads. It is the very essence of jingoism; civilization does not exist in and of itself, it is "white"; and the conclusions are directly at variance with the ideals that have been supposed to guide England and America. Incidentally the work speaks of the Negro and negroid population of Africa as "estimated at about 120,000,000." This low estimate has proved a common pitfall for writers. If we remember that Africa is three and a half times as large as the United States, and that while there are no cities as large as New York and Chicago, there are many centers of very dense population; if we omit entirely from the consideration the Desert of Sahara and make due allowance for some heavily wooded tracts in which live no people at all; and if we then take some fairly well-known region like Nigeria or Sierra Leone as the basis of estimate, we shall arrive at some such figure as 450,000,000. In order to satisfy any other points that might possibly be made, let us reduce this by as much as a third, and we shall still have 300,000,000, which figure we feel justified in advancing as the lowest possible estimate for the population of Africa; and yet most books tell us that there are only 140,000,000 people on the whole continent.

Darkwater may be regarded as the reply to such a position as that taken by Dr. Stoddard. If the white world conceives it to be its destiny to exploit the darker races of mankind, then it simply remains for the darker races to gird their loins for the contest. "What of the darker world that watches? Most men belong to this world. With Negro and Negroid, East Indian, Chinese, and Japanese they form two-thirds of the population of the world. A belief in humanity is a belief in colored men. If the uplift of mankind must be done by men, then the destinies of this world will rest ultimately in the hands of darker nations. What, then, is this dark world thinking? It is thinking that as wild and awful as this shameful war was, it is nothing to compare with that fight for freedom which black and brown and yellow men must and will make unless their oppression and humiliation and insult at the hands of the White World cease. The Dark World is going to submit to its present treatment just as long as it must and not one moment longer."

Both of these books are strong, and both are materialistic; and materialism, it must be granted, is a very important factor in the world just now. Somewhat different in outlook, however, is the book that labors under an economic subject, *Empire and Commerce in Africa.* In general the inquiry is concerned with the question, What do we desire to attain, particularly economically, in Africa, and how far is it attainable through policy? The discussion is mainly confined to the three powers: England, France, and Germany; and special merit attaches to the chapter on Abyssinia, probably the best brief account of this country ever written. Mr. Woolf announces such fundamental principles as that the land in Africa should be reserved for the natives; that there should be systematic education of the natives with a view to training them to take part in, and eventually control, the government of the country; that there should be a gradual expatriation of all Europeans and their capitalistic enterprises; that all revenue raised in Africa should be applied to the development of the country and the education and health of the inhabitants; that alcohol should be absolutely prohibited; and that Africa should be completely neutralized, that is, in no case should any military operations between European states be allowed. The difficulties of the enforcement of such a program are of course apparent to the author; but with other such volumes as this to guide and mold opinion, the time may indeed come at no distant date when Africa will cease to exist solely for exploitation and no longer be the rebuke of Christendom.

These four books then express fairly well the different opinions and hopes with which Africa and the world problem that the continent raises have recently been regarded. It remains simply to mention a conception that after the close of the war found many adherents in the United States and elsewhere, and whose operation was on a scale that forced recognition. This was the idea of the Provisional Republic of Africa, the Universal Negro Improvement Association and African Communities League of the World, the Black Star Line of steamships, and the Negro Factories Corporation, all of which activities were centered in New York, had as their organ the *Negro World,* and as their president and leading spirit Marcus Garvey, who was originally from Jamaica. The central thought that appealed to great crowds of people and won their support was that of freedom for the race in every sense of the word. Such freedom, it was declared, transcended the mere demand for the enforcement of certain political and social rights and could finally be realized only under a vast super-government guiding the destinies of the race in Africa, the United States, the West Indies, and everywhere else in the world. This was to control its people "just as the Pope and the Catholic Church control its millions in every land." The related ideas and activities were sometimes termed grandiose and they awakened much opposition on the part of the old leaders, the clergy, while conservative business stood aloof. At the same time the conception is one that deserves to be considered on its merits.

It is quite possible that if promoted on a scale vast enough such a Negro super-government as that proposed could be realized. It is true that England and France seem to-day to have a firm grip on the continent of Africa, but the experience of Germany has shown that even the mailèd fist may lose its strength overnight. With England beset with problems in Ireland and the West Indies, in India and Egypt, it is easy for the millions in equatorial Africa to be made to know that even this great power is not invincible and in time might rest with Nineveh and Tyre. There are things in Africa that will forever baffle all Europeans, and no foreign governor will ever know all that is at the back of the black man's mind. Even now, without the aid of modern science, information travels in a few hours throughout the length and breadth of the continent; and those that slept are beginning to be awake and restless. Let this restlessness increase, let intelligence also increase, let the natives be aided by their fever, and all the armies of Europe could be lost in Africa and this ancient mother still rise bloody but unbowed. The realization of the vision, however, would call for capital on a scale as vast as that of a modern war or an international industrial enterprise. At the very outset it would engage England in nothing less than a death-grapple, especially as regards the shipping on the West Coast. If ships can not go from Liverpool to Seccondee and Lagos, then England herself is doomed. The possible contest appalls the imagination. At the same time the exploiting that now goes on in the world can not go on forever.

CHAPTER XVII

It is probably clear from our study in the preceding pages that the history of the Negro people in the United States falls into well defined periods or epochs. First of all there was the colonial era, extending from the time of the first coming of Negroes to the English colonies to that of the Revolutionary War. This divides into two parts, with a line coming at the year 1705. Before this date the exact status of the Negro was more or less undefined; the system of servitude was only gradually passing into the sterner one of slavery; and especially in the middle colonies there was considerable intermixture of the races. By the year 1705, however, it had become generally established that the Negro was to be regarded not as a person but as a thing; and the next seventy years were a time of increasing numbers, but of no racial coherence or spiritual outlook, only a spasmodic insurrection here and there indicating the yearning for a better day. With the Revolution there came a change, and the second period extends from this war to the Civil War. This also divides into two parts, with a line at the year 1830. In the years immediately succeeding the Revolution there was put forth the first effective effort toward racial organization, this being represented by the work of such men as Richard Allen and Prince Hall; but, in spite of a new racial consciousness, the great mass of the Negro people remained in much the same situation as before, the increase in numbers incident to the invention of the cotton-gin only intensifying the ultimate problem. About the year 1830, however, the very hatred and ignominy that began to be visited upon the Negro indicated that at least he was no longer a thing but a person. Lynching began to grow apace, burlesque on the stage tended to depreciate and humiliate the race, and the South became definitely united in its defense of the system of slavery. On the other hand, the Abolitionists challenged the attitude that was becoming popular; the Negroes themselves began to be prosperous and to hold conventions; and Nat Turner's insurrection thrust baldly before the American people the great moral and economic problem with which they had to deal. With such divergent opinions, in spite of feeble attempts at compromise, there could be no peace until the issue of slavery at least was definitely settled. The third great period extends from the Civil War to the opening of the Great War in Europe. Like the others it also falls into two parts, the division coming at the year 1895. The thirty years from 1865 to 1895 may be regarded as an era in which the race, now emancipated, was mainly under the guidance of political ideals. Several men went to Congress and popular education began to be emphasized; but the difficulties of Reconstruction and the outrages of the KuKlux Klan were succeeded by an enveloping system of peonage, and by 1890-1895 the pendulum had swung fully backward and in the South disfranchisement had been arrived at as the concrete solution of the political phase of the problem. The twenty years from 1895 to 1915 formed a period of unrest and violence, but also of solid economic and social progress, the dominant influence being the work of Booker T. Washington. With the world war the Negro people came face to face with new and vast problems of economic adjustment and passed into an entirely different period of their racial history in America.

This is not all, however. The race is not to be regarded simply as existent unto itself. The most casual glance at any such account as we have given emphasizes the importance of the Negro in the general history of the United States. Other races have come, sometimes with great gifts or in great numbers, but it is upon this one that the country's history has turned as on a pivot. It is true that it has been despised and rejected, but more and more it seems destined to give new proof that the stone which the builders refused is become the head stone of the corner. In the colonial era it was the economic advantage of slavery over servitude that caused it to displace this institution as a system of labor. In the preliminary draft of the Declaration of Independence a noteworthy passage arraigned the king of England for his insistence upon the slave-trade, but this was later suppressed for reasons of policy. The war itself revealed clearly the fallacy of the position of the patriots, who fought for their rights as Englishmen but not for the fundamental rights of man; and their attitude received formal expression in the compromises that entered into the Constitution. The expansion of the Southwest depended on the labor of the Negro, whose history became inextricably bound up with that of the cotton-gin; and the question or the excuse of fugitives was the real key to the Seminole Wars. The long struggle culminating in the Civil War was simply to settle the status of the Negro in the Republic; and the legislation after the war determined for a generation the history not only of the South but very largely of the nation as well. The later disfranchising acts have had overwhelming importance, the unfair system of national representation controlling the election of 1916 and thus the attitude of America in the world war.

This is an astonishing phenomenon—this vast influence of a people oppressed, proscribed, and scorned. The Negro is so dominant in American history not only because he tests the real meaning of democracy, not only because he challenges the conscience of the nation, but also because he calls in question one's final attitude toward human nature itself. As we have seen, it is not necessarily the worker, not even the criminal, who makes the ultimate problem, but the simple Negro of whatever quality. If this man did not have to work at all, and if his race did not include a single criminal, in American opinion he would still raise a question. It is accordingly from the social standpoint that we must finally consider the problem. Before we can do this we need to study the race as an actual living factor in American life; and even before we do that it might be in order to observe the general importance of the Negro to-day in any discussion of the racial problems of the world.

i. *World Aspect*

Any consideration of the Negro Problem in its world aspect at the present time must necessarily be very largely concerned with Africa as the center of the Negro population. This in turn directs attention to the great colonizing powers of Europe, and especially to Great Britain as the chief of these; and the questions that result are of far-reaching importance for the whole fabric of modern civilization. No one can gainsay the tremendous contribution that England has made to the world; every one must respect a nation that produced Wycliffe and Shakespeare and Darwin, and that, standing for democratic principles, has so often stayed the tide of absolutism and anarchy; and it is not without desert that for three hundred years this country has held the moral leadership of mankind. It may now not unreasonably be asked, however, if it has not lost some of its old ideals, and if further insistence upon some of its policies would not constitute a menace to all that the heart of humanity holds dear.

As a preliminary to our discussion let us remark two men by way of contrast. A little more than seventy years ago a great traveler set out upon the first of three long journeys through central and southern Africa. He was a renowned explorer, and yet to him "the end of the geographical feat was only the beginning of the enterprise." Said Henry Drummond of him: "Wherever David Livingstone's footsteps are crossed in Africa the fragrance of his memory seems to remain." On one occasion a hunter was impaled on the horn of a rhinoceros, and a messenger ran eight miles for the physician. Although he himself had been wounded for life by a lion and his friends said that he should not ride at night through a wood infested with beasts, Livingstone insisted on his Christian duty to go, only to find that the man had died and to be obliged to retrace his footsteps. Again and again his party would have been destroyed if it had not been for his own unbounded tact and courage, and after his death at Chitambo's village Susi and Chuma journeyed for nine months and over eight hundred miles to take his body to the coast.

"We work for a glorious future," said he, "which we are not destined to see—the golden age which has not been, but will yet be. We are only morning-stars shining in the dark, but the glorious morn will break, the good time coming yet. For this time we work; may God accept our imperfect service."

About the time that Livingstone was passing off the scene another strong man, one of England's "empire builders," began his famous career. Going first to South Africa as a young man in quest of health, Cecil Rhodes soon made a huge fortune out of Kimberley diamonds and Transvaal gold, and by 1890 had become the Prime Minister of Cape Colony. In the pursuit of his aims he was absolutely unscrupulous. He refused to recognize any rights of the Portuguese in Matabeleland and Mashonaland; he drove hard bargains with the Germans and the French; he defied the Boers; and to him the native Africans were simply so many tools for the heaping up of gold. Nobody ever said of him that he left a "fragrant memory" behind him; but thousands of bruised bodies and broken hearts bore witness to his policy. According to the ideals of modern England, however, he was a great man. What the Negro in the last analysis wonders is: Who was right, Livingstone or Rhodes? And which is the world to choose, Christ or Mammon?

There are two fundamental assumptions upon which all so-called Western civilization is based—that of racial and that of religious superiority. Sight has been lost of the fact that there is really no such thing as a superior race, that only individuals are superior one to another, and a popular English poet has sung of "the white man's burden" and of "lesser breeds without the law." These two assumptions have accounted for all of the misunderstanding that has arisen between the West and the East, for China and Japan, India and Egypt can not see by what divine right men from the West suppose that they have the only correct ancestry or by what conceit they presume to have the only true faith. Let them but be accepted, however, let a nation be led by them as guiding-stars, and England becomes justified in forcing her system upon India, she finds it necessary to send missionaries to Japan, and the lion's paw pounces upon the very islands of the sea.

The whole world, however, is now rising as never before against any semblance of selfishness on the part of great powers, and it is more than ever clear that before there can be any genuine progress toward the brotherhood of man, or toward comity among nations, one man will have to give some consideration to the other man's point of view. One people will have to respect another people's tradition. The Russo-Japanese War gave men a new vision. The whole world gazed upon a new power in the East—one that could be dealt with only upon equal terms. Meanwhile there was unrest in India, and in Africa there were insurrections of increasing bitterness and fierceness. Africa especially had been misrepresented. The people were all said to be savages and cannibals, almost hopelessly degraded. The traders and the politicians knew better. They knew that there were tribes and tribes in Africa, that many of the chiefs were upright and wise and proud of their tradition, and that the land could not be seized any too quickly. Hence they made haste to get into the game.

It is increasingly evident also that the real leadership of the world is a matter not of race, not even of professed religion, but of principle. Within the last hundred years, as science has flourished and colonization grown, we have been led astray by materialism. The worship of the dollar has become a fetish, and the man or the nation that had the money felt that it was ordained of God to rule the universe. Germany was led astray by this belief, but it is England, not Germany, that has most thoroughly mastered the *Art of Colonization*. Crown colonies are to be operated in the interest of the owners. Jingoism is king. It matters not that the people in India and Africa, in Hayti and the Philippines, object to our benevolence; *we* know what is good for them and therefore they should be satisfied.

In Jamaica to-day the poorer people can not get employment; and yet, rather than accept the supply at hand, the powers of privilege import "coolie" labor, a still cheaper supply. In Sierra Leone, where certainly there has been time to see the working of the principle, native young men crowd about the wharves and seize any chance to earn a penny, simply because there is no work at hand to do—nothing that would genuinely nourish independence and self-respect.

It is not strange that the worship of industrialism, with its attendant competition, finally brought about the most disastrous war in history and such a breakdown of all principles of morality as made the whole world stand aghast. Womanhood was no longer sacred; old ideas of ethics vanished; Christ himself was crucified again—everything holy and lovely was given to the grasping demon of Wealth.

Suddenly men realized that England had lost the moral leadership of the world. Lured by the ideals of Rhodes, the country that gave to mankind *Magna Charta* seemed now bent only on its own aggrandizement and preservation. Germany's colonies were seized, and anything that threatened the permanence of the dominant system, especially unrest on the part of the native African, was throttled. Briton and Boer began to feel an identity of interest, and especially was it made known that American Negroes were not wanted.

Just what the situation is to-day may be illustrated by the simple matter of foreign missions, the policy of missionary organizations in both England and America being dictated by the political policy of the empire. The appointing of Negroes by the great American denominations for service in Africa has practically ceased, for American Negroes are not to be admitted to any portion of the continent except Liberia, which, after all, is a very small part of the whole. For the time being the little republic seems to receive countenance from the great powers as a sort of safety-valve through which the aspiration of the Negro people might spend itself; but it is evident that the present understanding is purely artificial and can not last. Even the Roman Empire declined, and Germany lost her hold in Africa overnight. Of course it may be contended that the British Empire to-day is not decadent but stronger than ever. At the same time there can be no doubt that Englishman and Boer alike regard these teeming millions of prolific black people always with concern and sometimes with dismay. Natives of the Congo still bear the marks of mutilation, and men in South Africa chafe under unjust land acts and constant indignities in their daily life.

Here rises the question for our own country. To the United States at last has come that moral leadership—that obligation to do the right thing—that opportunity to exhibit the highest honor in all affairs foreign or domestic—that is the ultimate test of greatness. Is America to view this great problem in Africa sympathetically and find some place for the groping for freedom of millions of human beings, or is she to be simply a pawn in the game of English colonization? Is she to abide by the principles that guided her in 1776, or simply seize her share of the booty? The Negro either at home or abroad is only one of many moral problems with which she has to deal. At the close of the war extravagance reigned, crime was rampant, and against any one of three or four races there was insidious propaganda. To add to the difficulties, the government was still so dominated by politics and officialdom that it was almost always impossible to get things done at the time they needed to be done. At the same time every patriot knows that America is truly the hope of the world. Into her civilization and her glory have entered not one but many races. All go forth against a common enemy; all should share the duties and the privileges of citizenship. In such a country the law can know no difference of race or class or creed, provided all are devoted to the general welfare. Such is the obligation resting upon the United States—such the challenge of social, economic, and moral questions such as never before faced the children of men. That she be worthy of her opportunity all would pray; to the fulfilment of her destiny all should help. The eyes of the world are upon her; the scepter of the ages is in her hand.

2. The Negro in American Life

If now we come to the Negro in the United States, it is hardly an exaggeration to say that no other race in the American body politic, not even the Anglo-Saxon, has been studied more critically than this one, and treatment has varied all the way from the celebration of virtues to the bitterest hostility and malignity. It is clearly fundamentally necessary to pay some attention to racial characteristics and gifts. In recent years there has been much discussion from the standpoint of biology, and special emphasis has been placed on the emotional temperament of the race. The Negro, however, submits that in the United States he has not been chiefly responsible for such miscegenation as has taken place; but he is not content to rest simply upon a *tu quoque*. He calls attention to the fact that whereas it has been charged that lynchings find their excuse in rape, it has been shown again and again that this crime is the excuse for only one-fourth or one-fifth of the cases of violence. If for the moment we suppose that there is no question about guilt in a fourth or a fifth of the cases, the overwhelming fraction that remains indicates that there are other factors of the highest importance that have to be considered in any ultimate adjustment of the situation. In every case accordingly the Negro asks only for a fair trial in court —not too hurried; and he knows that in many instances a calm study of the facts will reveal nothing more than fright or hysteria on the part of a woman or even other circumstances not more incriminating.

Unfortunately the whole question of the Negro has been beclouded by misrepresentation as has no other social question before the American people, and the race asks simply first of all that the tissue of depreciation raised by prejudice be done away with in order that it may be judged and estimated for its quality. America can make no charges against any element of her population while she denies the fundamental right of citizenship—the protection of the individual person. Too often mistakes are made, and no man is so humble or so low that he should be deprived of his life without due process of law. The Negro undoubtedly has faults. At the same time, in order that his gifts may receive just consideration, the tradition of burlesque must for the time being be forgotten. All stories about razors, chickens, and watermelons must be relegated to the rear; and even the revered and beloved "black mammy" must receive an affectionate but a long farewell.

The fact is that the Negro has such a contagious brand of humor that many people never realize that this plays only on the surface. The real background of the race is one of tragedy.

It is not in current jest but in the wail of the old melodies that the soul of this people is found. There is something elemental about the heart of the race, something that finds its origin in the forest and in the falling of the stars. There is something grim about it too, something that speaks of the lash, of the child torn from its mother's bosom, of the dead body swinging at night by the roadside. The race has suffered, and in its suffering lies its destiny and its contribution to America; and hereby hangs a tale.

If we study the real quality of the Negro we shall find that two things are observable. One is that any distinction so far won by a member of the race in America has been almost always in some one of the arts; and the other is that any influence so far exerted by the Negro on American civilization has been primarily in the field of æsthetics. The reason is not far to seek, and is to be found in the artistic striving even ot untutored Negroes. The instinct for beauty insists upon an outlet, and if one can find no better picture he will paste a circus poster or a flaring advertisement on the wall. Very few homes have not at least a geranium on the windowsill or a rosebush in the garden. If we look at the matter conversely we shall find that those things which are most picturesque make to the Negro the readiest appeal. Red is his favorite color simply because it is the most pronounced of all colors. The principle holds in the sphere of religion. In some of our communities Negroes are known to "get happy" in church. It is, however, seldom a sermon on the rule of faith or the plan of salvation that awakens such ecstasy, but rather a vivid portrayal of the beauties of heaven, with the walls of jasper, the feast of milk and honey, and the angels with palms in their hands. The appeal is primarily sensuous, and it is hardly too much to say that the Negro is thrilled not so much by the moral as by the artistic and pictorial elements in religion. Every member of the race is an incipient poet, and all are enthralled by music and oratory.

Illustrations are abundant. We might refer to the oratory of Douglass, to the poetry of Dunbar, to the picturesque style of DuBois, to the mysticism of the paintings of Tanner, to the tragic sculpture of Meta Warrick Fuller, and to a long line of singers and musicians. Even Booker Washington, most practical of Americans, proves the point, the distinguishing qualities of his speeches being anecdote and vivid illustration. It is best, however, to consider members of the race who were entirely untaught in the schools. On one occasion Harriet Tubman, famous for her work in the Underground Railroad, was addressing an audience and describing a great battle in the Civil War. "And then," said she, "we saw the lightning, and that was the guns; and then we heard the thunder, and that was the big guns; and then we heard the rain falling, and that was drops of blood falling; and when we came to git in the craps, it was dead men that we reaped." Two decades after the war John Jasper, of Richmond, Virginia, astonished the most intelligent hearers by the power of his imagery. He preached not only that the "sun do move," but also of "dry bones in the valley," the glories of the New Jerusalem, and on many similar subjects that have been used by other preachers, sometimes with hardly less effect, throughout the South. In his own way Jasper was an artist. He was eminently imaginative; and it is with this imaginative—this artistic—quality that America has yet to reckon.

The importance of the influence has begun to be recognized, and on the principle that to him that hath shall be given, in increasing measure the Negro is being blamed for the ills of American life, a ready excuse being found in the perversion and debasement of Negro music. We have seen discussions whose reasoning, condensed, was somewhat as follows: The Negro element is daily becoming more potent in American society; American society is daily becoming more immoral; therefore at the door of the Negro may be laid the increase in divorce and all the other evils of society. The most serious charge brought against the Negro intellectually is that he has not yet developed the great creative or organizing mind that points the way of civilization. He most certainly has not, and in this he is not very unlike all the other people in America. The whole country is still in only the earlier years of its striving. While the United States has made great advance in applied science, she has as yet produced no Shakespeare or Beethoven. If America has not yet reached her height after three hundred years of striving, she ought not to be impatient with the Negro after only sixty years of opportunity. But all signs go to prove the assumption of limited intellectual ability fundamentally false. Already some of the younger men of the race have given the highest possible promise.

If all of this, however, is granted, and if the Negro's exemplification of the principle of self-help is also recognized, the question still remains: Just what is the race worth as a constructive factor in American civilization? Is it finally to be an agency for the upbuilding of the nation, or simply one of the forces that retard? What is its real promise in American life?

In reply to this it might be worth while to consider first of all the country's industrial life. The South, and very largely the whole country, depends upon Negro men and women as the stable labor supply in such occupations as farming, sawmilling, mining, cooking, and washing. All of this is hard work, and necessary work. In 1910, of 3,178,554 Negro men at work, 981,922 were listed as farm laborers and 798,509 as farmers. That is to say, 56 per cent of the whole number were engaged in raising farm products either on their own account or by way of assisting somebody else, and the great staples of course were the cotton and corn of the Southern states. If along with the farmers we take those engaged in the occupations employing the next greatest numbers of men —those of the building and hand trades, saw and planing mills, as well as those of railway firemen and porters, draymen, teamsters, and coal mine operatives—we shall find a total of 71.2 per cent engaged in such work as represents the very foundation of American industry. Of the women at work, 1,047,146, or 52 per cent, were either farm laborers or farmers, and 28 per cent more were either cooks or washerwomen. In other words, a total of exactly 80 per cent were engaged in some of the hardest and at the same time some of the most vital labor in our home and industrial life. The new emphasis on the Negro as an industrial factor in the course of the recent war is well known. When immigration ceased, upon his shoulders very largely fell the task of keeping the country and the army alive. Since the war closed he has been on the defensive in the North; but a country that wishes to consider all of the factors that enter into its gravest social problem could never forget his valiant service in 1918. Let any one ask, moreover, even the most prejudiced observer, if he would like to see every Negro in the country out of it, and he will then decide whether economically the Negro is a liability or an asset.

Again, consider the Negro soldier. In all our history there are no pages more heroic, more pathetic, than those detailing the exploits of black men. We remember the Negro, three thousand strong, fighting for the liberties of America when his own race was still held in bondage. We remember the deeds at Port Hudson, Fort Pillow, and Fort Wagner. We remember Santiago and San Juan Hill, not only how Negro men went gallantly to the charge, but how a black regiment faced pestilence that the ranks of their white comrades might not be decimated. And then Carrizal. Once more, at an unexpected moment, the heart of the nation was thrilled by the troopers of the Tenth Cavalry. Once more, despite Brownsville, the tradition of Fort Wagner was preserved and passed on. And then came the greatest of all wars. Again was the Negro summoned to the colors—summoned out of all proportion to his numbers. Others might desert, but not he; others might be spies or strikers, but not he—not he in the time of peril. In peace or war, in victory or danger, he has always been loyal to the Stars and Stripes.

Not only, however, does the Negro give promise by reason of his economic worth; not only does he deserve the fullest rights of citizenship on the basis of his work as a soldier; he brings nothing less than a great spiritual contribution to civilization in America. His is a race of enthusiasm, imagination, and spiritual fervor; and after all the doubt and fear through which it has passed there still rests with it an abiding faith in God. Around us everywhere are commercialism, politics, graft —sordidness, selfishness, cynicism. We need hope and love, a new birth of idealism, a new faith in the unseen. Already the work of some members of the race has pointed the way to great things in the realm of conscious art; but above even art soars the great world of the spirit. This it is that America most sadly needs; this it is that her most fiercely persecuted children bring to her.

Obviously now if the Negro, if any race, is to make to America the contribution of which it is capable, it must be free; and this raises the whole question of relation to the rest of the body politic. One of the interesting phenomena of society in America is that the more foreign elements enter into the "melting pot" and advance in culture, the more do they cling to their racial identity. Incorporation into American life, instead of making the Greek or the Pole or the Irishman forget his native country, makes him all the more jealous of its traditions. The more a center of any one of these nationalities develops, the more wealthy and cultured its members become, the more do we find them proud of the source from which they sprang. The Irishman is now so much an American that he controls whole wards in our large cities, and sometimes the cities themselves. All the same he clings more tenaciously than ever to the celebration of March 17. When an isolated Greek came years ago, poor and friendless, nobody thought very much about him, and he effaced himself as much as possible, taking advantage, however, of any opportunity that offered for self-improvement or economic advance. When thousands came and the newcomers could take inspiration from those of their brothers who had preceded them and achieved success, nationality asserted itself. Larger groups now talked about Venizelos and a greater Greece; their chests expanded at the thought of Marathon and Plato; and companies paraded amid applause as they went to fight in the Balkans. In every case, with increasing intelligence and wealth, race pride asserted itself. At the same time no one would think of denying to the Greek or the Irishman or the Italian his full rights as an American citizen.

It is a paradox indeed, this thing of a race's holding its identity at the same time that it is supposed to lose this in the larger civilization. Apply the principle to the Negro. Very soon after the Civil War, when conditions were chaotic and ignorance was rampant, the ideals constantly held before the race were those of white people. Some leaders indeed measured success primarily by the extent to which they became merged in the white man's life. At the time this was very natural. A struggling people wished to show that it could be judged by the standards of the highest civilization within sight, and it did so. To-day the tide has changed. The race now numbers a few millionaires. In almost every city there are beautiful homes owned by Negroes. Some men have reached high attainment in scholarship, and the promise grows greater and greater in art and science. Accordingly the Negro now loves his own, cherishes his own, teaches his boys about black heroes, and honors and glorifies his own black women. Schools and churches and all sorts of coöperative enterprises testify to the new racial self-respect, while a genuine Negro drama has begun to flourish. A whole people has been reborn; a whole race has found its soul.

3. *Face to Face*

Even when all that has been said is granted, it is still sometimes maintained that the Negro is the one race that can not and will not be permitted to enter into the full promise of American life. Other elements, it is said, even if difficult to assimilate, may gradually be brought into the body politic, but the Negro is the one element that may be tolerated but not assimilated, utilized but not welcomed to the fullness of the country's glory.

However, the Negro has no reason to be discouraged. If one will but remember that after all slavery was but an incident and recall the status of the Negro even in the free states ten years before the Civil War, he will be able to see a steady line of progress forward. After the great moral and economic awakening that gave the race its freedom, the pendulum swung backward, and finally it reached its farthest point of proscription, of lawlessness, and inhumanity. No obscuring of the vision for the time being should blind us to the reading of the great movement of history.

To-day in the whole question of the Negro problem there are some matters of pressing and general importance. One that is constantly thrust forward is that of the Negro criminal.

On this the answer is clear. If a man—Negro or otherwise—
is a criminal, he is an enemy of society, and society demands
that he be placed where he will do the least harm. If execution is necessary, this should take place in private; and in
no case should the criminal be so handled as to corrupt the
morals or arouse the morbid sensibilities of the populace. At
the same time simple patriotism would demand that by uplift-
ing home surroundings, good schools, and wholesome recreation everything possible be done for Negro children as for
other children of the Republic, so that just as few of them
as possible may graduate into the criminal class.

Another matter, closely akin to this, is that of the astonishing lust for torture that more and more is actuating the American people. When in 1835 McIntosh was burned in St. Louis
for the murder of an officer, the American people stood aghast,
and Abraham Lincoln, just coming into local prominence,
spoke as if the very foundations of the young republic had
been shaken. After the Civil War, however, horrible lynchings became frequent; and within the last decade we have
seen a Negro boy stabbed in numberless places while on his
way to the stake, we have seen the eyes of a Negro man
burned out with hot irons and pieces of his flesh cut off, and
a Negro woman—whose only offense was a word of protest
against the lynching of her husband—while in the state of
advanced pregnancy hanged head downwards, her clothing
burned from her body, and herself so disemboweled that her
unborn babe fell to the ground. We submit that any citizens
who commit such deeds as these are deserving of the most
serious concern of their country; and when they bring their
little children to behold their acts—when baby fingers handle
mutilated flesh and baby eyes behold such pictures as we have
suggested—a crime has been committed against the very name
of childhood. Most frequently it will be found that the men
who do these things have had only the most meager educational advantages, and that generally—but not always—they
live in remote communities, away from centers of enlighten-
ment, so that their whole course of life is such as to cultivate
provincialism. With not the slightest touch of irony whatever we suggest that these men need a crusade of education

in books and in the fundamental obligations of citizenship. At present their ignorance, their prejudice, and their lack of moral sense constitute a national menace.

It is full time to pause. We have already gone too far. The Negro problem is only an index to the ills of society in America. In our haste to get rich or to meet new conditions we are in danger of losing all of our old standards of conduct, of training, and of morality. Our courts need to summon a new respect for themselves. The average citizen knows only this about them, that he wants to keep away from them. So far we have not been assured of justice. The poor man has not stood an equal chance with the rich, nor the black with the white. Money has been freely used, even for the changing of laws if need be; and the sentencing of a man of means generally means only that he will have a new trial. The murders in any American city average each year fifteen or twenty times as many as in an English or French city of the same size. Our churches need a new baptism; they have lost the faith. The same principle applies in our home-life, in education, in literature. The family altar is almost extinct; learning is more easy than sound; and in literature as in other forms of art any passing fad is able to gain followers and pose as worthy achievement. All along the line we need more uprightness— more strength. Even when a man has committed a crime, he must receive justice in court. Within recent years we have heard too much about "speedy trials," which are often nothing more than legalized lynchings. If it has been decreed that a man is to wait for a trial one week or one year, the mob has nothing to do with the matter, and, if need be, all the soldiery of the United States must be called forth to prevent the storming of a jail. Fortunately the last few years have shown us several sheriffs who had this conception of their duty.

In the last analysis this may mean that more responsibility and more force will have to be lodged in the Federal Government. Within recent years the dignity of the United States has been seriously impaired. The time seems now to have come when the Government must make a new assertion of its integrity and its authority. No power in the country can be stronger than that of the United States of America.

For the time being, then, this is what we need—a stern adherence to law. If men will not be good, they must at least be made to behave. No one will pretend, however, that an adjustment on such a basis is finally satisfactory. Above the law of the state—above all law of man—is the law of God. It was given at Sinai thousands of years ago. It received new meaning at Calvary. To it we must all yet come. The way may be hard, and in the strife of the present the time may seem far distant; but some day the Messiah will reign and man to man the world over shall brothers be "for a' that."

SELECT BIBLIOGRAPHY

Unless an adequate volume is to be devoted to the work, any bibliography of the history of the Negro Problem in the United States must be selective. No comprehensive work is in existence. Importance attaches to *Select List of References on the Negro Question,* compiled under the direction of A. P. C. Griffin, Library of Congress, Washington, 1903; *A Select Bibliography of the Negro American,* edited by W. E. B. DuBois, Atlanta, 1905, and *The Negro Problem: a Bibliography,* edited by Vera Sieg, Free Library Commission, Madison, Wis., 1908; but all such lists have to be supplemented for more recent years. Compilations on the Abolition Movement, the early education of the Negro, and the literary and artistic production of the race are to be found respectively in Hart's *Slavery and Abolition,* Woodson's *The Education of the Negro prior to 1861,* and Brawley's *The Negro in Literature and Art,* and the *Journal of Negro History* is constantly suggestive of good material.

The bibliography that follows is confined to the main question. First of all are given general references, and then follows a list of individual authors and books. Finally, there are special lists on topics on which the study in the present work is most intensive. In a few instances books that are superficial in method or prejudiced in tone have been mentioned as it has seemed necessary to try to consider all shades of opinion even if the expression was not always adequate. On the other hand, not every source mentioned in the footnotes is included, for sometimes these references are merely incidental; and especially does this apply in the case of lectures or magazine articles, some of which were later included in books. Nor is there any reference to works of fiction. These are frequently important, and books of unusual interest are sometimes considered in the body of the work; but in such a study as the present imaginative literature can be hardly more than a secondary and a debatable source of information.

I. General References

(Mainly in Collections, Sets, or Series)

Statutes at Large, being a Collection of all the Laws of Virginia from the first session of the Legislature, in the year 1619, by William Waller Hening. Richmond, 1819-20.

Laws of the State of North Carolina, compiled by Henry Potter, J. L. Taylor, and Bart. Yancey. Raleigh, 1821.

The Statutes at Large of South Carolina, edited by Thomas Cooper. Columbia, 1837.

The Pro-Slavery Argument (as maintained by the most distinguished writers of the Southern states). Charleston, 1852.

Files of such publications as Niles's *Weekly Register,* the *Genius of Universal Emancipation,* the *Liberator,* and DeBow's *Commercial Review,* in the period before the Civil War; and of the *Crisis,* the *Journal of Negro History,* the *Negro Year-Book,* the *Virginia Magazine of History,* the *Review of Reviews,* the *Literary Digest,* the *Independent,* the *Outlook,* as well as representative newspapers North and South and weekly Negro newspapers in later years.

Johns Hopkins University Studies in Historical and Political Science (some numbers important for the present work noted below).

Studies in History, Economics, and Public Law edited by the Faculty of Political Science of Columbia University (some numbers important for the present work noted below).

Atlanta University Studies of Negro Problems (for unusually important numbers note DuBois, editor, below, also Bigham).

Occasional Papers of the American Negro Academy (especially note Cromwell in special list No. 1 below and Grimké in No. 3).

Census Reports of the United States; also Publications of the Bureau of Education.

Annual Reports of the General Education Board, the John F. Slater Fund, the Jeanes Fund; reports and pamphlets issued by American Missionary Association, American Baptist Home Mission Society, Freedmen's Aid Society, etc.; catalogues of representative educational institutions; and a volume "From Servitude to Service" (the Old South lectures on representative educational institutions for the Negro), Boston, 1905.

Pamphlets and reports of National Association for the Advancement of Colored People, the National Urban League, the Southern Sociological Congress, the University Commission on Southern Race Questions, Hampton Conference reports, 1897-1907, and Proceedings of the National Negro Business League, annual since 1900.

The American Nation: A History from Original Sources by Associated Scholars, edited by Albert Bushnell Hart. 27 vols. Harper

& Bros., New York, 1907. (Volumes important for the present work specially noted below.)

The Chronicles of America. A Series of Historical Narratives edited by Allen Johnson. 50 vols. Yale University Press, New Haven, 1918—. (Volumes important for the present work specially noted below.)

The South in the Building of the Nation. 12 vols. The Southern Publication Society. Richmond, Va., 1909.

Studies in Southern History and Politics. Columbia University Press, New York, 1914.

New International and Americana Encyclopedias (especially on such topics as Africa, the Negro, and Negro Education).

II. INDIVIDUAL WORKS

(Note pamphlets at end of list; also special lists under III below.)

Adams, Alice Dana: The Neglected Period of Anti-Slavery in America (1808-1831), Radcliffe College Monograph No. 14. Boston, 1908 (now handled by Harvard University Press).

Adams, Henry: History of the United States from 1801 to 1817. 9 vols. Charles Scribner's Sons, New York, 1889-90.

Alexander, William T.: History of the Colored Race in America. Palmetto Publishing Co., New Orleans, 1887.

Armistead, Wilson: A Tribute for the Negro, being a Vindication of the Moral, Intellectual, and Religious Capabilities of the Colored Portion of Mankind, with particular reference to the African race, illustrated by numerous biographical sketches, facts, anecdotes, etc., and many superior portraits and engravings. Manchester, 1848.

Baker, Ray Stannard: Following the Color Line. Doubleday, Page & Co., New York, 1908.

Ballagh, James Curtis: A History of Slavery in Virginia. Johns Hopkins Studies, extra volume 24. Baltimore, 1902.

White Servitude in the Colony of Virginia. Johns Hopkins Studies, Thirteenth Series, Nos. 6 and 7. Baltimore, 1895.

Bassett, John Spencer: Anti-Slavery Leaders of North Carolina. Sixth Series, No. 6. Baltimore, 1898.

Slavery and Servitude in the Colony of North Carolina. Johns Hopkins Studies, Fourteenth Series, Nos. 4 and 5. Baltimore, 1896.

Slavery in the State of North Carolina. Johns Hopkins Studies, XIV: 179; XVII: 323.

Bigham, John Alvin (editor): Select Discussions of Race Problems, No. 20, of Atlanta University Publications. Atlanta, 1916.

Birney, William: James G. Birney and His Times. D. Appleton & Co., New York, 1890.

Blake, W. O.: The History of Slavery and the Slave-Trade. Columbus, O., 1861.

Blyden, Edward W.: Christianity, Islam, and the Negro Race. London, 1887.

Bogart, Ernest Ludlow: The Economic History of the United States. Longmans, Green & Co., New York, 1918 edition.

Bourne, Edward Gaylord: Spain in America, 1450-1580. Vol. 3 of American Nation Series.

Brackett, Jeffrey Richardson: The Negro in Maryland: A Study of the Institution of Slavery. Johns Hopkins Studies, extra volume 6. Baltimore, 1889.

Bradford, Sarah H.: Harriet, the Moses of Her People. New York, 1886.

Brawley, Benjamin: A Short History of the American Negro. The Macmillan Co., New York, 1913, revised 1919.

History of Morehouse College. Atlanta, 1917.

The Negro in Literature and Art. Duffield & Co., New York, 1918.

Your Negro Neighbor (in Our National Problems series). The Macmillan Co., New York, 1918.

Africa and the War. Duffield & Co., New York, 1918.

Women of Achievement (written for the Fireside Schools under the auspices of the Woman's American Baptist Home Mission Society). Chicago and New York, 1919.

Brawley, Edward M.: The Negro Baptist Pulpit. American Baptist Publication Society, Philadelphia, 1890.

Bruce, Philip Alexander: Economic History of Virginia in the Seventeenth Century. 2 vols. The Macmillan Co., New York, 1896.

Cable, George Washington: The Negro Question. Charles Scribner's Sons, New York, 1890.

Calhoun, William Patrick: The Caucasian and the Negro in the United States. R. L. Bryan Co., Columbia, S. C., 1902.

Chamberlain, D. H.: Present Phases of Our So-Called Negro Problem (open letter to the Rt. Hon. James Bryce of England), reprinted from *News and Courier,* Charleston, of August 1, 1904.

Cheyney, Edward Potts: European Background of American History. Vol. I of American Nation Series.

Child, Lydia Maria: An Appeal in Favor of That Class of Americans Called Africans. Boston, 1833.

The Oasis (edited). Boston, 1834.

Clayton, V. V.: White and Black under the Old Régime. Milwaukee, 1899.

Clowes, W. Laird: Black America: A Study of the Ex-Slave and His Late Master. Cassell & Co., London, 1891.

Coffin, Joshua: An Account of Some of the Principal Slave Insurrections, and others, which have occurred, or been attempted, in the United States and elsewhere, during the last two centuries, with various remarks. American Anti-Slavery Society, New York, 1860.

Collins, Winfield H.: The Domestic Slave Trade of the Southern States. Broadway Publishing Co., New York, 1904.

Coman, Katherine: The Industrial History of the United States. The Macmillan Co., New York, 1918 edition.

The Negro as a Peasant Farmer. American Statistical Association Publications, 1904:39.

Commons, John R.: Races and Immigrants in America. The Macmillan Co., 1907.

Coolidge, Archibald Cary: The United States as a World Power. The Macmillan Co., New York, 1918.

Cooper, Anna Julia: A Voice from the South, by a black woman of the South. Xenia, O., 1892.

Corey, Charles H.: A History of the Richmond Theological Seminary. Richmond, 1895.

Cornish, Samuel E., and Wright, T. S.: The Colonization Scheme Considered in Its Rejection by the Colored People. Newark, 1840.

Cromwell, John W.: The Negro in American History. The American Negro Academy, Washington, 1914.

Culp, Daniel W. (editor): Twentieth Century Negro Literature. Nichols & Co., Toronto, 1902.

Cutler, James E.: Lynch Law, an Investigation into the History of Lynching in the United States. Longmans, Green & Co., New York, 1905.

Daniels, John: In Freedom's Birthplace: A Study of the Boston Negroes. Houghton Mifflin Co., Boston and New York, 1914.

Dewey, Davis Rich: National Problems, 1885-1897. Vol. 24 in American Nation Series.

Dill, Augustus Granville. See DuBois, editor Atlanta University Publications.

Dodd, William E.: The Cotton Kingdom. Vol. 27 of Chronicles of America.

Expansion and Conflict. Vol. 3 of Riverside History of the United States. Houghton Mifflin Co., Boston, 1915.

Dow, Lorenzo ("Cosmopolite, a Listener"): A Cry from the Wilderness! A Voice from the East, A Reply from the West—Trouble in the North, Exemplifying in the South. Intended as a timely and solemn warning to the People of the United States. Printed for the Purchaser and the Public. United States, 1830.

DuBois, W. E. Burghardt: Suppression of the African Slave-Trade. Longmans, Green & Co., New York, 1896 (now handled by Harvard University Press).

DuBois, W. E. Burghardt: The Philadelphia Negro. University of Pennsylvania, Philadelphia, 1899.

The Souls of Black Folk. A. C. McClurg & Co., Chicago, 1903.

The Negro in the South (Booker T. Washington, co-author). George W. Jacobs & Co., Philadelphia, 1907.

John Brown (in American Crisis Biographies). George W. Jacobs & Co., Philadelphia, 1909.

The Negro (in Home University Library Series). Henry Holt & Co., New York, 1915.

Darkwater: Voices from within the Veil. Harcourt, Brace & Co., New York, 1920.

(Editor Atlanta University Publications).

The Negro Church, No. 8.

The Health and Physique of the Negro American, No. 11.

Economic Co-operation among Negro Americans, No. 12.

The Negro American Family, No. 13.

Efforts for Social Betterment among Negro Americans, No. 14.

The College-Bred Negro American, No. 15. (A. G. Dill, co-editor.)

The Negro American Artisan, No. 17. (A. G. Dill, co-editor.)

Morals and Manners among Negro Americans, No. 18. (A. G. Dill, co-editor.)

Dunbar, Alice Ruth Moore: Masterpieces of Negro Eloquence. The Bookery Publishing Co., New York, 1914.

Dunbar, Paul Laurence: Complete Poems. Dodd, Mead & Co., New York, 1913.

Dunning, William Archibald: Reconstruction, Political and Economic. Vol. 22 of American Nation Series.

Earnest, Joseph B., Jr.: The Religious Development of the Negro in Virginia (Ph.D. thesis, Virginia). Charlottesville, 1914.

Eckenrode, Hamilton James: The Political History of Virginia during the Reconstruction. Johns Hopkins Studies. Twenty-second Series, Nos. 6, 7, and 8. Baltimore, 1904.

Ellis, George W.: Negro Culture in West Africa. The Neale Publishing Co., New York, 1914.

Ellwood, Charles A.: Sociology and Modern Social Problems. American Book Co., New York, 1910.

Elwang, William W.: The Negroes of Columbia, Mo. (A.M. thesis, Missouri), 1904.

Epstein, Abraham: The Negro Migrant in Pittsburgh (in publications of School of Economics of the University of Pittsburgh). 1918.

Evans, Maurice S.: Black and White in the Southern States: A Study of the Race Problem in the United States from a South African Point of View. Longmans, Green & Co., London, 1915.

Ferris, William Henry: The African Abroad. 2 vols. New Haven, 1913.

Fleming, Walter L.: Documentary History of Reconstruction. 2 vols. Arthur H. Clark Co., Cleveland, O., 1906.

The Sequel of Appomattox. Vol. 32 of Chronicles of America.

Fletcher, Frank H.: Negro Exodus. Report of agent appointed by the St. Louis Commission to visit Kansas for the purpose of obtaining information in regard to colored emigration. No imprint.

Furman, Richard: Exposition of the Views of the Baptists Relative to the Colored Population in the United States, in a communication to the Governor of South Carolina. Second edition, Charleston, 1833. (Letter bears original date December 24, 1822; Furman was president of State Baptist Convention.)

Garrison, Wendell Phillips, and Garrison, Francis Jackson: William Lloyd Garrison; Story of His Life Told by His Children. 4 vols. Houghton, Mifflin & Co., 1894.

Garrison, William Lloyd: Thoughts on African Colonization: or An Impartial Exhibition of the Doctrines, Principles, and Purposes of the American Colonization Society, together with the Resolutions, Addresses, and Remonstrances of the Free People of Color. Boston, 1832.

Gayarré, Charles E. A.: History of Louisiana. 4 vols. New Orleans, 1885 edition.

Grady, Henry W.: The New South and Other Addresses, with biography, etc., by Edna H. L. Turpin. Maynard, Merrill & Co., New York, 1904.

Graham, Stephen: The Soul of John Brown. The Macmillan Co., New York, 1920.

Hallowell, Richard P.: Why the Negro was Enfranchised—Negro Suffrage Justified. Boston, 1903. (Reprint of two letters in the *Boston Herald*, March 11 and 26, 1903.)

Hammond, Lily Hardy: In Black and White: An Interpretation of Southern Life. Fleming H. Revell Co., New York, 1914.

Harris, Norman Dwight: Intervention and Colonization in Africa. Houghton, Mifflin Co., Boston, 1914.

Hart, Albert Bushnell: National Ideals Historically Traced. Vol. 26 in American Nation Series.

Slavery and Abolition. Vol. 16 in American Nation Series.

The Southern South. D. Appleton & Co., New York, 1910.

Hartshorn, W. N., and Penniman, George W.: An Era of Progress and Promise, 1863-1910. The Priscilla Publishing Co., Boston, 1910.

Haworth, Paul Leland: America in Ferment. Bobbs-Merrill Co., Indianapolis, 1915.

Haynes, George E.: The Negro at Work in New York City. Vol. 49, No. 3, of Columbia Studies, 1912.

Helper, Hinton Rowan: The Impending Crisis of the South: How to Meet It. New York, 1857.

Hickok, Charles T.: The Negro in Ohio, 1802-1870. (Western Reserve thesis.) Cleveland, 1896.

Higginson, Thomas Wentworth: Army Life in a Black Regiment, Boston, 1870. (Latest edition, Houghton, Mifflin Co., 1900.)

Hoffman, Frederick L.: Race Traits and Tendencies of the American Negro. American Economics Association Publications, XI, Nos. 1-3, 1896.

Hodge, Frederick W. (editor): Spanish Explorers in the Southern United States, 1528-1543 (in Original Narratives of Early American History), esp. The Narrative of Alvar Nuñez Cabeça de Vaca. Charles Scribner's Sons, New York, 1907.

Holland, Edwin C.: A Refutation of the Calumnies circulated against the Southern and Western States, respecting the institution and existence of slavery among them; to which is added a minute and particular account of the actual condition and state of their Negro Population, together with Historical Notices of all the Insurrections that have taken place since the settlement of the country. By a South Carolinian. Charleston, 1822.

Horsemanden, Daniel (Judge): A Journal of the Proceedings in the Detection of the Conspiracy Formed by Some White People, in conjunction with Negro and Other Slaves, for Burning the City of New York in America, and Murdering the Inhabitants. New York, 1744.

Hosmer, James K.: The History of the Louisiana Purchase. D. Appleton & Co., New York, 1902.

Hurd, John C.: The Law of Freedom and Bondage. 2 vols. Boston, 1858-1862.

Jay, William: Inquiry into the Character and Tendency of the American Colonization and Anti-Slavery Societies. New York, 1835.

Jefferson, Thomas: Writings, issued under the auspices of the Thomas Jefferson Memorial Association. 20 vols. Washington, 1903.

Jervey, Theodore D.: Robert Y. Hayne and His Times. The Macmillan Co., New York, 1909.

Johnson, Allen: Union and Democracy. Vol. 2 of Riverside History of the United States. Houghton, Mifflin Co., Boston, 1915.

Johnson, James W.: Autobiography of an Ex-Colored Man (published anonymously). Sherman, French & Co., Boston, 1912.

Fifty Years and Other Poems. The Cornhill Co., Boston, 1917.

Hayti. Four articles reprinted from the *Nation*, New York, 1920.

Johnston, Sir Harry Hamilton: The Negro in the New World. The Macmillan Co., New York, 1910.

Kelsey, Carl: The Negro Farmer (Ph.D. thesis, Pennsylvania). Jennings & Pye, Chicago, 1903.

Kemble, Frances A.: Journal of Residence on a Georgia Plantation, 1838-1839. Harper & Bros., 1863.

Kerlin, Robert T. (editor): The Voice of the Negro, 1919. E. P. Dutton & Co., New York, 1920.

Kimball, John C.: Connecticut's Canterbury Tale; Its Heroine Prudence Crandall, and Its Moral for To-Day. Hartford, Conn. (1886).

Krehbiel, Henry E.: Afro-American Folk-Songs. G. Schirmer, New York and London, 1914.

Lauber, Almon Wheeler: Indian Slavery in Colonial Times within the Present Limits of the United States. Vol. 54, No. 3, of Columbia University Studies, 1913.

Livermore, George: An Historical Research Respecting the Opinions of the Founders of the Republic on Negroes as Slaves, as Citizens, and as Soldiers. Boston, 1863.

Locke, Mary Stoughton: Anti-Slavery in America from the Introduction of African Slaves to the Prohibition of the Slave-Trade, 1619-1808. Radcliffe College Monograph No. 11. Boston, 1901 (now handled by Harvard University Press).

Lonn, Ella: Reconstruction in Louisiana. G. P. Putnam's Sons, New York, 1919.

Lugard, Lady (Flora L. Shaw): A Tropical Dependency. James Nisbet & Co., Ltd., London, 1906.

Lynch, John R.: The Facts of Reconstruction: The Neale Publishing Co., New York, 1913.

McConnell, John Preston: Negroes and Their Treatment in Virginia from 1865 to 1867 (Ph.D. thesis, Virginia, 1905). Printed by B. D. Smith & Bros., Pulaski, Va., 1910.

MacCorkle, William A.: Some Southern Questions. G. P. Putnam's Sons, New York, 1908.

McCormac, E. I.: White Servitude in Maryland. Johns Hopkins Studies, XXII, 119.

McDougall, Marion Gleason: Fugitive Slaves, 1619-1865. Fay House (Radcliffe College) Monograph, No. 3. Boston, 1891 (now handled by Harvard University Press).

McLaughlin, Andrew Cunningham: The Confederation and the Constitution, 1783-1789. Vol. 10 in American Nation Series.

McMaster, John Bach: A History of the People of the United States, from the Revolution to the Civil War. 8 vols. D. Appleton & Co., New York, 1883-1913.

Macy, Jesse: The Anti-Slavery Crusade. Vol. 28 in Chronicles of America.

Marsh, J. B. T.: The Story of the Jubilee Singers, with their songs. Boston, 1880.

Miller, Kelly: Race Adjustment. The Neale Publishing Co., New York and Washington, 1908.

Out of the House of Bondage. The Neale Publishing Co., New York, 1914.

Appeal to Conscience (in Our National Problems Series). The Macmillan Co., New York, 1913.

Moore, G. H.: Historical Notes on the Employment of Negroes in the American Army of the Revolution. New York, 1862.

Morgan, Thomas J.: Reminiscences of Service with Colored Troops in the Army of the Cumberland, 1863-65. Providence, 1885.

Moton, Robert Russa: Finding a Way Out: An Autobiography. Doubleday, Page & Co., Garden City, N. Y., 1920.

Murphy, Edgar Gardner: The Basis of Ascendency. Longmans, Green & Co., London, 1909.

Murray, Freeman H. M.: Emancipation and the Freed in American Sculpture. Published by the author, 1733 Seventh St., N.W., Washington, 1916.

Odum, Howard W.: Social and Mental Traits of the Negro. Columbia University Studies, Vol. 37, No. 3. New York, 1910.

Olmsted, Frederick Law: The Cotton Kingdom. 2 vols. New York, 1861.

A Journey in the Seaboard Slave States. New York, 1856.

Page, Thomas Nelson: The Old South. Charles Scribner's Sons, New York, 1892.

The Negro: the Southerner's Problem. Charles Scribner's Sons, New York, 1904.

Palmer, B. M. (with W. T. Leacock): The Rights of the South Defended in the Pulpits. Mobile, 1860.

Penniman, George W. See Hartshorn, W. N.

Phillips, Ulrich B.: American Negro Slavery. D. Appleton & Co., New York, 1918.

Plantation and Frontier. Vols. I and II of Documentary History of American Industrial Society. Arthur H. Clark Co., Cleveland, 1910.

Pike, G. D.: The Jubilee Singers and Their Campaign for $20,000. Boston, 1873.

Pike, J. S.: The Prostrate State: South Carolina under Negro Government. New York, 1874.

Pipkin, James Jefferson: The Negro in Revelation, in History, and in Citizenship. N. D. Thompson Publishing Co., St. Louis, 1902.

Platt, O. H.: Negro Governors. Papers of the New Haven Colony Historical Society, Vol. 6. New Haven, 1900.

Reese, David M.: A Brief Review of the First Annual Report of the American Anti-Slavery Society. New York, 1834.

Rhodes, James Ford: History of the United States from the Compromise of 1850 (1850-1877 and 1877-1896). 8 vols. The Macmillan Co., New York, 1893-1919.

Roman, Charles Victor: American Civilization and the Negro. F. A. Davis Co., Philadelphia, 1916.

Russell, John H.: The Free Negro in Virginia, 1619-1865. Johns Hopkins Studies, Series XXXI, No. 3. Baltimore, 1913.

Sandburg, Carl: The Chicago Race Riots, July, 1919. Harcourt, Brace & Howe, New York, 1919.

Schurz, Carl: Speeches, Correspondence,' and Political Papers, selected and edited by Frederic Bancroft. 6 vols. G. P. Putnam's Sons, New York and London, 1913.

Scott, Emmett J.: Negro Migration during the War (in Preliminary Economic Studies of the War—Carnegie Endowment for International Peace: Division of Economics and History). Oxford University Press, American Branch. New York, 1920.
  Official History of the American Negro in the World War. Washington, 1919.

Seligman, Herbert J.: The Negro Faces America. Harper Bros., New York, 1920.

Shaler, Nathaniel Southgate: The Neighbor: the Natural History of Human Contacts. Houghton, Mifflin Co., Boston, 1904.

Siebert, Wilbur H.: The Underground Railroad from Slavery to Freedom. The Macmillan Co., New York, 1898.

Sinclair, William A.: The Aftermath of Slavery. Small, Maynard & Co., Boston, 1905.

Smith, Justin H.: The War with Mexico. 2 vols. The Macmillan Co., New York, 1919.

Smith, Theodore Clarke: Parties and Slavery. Vol. 18 of American Nation Series.

Smith, T. W.: The Slave in Canada. Vol. 10 in Collections of the Nova Scotia Historical Society. Halifax, N. S., 1889.

Stephenson, Gilbert Thomas: Race Distinctions in American Law. D. Appleton & Co., New York, 1910.

Steward, T. G.: The Haitian Revolution, 1791-1804. Thomas Y. Crowell Co., New York, 1914.

Stoddard, Lothrop: The Rising Tide of Color against White World-Supremacy, with an Introduction by Madison Grant. Charles Scribner's Sons. New York, 1920.

Stone, Alfred H.: Studies in the American Race Problem. Doubleday, Page & Co., New York, 1908.

Storey, Moorfield: The Negro Question. An Address delivered before the Wisconsin Bar Association. Boston, 1918.
  Problems of To-Day. Houghton, Mifflin Co., Boston, 1920.

Thompson, Holland: The New South. Vol. 42 in Chronicles of America.

Tillinghast, Joseph Alexander: The Negro in Africa and America.

Publications of American Economics Association, Series 3, Vol. 3, No. 2. New York, 1902.

Toombs, Robert: Speech on The Crisis, delivered before the Georgia Legislature, Dec. 7, 1860. Washington, 1860.

Tucker, St. George: A Dissertation on Slavery, with a Proposal for the Gradual Abolition of it in the State of Virginia. Philadelphia, 1796.

Turner, Frederick Jackson: The Rise of the New West. Vol. 14 in American Nation Series.

Turner, Edward Raymond: The Negro in Pennsylvania, 1639-1861 (Justin Winsor Prize of American Historical Association, 1910). Washington, 1911.

Washington, Booker T.: The Future of the American Negro. Small, Maynard & Co., Boston, 1899.

The Story of My Life and Work. Nichols & Co., Naperville, Ill., 1900.

Up from Slavery: An Autobiography. Doubleday, Page & Co., New York, 1901.

Character Building. Doubleday, Page & Co., New York, 1902.

Working with the Hands. Doubleday, Page & Co., New York, 1904.

Putting the Most into Life. Crowell & Co., New York, 1906.

Frederick Douglass (in American Crisis Biographies). George W. Jacobs & Co., Philadelphia, 1906.

The Negro in the South (with W. E. B. DuBois). George W. Jacobs & Co., Philadelphia, 1907.

The Negro in Business. Hertel, Jenkins & Co., Chicago, 1907.

The Story of the Negro. 2 vols. Doubleday, Page & Co., New York, 1909.

My Larger Education. Doubleday, Page & Co., Garden City, N. Y., 1911.

The Man Farthest Down (with Robert Emory Park). Doubleday, Page & Co., Garden City, N. Y., 1912.

Weale, B. L. Putnam: The Conflict of Color. The Macmillan Co., New York, 1910.

Weatherford, W. D.: Present Forces in Negro Progress. Association Press, New York, 1912.

Weld, Theodore Dwight: American Slavery as It Is: Testimony of a Thousand Witnesses. Published by the American Anti-Slavery Society, New York, 1839.

Wiener, Leo: Africa and the Discovery of America, Vol. I. Innes & Sons, Philadelphia, 1920.

Williams, George Washington: History of the Negro Race in America from 1619 to 1880. 2 vols. G. P. Putnam's Sons, New York, 1883.

Wise, John S.: The End of an Era. Houghton, Mifflin Co., 1899.

Woodson, Carter G.: The Education of the Negro Prior to 1861. G. P. Putnam's Sons, New York, 1915.

A Century of Negro Migration. Association for the Study of Negro Life and History, Washington, 1918.

Woolf, Leonard: Empire and Commerce in Africa: A Study in Economic Imperialism. London, 1920. The Macmillan Co., New York.

Wright, Richard R.: Negro Companions of the Spanish Explorers. (Reprinted from the *American Anthropologist*, Vol. 4, April-June, 1902.)

Wright, Richard R., Jr.: The Negro in Pennsylvania: A Study in Economic History. (Ph.D. thesis, Pennsylvania.) A. M. E. Book Concern, Philadelphia.

Wright, T. S. See Cornish, Samuel E.

Zabriskie, Luther K.: The Virgin Islands of the United States of America. G. P. Putnam's Sons, New York, 1918.

An Address to the People of the United States, adopted at a Conference of Colored Citizens, held at Columbia, S. C., July 20 and 21, 1876. Republican Printing Co., Columbia, S. C., 1876.

Paper (letter published in a Washington paper) submitted in connection with the Debate in the United States House of Representatives, July 15th and 18th, 1776, on the Massacre of Six Colored Citizens at Hamburg, S. C., July 4, 1876.

Proceedings of the National Conference of Colored Men of the United States, held in the State Capitol at Nashville, Tenn., May 6, 7, 8, and 9, 1879. Washington, D. C., 1879.

Story of the Riot. Persecution of Negroes by roughs and policemen in the City of New York, August, 1900. Statement and Proofs written and compiled by Frank Moss and issued by the Citizens' Protective League. New York, 1900.

The Voice of the Carpet Bagger. Reconstruction Review No. 1, published by the Anti-Lynching Bureau. Chicago, 1901.

III. SPECIAL LISTS

1. On Chapter II, Section 3; Chapter III, Section 5; Chapter VIII and Chapter XI, the general topic being the social progress of the Negro before 1860. Titles are mainly in the order of appearance of works.

Mather, Cotton: Rules for the Society of Negroes, 1693. Reprinted by George H. Moore, Lenox Library, New York, 1888.

The Negro Christianized. An Essay to excite and assist that good work, the instruction of Negro-servants in Christianity. Boston, 1706.

Allen, Richard. The Life, Experience and Gospel Labors of the Rt. Rev. Richard Allen, written by himself. Philadelphia, 1793.

Hall, Prince. A Charge delivered to the African Lodge, June 24, 1797, at Menotomy, by the Right Worshipful Prince Hall. (Boston) 1797.

To the Free Africans and Other Free People of Color in the United States. (Broadside) Philadelphia, 1797.

Walker, David: Appeal, in four articles, together with a Preamble to the Colored Citizens of the World. Boston, 1829.

Garrison, William Lloyd: An Address delivered before the Free People of Color in Philadelphia, New York, and other cities, during the month of June, 1831. Boston, 1831.

Thoughts on African Colonization (see list above).

Minutes and Proceedings of the First Annual Convention of the People of Color, held by adjournments in the City of Philadelphia, from the sixth to the eleventh of June, inclusive, 1831. Philadelphia, 1831.

College for Colored Youth. An Account of the New Haven City Meeting and Resolutions with Recommendations of the College, and Strictures upon the Doings of New Haven. New York, 1831.

On the Condition of the Free People of Color in the United States. New York, 1839. (*The Anti-Slavery Examiner*, No. 13.)

Condition of the People of Color in the State of Ohio, with interesting anecdotes. Boston, 1839.

Armistead, Wilson: Memoir of Paul Cuffe. London, 1840.

Wilson, Joseph: Sketches of the Higher Classes of Colored Society in Philadelphia. Philadelphia, 1841.

National Convention of Colored Men and Their Friends. Troy, N. Y., 1847.

Garnet, Henry Highland: The Past and Present Condition and the Destiny of the Colored Race. Troy, 1848.

Delany, Martin R.: The Condition, Elevation, Emigration, and Destiny of the Colored People of the United States, Politically Considered. Philadelphia, 1852.

Cincinnati Convention of Colored Freedmen of Ohio. Proceedings, Jan. 14-19, 1852. Cincinnati, 1852.

Proceedings of the Colored National Convention, held in Rochester, July 6, 7, and 8, 1853. Rochester, 1853.

Cleveland National Emigration Convention of Colored People. Proceedings, Aug. 22-24, 1854. Pittsburg, 1854.

Nell, William C.: The Colored Patriots of the American Revolution, with sketches of several Distinguished Colored Persons: to which is added a brief survey of the Condition and Prospects of Colored Americans, with an Introduction by Harriet Beecher Stowe. Boston, 1855.

Stevens, Charles E.: Anthony Burns, a History. Boston, 1856.

Catto, William T.: A Semi-Centenary Discourse, delivered in the First African Presbyterian Church, Philadelphia, with a History of the church from its first organization, including a brief notice of Rev. John Gloucester, its first pastor. Philadelphia, 1857.

Bacon, Benjamin C.: Statistics of the Colored People of Philadelphia. Philadelphia, 1856. Second edition, with statistics of crime, Philadelphia, 1857.

Condition of the Free Colored People of the United States, by James Freeman Clarke, in Christian Examiner, March, 1859, 246-265. Reprinted as pamphlet by American Anti-Slavery Society, New York, 1859.

Brown, William Wells: Clotel, or The President's Daughter (a narrative of slave life in the United States). London, 1853.

The Escape; or A Leap for Freedom, a Drama in five acts. Boston, 1858.

The Black Man, His Antecedents, His Genius, and His Achievements. New York, 1863.

The Rising Son; or The Antecedents and Advancement of the Colored Race. Boston, 1874.

To Thomas J. Gantt, Esq. (Broadside), Charleston, 1861.

Douglass, William: Annals of St. Thomas's First African Church. Philadelphia, 1862.

Proceedings of the National Convention of Colored Men, held in the city of Syracuse, N. Y., October 4, 5, 6, and 7, 1864, with the Bill of Wrongs and Rights and the Address to the American People. Boston, 1864.

The Budget, containing the Annual Reports of the General Officers of the African M. E. Church of the United States of America, edited by Benjamin W. Arnett. Xenia, O., 1881. Same for later years.

Simms, James M.: The First Colored Baptist Church in North America. Printed by J. B. Lippincott Co., Philadelphia, 1888.

Upton, William H.: Negro Masonry, being a Critical Examination of objections to the legitimacy of the Masonry existing among the Negroes of America. Cambridge, 1899; second edition, 1902.

Brooks, Charles H.: The Official History and Manual of the Grand United Order of Odd Fellows in America. Philadelphia, 1902.

Cromwell, John W.: The Early Convention Movement. Occasional Paper No. 9 of American Negro Academy, Washington, D. C., 1904.

Brooks, Walter H.: The Silver Bluff Church, Washington, 1910.

Crawford, George W.: Prince Hall and His Followers. New Haven, 1915.

Wright, Richard R., Jr. (Editor-in-Chief): Centennial Encyclopædia of the African Methodist Episcopal Church. A. M. E. Book Concern, Philadelphia, 1916.

Also note narratives or autobiographies of Frederick Douglass, Sojourner Truth, Samuel Ringgold Ward, Solomon Northrup, Luns-
ford Lane, etc.; the poems of Phillis Wheatley (first edition,
London, 1773), and George M. Horton; Williams's History for
study of some more prominent characters; Woodson's bibliography for the special subject of education; and periodical literature, especially the articles remarked in Chapter XI in connection with the free people of color in Louisiana.

2. On Chapter V (Indian and Negro)

A standard work on the Second Seminole War is The Origin,
Progress, and Conclusion of the Florida War, by John T. Sprague,
D. Appleton & Co., New York, 1848; but also important as touching
upon the topics of the chapter are The Exiles of Florida, by Joshua
R. Giddings, Columbus, Ohio, 1858, and a speech by Giddings in the
House of Representatives February 9, 1841. Note also House Document No. 128 of the 1st session of the 20th Congress, and Document
327 of the 2nd session of the 25th Congress. The Aboriginal Races
of North America, by Samuel G. Drake, fifteenth edition, New York,
1880, is interesting and suggestive though formless; and McMaster
in different chapters gives careful brief accounts of the general
course of the Indian wars.

3. On Chapter VII (Insurrections)

(For insurrections before that of Denmark Vesey note especially
Coffin, Holland, and Horsemanden above. On Gabriel's Insurrection see article by Higginson (Atlantic, X. 337), afterwards included in Travellers and Outlaws.)

Denmark Vesey

1. An Official Report of the Trials of Sundry Negroes, charged
with an attempt to raise an Insurrection in the State of South Carolina. By Lionel H. Kennedy and Thomas Parker (members of the
Charleston Bar and the Presiding Magistrates of the Court).
Charleston, 1822.
2. An Account of the Late Intended Insurrection among a Portion of the Black of this City. Published by the Authority of the
Corporation of Charleston. Charleston, 1822 (reprinted Boston, 1822,
and again in Boston and Charleston).
The above accounts, now exceedingly rare, are the real sources of
all later study of Vesey's insurrection. The two accounts are sometimes identical; thus the list of those executed or banished is the
same. The first has a good introduction. The second was written
by James Hamilton, Intendant of Charleston.

3. Letter of Governor William Bennett, dated August 10, 1822. (This was evidently a circular letter to the press. References are to Lundy's *Genius of Universal Emancipation*, II, 42, Ninth month, 1822, and there are reviews in the following issues, pages 81, 131, and 142. Higginson notes letter as also in *Columbian Sentinel*, August 31, 1822; *Connecticut Courant*, September 3, 1822; and *Worcester Spy*, September 18, 1822.)

Three secondary accounts in later years are important:

1. Article on Denmark Vesey by Higginson (*Atlantic*, VII. 728) included in Travellers and Outlaws: Episodes in American History. Lee and Shepard, Boston, 1889.

2. Right on the Scaffold, or the Martyrs of 1822, by Archibald H. Grimké. No. 7 of the Papers of the American Negro Academy, Washington.

3. Book I, Chapter XII, "Denmark Vesey's Insurrection," in Robert Y. Hayne and His Times, by Theodore D. Jervey, The Macmillan Co., New York, 1909.

Various pamphlets were written immediately after the insurrection not so much to give detailed accounts as to discuss the general problem of the Negro and the reaction of the white citizens of Charleston to the event. Of these we may note the following:

1. Holland, Edwin C.: A Refutation of the Calumnies Circulated against the Southern and Western States. (See main list above.)

2. Achates (General Thomas Pinckney): Reflections Occasioned by the Late Disturbances in Charleston. Charleston, 1822.

3. Rev. Dr. Richard Furman's Exposition of the Views of the Baptists Relative to the Colored Population in the United States. (See main list above.)

4. Practical Considerations Founded on the Scriptures Relative to the Slave Population of South Carolina. By a South Carolinian. Charleston, 1823.

Nat Turner

1. The Confessions of Nat Turner, Leader of the Late Insurrection in Southampton, Va., as fully and voluntarily made to Thos. C. Gray, in the prison where he was confined—and acknowledged by him to be such, when read before the court at Southampton, convened at Jerusalem November 5, 1831, for his trial. (This is the main source. Thousands of copies of the pamphlet are said to have been circulated, but it is now exceedingly rare. Neither the Congressional Library nor the Boston Public has a copy, and Cromwell notes that there is not even one in the State Library in Richmond. The copy used by the author is in the library of Harvard University.)

2. Horrid Massacre. Authentic and Impartial Narrative of the Tragical Scene which was witnessed in Southampton County (Virginia) on Monday the 22nd of August last. New York, 1831. (This

gives a table of victims and has the advantage of nearness to the event. This very nearness, however, has given credence to much hearsay and accounted for several instances of inaccuracy.)

To the above may be added the periodicals of the day, such as the Richmond *Enquirer* and the *Liberator;* note *Genius of Universal Emancipation,* September, 1831. Secondary accounts or studies would include the following:

1. Nat Turner's Insurrection, exhaustive article by Higginson (*Atlantic,* VIII. 173) later included in Travellers and Outlaws.

2. Drewry, William Sidney: Slave Insurrections in Virginia (1830-1865). A Dissertation presented to the Board of University Studies of the Johns Hopkins University for the Degree of Doctor of Philosophy. The Neale Company, Washington, 1900. (Unfortunately marred by a partisan tone.)

3. The Aftermath of Nat Turner's Insurrection, by John W. Cromwell, in *Journal of Negro History,* April, 1920.

Amistad and *Creole* Cases

1. Argument of John Quincy Adams before the Supreme Court of the United States, in the case of the United States, Apellants, vs. Cinque, and others, Africans, captured in the Schooner *Amistad,* by Lieut. Gedney, delivered on the 24th of February and 1st of March, 1841. New York, 1841.

2. Africans Taken in the *Amistad.* Document No. 185 of the 1st session of the 26th Congress, containing the correspondence in relation to the captured Africans. (Reprinted by Anti-Slavery Depository, New York, 1840.)

3. Senate Document 51 of the 2nd session of the 27th Congress.

4. On Chapter IX (Liberia)

Much has been written about Liberia, but the books and pamphlets have been very uneven in quality. Original sources include the reports of the American Colonization Society to 1825; *The African Repository,* a compendium issued sometimes monthly, sometimes quarterly, by the American Colonization Society from 1825 to 1892, and succeeded by the periodical known as *Liberia;* the reports of the different state organizations; J. Ashmun's History of the American Colony in Liberia from December, 1821 to 1823, compiled from the authentic records of the colony, Washington, 1826; Ralph Randolph Gurley's Life of Jehudi Ashmun, Washington, 1835, second edition, New York, 1839; Gurley's report on Liberia (a United States state paper), Washington, 1850; and the Memorial of the Semi-Centennial Anniversary of the American Colonization Society, celebrated at Washington, January 15, 1867, with documents concerning Liberia, Washington, 1867; to all of which might be added Journal of Daniel

Coker, a descendant of Africa, from the time of leaving New York, in the ship *Elizabeth,* Capt. Sebor, on a voyage for Sherbro, in Africa, Baltimore, 1820. J. H. B. Latrobe, a president of the American Colonization Society, is prominent in the Memorial volume of 1867, and after this date are credited to him Liberia: its Origin, Rise, Progress, and Results, an address delivered before the American Colonization Society, January 20, 1880, Washington, 1880, and Maryland in Liberia, Baltimore, 1885. An early and interesting compilation is G. S. Stockwell's The Republic of Liberia: Its Geography, Climate, Soil, and Productions, with a history of its early settlement, New York, 1868; a good handbook is Frederick Starr's Liberia, Chicago, 1913; mention might also be made of T. McCants Stewart's Liberia, New York, 1886; and George W. Ellis's Negro Culture in West Africa, Neale Publishing Co., New York, 1914, is outstanding in its special field. Two Johns Hopkins theses have been written: John H. T. McPherson's History of Liberia (Studies, IX, No. 10), 1891, and E. L. Fox's The American Colonization Society 1817-1840 (Studies, XXXVII, 9-226), 1919; the first of these is brief and clearcut and especially valuable for its study of the Maryland colony. Magazine articles of unusual importance are George W. Ellis's Dynamic Factors in the Liberian Situation and Emmett J. Scott's Is Liberia Worth Saving? both in *Journal of Race Development,* January, 1911. Of English or continental works outstanding is the monumental but not altogether unimpeachable Liberia, by Sir Harry H. Johnston, with an appendix on the Flora of Liberia by Dr. Otto Stapf, 2 vols., Hutchinson & Co., London, 1906; while with a strong English bias and incomplete and unsatisfactory as a general treatise is R. C. F. Maughan's The Republic of Liberia, London (1920?), Charles Scribner's Sons, New York. Mention must also be made of the following publications by residents of Liberia: The Negro Republic on West Africa, by Abayomi Wilfrid Karnga, Monrovia, 1909; New National Fourth Reader, edited by Julius C. Stevens, Monrovia, 1903; Liberia and Her Educational Problems, by Walter F. Walker, an address delivered before the Chicago Historical Society, October 23, 1916; and Catalogue of Liberia College for 1916, and Historical Register, printed at the Riverdale Press, Brookline, Mass., 1919; while Edward Wilmot Blyden's Christianity, Islam, and the Negro Race is representative of the best of the more philosophical dissertations.

INDEX

409

A CATALOG OF SELECTED
DOVER BOOKS
IN ALL FIELDS OF INTEREST

A CATALOG OF SELECTED DOVER
BOOKS IN ALL FIELDS OF INTEREST

CONCERNING THE SPIRITUAL IN ART, Wassily Kandinsky. Pioneering work by father of abstract art. Thoughts on color theory, nature of art. Analysis of earlier masters. 12 illustrations. 80pp. of text. 5⅜ x 8½.   23411-8 Pa. $4.95

ANIMALS: 1,419 Copyright-Free Illustrations of Mammals, Birds, Fish, Insects, etc., Jim Harter (ed.). Clear wood engravings present, in extremely lifelike poses, over 1,000 species of animals. One of the most extensive pictorial sourcebooks of its kind. Captions. Index. 284pp. 9 x 12.   23766-4 Pa. $14.95

CELTIC ART: The Methods of Construction, George Bain. Simple geometric techniques for making Celtic interlacements, spirals, Kells-type initials, animals, humans, etc. Over 500 illustrations. 160pp. 9 x 12. (Available in U.S. only.)   22923-8 Pa. $9.95

AN ATLAS OF ANATOMY FOR ARTISTS, Fritz Schider. Most thorough reference work on art anatomy in the world. Hundreds of illustrations, including selections from works by Vesalius, Leonardo, Goya, Ingres, Michelangelo, others. 593 illustrations. 192pp. 7⅛ x 10¼.   20241-0 Pa. $9.95

CELTIC HAND STROKE-BY-STROKE (Irish Half-Uncial from "The Book of Kells"): An Arthur Baker Calligraphy Manual, Arthur Baker. Complete guide to creating each letter of the alphabet in distinctive Celtic manner. Covers hand position, strokes, pens, inks, paper, more. Illustrated. 48pp. 8¼ x 11.   24336-2 Pa. $3.95

EASY ORIGAMI, John Montroll. Charming collection of 32 projects (hat, cup, pelican, piano, swan, many more) specially designed for the novice origami hobbyist. Clearly illustrated easy-to-follow instructions insure that even beginning papercrafters will achieve successful results. 48pp. 8¼ x 11.   27298-2 Pa. $3.50

THE COMPLETE BOOK OF BIRDHOUSE CONSTRUCTION FOR WOOD-WORKERS, Scott D. Campbell. Detailed instructions, illustrations, tables. Also data on bird habitat and instinct patterns. Bibliography. 3 tables. 63 illustrations in 15 figures. 48pp. 5¼ x 8½.   24407-5 Pa. $2.50

BLOOMINGDALE'S ILLUSTRATED 1886 CATALOG: Fashions, Dry Goods and Housewares, Bloomingdale Brothers. Famed merchants' extremely rare catalog depicting about 1,700 products: clothing, housewares, firearms, dry goods, jewelry, more. Invaluable for dating, identifying vintage items. Also, copyright-free graphics for artists, designers. Co-published with Henry Ford Museum & Greenfield Village. 160pp. 8¼ x 11.   25780-0 Pa. $12.95

HISTORIC COSTUME IN PICTURES, Braun & Schneider. Over 1,450 costumed figures in clearly detailed engravings–from dawn of civilization to end of 19th century. Captions. Many folk costumes. 256pp. 8⅜ x 11¾.   23150-X Pa. $12.95

THE CLARINET AND CLARINET PLAYING, David Pino. Lively, comprehensive work features suggestions about technique, musicianship, and musical interpretation, as well as guidelines for teaching, making your own reeds, and preparing for public performance. Includes an intriguing look at clarinet history. "A godsend," *The Clarinet,* Journal of the International Clarinet Society. Appendixes. 7 illus. 320pp. 5⅜ x 8½. 40270-3 Pa. $9.95

HOLLYWOOD GLAMOR PORTRAITS, John Kobal (ed.). 145 photos from 1926-49. Harlow, Gable, Bogart, Bacall; 94 stars in all. Full background on photographers, technical aspects. 160pp. 8⅜ x 11¼. 23352-9 Pa. $12.95

THE ANNOTATED CASEY AT THE BAT: A Collection of Ballads about the Mighty Casey/Third, Revised Edition, Martin Gardner (ed.). Amusing sequels and parodies of one of America's best-loved poems: Casey's Revenge, Why Casey Whiffed, Casey's Sister at the Bat, others. 256pp. 5⅜ x 8½. 28598-7 Pa. $8.95

THE RAVEN AND OTHER FAVORITE POEMS, Edgar Allan Poe. Over 40 of the author's most memorable poems: "The Bells," "Ulalume," "Israfel," "To Helen," "The Conqueror Worm," "Eldorado," "Annabel Lee," many more. Alphabetic lists of titles and first lines. 64pp. 5$\frac{3}{16}$ x 8¼. 26685-0 Pa. $1.00

PERSONAL MEMOIRS OF U. S. GRANT, Ulysses Simpson Grant. Intelligent, deeply moving firsthand account of Civil War campaigns, considered by many the finest military memoirs ever written. Includes letters, historic photographs, maps and more. 528pp. 6⅛ x 9¼. 28587-1 Pa. $12.95

ANCIENT EGYPTIAN MATERIALS AND INDUSTRIES, A. Lucas and J. Harris. Fascinating, comprehensive, thoroughly documented text describes this ancient civilization's vast resources and the processes that incorporated them in daily life, including the use of animal products, building materials, cosmetics, perfumes and incense, fibers, glazed ware, glass and its manufacture, materials used in the mummification process, and much more. 544pp. 6⅛ x 9¼. (Available in U.S. only.) 40446-3 Pa. $16.95

RUSSIAN STORIES/PYCCKNE PACCKA3bl: A Dual-Language Book, edited by Gleb Struve. Twelve tales by such masters as Chekhov, Tolstoy, Dostoevsky, Pushkin, others. Excellent word-for-word English translations on facing pages, plus teaching and study aids, Russian/English vocabulary, biographical/critical introductions, more. 416pp. 5⅜ x 8½. 26244-8 Pa. $9.95

PHILADELPHIA THEN AND NOW: 60 Sites Photographed in the Past and Present, Kenneth Finkel and Susan Oyama. Rare photographs of City Hall, Logan Square, Independence Hall, Betsy Ross House, other landmarks juxtaposed with contemporary views. Captures changing face of historic city. Introduction. Captions. 128pp. 8¼ x 11. 25790-8 Pa. $9.95

AIA ARCHITECTURAL GUIDE TO NASSAU AND SUFFOLK COUNTIES, LONG ISLAND, The American Institute of Architects, Long Island Chapter, and the Society for the Preservation of Long Island Antiquities. Comprehensive, well-researched and generously illustrated volume brings to life over three centuries of Long Island's great architectural heritage. More than 240 photographs with authoritative, extensively detailed captions. 176pp. 8¼ x 11. 26946-9 Pa. $14.95

NORTH AMERICAN INDIAN LIFE: Customs and Traditions of 23 Tribes, Elsie Clews Parsons (ed.). 27 fictionalized essays by noted anthropologists examine religion, customs, government, additional facets of life among the Winnebago, Crow, Zuni, Eskimo, other tribes. 480pp. 6⅛ x 9¼. 27377-6 Pa. $10.95

FRANK LLOYD WRIGHT'S DANA HOUSE, Donald Hoffmann. Pictorial essay of residential masterpiece with over 160 interior and exterior photos, plans, elevations, sketches and studies. 128pp. 9¼ x 10¾. 29120-0 Pa. $14.95

THE MALE AND FEMALE FIGURE IN MOTION: 60 Classic Photographic Sequences, Eadweard Muybridge. 60 true-action photographs of men and women walking, running, climbing, bending, turning, etc., reproduced from rare 19th-century masterpiece. vi + 121pp. 9 x 12. 24745-7 Pa. $12.95

1001 QUESTIONS ANSWERED ABOUT THE SEASHORE, N. J. Berrill and Jacquelyn Berrill. Queries answered about dolphins, sea snails, sponges, starfish, fishes, shore birds, many others. Covers appearance, breeding, growth, feeding, much more. 305pp. 5¼ x 8¼. 23366-9 Pa. $9.95

ATTRACTING BIRDS TO YOUR YARD, William J. Weber. Easy-to-follow guide offers advice on how to attract the greatest diversity of birds: birdhouses, feeders, water and waterers, much more. 96pp. 5³⁄₁₆ x 8¼. 28927-3 Pa. $2.50

MEDICINAL AND OTHER USES OF NORTH AMERICAN PLANTS: A Historical Survey with Special Reference to the Eastern Indian Tribes, Charlotte Erichsen-Brown. Chronological historical citations document 500 years of usage of plants, trees, shrubs native to eastern Canada, northeastern U.S. Also complete identifying information. 343 illustrations. 544pp. 6½ x 9¼. 25951-X Pa. $12.95

STORYBOOK MAZES, Dave Phillips. 23 stories and mazes on two-page spreads: Wizard of Oz, Treasure Island, Robin Hood, etc. Solutions. 64pp. 8¼ x 11. 23628-5 Pa. $2.95

AMERICAN NEGRO SONGS: 230 Folk Songs and Spirituals, Religious and Secular, John W. Work. This authoritative study traces the African influences of songs sung and played by black Americans at work, in church, and as entertainment. The author discusses the lyric significance of such songs as "Swing Low, Sweet Chariot," "John Henry," and others and offers the words and music for 230 songs. Bibliography. Index of Song Titles. 272pp. 6½ x 9¼. 40271-1 Pa. $10.95

MOVIE-STAR PORTRAITS OF THE FORTIES, John Kobal (ed.). 163 glamor, studio photos of 106 stars of the 1940s: Rita Hayworth, Ava Gardner, Marlon Brando, Clark Gable, many more. 176pp. 8⅜ x 11¼. 23546-7 Pa. $14.95

BENCHLEY LOST AND FOUND, Robert Benchley. Finest humor from early 30s, about pet peeves, child psychologists, post office and others. Mostly unavailable elsewhere. 73 illustrations by Peter Arno and others. 183pp. 5⅜ x 8½. 22410-4 Pa. $6.95

YEKL and THE IMPORTED BRIDEGROOM AND OTHER STORIES OF YIDDISH NEW YORK, Abraham Cahan. Film Hester Street based on *Yekl* (1896). Novel, other stories among first about Jewish immigrants on N.Y.'s East Side. 240pp. 5⅜ x 8½. 22427-9 Pa. $7.95

SELECTED POEMS, Walt Whitman. Generous sampling from *Leaves of Grass*. Twenty-four poems include "I Hear America Singing," "Song of the Open Road," "I Sing the Body Electric," "When Lilacs Last in the Dooryard Bloom'd," "O Captain! My Captain!"–all reprinted from an authoritative edition. Lists of titles and first lines. 128pp. 5³⁄₁₆ x 8¼. 26878-0 Pa. $1.00

CATALOG OF DOVER BOOKS

THE BEST TALES OF HOFFMANN, E. T. A. Hoffmann. 10 of Hoffmann's most important stories: "Nutcracker and the King of Mice," "The Golden Flowerpot," etc. 458pp. 5⅜ x 8½. 2179 P $9.95

FROM FETISH TO GOD IN ANCIENT EGYPT, E. A. Wallis Budge. Rich detailed survey of Egyptian conception of "God" and gods, magic, cult of animals, Osiris, more. Also, superb English translations of hymns and legends. 240 illustrations. 545pp. 5⅜ x 8½. 25803-3 Pa. $13.95

FRENCH STORIES/CONTES FRANÇAIS: A Dual-Language Book, Wallace Fowlie. Ten stories by French masters, Voltaire to Camus: "Micromegas" by Voltaire; "The Atheist's Mass" by Balzac; "Minuet" by de Maupassant; "The Guest" by Camus, six more. Excellent English translations on facing pages. Also French-English vocabulary list, exercises, more. 352pp. 5⅜ x 8½. 26443-2 Pa. $9.95

CHICAGO AT THE TURN OF THE CENTURY IN PHOTOGRAPHS: 122 Historic Views from the Collections of the Chicago Historical Society, Larry A. Viskochil. Rare large-format prints offer detailed views of City Hall, State Street, the Loop, Hull House, Union Station, many other landmarks, circa 1904-1913. Introduction. Captions. Maps. 144pp. 9⅜ x 12¼. 24656-6 Pa. $12.95

OLD BROOKLYN IN EARLY PHOTOGRAPHS, 1865-1929, William Lee Younger. Luna Park, Gravesend race track, construction of Grand Army Plaza, moving of Hotel Brighton, etc. 157 previously unpublished photographs. 165pp. 8⅞ x 11¾. 23587-4 Pa. $13.95

THE MYTHS OF THE NORTH AMERICAN INDIANS, Lewis Spence. Rich anthology of the myths and legends of the Algonquins, Iroquois, Pawnees and Sioux, prefaced by an extensive historical and ethnological commentary. 36 illustrations. 480pp. 5⅜ x 8½. 25967-6 Pa. $10.95

AN ENCYCLOPEDIA OF BATTLES: Accounts of Over 1,560 Battles from 1479 B.C. to the Present, David Eggenberger. Essential details of every major battle in recorded history from the first battle of Megiddo in 1479 B.C. to Grenada in 1984. List of Battle Maps. New Appendix covering the years 1967-1984. Index. 99 illustrations. 544pp. 6½ x 9¼. 24913-1 Pa. $16.95

SAILING ALONE AROUND THE WORLD, Captain Joshua Slocum. First man to sail around the world, alone, in small boat. One of great feats of seamanship told in delightful manner. 67 illustrations. 294pp. 5⅜ x 8½. 20326-3 Pa. $6.95

ANARCHISM AND OTHER ESSAYS, Emma Goldman. Powerful, penetrating, prophetic essays on direct action, role of minorities, prison reform, puritan hypocrisy, violence, etc. 271pp. 5⅜ x 8½. 22484-8 Pa. $8.95

MYTHS OF THE HINDUS AND BUDDHISTS, Ananda K. Coomaraswamy and Sister Nivedita. Great stories of the epics; deeds of Krishna, Shiva, taken from puranas, Vedas, folk tales; etc. 32 illustrations. 400pp. 5⅜ x 8½. 21759-0 Pa. $12.95

THE TRAUMA OF BIRTH, Otto Rank. Rank's controversial thesis that anxiety neurosis is caused by profound psychological trauma which occurs at birth. 256pp. 5⅜ x 8½. 27974-X Pa. $7.95

A THEOLOGICO-POLITICAL TREATISE, Benedict Spinoza. Also contains unfinished Political Treatise. Great classic on religious liberty, theory of government on common consent. R. Elwes translation. Total of 421pp. 5⅜ x 8½. 20249-6 Pa. $10.95

PERSPECTIVE FOR ARTISTS, Rex Vicat Cole. Depth, perspective of sky and sea, shadows, much more, not usually covered. 391 diagrams, 81 reproductions of drawings and paintings. 279pp. 5⅜ x 8½. 22487-2 Pa. $9.95

DRAWING THE LIVING FIGURE, Joseph Sheppard. Innovative approach to artistic anatomy focuses on specifics of surface anatomy, rather than muscles and bones. Over 170 drawings of live models in front, back and side views, and in widely varying poses. Accompanying diagrams. 177 illustrations. Introduction. Index. 144pp. 8⅜ x11¼. 26723- P $9.95

GOTHIC AND OLD ENGLISH ALPHABETS: 100 Complete Fonts, Dan X. Solo. Add power, elegance to posters, signs, other graphics with 100 stunning copyright-free alphabets: Blackstone, Dolbey, Germania, 97 more–including many lower-case, numerals, punctuation marks. 104pp. 8⅛ x 11. 24695-7 Pa. $9.95

HOW TO DO BEADWORK, Mary White. Fundamental book on craft from simple projects to five-bead chains and woven works. 106 illustrations. 142pp. 5⅜ x 8. 20697-1 Pa. $5.95

THE BOOK OF WOOD CARVING, Charles Marshall Sayers. Finest book for beginners discusses fundamentals and offers 34 designs. "Absolutely first rate . . . well thought out and well executed."–E. J. Tangerman. 118pp. 7¾ x 10⅝. 23654-4 Pa. $7.95

ILLUSTRATED CATALOG OF CIVIL WAR MILITARY GOODS: Union Army Weapons, Insignia, Uniform Accessories, and Other Equipment, Schuyler, Hartley, and Graham. Rare, profusely illustrated 1846 catalog includes Union Army uniform and dress regulations, arms and ammunition, coats, insignia, flags, swords, rifles, etc. 226 illustrations. 160pp. 9 x 12. 24939-5 Pa. $12.95

WOMEN'S FASHIONS OF THE EARLY 1900s: An Unabridged Republication of "New York Fashions, 1909," National Cloak & Suit Co. Rare catalog of mail-order fashions documents women's and children's clothing styles shortly after the turn of the century. Captions offer full descriptions, prices. Invaluable resource for fashion, costume historians. Approximately 725 illustrations. 128pp. 8⅜ x 11¼. 27276-1 Pa. $12.95

THE 1912 AND 1915 GUSTAV STICKLEY FURNITURE CATALOGS, Gustav Stickley. With over 200 detailed illustrations and descriptions, these two catalogs are essential reading and reference materials and identification guides for Stickley furniture. Captions cite materials, dimensions and prices. 112pp. 6½ x 9¼. 26676-1 Pa. $9.95

EARLY AMERICAN LOCOMOTIVES, John H. White, Jr. Finest locomotive engravings from early 19th century: historical (1804–74), main-line (after 1870), special, foreign, etc. 147 plates. 142pp. 11⅜ x 8¼. 22772-3 Pa. $12.95

THE TALL SHIPS OF TODAY IN PHOTOGRAPHS, Frank O. Braynard. Lavishly illustrated tribute to nearly 100 majestic contemporary sailing vessels: Amerigo Vespucci, Clearwater, Constitution, Eagle, Mayflower, Sea Cloud, Victory, many more. Authoritative captions provide statistics, background on each ship. 190 black-and-white photographs and illustrations. Introduction. 128pp. 8⅞ x 11¾. 27163-3 Pa. $14.95

CATALOG OF DOVER BOOKS

LITTLE BOOK OF EARLY AMERICAN CRAFTS AND TRADES, Peter Stockham (ed.). 1807 children's book explains crafts and trades: baker, hatter, cooper, potter, and many others. 23 copperplate illustrations. 140pp. 4⅝ x 6.
23336-7 Pa. $4.95

VICTORIAN FASHIONS AND COSTUMES FROM HARPER'S BAZAR, 1867–1898, Stella Blum (ed.). Day costumes, evening wear, sports clothes, shoes, hats, other accessories in over 1,000 detailed engravings. 320pp. 9⅜ x 12¼.
22990-4 Pa. $16.95

GUSTAV STICKLEY, THE CRAFTSMAN, Mary Ann Smith. Superb study surveys broad scope of Stickley's achievement, especially in architecture. Design philosophy, rise and fall of the Craftsman empire, descriptions and floor plans for many Craftsman houses, more. 86 black-and-white halftones. 31 line illustrations. Introduction 208pp. 6½ x 9¼.
27210-9 Pa. $9.95

THE LONG ISLAND RAIL ROAD IN EARLY PHOTOGRAPHS, Ron Ziel. Over 220 rare photos, informative text document origin (1844) and development of rail service on Long Island. Vintage views of early trains, locomotives, stations, passengers, crews, much more. Captions. 8⅞ x 11¾.
26301-0 Pa. $14.95

VOYAGE OF THE LIBERDADE, Joshua Slocum. Great 19th-century mariner's thrilling, first-hand account of the wreck of his ship off South America, the 35-foot boat he built from the wreckage, and its remarkable voyage home. 128pp. 5⅜ x 8½.
40022-0 Pa. $5.95

TEN BOOKS ON ARCHITECTURE, Vitruvius. The most important book ever written on architecture. Early Roman aesthetics, technology, classical orders, site selection, all other aspects. Morgan translation. 331pp. 5⅜ x 8½. 20645-9 Pa. $9.95

THE HUMAN FIGURE IN MOTION, Eadweard Muybridge. More than 4,500 stopped-action photos, in action series, showing undraped men, women, children jumping, lying down, throwing, sitting, wrestling, carrying, etc. 390pp. 7⅞ x 10⅝.
20204-6 Clothbd. $29.95

TREES OF THE EASTERN AND CENTRAL UNITED STATES AND CANADA, William M. Harlow. Best one-volume guide to 140 trees. Full descriptions, woodlore, range, etc. Over 600 illustrations. Handy size. 288pp. 4½ x 6⅜.
20395-6 Pa. $6.95

SONGS OF WESTERN BIRDS, Dr. Donald J. Borror. Complete song and call repertoire of 60 western species, including flycatchers, juncoes, cactus wrens, many more–includes fully illustrated booklet.   Cassette and manual 99913-0 $8.95

GROWING AND USING HERBS AND SPICES, Milo Miloradovich. Versatile handbook provides all the information needed for cultivation and use of all the herbs and spices available in North America. 4 illustrations. Index. Glossary. 236pp. 5⅜ x 8½.
25058-X Pa. $7.95

BIG BOOK OF MAZES AND LABYRINTHS, Walter Shepherd. 50 mazes and labyrinths in all–classical, solid, ripple, and more–in one great volume. Perfect inexpensive puzzler for clever youngsters. Full solutions. 112pp. 8⅛ x 11.
22951-3 Pa. $5.95

PIANO TUNING, J. Cree Fischer. Clearest, best book for beginner, amateur. Simple repairs, raising dropped notes, tuning by easy method of flattened fifths. No previous skills needed. 4 illustrations. 201pp. 5⅜ x 8½. 23267-0 Pa. $6.95

HINTS TO SINGERS, Lillian Nordica. Selecting the right teacher, developing confidence, overcoming stage fright, and many other important skills receive thoughtful discussion in this indispensible guide, written by a world-famous diva of four decades' experience. 96pp. 5⅜ x 8½. 40094-8 Pa. $4.95

THE COMPLETE NONSENSE OF EDWARD LEAR, Edward Lear. All nonsense limericks, zany alphabets, Owl and Pussycat, songs, nonsense botany, etc., illustrated by Lear. Total of 320pp. 5⅜ x 8½. (Available in U.S. only.) 20167-8 Pa. $7.95

VICTORIAN PARLOUR POETRY: An Annotated Anthology, Michael R. Turner. 117 gems by Longfellow, Tennyson, Browning, many lesser-known poets. "The Village Blacksmith," "Curfew Must Not Ring Tonight," "Only a Baby Small," dozens more, often difficult to find elsewhere. Index of poets, titles, first lines. xxiii + 325pp. 5⅝ x 8¼. 27044-0 Pa. $12.95

DUBLINERS, James Joyce. Fifteen stories offer vivid, tightly focused observations of the lives of Dublin's poorer classes. At least one, "The Dead," is considered a masterpiece. Reprinted complete and unabridged from standard edition. 160pp. 5³⁄₁₆ x 8¼. 26870-5 Pa. $1.50

GREAT WEIRD TALES: 14 Stories by Lovecraft, Blackwood, Machen and Others, S. T. Joshi (ed.). 14 spellbinding tales, including "The Sin Eater," by Fiona McLeod, "The Eye Above the Mantel," by Frank Belknap Long, as well as renowned works by R. H. Barlow, Lord Dunsany, Arthur Machen, W. C. Morrow and eight other masters of the genre. 256pp. 5⅜ x 8½. (Available in U.S. only.) 40436-6 Pa. $8.95

THE BOOK OF THE SACRED MAGIC OF ABRAMELIN THE MAGE, translated by S. MacGregor Mathers. Medieval manuscript of ceremonial magic. Basic document in Aleister Crowley, Golden Dawn groups. 268pp. 5⅜ x 8½. 23211-5 Pa. $9.95

NEW RUSSIAN-ENGLISH AND ENGLISH-RUSSIAN DICTIONARY, M. A. O'Brien. This is a remarkably handy Russian dictionary, containing a surprising amount of information, including over 70,000 entries. 366pp. 4½ x 6⅛. 20208-9 Pa. $10.95

HISTORIC HOMES OF THE AMERICAN PRESIDENTS, Second, Revised Edition, Irvin Haas. A traveler's guide to American Presidential homes, most open to the public, depicting and describing homes occupied by every American President from George Washington to George Bush. With visiting hours, admission charges, travel routes. 175 photographs. Index. 160pp. 8¼ x 11. 26751-2 Pa. $13.95

NEW YORK IN THE FORTIES, Andreas Feininger. 162 brilliant photographs by the well-known photographer, formerly with *Life* magazine. Commuters, shoppers, Times Square at night, much else from city at its peak. Captions by John von Hartz. 181pp. 9¼ x 10¾. 23585-8 Pa. $13.95

INDIAN SIGN LANGUAGE, William Tomkins. Over 525 signs developed by Sioux and other tribes. Written instructions and diagrams. Also 290 pictographs. 111pp. 6⅛ x 9¼. 22029-X Pa. $3.95

ANATOMY: A Complete Guide for Artists, Joseph Sheppard. A master of figure drawing shows artists how to render human anatomy convincingly. Over 460 illustrations. 224pp. 8⅜ x 11¼. 27279-6 Pa. $11.95

MEDIEVAL CALLIGRAPHY: Its History and Technique, Marc Drogin. Spirited history, comprehensive instruction manual covers 13 styles (ca. 4th century through 15th). Excellent photographs; directions for duplicating medieval techniques with modern tools. 224pp. 8⅜ x 11¼. 26142-5 Pa. $12.95

DRIED FLOWERS: How to Prepare Them, Sarah Whitlock and Martha Rankin. Complete instructions on how to use silica gel, meal and borax, perlite aggregate, sand and borax, glycerine and water to create attractive permanent flower arrangements. 12 illustrations. 32pp. 5⅜ x 8½. 21802-3 Pa. $1.00

EASY-TO-MAKE BIRD FEEDERS FOR WOODWORKERS, Scott D. Campbell. Detailed, simple-to-use guide for designing, constructing, caring for and using feeders. Text, illustrations for 12 classic and contemporary designs. 96pp. 5⅜ x 8½. 25847-5 Pa. $3.95

SCOTTISH WONDER TALES FROM MYTH AND LEGEND, Donald A. Mackenzie. 16 lively tales tell of giants rumbling down mountainsides, of a magic wand that turns stone pillars into warriors, of gods and goddesses, evil hags, powerful forces and more. 240pp. 5⅜ x 8½. 29677-6 Pa. $6.95

THE HISTORY OF UNDERCLOTHES, C. Willett Cunnington and Phyllis Cunnington. Fascinating, well-documented survey covering six centuries of English undergarments, enhanced with over 100 illustrations: 12th-century laced-up bodice, footed long drawers (1795), 19th-century bustles, l9th-century corsets for men, Victorian "bust improvers," much more. 272pp. 5⅜ x 8¼. 27124-2 Pa. $9.95

ARTS AND CRAFTS FURNITURE: The Complete Brooks Catalog of 1912, Brooks Manufacturing Co. Photos and detailed descriptions of more than 150 now very collectible furniture designs from the Arts and Crafts movement depict davenports, settees, buffets, desks, tables, chairs, bedsteads, dressers and more, all built of solid, quarter-sawed oak. Invaluable for students and enthusiasts of antiques, Americana and the decorative arts. 80pp. 6½ x 9¼. 27471-3 Pa. $8.95

WILBUR AND ORVILLE: A Biography of the Wright Brothers, Fred Howard. Definitive, crisply written study tells the full story of the brothers' lives and work. A vividly written biography, unparalleled in scope and color, that also captures the spirit of an extraordinary era. 560pp. 6⅛ x 9¼. 40297-5 Pa. $17.95

THE ARTS OF THE SAILOR: Knotting, Splicing and Ropework, Hervey Garrett Smith. Indispensable shipboard reference covers tools, basic knots and useful hitches; handsewing and canvas work, more. Over 100 illustrations. Delightful reading for sea lovers. 256pp. 5⅜ x 8½. 26440-8 Pa. $8.95

FRANK LLOYD WRIGHT'S FALLINGWATER: The House and Its History, Second, Revised Edition, Donald Hoffmann. A total revision–both in text and illustrations–of the standard document on Fallingwater, the boldest, most personal architectural statement of Wright's mature years, updated with valuable new material from the recently opened Frank Lloyd Wright Archives. "Fascinating"–*The New York Times*. 116 illustrations. 128pp. 9¼ x 10¾. 27430-6 Pa. $12.95

THE WIT AND HUMOR OF OSCAR WILDE, Alvin Redman (ed.). More than 1,000 ripostes, paradoxes, wisecracks: Work is the curse of the drinking classes; I can resist everything except temptation; etc. 258pp. 5⅜ x 8½. 20602-5 Pa. $6.95

SHAKESPEARE LEXICON AND QUOTATION DICTIONARY, Alexander Schmidt. Full definitions, locations, shades of meaning in every word in plays and poems. More than 50,000 exact quotations. 1,485pp. 6½ x 9¼. 2-vol. set.

Vol. 1: 22726-X Pa. $17.95
Vol. 2: 22727-8 Pa. $17.95

SELECTED POEMS, Emily Dickinson. Over 100 best-known, best-loved poems by one of America's foremost poets, reprinted from authoritative early editions. No comparable edition at this price. Index of first lines. 64pp. 5³⁄₁₆ x 8¼.

26466-1 Pa. $1.00

THE INSIDIOUS DR. FU-MANCHU, Sax Rohmer. The first of the popular mystery series introduces a pair of English detectives to their archnemesis, the diabolical Dr. Fu-Manchu. Flavorful atmosphere, fast-paced action, and colorful characters enliven this classic of the genre. 208pp. 5³⁄₁₆ x 8¼. 29898-1 Pa. $2.00

THE MALLEUS MALEFICARUM OF KRAMER AND SPRENGER, translated by Montague Summers. Full text of most important witchhunter's "bible," used by both Catholics and Protestants. 278pp. 6⅝ x 10. 22802-9 Pa. $12.95

SPANISH STORIES/CUENTOS ESPAÑOLES: A Dual-Language Book, Angel Flores (ed.). Unique format offers 13 great stories in Spanish by Cervantes, Borges, others. Faithful English translations on facing pages. 352pp. 5⅜ x 8½.

25399-6 Pa. $9.95

GARDEN CITY, LONG ISLAND, IN EARLY PHOTOGRAPHS, 1869–1919, Mildred H. Smith. Handsome treasury of 118 vintage pictures, accompanied by carefully researched captions, document the Garden City Hotel fire (1899), the Vanderbilt Cup Race (1908), the first airmail flight departing from the Nassau Boulevard Aerodrome (1911), and much more. 96pp. 8⅞ x 11¾. 40669-5 Pa. $12.95

OLD QUEENS, N.Y., IN EARLY PHOTOGRAPHS, Vincent F. Seyfried and William Asadorian. Over 160 rare photographs of Maspeth, Jamaica, Jackson Heights, and other areas. Vintage views of DeWitt Clinton mansion, 1939 World's Fair and more. Captions. 192pp. 8⅞ x 11. 26358-4 Pa. $14.95

CAPTURED BY THE INDIANS: 15 Firsthand Accounts, 1750-1870, Frederick Drimmer. Astounding true historical accounts of grisly torture, bloody conflicts, relentless pursuits, miraculous escapes and more, by people who lived to tell the tale. 384pp. 5⅜ x 8½. 24901-8 Pa. $9.95

THE WORLD'S GREAT SPEECHES (Fourth Enlarged Edition), Lewis Copeland, Lawrence W. Lamm, and Stephen J. McKenna. Nearly 300 speeches provide public speakers with a wealth of updated quotes and inspiration—from Pericles' funeral oration and William Jennings Bryan's "Cross of Gold Speech" to Malcolm X's powerful words on the Black Revolution and Earl of Spenser's tribute to his sister, Diana, Princess of Wales. 944pp. 5⅜ x 8⅜. 40903-1 Pa. $15.95

THE BOOK OF THE SWORD, Sir Richard F. Burton. Great Victorian scholar/adventurer's eloquent, erudite history of the "queen of weapons"–from prehistory to early Roman Empire. Evolution and development of early swords, variations (sabre, broadsword, cutlass, scimitar, etc.), much more. 336pp. 6⅛ x 9¼.

25434-8 Pa. $9.95

THE INFLUENCE OF SEA POWER UPON HISTORY, 1660–1783, A. T. Mahan. Influential classic of naval history and tactics still used as text in war colleges. First paperback edition. 4 maps. 24 battle plans. 640pp. 5⅜ x 8½. 25509-3 Pa. $14.95

THE STORY OF THE TITANIC AS TOLD BY ITS SURVIVORS, Jack Winocour (ed.). What it was really like. Panic, despair, shocking inefficiency, and a little heroism. More thrilling than any fictional account. 26 illustrations. 320pp. 5⅜ x 8½. 20610-6 Pa. $8.95

FAIRY AND FOLK TALES OF THE IRISH PEASANTRY, William Butler Yeats (ed.). Treasury of 64 tales from the twilight world of Celtic myth and legend: "The Soul Cages," "The Kildare Pooka," "King O'Toole and his Goose," many more. Introduction and Notes by W. B. Yeats. 352pp. 5⅜ x 8½. 26941-8 Pa. $8.95

BUDDHIST MAHAYANA TEXTS, E. B. Cowell and others (eds.). Superb, accurate translations of basic documents in Mahayana Buddhism, highly important in history of religions. The Buddha-karita of Asvaghosha, Larger Sukhavativyuha, more. 448pp. 5⅜ x 8½. 25552-2 Pa. $12.95

ONE TWO THREE . . . INFINITY: Facts and Speculations of Science, George Gamow. Great physicist's fascinating, readable overview of contemporary science: number theory, relativity, fourth dimension, entropy, genes, atomic structure, much more. 128 illustrations. Index. 352pp. 5⅜ x 8½. 25664-2 Pa. $9.95

EXPERIMENTATION AND MEASUREMENT, W. J. Youden. Introductory manual explains laws of measurement in simple terms and offers tips for achieving accuracy and minimizing errors. Mathematics of measurement, use of instruments, experimenting with machines. 1994 edition. Foreword. Preface. Introduction. Epilogue. Selected Readings. Glossary. Index. Tables and figures. 128pp. 5⅜ x 8½. 40451-X Pa. $6.95

DALÍ ON MODERN ART: The Cuckolds of Antiquated Modern Art, Salvador Dalí. Influential painter skewers modern art and its practitioners. Outrageous evaluations of Picasso, Cézanne, Turner, more. 15 renderings of paintings discussed. 44 calligraphic decorations by Dalí. 96pp. 5⅜ x 8½. (Available in U.S. only.) 29220-7 Pa. $5.95

ANTIQUE PLAYING CARDS: A Pictorial History, Henry René D'Allemagne. Over 900 elaborate, decorative images from rare playing cards (14th–20th centuries): Bacchus, death, dancing dogs, hunting scenes, royal coats of arms, players cheating, much more. 96pp. 9¼ x 12¼. 29265-7 Pa. $12.95

MAKING FURNITURE MASTERPIECES: 30 Projects with Measured Drawings, Franklin H. Gottshall. Step-by-step instructions, illustrations for constructing handsome, useful pieces, among them a Sheraton desk, Chippendale chair, Spanish desk, Queen Anne table and a William and Mary dressing mirror. 224pp. 8⅛ x 11¼. 29338-6 Pa. $16.95

THE FOSSIL BOOK: A Record of Prehistoric Life, Patricia V. Rich et al. Profusely illustrated definitive guide covers everything from single-celled organisms and dinosaurs to birds and mammals and the interplay between climate and man. Over 1,500 illustrations. 760pp. 7½ x 10⅛. 29371-8 Pa. $29.95

Prices subject to change without notice.

Available at your book dealer or write for free catalog to Dept. GI, Dover Publications, Inc., 31 East 2nd St., Mineola, N.Y. 11501. Dover publishes more than 500 books each year on science, elementary and advanced mathematics, biology, music, art, literary history, social sciences and other areas.